MW01116371

CLASSIC ESSAYS
ON THE
JEWISH QUESTION

BOOKS FROM CLEMENS & BLAIR
(www.clemensandblair.com)

Pan-Judah! Political Cartoons of Der Stürmer, by Robert Penman
Passovers of Blood, by Ariel Toaff
The Poisonous Mushroom, by Ernst Hiemer
On the Jews and Their Lies, by Martin Luther
Mein Kampf, by Adolf Hitler
Mein Kampf (Dual English-German edition), by Adolf Hitler
The Essential Mein Kampf, by Adolf Hitler
The Myth of the 20th Century, by Alfred Rosenberg

BOOKS BY THOMAS DALTON
(www.thomasdaltonphd.com)

Debating the Holocaust
The Holocaust: An Introduction
The Jewish Hand in the World Wars
Eternal Strangers: Critical Views of Jews and Judaism
Hitler on the Jews
Goebbels on the Jews
Streicher, Rosenberg, and the Jews: The Nuremberg Transcripts

CLASSIC ESSAYS ON THE JEWISH QUESTION

1850 to 1945

Edited by
Thomas Dalton

Clemens & Blair, LLC
— 2022 —

CLEMENS & BLAIR, LLC

Clemens & Blair, LLC, is a non-profit educational publisher.
www.clemensandblair.com

Library of Congress Cataloging-in-Publication Data

Dalton, Thomas B., editor
Classic Essays on the Jewish Question: 1850 to 1945

p. cm.
Includes bibliographical references

ISBN 978-1737-4461-87
(hbk.: alk. paper)

1. Jews and Judaism
2. History, General

Printing number: 9 8 7 6 5 4 3 2 1

Printed in the United States of America on acid-free paper.

ACKNOWLEDGEMENTS

The editor would like to acknowledge the extensive assistance on editing and text production by WC, whose efforts are greatly appreciated.

Thanks also to Karl Haemers for his aid in preparing the Ravage essays.

Skillful translations of essays by Fritsch (both), Himmler, and Ley were done by Alexander Jacob.

Many thanks to all for their diligent and valuable support.

CONTENTS

INTRODUCTION
THOMAS DALTON

Given the situation in the world today, one can make a very good case that the single most urgent problem facing humanity is what the Germans used to call the *Judenfrage*—the Jewish Question. East or West, rich nation or poor, urban or rural, white collar or blue…nothing seems to be more consequential than this question. Regardless of social standing, regardless of age or gender, regardless of education or training, people everywhere are profoundly affected by the policies and actions of Jews around the world, and especially Jews in the industrial West. Their personal wealth, their access to power, and their roles in media and academia all combine with a broadly misanthropic outlook to wreak havoc on the globe. Political strife (both domestic and international), warfare, terrorism, economic gyrations, global pandemics, wealth disparities, declines in physical and mental health, environmental degradation, unrestrained technological development, cultural decline, crude materialism—all these things have roots in Jewish power and Jewish action. Nothing is more pressing than for people everywhere to address, and to work to resolve, the Jewish Question.

But what, exactly, is the Jewish Question? In short, it is this: How should society deal with the presence of a wealthy and powerful but malevolent, manipulative, corrupting, debasing, and malicious Jewish minority? Virtually every nation on Earth has its share of Jews—most well under 1% of population, but in some cases, like the US, up to nearly 2%. Though numerically small, Jews have hugely disproportionate wealth, and thus influence, in every country in which they reside. They furthermore work, notoriously, collectively in their own best interests; these interests are often at odds with, and sometimes in direct opposition to, the interests of native peoples. As has been demonstrated in countless studies over the centuries, Jews in general strive for wealth and power, using this to secure yet more wealth and power. Doing so often demands that they neglect, cheat, debase, sicken, or even kill non-Jews in their path. And as supreme misanthropes, Jews do so without compunction. The Jewish Question, then, can be rephrased as follows: How should societies around the globe confront this most troublesome and pernicious minority?

The initial steps are fairly obvious. We must, first of all, treat the Jewish Question as a very real and a very serious matter. There can be no pussy-footing, no side-stepping, no polite maneuvers. The Jewish Question must be tackled head-on. Second, the extent and degree of Jewish influence must be openly stated and discussed. Wealthy Jews must be 'outed' as Jews. Jewish politicians—or half-Jews, or those with Jewish spouses—must be outed as such. Jewish media personalities, Jewish academicians, and Jewish celebrities must be clearly and openly cited as Jews. This is particularly urgent in the industrial West, where Jews can otherwise move with relative invisibility among a majority White population. Third, there must be open discussion and open debate on policies that benefit Jewish constituencies at the expense of Gentile masses. Eventually, it is hoped, such initial steps may lead to actual policies for reigning in and constraining adverse Jewish influence, permanently. Some such process is the long-term objective.

But perhaps even before all this, there is a preliminary step: *Know your history.* The legacy of malicious Jewish influence goes back literally millennia. At least since the time of ancient Greece, Jews were recognized as a dangerous, corrupt, degrading influence on society. This situation has been examined and documented by some of our greatest thinkers in history; my book *Eternal Strangers* (2020) summarizes and documents many of the more compelling statements. Classic writers had a litany of complaints: Jews were morally corrupt; they bore a "hatred of humanity"; they were master liars; they were swindlers; they were agitators and war-mongers; they were "superstitious"; they were enemies of Christianity; they were shameless manipulators; they were brute materialists; on and on. The remarkable consistency of such complaints, across cultures and across eras, suggests that they are grounded in intrinsic Jewish qualities—qualities that certainly have a genetic basis.

For much of history, commentary on the Jewish Question was limited to brief remarks or passing comments. The relative handful of books dedicated to the topic were generally by Christian theologians of the Middle Ages or Renaissance, and thus relied heavily on theological disputations. While interesting, these studies are less relevant today; in the current world, we are less concerned with the theological inanities of Judaism than we are with secular Jewish traits, behaviors, and values. Thus we see a shift in Jewish critiques from the beginning of the 1800s: complaints became less focused on religion and more on behavior and action. Thinkers around the world began to realize that it was not Judaism per se that was the problem, but rather *the Jews themselves.* This realization is the modern basis for discussions of the Jewish Question.

Thanks to pervasive Jewish influence in media and academia—a condition that has existed for well over 200 years in the West—readers are often unfamiliar with detailed critiques of the Jews. Many people, for example, have a vague impression that "Richard Wagner was an anti-Semite" but they have no idea what he actually said or wrote. Many suspect that there were longstanding references to Jews as financial manipulators or political corruptors or war agitators, but they have no idea where those ideas came from, nor what the basis might be for such claims. Many know that the Nazis were anti-Semitic in the extreme, but very few know the context from which Hitler's (and others') ideas emerged. The few people who might be interested in details find it hard to locate full and unbiased translations of the relevant material, even on the Internet.

The objective of the present volume is to begin to remedy these problems. Here, we present a selection of truly classic essays on the Jewish Question, from the years 1850 to 1945. When not limited by reasons of space, we have presented these essays in full. In each case, we offer honest and sympathetic translations in highly-readable modern American English. We have preserved as many of the original footnotes as possible and added a number of our own, to further illuminate the subjects at hand. The essays are presented here chronologically, in order that the reader might get a better sense of the flow and progression of ideas over time.

If indeed the Jewish Question is the most pressing matter of our day, we hope that this selection will shed some badly needed light on the topic, and serve as a stimulus to action. It is in neither Gentile nor Jewish interests that corrupt Jews dominate society. All are well-served by carefully considering these issues, and by moving global society toward a more balanced and more just future.

CLASSIC ESSAYS ON THE JEWISH QUESTION

JEWRY IN MUSIC

Richard Wagner
(1850/1869)

Editor: Renowned German composer Richard Wagner (1813-1883) was often confronted, and even surrounded, by Jews in the music business—as composers, journalists, theater owners, and promoters. But for the first several years of his professional life, he was generally able to ignore them. Both his 'early' (pre-1843) and 'middle' (1843-1850) works were composed without apparent reference to the Jewish Question. Wagner's middle period, which included such classic operas as *Tannhäuser* and *Lohengrin*, was effectively complete by 1850, when he was just 37 years old. It was just around this time that a student of his, Theodor Uhlig, wrote a series of articles critical of Jewish composer Giacomo Meyerbeer and his "Hebraic taste in art." Wagner was notably impressed—sufficiently so that he decided to write his own essay, under a pseudonym, to be titled *Das Judenthum in der Musik* (Jewry in Music). In it, he would address the broader question of negative Jewish influence on music and culture generally, within a specifically German context.

The word *Judenthum,* incidentally, is often translated as 'Judaism,' and sometimes as 'Jewishness,' rather than 'Jewry' as we have here. But the former term refers to the Jewish religion, which is not at issue here; and the latter suggests a kind of Jewish quality or aspect to music, when the real concern is involvement and degradation of music (and culture) by Jews themselves. Literally, 'Jewdom' might be appropriate, but this is not a proper English word. It is the collective body of Jews, as members of a specific ethnicity, that is at issue—hence, 'Jewry.'

Despite the use of a penname, most people suspected that Wagner had authored the offending essay; it was something of an open secret in German music circles, at least. From that time on, Jewish critics, producers, and journalists took every opportunity to disparage or discredit Wagner and his compositions—and just as he was entering his mature and most productive period of life. Still, for nearly 20 years afterward, Wagner said little publicly on the Jews.

Eventually, after years of frustration, he decided to speak out once again, and this time openly, in his own name. Thus it was that, in 1869, at age 56, he published both the original essay and a lengthy follow-up piece that was originally composed as a letter from himself to a close friend, and part-Jew, Marie Muchanoff (or Muchanow; née Kalergis). The new essay—now considered Part 2 of *Jewry in Music*—is a prescient discussion of Jewish underhanded attacks and petty assaults on Wagner's character and career. It is an instructive and enlightening commentary on the diverse tactics employed by Jews in positions of influence against people that oppose their dominance.

The combined two-part essay, presented here in full, has rarely been published; at best, one can find short quotations or excerpts, carefully selected to give a maximum negative connotation to the author. In any case, *Jewry in Music* is widely considered "an important landmark" in the emergence of German critiques of Jewry in the late 1800s. Wagner's status contributed in no small part to its legacy, and his name was often invoked by supporters over subsequent decades. It is an entirely appropriate essay to open this book. All notes are the editor's, unless otherwise specified.

PART ONE

In the *Neue Zeitschrift für Musik* not long ago, mention was made of a "Hebraic taste in art": an attack and a defense of that expression neither did, nor could, be avoided. Now, it seems to me not unimportant to clear up the matter lying at bottom of all this—a matter either hitherto glossed over by our critics, or touched with a certain burst of excitement. It's not a question, however, of saying something new, but of explaining that unconscious feeling that proclaims itself among the people as a rooted dislike of the Jewish nature; thus, of saying something really existent, and by no means of attempting to artfully breathe life into an unreality through the force of any sort of fancy. Criticism goes against its very essence, if, in attack or defense, it tries for anything else.

Since it here is merely with respect to art, and especially to music, that we want to explain to ourselves the popular dislike of the Jewish nature,[1] even at the present day, we may completely pass over any dealing with this same phenomenon in the field of religion and politics. In religion, the Jews have long ceased to be our hated foes, thanks to all those within the Christian religion itself who have drawn upon themselves the people's hatred. In pure politics, we have never come to actual conflict with the Jews; we have even granted them the erection of a new Jewish kingdom, and in this respect, we have rather had to regret that Herr von Rothschild was too keen-witted to make himself King of the Jews, preferring, as is well known, to remain "the Jew of Kings".[2]

It is another matter, however, where politics become a question of society. Here the isolation of the Jews has been held by us a challenge to the exercise of human justice, for just as long as in ourselves the thrust toward social liberation has awoken into clearer consciousness. When we strove for the emancipation of the Jews, however, we were more the champions of an abstract principle than of a concrete case. Just as all our liberalism was a not very lucid mental sport—since we went for freedom of the people without knowledge of that people itself; nay, with a dislike of any genuine contact with it—so our eagerness to equalize the rights of Jews was rather more stimulated by a general idea than by any real sympathy. For, with all our speaking and writing in favor of the Jews' emancipation, we always felt instinctively repelled by any actual, operative contact with them.[3]

Here, then, we touch on a point that brings us closer to our main inquiry. We have to explain to ourselves our *involuntary repellence* toward the nature and personality of the Jews, so as to vindicate that instinctive dislike that we plainly recognize as stronger and more overpowering than our conscious zeal to rid ourselves of it. Even today we only purposely contradict ourselves in this regard, when we think it necessary to hold as immoral and

---

[1] Jews have, for millennia, been renowned for their "hatred of humanity." This hatred has always engendered a counter-hatred against the Jews themselves. See *Eternal Strangers* (T. Dalton, 2020) for the full story.

[2] A reference to Amschel Mayer von Rothschild (1773-1855). As a wealthy banker, Rothschild found it profitable to curry favor with royals by providing large loans and other financial services.

[3] Germans Jews had long sought legal equality and 'emancipation,' which they were in the process of attaining. They had already received this in Prussia (in 1812) and in Württemberg (in 1826), but full rights across Germany would not come until 1870.

taboo all open proclamation of our natural repugnance against the Jewish nature. Only in recent times do we seem to have reached an insight, that it is more rational to rid ourselves of that strenuous self-deception, so as to instead quite soberly view the object of our violent sympathy and bring ourselves to understand a repugnance still abiding with us, despite all our liberal bedazzlements. To our astonishment, we perceive that, in our liberal battles, we have been floating in the air and fighting clouds, whereas the whole fair soil of material reality has found in the Jews an appropriator who found our aerial flights very amusing, no doubt, yet who hold us far too foolish to reward us by relaxing one iota of their usurpation of that material soil. Quite imperceptibly, the "Creditor of Kings" has become the King of Creeds, and we really cannot take this monarch's pleading for emancipation as other than uncommonly naïve, seeing that it is rather *we* who are shifted into the necessity of fighting for emancipation from the Jews.

According to the present constitution of this world, the Jew in truth is already more than emancipated; *he rules*, and will rule, so long as money remains the power before which all our doings and our dealings lose their force. That the historical adversity of the Jews, and the rapacious rawness of Christian-German potentates, have brought this power within the hands of Israel's sons—this needs no argument to prove. That the impossibility of carrying further any natural, 'necessary,' and truly beauteous thing, upon the basis of that stage where the evolution of our arts has now arrived, and without a total alteration of that basis, is clear. That this has also brought the public art-taste of our time, between the busy fingers of the Jew, however, is the matter whose grounds we have here to consider somewhat closer.

What which the lords of the Roman and medieval world extracted from their bondmen through toil and labor is today turned into money by the Jew. Who thinks of noticing that the guileless-looking scrap of paper is slimy with the blood of countless generations? What the heroes of the arts, with untold life-consuming strain, have wrested from two millennia of misery, today the Jew converts into an art-bazaar. Who sees it in the mannered bric-a-brac that it is glued together by the hallowed brow-sweat of the genius of 2,000 years?

We have no need to first substantiate the Jewification of modern art; it springs to the eye, and thrusts itself upon the senses. It would take us too far afield to attempt to explain this phenomenon by a demonstration of the character of our art history itself. But if emancipation from the yoke of Jewry appears to us the greatest of necessities, we must hold it, above all, to prove our forces for this war of liberation.

Now, we shall never win these forces from an abstract definition of that phenomenon per se, but only from an accurate acquaintance with the nature of that involuntary feeling of ours that utters itself as an instinctive repugnance against the Jew's prime essence. Through it, through this unconquerable feeling—if we avow it quite honestly—it will become clear to us what we hate in that essence. What we then know definitely, we can make headway against. Nay, through his very laying-bare, may we even hope to rout the demon from the field, whereon he has only been able to maintain his stand beneath the shelter of a twilight darkness—a darkness we good-natured humanists ourselves have cast upon him, to make his appearance less loathsome.

*****

The Jew—who, as everyone knows, has a God all to himself—in ordinary life strikes us primarily by his outward appearance, which, no matter to what European nationality we belong, contains something disagreeably foreign. Instinctively we wish to have nothing in common with a man who looks like that. This must heretofore have passed as a misfortune for the Jew. In more recent times, however, we perceive that in the midst of this misfortune he feels entirely well; after all his successes, he necessarily deems his difference from us a pure and beneficial distinction.

Passing over the moral side, in the effect of this intrinsically unpleasant freak of nature, and coming to its bearing upon art, we here will merely observe that, to us, this exterior is unthinkable as a subject for the representative arts. If plastic art wants to present us with a Jew, it mostly takes its model from sheer fantasy, with a prudent ennobling, or entire omission, of everything that commonly characterizes the Jew's appearance. But the Jew never wanders on to the theatrical stage; the exceptions are so rare and special that they only confirm the general rule. We can conceive no representation of an antique or modern stage-character by a Jew, be it as hero or lover, without instinctively feeling the incongruity of such a notion. This is highly significant; a man whose appearance we must hold unfitted for artistic treatment—not merely in this or that personality, but according to his kind in general—neither can we hold him capable of any sort of artistic expression of his inner essence.

But far weightier, and quite decisive for our inquiry, is the effect the Jew produces on us through his speech; and this is the essential point in considering Jewish influence on music. The Jew speaks the language of the nation in which he dwells over generations, but he always speaks it as an alien. As it lies beyond our present scope to occupy ourselves with the cause of this phenomenon, we may also abstain from an accusation of Christian civilization for having kept the Jew in violent separation from it. On the other hand, in touching on the nature of that separation, we can scarcely propose to hold the Jews responsible.

Our only object here is to throw light on the aesthetic character of the results. In the first place, then, the general circumstance that the Jew speaks modern European languages merely as learned, and not as native tongues, must necessarily restrict him from expressing himself idiomatically, independently, and in conformance with his nature. A language, with its expression and evolution, is not the work of scattered units but of a historical community; only he who has unconsciously grown up within the bond of this community takes any share in its creations. But the Jew has stood outside the pale of any such community; he has stood solitarily with his Jehovah in a splintered, rootless stock, to which all self-generated evolution is denied, just as even the peculiar language of that stock—Hebrew—has been preserved for him merely as something dead.

Now, to make poetry in a foreign tongue has hitherto been impossible, even to geniuses of highest rank. Our whole European art and civilization, however, have remained a foreign tongue to the Jew. Just as he has taken no part in the evolution of the one, so has he taken none in that of the other. At most, the homeless creature has been a cold, hostile on-looker. In such language or such art, the Jew can naturally but echo and imitate, and is perforce barred from fluent expression and pure creative work.

The purely physical aspect of the Jewish mode of speech is particularly repellent to us. Throughout an intercourse of two millennia with European nations, culture has not succeeded in breaking the remarkable stubbornness of the Jewish nature as regards the peculiarities of Semitic pronunciation. The first thing that strikes our ear as quite outlandish and unpleasant is a creaking, squeaking, buzzing snuffle. Add to this a usage of words in a sense quite foreign to our nation's tongue, and an arbitrary twisting of the structure of our phrases—and this mode of speaking acquires at once the character of an intolerably jumbled blabber. When we hear this Jewish talk, our attention involuntarily dwells on its repulsive manner, rather than on any intrinsic meaning.

It must be recognized and borne in mind, above all, how exceptionally important this circumstance is, particularly for explaining the impression made on us by the musical works of modern Jews. If we hear a Jew speak, we are unconsciously offended by the entire lack of purely human expression in his discourse. The cold indifference of its peculiar blabber never rises, even by accident, to the ardor of a higher, heartfelt passion. If, on the other hand, we find ourselves driven to this more heated expression in a conversation with a Jew, he will always shuffle off, since he is incapable of replying in kind. The Jew never bothers himself in mutual interchange of feelings with us, but—so far as we are concerned—only in the altogether special egoistic interest of his vanity or profit. This is something which, coupled with the wry expression of his daily mode of speech, always gives to such excitement a tinge of the ridiculous, and may arouse anything except sympathy with the interests of the speaker. Though it may well be conceivable that, in intercourse with one another, and particularly where domestic life brings purely-human feelings to an outburst, even the Jews may be able to give expression to their emotions in a manner effective enough among themselves. Yet, this is irrelevant here, since we Germans are listening to the Jew who, in the intercourse of life and art, speaks expressly to us.

Now, if the aforesaid defects of his dialect make the Jew almost incapable of giving artistic enunciation to his thoughts and feelings through speech, his aptitude is necessarily infinitely smaller with respect to *song*. Song is just speech aroused to highest passion. Music is the speech of passion. If the Jew, in allowing himself a greater intensity of expression through the medium of speech, may make himself ridiculous without exciting our sympathy in the least degree, he will, should he proceed to the height of song, become entirely unsupportable. In the latter, everything that had previously moved us unfavorably, whether relating to his speech or to his outward appearance, becomes intensified. We are either driven from the scene or else chained to the spot by the utter absurdity of such a manifestation. In song, the peculiarity of the Jewish nature that affects us so disagreeably is very naturally at its height, considering that song is the most vivid and unquestionably the truest expression of personal feeling. Consequently, to whatever branch of art we may feel inclined to admit the Jews as capable, that of song, at all events, must, by a natural admission, be eternally denied to him.

*****

The Jews' sense perception has never been of such a kind as to allow plastic artists to arise among them. Their eyes have always been busied with far more practical affairs than beauty and the spiritual substance of the world. We know nothing of a Jewish architect or sculptor in our times, as far as I am aware. Whether recent painters of Jewish descent have been truly creative in their art, I must leave to connoisseurs to judge; presumably, however, these artists occupy no other standing toward their art than that of modern Jewish composers toward music—to whose plainer investigation we now will turn.

The Jew, who is innately incapable of articulating himself to us artistically through either his outward appearance or his speech, and least of all through his singing, has nevertheless been able, in the broad spread of modern types of art, especially in music, to attain the dictatorship of public taste. To explain this phenomenon, let us first consider how it became possible for the Jew to become a musician. From that turning-point in our social evolution where money, with less and less disguise, was raised to the virtual level of nobility, the Jews—to whom money-making without actual labor, i.e. usury, had been left as their only trade—the Jews not merely could no longer be denied standing in a new society that needed little but gold, but they brought it with them in their pockets. Thus our modern culture, accessible to no one but the well-to-do, remained an open book to them, as it sank into a venal article of luxury.

Henceforward, then, the *cultured Jew* appears in our society; and his distinction from the uncultured, common Jew is something we now have to closely observe. The cultured Jew has spared no pains to strip off all the obvious tokens of his lower co-religionists. In many cases, he has even deemed it wise to become baptized as a Christian in order to wash away the traces of his origin. This zeal, however, has never got so far as to let him reap the anticipated fruits. It has conducted only to his utter isolation, and to making him the most heartless of all human beings—to such a point that we have been bound to lose even our earlier sympathy for the tragic history of his stock. His connection with his former comrades in suffering, which he arrogantly tore asunder, it has made it impossible for him to replace with a new connection with that society in which he has prospered.

He maintains good standing with none but those who need his money. And never yet has money risen to the point of knitting a good bond between man and man. The educated Jew stands alien and apathetic in the midst of a society he does not understand, with whose tastes and aspirations he does not sympathize, and whose history and evolution have always been indifferent to him. In such a situation, have we seen the Jews give birth to thinkers. The thinker is a backward-looking poet; but the true poet is a foretelling prophet. Nothing but deep and entire sympathy with the common strivings of a great community can form a sufficient qualification for the exercise of this high office, for it is by this sympathy that the poet is enabled to give unconscious expression to such aspirations. But from such a community of sentiment, the higher Jew is, by the very nature of his position, completely shut out. He has separated himself from all connection with his own race; the education he has acquired and paid for is to him a mere luxury—and one, moreover, for which he is somewhat at a loss to find a suitable employment.

Now, our modern arts have likewise become a portion of this culture, and among them more particularly that art which is just the very easiest to learn—the art of *music*. Indeed, that music which, severed from her sister arts, had been lifted by the force and stress of grandest geniuses to a stage in her universal faculty of expression where either, in new conjunction with the other arts, she might speak aloud the most sublime, or also, in continued separation from them, to become that for the communication of the trivial and indifferent. Naturally, what the cultured Jew had to say in his aforesaid situation could be nothing but the trivial and indifferent, because his whole artistic bent was a mere luxurious, needless thing. Exactly as his whim inspired, or some interest lying outside art, could he express himself now this way, and now otherwise. Never was he driven to say a definite, real, and necessary thing, but he just merely wanted to speak, no matter what; so that, naturally, the *how* was the only 'moment' left for him to care about.

At present, no art affords such possibilities of "speaking without saying anything" as music, since the greatest geniuses have already said whatever there was to say in it as an absolutely separate art. When this had once been said, there was nothing left but to babble after—and indeed, with quite distressing accuracy and deceptive likeness, just as parrots reel off human words and phrases, but also with just as little real feeling and expression as these foolish birds. Only, in the case of our Jewish music makers, this mimicked speech presents one marked peculiarity—that of the Jewish style of speech in general, which we have more precisely characterized above.

Although the peculiarities of the Jewish mode of speaking and singing appear most glaringly in the commoner class of Jew, who has remained faithful to his fathers' stock, and though cultured Jewry takes untold pains to strip them off, nevertheless they show an impertinent obstinacy in sticking to him. Physiology may explain part of this, yet it also has its reason in the aforesaid social situation of the educated Jew. However much our luxury-art may float in well-nigh nothing but the ether of our self-willed fantasy, still it keeps a connection to the genuine Folk spirit. The true poet, no matter in what branch of art, still gains his stimulus from nothing but a faithful, loving contemplation of instinctive life, of that life that only greets his sight amid the Folk.

Now, where is the cultured Jew to find this Folk? Not, surely, on the soil of that society in which he plays his artistic role. If he has any connection at all with this society, it is merely with an offshoot of it, entirely loosened from the real, healthy stem; but this connection is entirely loveless, and this lovelessness must ever become more obvious to him, if he approaches society for the sake of feeding his artistic cravings. Not only does he here find everything stranger and more unintelligible, but the instinctive ill-will of the Folk confronts him here in all its wounding nakedness, since—unlike its fellow in the richer classes—it is neither weakened nor broken down here by reckonings of advantage and regard for the common interest.

*****

Repulsed therefore in a manner most hurtful to his feelings by a society of which he is unable to seize the spirit, the educated Jew is driven back to his own race, where at least everything is immeasurably clearer. Whether he will or not, this is the source from which he must draw what he requires, but here again he is confronted by the dearth of material for "What to say"; assistance in the direction of "How to speak" is all that is offered to him. The fact is that the Jews have never had an art of their own—never a life replete with artistic possibilities. Features of universal human application are not to be found amongst them, the sum of their resource being the peculiar mode of expression indicated above.

Only one source may be said to offer itself to the Jewish composer, and that lies in the solemn musical service dedicated to his Jehovah. After all, it is to the synagogue that he must look if he hopes to obtain motives that are both comprehensible and of true folk-character.

Now, however much we may feel inclined to regard this musical divine-service as noble and inspired in its condition of original purity, we cannot fail to observe that the condition in which it has come down to us is one of the greatest corruption. In this domain, thousands of years have passed without any development or movement of inner life; and, like everything else in Judah, it has stood still both as to form and content. But a form that is never enlivened by renewal of its contents becomes ever disintegrated at last, just as words that no longer represent a living feeling are liable to become distorted and obsolete in the same way. Who, for example, has not had occasion to become convinced that what goes on in the present day in an ordinary synagogue is the merest caricature of church-song? Who has not been shocked and held to the spot, partly by horror and partly by a sense of their absurdity, at hearing those gurgling, yodeling, and babbling sounds bereft of all trace of sense and spirit, and which no intentional caricature could depict so horribly as all appears in fact, and which may easily be witnessed going on with the most perfect naiveté and earnestness?

It may be admitted that a spirit of reform has recently shown itself and has taken the legitimate direction of trying to restore the primitive purity of this Divine Song. From the viewpoint of the higher and more reflective Jewish intelligence, the result is, however, mere fruitless labor. It is merely that of an effort on the part of culture to improve the people; but the improvement of the latter can obviously never be such that the higher Jew, seeking the satisfaction of his art-needs at their proper source in the instinctive life of his people, can find amongst them anything more than the reflection of his own efforts. But it is the Instinctive and not the Reflected that he longs to find; the latter is simply his own creation. Yet, all of the former that he can hope to meet is the same distorted expression as before.

If, like artists in general, the educated Jew has been led back to the folk source, not premeditatedly but instinctively, and from the very nature of the necessities which press upon him, the impression produced may be applied to the art productions of his race. Those melisma and rhythms of the synagogue captivate the musical fancy of the Jewish composer quite in the same way as an instinctive familiarity with the melodies and rhythms of our own folk-song and dance constitutes a nucleus of power for the creators of our musical works of art, whether vocal or instrumental.

Out of our copious range of folk-song, only such material is open to the musical faculty of perception of the educated Jew as may happen to strike his fancy as intelligible; but only that can be intelligible to him, in the sense of being able to be applied artistically, that is found to present some aspect of approach to Jewish musical peculiarities. Were the Jew, by listening either to our simple or our artistic music, to attempt to trace the heart and soul of its inner life, he would be inevitably driven to the conclusion that these present nothing in common with his own musical nature. The total strangeness of such a manifestation might be counted upon to persuade him that it would probably be impossible in the future for him to sustain sufficient courage to attempt to compete with us in our art-creation.

The Jew, however, is never induced by his position in general amongst us to indulge in any such deep reflections. Whether it be by design, as happens when he recognizes his real position, or whether instinctively, as happens when he lacks the capacity to understand it—in either case, he listens to our art-productions and their life-giving inner organism in a merely superficial manner. But such an unsympathetic hearing can necessarily convey to him no more than exterior resemblances with what may be either intelligible to him or consonant with his nature.

Thus it happens that he mistakes the *exterior* of the manifestations in our musical life and art-domain for the real substance of them. Thus it is that his conceptions of them, when he ventures upon a reproduction, strike us as strange, odd, indifferent, unnatural, and distorted—to such a degree that Jewish musical works often produce upon us an impression similar to that which we might expect from a Goethe poem, if recited before us in the Jewish gibberish. Just as a confused heap of words and phrases are hurled together in this jargon, the Jew composer makes a confused heap of the forms and styles of all ages and masters. Cheek-by-jowl we meet them in the loveliest chaos—formal peculiarities of the various schools all huddled together. The intention in these productions was merely to *speak*, and to do so at all hazards, and therefore to the exclusion of all consideration of any object sufficiently worthy of conferring some value. The only means of rendering such babble at all exciting to the ear is to continually change the means and mode of expression.

Heartfelt excitement and true passion find their own appropriate tongue when, striving to make themselves intelligible, they formulate an utterance. The Jew, however, as already described in this connection, has no real passion—or, in any case, no passion of a nature to impel him to artistic creation. But without such passion there can also be no repose, for a genuine and noble stillness is nothing else than passion that has subsided and become resigned. Where there has been no previous passion, we recognize no calm—but only dullness. The usual contrast to this, in Jewish work, is a pungent unrest that is so noticeable from beginning to end; it only ceases, in fact, to make way for the aforesaid dullness, which is devoid of both spirit and feeling.

All that the Jew's ambition to engage in art has really yielded must therefore necessarily possess the properties of coldness and indifference, if not even those of triviality and nonsense. Hence the period of Jewry in modern music can only be described historically as one of complete unfruitfulness and of a stability gone to ruin.

*****

Where is the manifestation by which all the preceding could be rendered clearer? Where is one to be found more instantly calculated to convince us, than that presented to us in the works of a composer of Jewish extraction who was endowed by Nature with specific musical gifts to a degree hitherto equaled by few? Everything that in the course of our enquiry into the antipathy we feel towards the Jewish character gave ground for reflection—whether the contradictions of this character within itself and towards us, or its incapacity, whilst outside our domain, to deal with us on that ground—or, its lack of the power even to formulate so much as an earnest desire to further develop the productions that have sprung from us. All these accumulated considerations rise up with the importance of a tragic conflict as we find them exhibited in the nature, life, and artistic career of the composer who was taken from our midst at such an early age—Felix Mendelssohn-Bartholdy.[4]

By him we have been shown that a Jew may be gifted with the ripest specific talent, he may have acquired the finest and most varied education, and he may possess the highest and most finely-tempered sense of honor. And yet, notwithstanding all these advantages, he may remain unable, even in so much as *one solitary instance*, to bring forth that deep effect upon our hearts and souls that we expect from art because we know its capability in that direction—because we have experienced it many times. In fact, this has happened whenever a hero of our craft has deigned, as it were, to open his mouth to speak to us.

To the professional music critics, who must necessarily have arrived at a similar view, the duty of confirming this unquestionable fact comes by references to individual instances among Mendelssohn's productions. The general statement, however, will be made sufficiently clear here if we recall that, in hearing a piece by this composer, our attention is only fixed, while graceful, smooth, and artificial figures are in progress. These are brought forward, ordered, and combined, more or less for the entertainment of our fancy; their changes are akin to those of the kaleidoscope. But never do we

---

[4] Mendelssohn (1809-1847) died at age 38 from a series of strokes.

feel moved at those situations where the figures are intended to express any deep or pithy heart-sensation. At that point, even formal productive capacity for Mendelssohn entirely ceased. For this reason, wherever, as in Oratorio, he approached Drama, he was obliged to appropriate without scruple any individual feature that he could gather from this or that predecessor, according to whom he had taken as his temporary model. In doing so, it is to be well observed that, in his expressionless modern speech, he had a marked preference for our old master, Bach, as model. Bach's musical language grew up at that period of our musical history when the universal musical tongue was still struggling for the power of individual and exact expression. The purely formal and pedantic still had so strong a hold upon it that, even in the case of Bach, it was only through the stupendous power of his genius that purely human expression was able to break through such an obstacle. The language of Bach stands to the language of Mozart, and finally to that of Beethoven, in the same relation as did the Egyptian Sphinx to Grecian sculpture. And, in the same way as the Sphinx with human face seems to strive to quit its animal body, so does the noble human figure of Bach seem to strive to quit its ancient periwig.

The luxurious musical taste of our time is subject to an inconceivable and thoughtless confusion, which lies in the fact that we complacently listen, at one and the same time, to discussion of Bach and Beethoven's mode of expression. We actually make ourselves believe that the difference between them was merely an individual and formal one, losing sight of the fact that it really stands for an important landmark in the history of our culture.

The reason for this is, however, obvious enough. Beethoven's speech was the musical language of a complete, finished, warm-feeling man, and could necessarily proceed from no one else. It was the speech of a musical man so perfect that, of irresistible impulse, he had pressed forward beyond the domain of absolute music, the limits of which he had measured and extended to their utmost. In doing so, he showed us the way to the fruition of all arts through music as their only successful extension.

Bach's speech, on the other hand, can be suitably imitated by any well-equipped musician, even though it be not in the same sense that Bach employed it. In it, the formal element predominates; the purely human element, being not so completely the governing feature, that the "What to say" is able to assert itself quite unconditionally, and this for the reason that it is still too much engaged in the throes of "How to speak." The flimsiness and waywardness of our musical style has been, in consequence of Mendelssohn's attempt to deliver unclear and worthless material in the most agreeable manner possible, or if not actually introduced, at all events, pushed to its utmost limits. Beethoven, the last in the chain of our genuine music-heroes, with the most intense longing and miraculous powers, strove ever for the clearest and most accurate expression of that which was otherwise unspeakable with the sharply-cut plastic form of his tone-pictures. Mendelssohn, by contrast, dwindles these trophies in his productions, thus reducing his effects to the level of disintegrating views and of fantastic shadow-pictures. By such uncertain tints, our capricious imaginative powers may be excited, but our pure and manly longing for clearer artistic insight is scarcely so much as moved to any hope of fulfilment.

Only when the irksome consciousness of this limitation of power appears to influence the composer's mood, compelling him to the expression of a soft and melancholy resignation, does Mendelssohn present himself to us characteristically. And he does so then in the subjective sense of a refined character which, confronted by the impossible, makes a confession of its own impotence. This, as has been said, constitutes the tragic feature in Mendelssohn's life. And, should we desire to extend our sympathy to any personality within the domain of art, we could not refuse it in strong measure to him, notwithstanding that its force is likely to be diminished when we reflect that, in his case, the Tragic was rather a passive resultant feeling than one leading to active, suffering, and enlightening conviction.

*****

No other Jewish composer has, however, been able to awaken a similar sympathy in us. A celebrated Jewish music-setter of our day has, in his productions, had a portion of our public in view whose entire confusion of musical taste was less a matter for him to *accommodate* than to *exploit*.[5] The present opera-going public has now for a long time been gradually more and more and, at last, totally drawn away from the claims that should rightly be addressed—not only in dramatic art-work, but in all work of good taste. The seats at these places of amusement are generally occupied by that portion of our middle-class society with whom utter boredom is the only reason for

---

[5] Wagner refers here, without specific mention, to Giacomo Meyerbeer (1791-1864), a wealthy and popular Jewish composer of the time. Today, Meyerbeer has been consigned to utter obscurity. It is revealing that Wagner refuses to mention him by name.

preferring one occupation to another. The infirmity of boredom, however, is not one to be cured by art-enjoyment, and any deliberate attempt to disperse it merely results in the deception of reproducing it in another form. The cultivation of this deception has formed the artistic life-study of the renowned opera-composer alluded to [i.e. Meyerbeer].

It could serve no useful purpose to describe in detail the array of artistic means that he has employed for the attainment of the object of his ambition. His success sufficiently shows that he thoroughly understood this form of deceit. This was principally attained by serving up to his jaded audience in the jargon that has already been described, and as if they were modern sayings of a pointed description, all the trivialities which, in their original inanity, had been represented before them over and over again. It is unsurprising that this composer was also intent upon utilizing the effect of catastrophes and contrived emotional situations. Anyone who knows how necessary such features are to those who are bored will feel no astonishment at the success of his intention, which, if they consider well the circumstances, they will regard as a foregone conclusion. This deceiver amongst composers succeeds, in fact, so well that he deceives himself, and does so perhaps with an intention as deliberate as that which he applies to the deceit of his audience.

In reality, we believe that he would like to produce true works of art, knowing at the same time, that he cannot do it. Thus, in order to escape from this painful conflict between what he would like and what he is able to do, he writes operas for Paris that can then easily get played in other parts of the world. This, nowadays, is the surest means of making oneself an art-celebrity—without the necessity of becoming an artist beforehand. Under the stress of this self-deception (which is not so trouble-free as might be supposed) he appears to us, moreover, in a tragic light, though the effect is rendered tragi-comic by his wounded vanity. As it is, the would-be-emotional and the really laughable are the features by which we recognize the Jewishness of this renowned composer in his music.

A more precise examination of the various instances brought forward—instances which we can now appreciate in detail, having by this time ascertained the basis of and justification for our invincible dislike of the Jewish nature—will result in showing us, firstly, the ineptitude of our musical art-epoch. For, if our music had really been advanced to a higher degree of flowering by the two Jewish composers alluded to [Mendelssohn and Meyerbeer], we would have to admit that our remaining behind them indicated some organic incapacity on our part. That, however, is not the case. On the contrary, the individual and purely musical capacity that we possess, as compared with that of past art-epochs, must be declared to represent an *increase* of power rather than its diminution.

Our present ineptitude lies in the very spirit of our art, longing as it does for a life quite different from the artificial one which, with such toil, is at present upheld. The shortcomings of our art-style are already sufficiently evident to us in the works of Mendelssohn—that specially and remarkably gifted musician. But the successes of the renowned Jewish composer we have mentioned [Meyerbeer] make the worthlessness of our public taste, with its absolutely inartistic existence and requirements, abundantly clear. Such are the weighty points which everyone who feels sincerely towards art must take upon himself personally. Upon these we have to enquire and to question ourselves until we come to a right understanding.[6] Whoever declines this trouble, whoever turns away from this enquiry—either because no direct necessity forces him to it or because he dreads the increased knowledge of himself that might result, driving him from the lazy ruts of an old custom devoid of thought or feeling—that person we include in the category of "Jews" in regard to music.

The Jews were utterly unable to secure a footing in this art until the time arrived when it was demonstratively incapable of an inner life. During the whole period that music as a separate art possessed a really organized necessity for existence, right down to the time of Mozart and Beethoven, we find no trace of any Jewish composer. It was impossible that an element so

---

[6] Wagner adds this footnote: "Characteristic enough is the attitude adopted by the remaining Jew musicians, nay, by the whole of cultured Jewry, toward their two most renowned composers. To the adherents of Mendelssohn, that famous opera-composer [Meyerbeer] is an atrocity; with a keen sense of honor, they feel how much he compromises Jewry in the eyes of better-trained musicians, and therefore they show no mercy in their judgment. But far more cautiously do that composer's retainers express themselves concerning Mendelssohn, regarding more with envy, than with manifest ill-will, the success he has made in the 'more solid' music-world. To a third faction, that of the composition-at-any-price Jews, it is their visible object to avoid all internecine scandal, and all self-exposure in general, so that their music-producing may take its even course without occasioning any painful fuss. The undeniable successes of the great opera-composer they let pass as worth only slight attention, allowing that there is something in them, although one cannot approve of much or dub it 'solid.' In truth, the Jews are far too clever not to know how to line their own pockets!"

foreign to that life should form part of its living organism. It is only when the inner death of a body becomes apparent that external elements have the power to seize upon it—though only to destroy it. Then it is, perhaps, that the flesh of this body is transformed into a wormy mass. But at sight of that, who would dare assert that the body still lives? The spirit that was its life has taken refuge with kindred other bodies. Only in active life shall we ever be able to meet that spirit again—and never aside the worm-ridden corpse.

*****

Having stated above that the Jews had produced no genuine poet, I must say something of Heinrich Heine. At the time of Goethe and Schiller's poetical creations, at all events, no one had heard of any poetical Jew. But when poetry became a lie, there was no limit to what might spring from the unpoetical life-standard we had adopted. Then it was that a highly-gifted poetical Jew undertook to cover with scathing irony the counterfeit moderation and Jesuitical hypocrisy of verse, still fondly regarded as poetical. He also unmercifully savaged the celebrated musical members of his own race for indulging the idea that they were artists. No deception could stand against him, for it seemed as though he were restlessly urged on by some merciless demon to seek out whatever might seem worthy of denial. He went through all the illusions of modern life, until at last he lied himself into being a poet, and was duly rewarded by having his poetical lies set to music by our own composers. He was the conscience of Jewry, in the same way that Jewry itself is the evil conscience of our modern civilization.

Another Jew remains to be mentioned, one who appeared amongst us as an author.[7] He came forth from his isolation as a Jew seeming to seek deliverance amongst us, but he did not find it. He had to convince himself, perforce, that only with our own deliverance as true men could he ever find it. But to a Jew, the idea of becoming a man in common with us is very nearly the same thing as that of ceasing to be a Jew. Börne fulfilled this.[8] But his case precisely shows us that deliverance cannot be attained in comfort or in cool, indifferent ease; as with us, it exacts a price in terms of toil, want, anxiety, and fulness of suffering and pain. If we participate frankly in this work

---

[7] As we see below, Wagner refers here to Ludwig Börne (1786-1837).
[8] Börne converted to Christianity at age 32, changed his name (from Loeb Baruch), and disavowed all connections with Judaism.

of deliverance—which, beginning in self-effacement, continues by being again productive—we remain one and undivided!

But remember that only one real thing can redeem you from the curse that befalls you: the redemption of Ahasuerus—*the "going under"!*[9]

PART TWO

The foregoing essay appeared, as I said, and in a form essentially the same as presented here, in the *Neue Zeitschrift für Musik*—now slightly more than 18 years ago.

It still remains almost inconceivable to me that my friend, Franz Brendel,[10] the editor of that journal, and now recently deceased, should have ever prevailed upon himself to risk its publication. In any case, this earnest-

---

[9] Wagner's cryptic closing sentence has instigated much speculation. First, the name Ahasuerus is ambiguous, given that there are two possible referents. It first appears in the Old Testament, in the Book of Esther, as the putative name of a Persian king, presumed to represent the actual king Xerxes (circa 475 BC). As the story goes, Ahasuerus comes to take a Jewish girl, Esther, as his queen—though she cleverly hides her ethnicity. Somewhat later, Ahasuerus' second-in-command, Haman, became highly disturbed at the actions of the many Jews in the realm, and consequently "sought to destroy all the Jews" (Esther 3:6), including, especially, Esther's cousin Mordecai. Esther and Mordecai then plotted against Haman, finally succeeding in having him hung on the gallows. (The Jews then acted in retaliation, killing "75,000 of those who hated them" [9:16]).

Much later, in the 1200s, a second Ahasuerus (or Ahasver) came to be associated with the image of "the wandering Jew," and especially with a particular Jew who allegedly taunted Jesus on his way to the crucifixion—though there is no Biblical source for such a story. As eternal wanderers, the Jews were cursed, perhaps by God, for their blasphemy against Jesus and Christianity more broadly.

So Wagner's "redemption of Ahasuerus" could refer to the biblical king and his entanglement with Jews. Or it could refer to the Wandering Jew, the cursed and rootless Hebrew who distorts and ultimately corrupts the culture of those with whom he lives.

The "going under" (*Untergang*) is another source of dispute. On a benign reading, it could mean that the German Jews are expected, like Börne, to deny their Jewish religion and heritage, becoming fully assimilated Europeans. Or, less charitably, it could be a call for a kind of elimination or destruction of European Jewry—much as Haman (with Ahasuerus' implicit consent) had attempted to eliminate the Jews of his realm.

[10] Brendel (1811-1868) was a prominent musicologist, professor, and journalist.

minded man, motivated as he was by the most honorable intentions and in the habit of addressing every question straight on, had no other object in view than merely to provide the necessary space for consideration of a subject referring to music history—a topic well worth attention. But the consequences soon showed him the kind of people with whom he had to deal.

Brendel at that time held an appointment as professor at the conservatory of Leipzig, where, as a consequence of prolonged activity there, the name of Mendelssohn was deservedly held in the greatest honor and esteem. Leipzig may be described as having, in a sense, received a Jewish baptism; and, as a writer once complained, fair-haired musicians in that place were becoming ever rarer. This city, which occupied so important a place in all German life, both by virtue of its university and its important book-trade, had, with respect to music, forsaken the most natural sympathies of local patriotism so dear to every other German town, and become exclusively a Jewish musical metropolis. The charges that now arose against Brendel extended even to the threatening of his civic existence. With all his firmness and calm in the statement of his convictions, it was with considerable trouble that he retained his position at the conservatory.

After the first ill-considered explosion of anger from the offended party, what helped Brendel return to a condition of apparent repose was a very characteristic phase that the matter assumed. I had never had the least intention of denying myself as author of the pamphlet, should the question arise. All that I desired was to prevent any purely personal element from being immediately injected into the matter. As I have earnestly and openly stated, this would undoubtedly have occurred, had my name—that of "a composer jealous of the reputation of others"—been cast into the arena straight away. For that reason, I signed with the obvious pseudonym K. Freigedank.[11] I communicated my view in this respect to Brendel and, although he might at once have freed himself from the effects of the storm by redirecting its force toward me, he was courageous enough to bear the brunt of it entirely himself.

Soon there appeared not only signs but clear indications that I had been recognized as the author; and I never denied such charges. This discovery resulted in an entire change in the tactics hitherto pursued. Until now, only the Jews' coarsest weapons had been brought into the fray, no sign appearing of any desire to reply to my article in any intellectual or even commonly decorous manner. With the exception of absurd distortions and misstatements

---

[11] "K. Free-thought."

of what the article contained, coarse attacks and insulting rebuffs were the exclusive methods used against the author [Wagner], who was meant to suffer for his alleged medieval, Jew-hating tendency—bringing much disgrace upon our enlightened age.

Soon, however, things were different. It was evident that higher Jewry was about to appear upon the scene. What it found most annoying was that so much attention had been aroused; in particular, as soon as my name was mentioned, there was a fear that, by drawing it in, attention would be increased. But the means of avoiding all this had been already placed in their hands by my having substituted a pseudonym for my own name.

It seemed now that the most desirable course was to ignore me henceforth as the author of the essay, simultaneously letting all talk about it quietly subside. In parallel, they investigated my vulnerability on different points, for I had recently published art-writings and composed operas—the latter of which I certainly wanted to see produced. The best chance for inflicting the desired punishment upon me seemed to be offered by systematic libel and persecution in this domain, coupled with a total suppression of the obnoxious Jewish Question.[12]

It would certainly be presumptuous on my part, considering that at the time I was living in retirement at Zürich, to attempt a more exact description of the inner machinery arrayed against me in pursuit of this inverted Jewish persecution, now in an ever-increasing scope.[13] I will therefore confine myself to experiences that are already public knowledge.

After the production of *Lohengrin* at Weimar in the summer of 1850, there came forward, somewhat ominously in the press, and for the special purpose of drawing the attention of the German public upon me and my work, certain men of important literary and artistic reputation, such as Adolf Stahr and Robert Franz. Even musical journals of dubious relevance became suddenly and seriously interested in me. This happened, however, so far as individual authors were concerned, only on single occasions; immediately

---

[12] The process that Wagner is about to describe is remarkably similar to the tactics of present-day Jews, who use all varieties of libel, defamation, and accusations of anti-Semitism in order to discredit their opponents. And the threat to boycott Wagner's future operas prefigures the "cancel culture" of today. Little has changed in 150 years.

[13] The persecution was "inverted" in the sense that the historical victims—the Jews—had now become the victimizers.

after which, each was silent again, conducting himself as things went on, and according to circumstances, with more or less hostility towards me.

Apart from this, the next thing was that a certain professor Bischoff, a friend and admirer of Ferdinand Hiller, started off the *Kölnische Zeitung* with systemic slander against me, something that has since then been steadily pursued. He dwelt specially upon my art-writings, distorting my idea about an "art-work of the future" into a ridiculous notion about "music of the future"—or, if you will, a sort of music which, though it sounds badly now, will improve in time. He said not a single word about Jewry; on the contrary, he took delight in posing as a Christian. I furthermore had allegedly described Mozart and even Beethoven as bunglers; I wanted to abolish melody completely and to allow nothing but the singing of psalms.

Even to this day, honored madam,[14] whenever "music of the future" is discussed you will hear these sayings repeated. Reflect, then, what must have been the mighty stubbornness with which this absurd libel was originally established and promulgated. Especially so, considering that, side by side with the actual and popular spread of my operas, as soon as my name was ever mentioned, and in nearly the entire European press, it continually cropped up with such renewed strength as to give it an indisputable air of undeniability.

As such senseless theories were ascribed to me, it followed that my musical works must also be of the most disgusting character. Thus, whatever might be their success, the press maintained that my music must be as horrible as my theories. This, then, was the point that they stressed. It was necessary for them to win over the especially cultured intellectuals to this view. This part of the plan was carried out by a Viennese jurist who was a great musical amateur and a student of Hegel's Dialectics.[15] Apart from this, his gracefully hidden Jewish descent rendered him appropriate for the purpose.[16] He was, moreover, one of those who at first had evinced an almost enthusiastic inclination towards me, so that I was quite startled at his apostasy, happening, as it did, so suddenly and pronouncedly.

---

[14] We recall that Part II is a letter composed to Wagner's friend, Madame Muchanoff.

[15] The jurist was music critic Eduard Hanslick (1825-1904)—whom, like Meyerbeer, Wagner is loath to mention by name.

[16] Hanslick publicly denied being a Jew, even though his mother was ethnically Jewish. It seems that he played the typical "race/religion" ploy: denying to be a religious Jew even as he was, technically, an ethnic Jew.

This gentleman then wrote a booklet on "The beautiful in music" that played into the hands of music-Jewry with extraordinary skill. Firstly, his most elegant dialectic form, by appearing to be in accordance with the finest philosophic spirit, deceived the entire Viennese intelligentsia into believing that, at last, a prophet had arisen among them—which was precisely the intended effect. But what he actually decked out with such elegant dialectic colors consisted of the most trivial banalities, such as could be seriously propounded only in a field like that of music, in which any attempt to talk about aesthetics has always resulted in nonsense. There was certainly nothing particularly clever in advancing "the beautiful" as the chief postulate for music; but the author did it in such a manner that everyone marveled at such brilliant wisdom. Here, however, he also succeeded in a far more difficult task—that of holding up modern Jewish music as the truly "beautiful." The tacit recognition of this dogma was attained quite imperceptibly by taking a series of men—Haydn, Mozart, and Beethoven—and not only tacking on to it Mendelssohn in the most natural possible manner, but, if we rightly understand his theory of the beautiful, he ascribed to Mendelssohn the peculiarly benevolent office of rearranging the Web of Beauty, which had been left somewhat in confusion by his immediate predecessor.

With Mendelssohn so enthroned—which was effected with a special grace by means of placing him in company with Christian notables like Robert Schumann—many further traits in the realm of modern music could be rendered believable. But the main thing was that the grand object of the whole aesthetic undertaking had now been attained. By means of his ingenious lampooning, the author had attained a general respect and created for himself a public image of some importance. Henceforth, as a widely-admired aesthete, he assumed the office of critic in a widely-circulated political journal and immediately proceeded to pronounce both me and all my doings to be simply null and void. The fact that he was not misled by the applause that the public gave to my works only added to his aura.

And in all this he succeeded so well (or rather, they succeeded so well through him) that far and wide—at least wherever newspapers are read in the world—this especially hostile attitude toward me which, honored Madam, you have been so astonished at seeing, has everywhere become the fashion.

The talk was always now of my contempt for the great masters, my hostility to melody, my horrible composition—in short, of "music of the future." But of my essay "Jewry in Music" there was never again the slightest sign. The latter, however, worked all the more effectively in secret, as may be observed in all such sudden works of conversion. It was the Medusa's head, promptly held up to anyone showing even the slightest movement in my favor.[17]

*****

It would certainly not be uninstructive, as bearing upon the culture-history of our time, to trace this curious propaganda a bit more closely. This is so because it has resulted in the formation of a peculiar party within the musical domain—a territory hitherto held by the Germans with such considerable renown. But the party in question—which is strangely divided, having been constructed out of the most varied elements—now seems to have assured itself an entire lack of both productiveness and power.

The next thing, honored Madam, that will likely occur to you is this: How can it be that my indubitable success, and the many friends that my works quite openly gained for me, could not be applied to rebut these hostile machinations? This is not altogether easy to reply to, in short. Note, however, in the first place, how it went with my great friend and most enthusiastic champion, Franz Liszt. It was especially due to the big-hearted confidence that he always displayed that he supplied the enemy (who was always on the alert to draw profit from the slightest circumstance) with just the weapons they wanted. The isolation of the distasteful Jewish Question, which the enemy so urgently desired, happened to be also agreeable to Liszt—though, of course, for quite an opposite reason. His desire was to remove all embittering personalities from an honorable art-dispute; whereas all that the enemy had in view was to conceal the motive of a dishonorable quarrel and prevent the real explanation of the slanders uttered against us from ever coming to light. That will explain why, on our side as well, silence was preserved regarding the mainspring of the whole commotion.

On the other hand, it was Liszt's playful idea to accept the nickname of *"Zukunfts-musiker"* [musicians of the future] that had been applied to us, very much in the same way as that of *"gueux"* [beggar] was once adopted by the Netherlanders. My friend's good-natured adoption of this description

---

[17] The mythological Medusa's head, chopped off by Greek hero Perseus, was used by him as a weapon; anyone gazing at it was turned to stone by its horrifying appearance. In similar fashion, Jews used Wagner's essay as a weapon against any perceived enemies.

was extremely welcome to the enemy, who was thus relieved of the trouble of all further slander in this respect. With the title of *Zukunftsmusiker* thus fastened upon him, it was now so much easier to attack this zealous and untiring artist. The agitation against him started with the defection of a hitherto warmly-devoted friend, a great violin virtuoso, upon whom the Medusa-head may be presumed to have finally worked. Liszt proved to be in every respect courageously unconcerned; but in the end, he had, nevertheless, to suffer a sad awakening to the disappointment of seeing all his splendid efforts for the improvement of music in Weimar frustrated.

And now, honored Madam, may I ask if you are less astonished at the hostilities to which our great friend was separately exposed than at those which fell to me? You might perhaps be misled by the fact that Liszt had certainly, by the brilliancy of his outward artistic career, excited the envy of his stick-in-the-mud German colleagues. The fact of giving up his place in the race for virtuosity having been attended only by mere preliminaries for an appearance as composer might also cause a doubt as to his vocation in that line—and this feeling, being an easy target for envy, had already been excited to a fair degree.

I believe, however, that the explanations to follow will prove that, behind this doubt, no less than my own art-theories, constituted a mere pretext for a war of persecution. A closer examination of either case, an estimation of our doings made in light of correct impressions of them, would have been enough to place the question upon quite a different footing. Then it would have been possible to judge, to discuss, to urge for and against—in short, to really do something. But that's not what was wanted. On the contrary, this closer examination of the new productions was not to be allowed at any price. But with a meanness of expression and insinuation that has never before been seen in a similar field, the whole press proclaimed that the case was unworthy of discussion by intelligent men. I may therefore confidently assure you that what Liszt suffered also originated with that article on "Jewry in Music."

Even we, however, did not find all this out very quickly. There are always many interests in natural opposition to any new manifestation. They quickly proceed to fix the taint of heresy upon whatever it may contain—such that even we thought we were only encountering the effects of having disturbed the comfort and lethargy of the ordinary art business. As the hostility came principally from the press, and particularly from the most influential political journals, those of our friends who were deeply interested in the forthcoming appearance of Liszt as an instrumental composer were of the opinion that it was necessary for them to adopt some contrary position. With the exception of a few cases, happening by accident, it soon became apparent that even the best-reasoned criticism of a Liszt composition could find no space in the bigger journals. Their space, on the contrary, was all occupied and sequestered beforehand, in a hostile sense.

Now, who can seriously entertain the notion that, in this attitude of the great newspapers, there was any genuine concern about a possible injury to the good art-taste of Germany, which the new direction in art might inflict? I know what it is to experience the impossibility in these papers of alluding even to Offenbach in a suitable way.[18] Will anyone dare, after that, to think that there was any concern about taste in art? Matters had, in fact, proceeded so far that we were completely barred from the great German press.

But to whom does this press belong? Our Liberals and Progressivists are called upon to bitterly compensate their having left the old Conservative opposition party by being thrown into one pot along with Jewry and its specific interests. And, if the Roman Ultramontanes seek to know how a press entirely directed by Jews can be justified in joining in a discussion over Christian matters, the enquiry bears an ominous meaning; it gives an accurate perception of how these great newspapers are operated.

The remarkable thing in all this is that these disclosures lie open to everyone. Who has not had some experience of them? It is not for me to say how far this factitious relation applies to the treatment of matters of great political importance; although the stock market is a fairly open index of this. But within the domain of music, abandoned as it is to the most dishonorable prattle, no sensible person can entertain a doubt of the existence of this highly energetic organization and control to which everything is subject, the action of which extends to the remotest circles, operating amongst them with uniform exactitude.

*****

In Paris, to my astonishment, I found that no secret whatsoever was made of this control. Everyone there had some astounding tale of its doings, particularly with respect to the stringent precautions that were exercised to prevent the secret from being publicly disclosed—given that it was known to so many persons and therefore in the greatest danger of being found out. The

---

[18] Jacques Offenbach (1819-1880) was a Jewish, German-born French composer.

slightest crevice by which it might leak into a journal was accordingly stopped up, even though it might be only by means of a calling card thrust through the key-hole. Thus, everyone there acted with the same obedience as reigns in the best-disciplined army during a battle. You are already aware of the bullets directed against me by the Paris journals, and which this 'solicitude for good taste in art' exacted from them.

In London, I was met at the time with great frankness on this point. The music critic of the *Times* (and I beg you to reflect of what a colossal world-newspaper I am now speaking!) attacked me with a shower of insults as soon as I arrived; and in the course of his outpourings, Mr. Davison considered himself justified in holding me up to popular insult as the blasphemer of the greatest composers on account of their Jewishness. As far as his own position with the English public was concerned, he had, in any case, far more to gain than to lose—firstly, on account of the great honor in which Mendelssohn is held there, and secondly, because of the peculiar character of the English religion which, to those who know it, seems to be based more upon the Old than upon the New Testament.

Only in St. Petersburg and Moscow did I find that Jewish influences had neglected to exploit the musical press. I experienced there the miracle of receiving as warm a welcome from the press as from the public. But the Jews had never been able to prevent my good reception by the public, save only in one place: my native town of Leipzig, where people simply kept away.

The ludicrous features of the matter having thus led me, in describing it, to adopt an almost playful tone, this, honored Madam, I must now forsake. I may permit myself, now, to draw your attention to its more serious side. This brings us to the point where, moving away from my persecuted self, we proceed to contemplate the *effect* of this remarkable persecution, insofar as it exercises an influence upon the very spirit of our art.

In taking up this road, my personal interest must necessarily be touched upon once more. As I said just now, the persecution brought against me on the part of the Jews had not hitherto succeeded in estranging from me the cordial public favor that awaited me everywhere. That is correct, but it is necessary to add, nevertheless, that such persecution is obviously calculated to bar my way to the public—or to render that access so difficult that I can never be assured that their spiteful activities, even in this respect, may not ultimately succeed. Already you cannot fail to note that, even though my earlier operas had carved out for themselves a road to the German stage, where a uniform success had attended their production, the very same theaters exhibit a cold and even unfriendly demeanor toward my recent works. The reason for this is simply that my earlier works were introduced to the stage before commencement of the Jew agitation. The attempt, however, was to show that my new works had been written after the formulation of my "senseless" theories; consequently, I had fallen away from my original innocence, and that henceforth it was every man's duty to shun my music.

As always, it is by utilizing the weakness and defects of our social conditions that Jewry in general succeeds in undermining us. So too, here, a ground was easily found upon which—to our shame—everything stood as if especially prepared to ensure its success. Whose hands direct our theaters? And what is the real tendency followed by them? Often and profusely have I expressed myself upon this subject; and again, quite recently, I have expounded in detail, in my larger treatise on "German Art and Politics," the various reasons that exist for the decadence of our theatrical art. Do you think that I have, by such measures, endeared myself to the parties concerned? They have proved that it is only with great reluctance that theatrical administrations now proceed to present any new work of mine.[19] But, as they might be otherwise compelled to allow it, as a consequence of the universally favorable attitude of the public in regard to my operas, how easy it must be for them, given the fact that my newer works are viewed so skeptically—not merely in the press generally, but even in the most influential sections of it? Can't you already hear the cry arising in Paris, why they should be expected to continue importing my operas into France—an undertaking sufficiently risky in itself—when my artistic value is not even recognized at home?

The state of affairs has now become even more difficult. At present, I do not simply offer my new works to any theater. On the contrary, I am

---

[19] Wagner adds this note: "It may not be uninstructive, and will in any case show how we stand in matters of art, if I describe to you more fully the treatment which, to my great astonishment, I lately had to experience from the two great theaters of Berlin and Vienna with regard to my *Meistersinger*. It took me some time, in my dealings with the leaders of these two Court theaters, before I perceived, from the tricks that they employed, that they were concerned not only to avoid producing my works themselves but also to prevent other theaters from doing so. You cannot fail to draw the obvious conclusion that a positive influence was at work. And it was evident that the appearance of a new work of mine was regarded with consternation. It may possibly amuse you, one of these days, to hear more details of my experiences."

obliged to reserve to myself the right to couple my consent to the production with conditions that never before have been considered necessary, and which are now required to guarantee for me a truly correct and proper performance.

But here I touch upon the most serious aspect of the pernicious consequences that arise when allowing the Jewish essence to become mixed up with matters of art.

*****

In the older essay with which I began [the original "Jewry in Music"], I concluded by showing that it was a weakness and incapacity that marked the period of German musical production since Beethoven that allowed the Jew to appear at all. I mentioned all those musicians who found, in the obliteration of the great plastic style of Beethoven, the ingredients for the construction of the newer, formless, shallow manner. This was the style in which, lacking in life or tension, they now, with a syrupy comfort, went on composing. All such writers were addressed by me in my definition of musical Jewry, no matter to what particular nationality they might happen to belong. Combined, they form that peculiar community that seems nowadays to comprise everyone who either composes music or, unfortunately, directs it.

I believe that many of these people have been thoroughly confused and startled by my writings. The Jews, angry about my article, grabbed ahold of these feelings to immediately stifle all respectful discussion of my theorizing on other subjects—something that had just begun to occur amongst certain honorable German musicians. With this pair of catchwords ['Jewry', 'music'], every fruitful, explanatory, enlightening, or formal discussion—along with any chance of mutual understanding about the whole subject—was destroyed.

The same enfeebled spirit continued to be displayed as a result of the havoc wrought in the German mind (already so prone to abstract meditation) by Hegelian philosophy, both in this and in the neighboring domain of aesthetics. At the same time, Kant's great idea—that Schiller had so cleverly utilized for the founding of aesthetic views of the Beautiful[20]—was obliged to make way for a confused wilderness of dialectic nothings.

Even in this quarter, I initially met with an inclination to approach the views laid down in my artistic writings with a certain amount of good-will. But, as the booklet on the aforementioned "Beauty in Music," written by

---

[20] See Schiller's essay "On the sublime" (1801).

Dr. Hanslick of Vienna, was written with a deliberate objective in mind, it had also been rushed into a high degree of celebrity. As a result, a thoroughly blond German aestheticist, Herr Vischer—though we cannot blame him—incorporated the ideas of the much-praised Viennese aesthete [Hanslick] into his 'grand system' of aesthetics, thinking thereby to secure some comfort for himself as well as security for his great work. Thus it was that the musical Jew-beauty became integrated into the heart of a full-blown German system of aesthetics, which naturally contributed even more to the glory of its creator, being now praised very loudly in the papers. This was so, even though, in consequence of the work's unamusing character, no one ever troubled very much to read it. The increase of protection afforded by this not only new, but also "Christian" German, thus promoted the musical Jew-beauty to the level of unquestioned dogma. The most peculiarly difficult questions relating to musical aesthetics—questions upon which the greatest philosophers, whenever they wished to say anything of serious import, always expressed themselves in measured terms of uncertainty—were now taken in hand by Jews and confused Christians with the greatest of confidence.

This went on to such a degree that, if anyone had desired to think through the matter, and in particular, to explain to himself the overpowering effect of Beethoven's music on his feelings, he would have inevitably been made to feel as if he were bartering for the Savior's garments at the foot of the Cross. This is a subject upon which, presumably, the celebrated Biblical critic, David Strauss, would be just about as well able to express himself as upon the Ninth Symphony of Beethoven.

Now, all this was bound to ultimately have the effect that when, in contrast to these sterile though exciting proceedings, an attempt was made to strengthen the nerves of Art, we not only encountered the natural obstacles that at all times interpose themselves, but also a completely organized opposition—each separate element of which was quite able to operate effectively on its own behalf. If we appeared dumbfounded and resigned, nothing went on in the opposite camp that could be regarded as indicative of a will, an attempt, or an accomplishment. It might rather be said that they allowed anything whatever to happen on the part of the connoisseurs of Jew-music-beauty; and each new calamity (á la Offenbach) would break over the heads of the German art-body without producing the least stir among them—a fact which, in any case, will be found *selbstverständlich* [self-intelligible].[21]

---

[21] That is, no one fought back against the attack on true German art-music.

If, on the other hand, anyone like myself, being encouraged by a favorable combination of circumstances, took artistic powers in hand in order to lead them into energetic action, you have seen for yourself, honored Madam, what an outcry this provoked on all sides. Then it was that real fire and fury were displayed within the tents of modern Israel! Its principal feature was the deprecatory and extremely contemptuous tone that I believe to have been prompted, not merely by blind passion but by a shrewd calculation of its inevitable effect upon my patrons' minds. And who can fail to become ultimately affected if he always hears a most disdainful tone deployed against a man, by all accounts, worthy of trust and respect?

Everywhere and in all the circumstances necessary for complicated undertakings, the natural elements of ill will are present—both among those unconcerned and those who are vitally concerned. How easy is it, then, by critical comments in the press, to give the undertaking a dubious appearance in the eyes of both these groups? Can anything of that kind happen in France, in the case of a Frenchman honored by the public? Or in Italy, to a lauded Italian composer? This form of opposition, being only possible for a German composer in Germany, was so new that we have to inquire into the causes that brought it about.

You, honored Madam, were astonished at all this. But those who, in this battle ostensibly waged about art-interests, though otherwise disinterested, nevertheless have their own good reasons for hindering my undertakings—and they are not astonished at all, but find everything quite natural.

The outcome of the preceding affair is therefore this: more and more resolutely sustained opposition of every undertaking that I might hazard to take, either for my works or for my influence upon the condition of theatrical or musical art. What does all this amount to? A great deal, in my view; which I believe I am justified in offering without any pretension.

There is one additional fact that I perceive from all this: the earnest avoidance of all comment upon those of my publications in which, from time to time, I have addressed this subject.

*****

I have related how, at the beginning—that is to say, before commencement of this strange and covertly-designed persecution of me by the Jews—there had been signs of a movement in favor of a treatment and estimation of the views laid down in my art-writings, both honorable in intention and conducted

in a truly German spirit. Let us assume that this agitation had not arisen; or
that, having arisen, it had reasonably confined itself to its initial outburst. We
would then have to ask ourselves, after the analogy of similar previous oc-
currences in tranquil German culture-life, how the matter would have proceeded. I am not of the optimistic view that, in that case, very much would
have resulted. Something, however, might fairly have been expected—and
in any case, something different from what did happen.

If we properly understand the matter, a period devoted to the collection
of the works bequeathed to us by the incomparable great masters had set in.
Both in music and in poetical literature, it was felt to be a duty that the value
of the works of these great men—who, following one another in quick succession, had brought the renaissance in German art to the heights of a national treasure—should be offered for the common good of the nation, and
for all the world. The question then was, in what sense this value should be
established.

For music in particular, this question was of the greatest urgency. The
fact is that, with the last period of Beethoven's life-work, an all-new phase of
development of the art had emerged, eclipsing all the views and prospects
that were previously established. Music had become, under the influence of
the Italian vocal style, an art of mere agreeableness. Its capacity to bear a
significance equal to the art of Dante, or of Michelangelo, was denied by that
very fact; accordingly, it was relegated to the lower rank of the arts.

A totally new acknowledgment of the nature of music was therefore
required, based upon our great Beethoven's achievements. It was urgent to
thoughtfully follow, from Bach to Palestrina, the root from which the art had
sprung to its present height and meaning. A totally different system for aesthetic judgment had to be created—a system that had nothing in common
with one that recognized a description of musical development outside these
masters' path.

A proper feeling respecting this was vividly and instinctively planted in
the German masters of this period. As the most sensible and highly gifted of
these, I name to you—Robert Schumann. From the course of his development as a composer, we may unmistakably prove the effect of Jewish influences upon our art. Compare the Robert Schumann of the first and second
half of his life-work. In the first, there is an aiming at plastic form; in the last,
a gradual degeneration into bombastic superficiality and shallowness. It ac-
cords entirely with this view that, during his second period, Schumann
should have looked with disfavor, discontent, and general ill-will upon those

to whom, in his first period, and as editor of the *Neue Zeitschrift für Musik*, he had extended his hand with such truly German amiability. By the attitude of his journal—in which, with instinctive correctness, he also occupied himself as writer for the furtherance of this all-absorbing topic—you can likewise perceive with what sort of spirit I would have had to take counsel, had it only been a question of coming to a personal understanding with him upon the problem that interested me. In his writings, we meet with a language far removed from that of the dialectic Jewish jargon with which the new aesthetical doctrines have been introduced. And I continue to insist that the adoption of this language would have led to a helpful understanding.

But what was it that imparted such power to the Jewish influence? Unfortunately, one of the German's principal virtues is also the source of his weakness. The peaceful, trusty self-confidence that causes him to disregard all evil forebodings, and leads his even and undisturbed nature to many a deed of inward truth may, if but slightly lacking the necessary fire, easily transform itself into a surprising passivity. Here, most, nay, nearly all those fallen spirits who, during the continued neglect of all higher aspirations of the German spirit on the part of political authorities, had remained true to the German character.

Robert Schumann's genius also sank into this passivity, as it weighed on him to make a stand against the frantic, restless Jewish spirit. He found it too much trouble to discern, by the thousand features that came closely under his observation, what was really happening. So he unconsciously lost his noble freedom, and his old friends—disowned by him in the end—are also now compelled to suffer once more, seeing him carried off in triumph by the music-Jews as one of their own!

Now, honored friend, it seems to me that this is highly significant. The introduction of this instance makes it unnecessary to examine lesser cases of subjugation, because, in consequence of this most important one, they become so much easier to obtain.

The success in personal cases, however, finds its natural completion in those of Associations and Societies. In this field also, the German spirit, according to its bent, showed itself disposed for action. The idea that I set before you, as the problem of our post-Beethoven period, actually brought together, for the first time, a large and increasing number of German musicians and friends of music for objectives that gained in importance by that task alone.

It is to the eternal credit of the excellent Franz Brendel, who bravely gave the impetus to this movement (and who was accordingly vilified by the Jewish journals), that he also realized what was necessary in this direction. The defect, common to all German Associations, was obliged, however, to be felt much more in this case. A competition was thus set up, not only between this union of German musicians and the mighty sphere of State organizations under government control—by which other free unions are also rendered ineffectual—but also between it and the mightiest organization of our time, Jewry itself. Obviously, any largescale union of musicians could only pursue a useful existence by the practical method of giving absolutely finished performances of works of the highest importance, calculated to assist the cultivation of German musical style. Funds were necessary for this. But for the typical German musician, being poor, the question was, who would help him? No amount of talking and disputing about art interests could do so; these things have, for many people, no sense at all, and easily lead to the ridiculous. The power that we lacked was, however, possessed by the Jews.

With the theater given over to the young squires and the scum of the stage-set, with the concert-institutions entirely owned by the Jews, what remained for us? Just one little music journal in which to report the outcome of our conferences—once every two years.

*****

As you see, honored Madam, I bear witness to you of the complete triumph of Jewry in every sense; and the fact that I once more raise my voice against it does not proceed from any belief in my power to stem the completeness of this victory in any way.

On the other hand, my present exposition of the course of this peculiar episode in German culture seems to be the result of the agitation amongst the Jews provoked by my original article, a new question, equally astonishing, may well come to you: Why did I originally stir up this agitation by my challenge?

I might excuse myself for this by pleading that I based my resolution for the attack not upon any estimation of the "final cause" but upon the inherent force of the "efficient cause"—as the philosophers might say. I certainly did not indulge the notion that, in writing and publishing that essay, I had any chance of successfully waging war with the Jews' influence upon our music. The foundation for all their successes in the meantime were, even then, so clear to me that I have some satisfaction in testifying to the truth of this by republishing now my description of them. I am unable, therefore, to state any express objective; though I may plead, on the other hand, that an acute perception of impending ruin in our music matters compelled me to state the causes of it. Possibly I may also have had, at heart, the desire of uniting it with a hopeful reception, as you may gather from my conclusion here, in which I turn to the Jews themselves.

In the same way that humane friends of the Church believed that, by an appeal to the oppressed lower clergy, its wholesome reform might be effect-ed, so I kept in view the great endowments of heart and mind that have ema-nated from Jewish circles to my own true comfort. I am, further, also of the emphatic opinion that whatever has hitherto oppressed the German character bears upon the intellectual and sympathetic Jew in a still more frightful de-gree. I fancied at the time that there were indications of my appeal having been both understood and deeply felt. Dependence in any position is a great evil and an impediment to free development, but that of the Jews amongst themselves appears to be an extreme and slavish misery. In view of the deci-sion to live not only *with* us but *in* us, much should be both granted to, and excused in, the intelligent Jew by his more enlightened race-associates. We hear from them the most entertaining Jewish anecdotes, for instance, and are also familiarized with a certain amount of unrestrained free talk, regarded as permissible on their part, and which in general refers as much to themselves as it does to us.

Still, to make a close friend of anyone who is an outlaw of one's own race must necessarily be regarded by the Jew as a mortal offence. I have had many moving experiences on this subject. But in order to describe this tyr-anny, one example will have to suffice.

An admittedly highly-gifted, truly talented, and intellectual author of Jewish extraction, who seems almost as if he had grown up amid characteris-tic German folk-life, and with whom I had long communicated, in many ways, about the Jewish Question, proceeded to read my poems "Der Ring des Nibelungen" and "Tristan und Isolde." He expressed himself about them with such appreciative warmth, as well as with such conspicuous intelligence, that he was inclined to respond to the invitation of my friends to publicly state his views about these poems that were so strangely ignored by our literary circles. But this was impossible for him to do![22]

You will understand, honored Madam, from these indications, that, in replying to your question respecting the enigmatical origin of the hostilities directed against me, and particularly of those of the press, I would not have allowed myself the risk of almost exhausting your patience by such an exposition, had I not been impelled by a hope still dear to my heart—though one difficult to express. If I were to attempt to describe it, I would, in the first place, remove all appearance of its seeming to be founded upon any concealment of my relation to Jewry; for it is this very concealment that has contributed to the present confusion—not only of yourself, but of nearly all my sympathetic friends.

If this confusion is due to my former pseudonym—if the employment of the latter gave the enemy strategic means for a successful attack against me—it follows that I was now obliged to reveal to my friends that which is already too well known to the opposite party. In believing that this openness is capable, not so much of drawing friends for me from the opposite camp as of strengthening them in the struggle for their own true emancipation, it may perhaps be found pardonable in me if a broad view of our culture-history conceals from me an illusion hiding in my heart. For, about one thing I am perfectly clear: In the same way that the influence upon our spiritual life that the Jews have won is shown, by the deviation or falsity of our highest culture-tendencies, to be no mere physiological accident, so it is also to be recognized as undeniable and decisive.

*****

Whether the decadence of our culture can be prevented by forcible expulsion of foreign elements of pernicious character, I cannot say. I have no acquaintance with the forces required for this. If, on the other hand, this element was to become so assimilated with us as to render it possible for both, in common, to ripen toward the higher cultivation of the nobler human talents, it is clearly not by hiding the difficulties of this assimilation, but only by their most candid disclosure.

In the event of my having caused an earnest impulse in this direction to emerge from what our newest aesthetics describes as the harmless and

---

[22] In other words, that Jewish peer pressure was too extreme, and that they would not allow it.

agreeable domain of music, the circumstance might appear as not altogether unfavorable to my personal view of the importance of this art. And you, in any case, most honored Madam, might be induced to accept it as an excuse for my having detained you so long with such an apparently abstruse subject.

Tribschen, near Lucerne, Switzerland, New Year, 1869.
Richard Wagner[23]

---

[23] For more on Wagner's views on the Jews, see *Eternal Strangers* (pp. 90-91).

— 2 —
THE CONQUEST OF THE WORLD BY THE JEWS

Frederick Millingen (aka Osman Bey)
(1873)

Editor: As important and influential as Wagner's *Jewry in Music* was, it was limited in scope. In that extended essay, Wagner did not examine the larger question of Jewish influence on society in general. Among the very first men to do so was a relative unknown, Frederick Millingen (1832-1901). Son of a British physician, he was apparently raised in Italy, dabbled in religion—both Islam and Orthodox Christianity—and came to be highly interested in the emergence of Jewish power in Europe and elsewhere. As a young man, Millingen spent some time in America during the last phase of its Civil War, circa 1865. He then returned to Europe and decided to write a lengthy essay on the 'Jewish Question'—a term that had been in circulation at least since 1842, when Bruno Bauer wrote a booklet of the same name.

Millingen's milestone work was preceded by many intimations of growing Jewish power looming over Europe. As early as 1798, German philosopher Immanuel Kant could make this surprising assessment: "the wealth of the Jews... apparently exceeds per capita that of any other nation at the present time" (*Anthropology* 1798/1978: 102). In 1823, Lord Byron's poem *The Age of Bronze* included an observation that "all states, all things, all sovereigns they [the Jews] control." Indeed: "'Tis gold, not steel that rears the conqueror's arch." In 1843, Bauer wrote, "The Jew...determines the fate of the whole [Austrian] Empire by his financial power. The Jew...decides the destiny of Europe" (cited in Marx's *On the Jewish Question*). And perhaps even beyond Europe. In an essay of 1860, Ralph Waldo Emerson remarked on Jewish toughness, brought on by years of persecution and suffering: "The sufferance which is the badge of the Jew, has made him, in these days, the ruler of the rulers of the earth" ("Fate", in *Conduct of Life*).

But it was left to Millingen to write the first extended, detailed essay on the topic of Jewish global dominance. Writing under the pseudonym 'Osman Bey,' Millingen set out to document the history, ethics, and sociology of the Jews that allowed them to ascend to a position of virtual world-rule. The result was the present essay, first published in German as *Die Eroberung der Welt durch die Juden*. A bestseller, it soon appeared in French and English, earning a wide circulation. It would go on to influence many later anti-Jewish writers, and perhaps even the anonymous author of the notorious "Protocols of the Elders of Zion," which first appeared early in the 20th century.

Preliminary Remarks

In obedience to an unchangeable law of nature, men strive to ameliorate their own condition at the expense of others. From this fact originated the many jealous contests and wars wherein men seek to excel each other. The manner in which these wars and contests are conducted is determined by principles that differ from each other according to geographical position, social and political condition, and the spirit peculiar to the contesting people. These principles that thus form the basis of the work of conquest are of three kinds:

1. *The Principle of Physical Force*
2. *The Theocratic Principle*, whereby the masses are subjected to a religious faith
3. *The Principle of Material Interests* that enslaves people by financial oppression

The first two principles are well-known, for the history of Rome and Greece in ancient times, as well as the history of the Papacy and of Russia and Germany in modern times, is simply an illustration of the application of those principles. They are the causes that gave rise to those Powers, and founded their predominance by physical and moral means.

But the conquests of the third category—that is, those that result from the application of the principle of material interests—show us a peculiar and altogether novel phenomenon. In this case, material interests take the place of physical force, or religious faith, and become the basis as well as the moving springs of the work of conquest. But the principle of material interests is in itself much more powerful than the other principles, no one being able to escape from its power. For a principle that is based on the necessity of existence, on the element of life, is a universal principle to which we all are subject at present. Our material interests form a central point toward which all human inclinations and desires tend; and hence their possession is equivalent to universal dominion. A conquest founded on the principle of material interests is not a victory of strength over weakness, nor a victory of knowledge over ignorance, but a victory of cunning over confidence and carelessness. Its endeavor is to obtain control of all the means of existence, and to absorb all the wealth of nations, thereby subjecting them, in the end, to the arbitrary rule of the conqueror.

It is my purpose in this essay to explain the mode and manner of this conquest, and to expose clearly and strikingly the rise of Jewish power and its wonderful development in our days.

The Jewish people has, in all probability, been the first one to discover that secret power—*the principle of material interests*. At any rate, this people is the only one that has understood how to utilize that principle as a means of conquest. If we examine history closely, we are struck by the fact that the Jews have, from the earliest times, used this principle as a weapon to fight other people, and as a basis for the erection of their religious, social, and political structure.

An attentive study of Jewish history enables us to become acquainted with the spirit and character of the Jewish people, and to properly appreciate its endeavors and purposes. Unfortunately, in following this study we are left exclusively to the documents and reports that the Jews themselves have seen fit to transmit to us. If the Philistines, the Pharaohs, and the other opponents of the Jews had left us historical memorials, the history of the "chosen people" would sound quite differently from how we read it today. But a philosophical analysis of the Old Testament will, after all, be amply sufficient to give us a correct estimation of the achievements of the Jewish people.

Origin of the Jews

The Jews were, at one time, an Arab tribe, living like the other Arab tribes upon plunder and the productions of their herds. The Old Testament makes no statements from which we might gather the descent of the Jews from the Arabs. Arabic tradition, however, and especially the Koran, fixes the fact that Abraham, an Arab patriarch, lived with his tribe and his herds in Arabia and laid the foundation of the holy Raaba, the temple in Mecca that has, at all times, been the seat of monotheistic worship, and where, to this day, prayers are offered up to the God of Abraham, Ismael, and Mohammed.

We do not know the circumstances that induced Abraham to leave Arabia with his tribe, but it was doubtless a desire to improve their condition that led them to emigrate. This assumption is all the more justified, as the same desire has, at all times, impelled the nomadic populations to invade the lands adjoining the Arabian Peninsula.

Characteristics of the Jews

The Arabs are endowed by nature with an unusual degree of mental faculties that throw those of all other races in the shade. The faculties that are thus peculiar to the Arabs are "a strength of mind that is not deterred by any mystery, or any distance; a ready and immediate comprehension of a plan; a fiery and energetic mode of acting; and finally an unparalleled cunning and craftiness." These faculties that belong to the Arabs in general, were necessarily also inherent in the Jews, but together with these they possess certain other special qualities that give them additional advantages. Thus the Arab is quick at the start, but lacks toughness and perseverance; whereas the Jew combines with a fiery temperament an obstinacy so inflexible that it may well be said that the Jew never gives way, and knows neither forgiving nor forgetting.

Another distinction that may be observed in the character of these two children of the desert is that the Arabs incline more to the ideal and abstract, while the Jews are essentially material and practical. From this divergence of character, it results that while the Arab experiences a platonic and spiritual reverence for the beautiful, the Jew sees in it only the useful. A Jew may well stop to admire a flower, or any other object; but at the same moment, he will be asking himself: *How much can I make from it?*

Rapacity is a passion that has become the Jew's second nature, and to that he instinctively lends obedience. The lust of gain is so strongly rooted in his organism that it extinguishes every other feeling, every other passion. The Jew knows, for instance, no self-love. If you sneer at him, he pays no attention to it; if you praise him, he laughs at you; but if you venture to keep a penny from him, he rages like a tiger. His only aim in life is gain. Hence everything that does not have this object in view deserves no attention. This unlimited rapacity places the Jews in an everlasting antagonism to the rest of mankind, and hence the Jew wages war to the uttermost against all other men. This rage leads the Jews to believe that men are created only to cheat and devour each other. In this rivalry between men, it is the Jews' opinion that the most cunning and rapacious must, in the end, devour the others.

Besides, this belief in an endless antagonism between men is an idea inborn in the mind of the Arabs, for we find it prevailing in the doctrines of the Talmud as well as the Koran—two books that are a rich mine of Semitic ideas and traditions. But if the Arabs and Jews are agreed on this point, the manner and way in which they apply that doctrine practically is not quite the same. Thus the Arab, with his spirit of chivalry, draws a line of distinction between the states of war and peace, whereas the Jew recognizes no armistice, and keeps up the battle without intermission.

The Principle of Material Interests

A people endowed with natural gifts of such an extraordinary character naturally excite expectations of wonderful achievements. But the greatest miracle that the Jewish people has ever accomplished is surely this: that it has discovered the principle of Material Interests and its power as a social and political tie, and as a means of the conquest of the world. This discovery was a result of the gradual development of the faculties peculiar to this people. In the midst of their intercourse with neighboring tribes, the Jews were able to keep in view these political-economical truths:

"Not those who acquire, but those who save, attain wealth."

"Those who save obtain supremacy over those who squander."

They, furthermore, observed that men in general place little value upon that which they possess, for the desire to acquire what they do *not* possess causes them to lose sight of what they hold in their hands. From these phenomena, the Jews derived those principles that have since become the basis of their commercial, social, and political system.

When their first attempts were crowned with success, they endeavored to extend their operations by emigration into a rich and fertile country, and hence resolved to abandon their native land—Arabia. It is proper enough to assume that Abraham and his tribe, before engaging in an enterprise of this kind, mapped out some sort of plan that accorded with their natural gifts and the purposed undertaking. The plan that the invaders adopted was this: to seize all the gold and valuables of every country that they might invade, but to leave to the inhabitants their life and their immoveable property. The Jews argued thus: If we take the gold and the fruits of their labor from the inhabitants, we may safely leave them their fields and vineyards. If we succeed in making their riches our own, we shall become the masters and they will become our slaves.

In adopting this plan, the Jews evinced an over whelming genius, for they thereby rejected the utterly different principles on which their predecessors had acted in making conquests, and formulated a new principle—that of material interests. Moreover, they applied it in its pure and simple form— that is, without support by physical force or religious influence.

Let us now see how this principle, using the weapons of cunning and activity, has accomplished in the first period of its existence such astonishing triumphs, and has completed, in the 19th century, the conquest of the world.

The Period of Abraham

Upon their departure from Arabia, Abraham and his people turned towards Mesopotamia. But their stay there was of short duration, the proverbial fruitfulness of the land of Canaan [Palestine] having attracted them. This first peaceful invasion accorded, in a remarkable manner, with their purposes. Once having entered into that country, they managed to utilize the dissensions and internal wars that their depredations excited amongst the people of Syria, so well to their own advantage that they were soon able to put their hands upon all the riches of the country.

We learn, however, that sometime afterwards, Abraham and his tribe turned towards Egypt—a country that had always been celebrated because of its wealth and fertility. It is true that the Jews explain this strange excursion by alleging a famine that then raged in Canaan.[1] It seems, however that this famine was, in truth, nothing but the burning thirst that the Jews longed to quench at the stream of the treasures of Pharaoh. At first, the Jews were as successful in Egypt as they had expected to be, for a short time sufficed to gather in a great amount of gold and silver and a large number of cattle.[2] But

---

[1] Gen (12:10).
[2] Gen (13:2).

their rapacity soon excited the wrath of the Egyptians against them to such an extent that King Pharaoh drove the Jews out of the country, their bad morals and their intrigues serving as a pretext.

After their return from Egypt, the Jews fell with renewed rage upon the rich lands of Canaan, where they became wealthy and powerful at the expense of the native-born inhabitants.

The Period of Isaac

Isaac, like Abraham, endeavored to carry on a financial conquest and to appropriate the riches that were in the possession of the natives.[3] To this end he redoubled his exertions and made an excursion into the land of the Philistines. In order to conceal his purpose, however, he considered it necessary to plead a famine[4] once more as a pretext under which to fasten his people upon that country.

At first, the king of the Philistines, Abimelech, received the Jews as friends, but a short time sufficed to change his mind and induce him to expel them, for the intrigues and rapacity of the Jewish people were exhibited in their true form very soon after their arrival. Abimelech, with a certain naiveté characteristic of his times, on no account made a secret of the motive that led him to get rid of the Jews, for he told them quite frankly, "You are more powerful," that is, "richer than I am".[5] Moreover, his people were so embittered against the Jews that they would have murdered them all if the Jews had not concluded to leave the country.[6]

Before I proceed further in our historical exposition, I must introduce here two very significant facts that occur in all these invasions and subsequent expulsions of the Jews. I want to direct the attention of the public to these facts, for they serve to expose the policy of the Jews and the clever tricks managed by them in order to effect their financial conquest of the world.

---

[3] *Ed.:* In Biblical lore, the likely-mythical Abraham had a son, Isaac (Gen 21). Isaac, in turn, had two sons: Esau and Jacob (aka "Israel")—see Gen 25. Jacob's alleged "12 sons" became the patriarchs of the "12 Tribes of Israel" (Gen 35).
[4] Gen (26:1).
[5] Gen (26:16). [*Ed*: If historically accurate, this would have occurred in the 1300s BC].
[6] Gen (26:20, 21, and 27).

The first remarkable fact is the special care with which the Jews avoided every armed conflict with the people whom they proposed to conquer. During the period referred to, their enterprises preserved an essentially moral character, for physical force was never applied by the Jews. Cunning was, at that time, their favorite weapon, it being evidently in the interest of the Jews to avoid all bloodshed; and hence we see none of those armed conflicts that constitute the physical principle as opposed to the principle of material interests.

The other remarkable fact is the tact exhibited by the Jews when they were forced to retire from a conquered country. They succeeded not only in carrying along with them their plunder, but also, in retiring with a moral victory over their opponents, by throwing all the blame upon their enemies and representing themselves as a persecuted people. This Jewish policy is a true masterpiece of Machiavellianism that no other race, no other sect, has ever been able to excel. This policy constitutes, indeed, even in our own times, the soul and spirit of Judaism.

The Egyptian Period

The aggressive movement that the Jews undertook against Egypt may be summed up in the following chief facts:

- An advance guard, consisting of Jewish adventurers, first entered Egypt on a reconnaissance in order to sneak into that country under the pretext of a famine.
- This advance-guard had a wonderful success, for they not only enriched themselves at the expense of the inhabitants, but also succeeded in gaining control of supreme power.

The elevation of Joseph to the rank of a Viceroy of Egypt called forth an aggressive movement on the part of Jacob and his whole tribe. From that moment, the Egyptians became the prey of the Jews, who plundered them at their pleasure.[7] The rapacity of these conquerors, however, soon provoked the resistance of the natives, who only too late recognized in the Jews a social plague and a political danger. Upon that, the Pharaonic government took measures for its own protection, and it was decided to expel the Jews from the country. But such a measure would have involved the Egyptians in the greatest financial difficulties. The expulsion of the Jews would have led to

---

[7] Gen (47:18).

great financial commotions in government affairs. Was it, then, more advisable to let the Jews depart with their extorted treasures, or to watch calmly the complete ruin of Egypt by the Jews?

While the unhappy Pharaoh was still looking for a way to escape from so terrible a dilemma, the Jews gathered together all the valuables of which they could get hold, and fled with them from Egypt. Having thus shown in what manner the Jewish people began to attack the finances from its very first appearance in history, we shall now follow it in the second period of its history.

*****

The Mosaic Period

This second period signifies a total revolution in the policy of the Jewish people. The changes introduced by Moses [ca. 1200s BC?] were nothing but a formal abjuration of the Jewish principle. This revolution did completely away with the chief motive principle of the Jewish people—the Principle of Material Interests—in order to put in its place a new one, formed out of a union of the physical and theocratic principles. This change was the result of a reaction that had taken place in the minds of the men who guided the fate of the "chosen people." These noble men shuddered as they beheld their race lowering itself so far as to indulge in highway robbery and usury. A people, they thought, that pretends to belong to the foremost of nations must enter openly and honestly upon the career that leads to prosperity and civilization. It must declare as unworthy of its aims a principle of cowardice that, in the eyes of mankind, deserves excommunication.

But the victory of the Mosaic idea could be secured only by the complete extinction of the adherents of the old Jewish idea. They were, therefore, annihilated, together with their Golden Calf—the symbol of the spirit of usury—that is the same as the principle of material interests. The application of the principle of conquest by armed force led to the occupation of Canaan and the foundation of the kingdom of Judah [ca. 930 BC].

But as this period serves only to explain the application of a principle that does not lie within the scope of my essay, I shall resume the thread of our investigation from the time when the kingdom of Judah vanished, in order to make room again for the reappearance of the Jewish idea, that is, the principle of material interests.

Reaction of the Jewish Idea

With the fall of the kingdom of Judah, its stay and support, the principle of physical force, fell also, and the Jews again turned their eyes towards that peculiarly Jewish principle that was to secure them the conquest of the world—the principle of material interests. When they were attacked by the Assyrians and Persians, there was, perhaps, still a party amongst the Jews that held a conquest by armed force possible, but this party was soon silenced by the adherents of the old idea. These latter partisans maintained that if the prophecies were to be fulfilled, and the sons of Israel were to acquire the conquest of the world, such an object could not be accomplished by the application of arms but only by the application of the principle of material interests.

"What use is it to us," they said, "to possess a country of our own, a kingdom, fortresses, and armies that a single storm can destroy in a moment, making us the slaves of the conqueror? No, the Mosaic principle may appear beautiful, but it is only a chimera. Our riches and our power must *not* be concentrated at one point; they must be everywhere and nowhere, so that they cannot become the prey of our enemies. No country, no kingdom, must be our own, but we must try to possess ourselves of the riches of all the countries and of all the empires of the world. Scattered over the whole face of the Earth, we must possess no fixed habitation, but hurry towards those spots where the harvest is most bountiful. Only through the principle indicated by Abraham, Isaac, and Jacob, and only in this manner, can, and will, the prophecies be fulfilled that promise to the sons of Israel the conquest of the world."

The conflict between these two principles divided the Jewish nation into two parties that long struggled for supremacy. The consequence of this conflict was that the Jews saw themselves at one time forced to decide upon a cosmopolitan emigration, and at another time felt drawn again towards Zion, the visible central point of their nationality. The tendency towards decentralization held, at a certain time, the upper hand, and became the cause of that kind of emigration that is known as the Babylonian captivity [ca. 600 BC].

But this captivity was, in fact, nothing else than an aggressive movement on the part of the Jews, having for its object to reduce their conquerors to subjection by means of cunning and usury. Beaten on the field of policy and war, the Jews endeavored to repay themselves by plundering the Assyrians, and it is a fact that, once established in the center of the Assyrian empire, the Jews possessed themselves of the riches of the country, and finally laid their grasp even on its administration and political power. This victory was accomplished by the assistance of the intrigues of Esther and Mordecai, who used the old king Ahasuerus [ca. 475 BC] as their tool, taking the reins of the State into their own hands.

The Roman Period

The conquest of Judea by the Romans gave a decisive direction to the Jews' cosmopolitan tendency. They now penetrated into all the Eastern and Western provinces of the Roman Empire. In all countries, they soon stole amongst their conquerors, and the vassals of those conquerors, and preyed upon them with cunning and usury to their hearts' content. It is to this influx of the Jews, as well as to their rebellious spirit, that we must ascribe the hatred that the Romans began to cherish towards them. When this hatred had reached its climax, the Romans undertook that campaign that had in view the destruction of a race that had grown to be a real plague of the Empire.

The campaign of Titus [66 to 70 AD] was intended to destroy the capital of the Jewish people, regarded by the Romans as the point of action of the Jewish race. But this campaign missed its intended purpose, and for this reason Jerusalem had long since ceased to be the central point of action of the Jewish nationality. For amongst the Jews, the movement of cosmopolitan decentralization had long ago taken the place of the system of centralization, and the principles of physical force had given way to the principle of material interests. This change having taken place, the Jews had no more use for the fortresses of Judea and the walls of Jerusalem in their aggressive movement. They had already boldly assumed the offensive on all points, and had decided to employ in their project of the conquest of the world only the weapons of cunning and usury. Moreover, Roman policy committed a great mistake when it turned its arms against a single point, the destruction of which could no longer weaken Jewish power.

For the Jews, having long ago exchanged their point of action for a principle, that principle now constituted their sole basis of operations, and the Romans ought to have fought and annihilated that principle. But such an undertaking was not within the power of the Romans; and Titus, in destroying Jerusalem, destroyed the only obstacle in the way of the Jews for a free aggressive movement upon all other nations. From that moment, the Jewish people forever renounced their native country and their Mosaic traditions, and began the great work of conquering the world by means of the principle of material interests.

A Christian Prejudice

The motives that, as I have stated in the foregoing, compelled the Jews to abandon their native country, gives the lie to a prejudice that has taken root amongst the Christians—namely the universal belief that the Jews have been scattered over the whole face of the world because of their stubbornness in refusing to recognize the divine mission of Christ.

History shows that this belief is a mere prejudice; for innumerable proofs might be cited to establish the fact that the dispersion of the Jews has been nothing but a voluntary and predetermined emigration. One proof of the fact that this scattering was voluntary is the circumstance that, 400 years before the conquest of Jerusalem (at the time of the Maccabees [167 to 63 BC]), the Jewish people had already begun to scatter towards all the regions of the world.

Another proof that brute force was not the cause of the dispersion is the fact that Titus took along only a few thousand Jewish prisoners for his triumphal entry into Rome. But there is a vast distinction between a few thousand Jews and the whole population of Judea—a distinction that may well be sufficient to override every other proof that may be brought forward to show that the Jews were dispersed by force. If we furthermore consider the fact that the Romans never drove from their countries the people whom they subjected, we are all the less slow to believe that they made an exception in the case of the Jews, of whom they never stood much in fear anyway.

Having thus shown that the dispersion of the Jewish people must be regarded only as an aggressive movement that had the universal conquest of the world for its object, I shall now follow the fate of the Jews and their progress in the later times of the Roman Empire and the Middle Ages.

*****

The Period of the Middle Ages

The weakening of Roman rule and the invasions of the barbarians brought about a period of transition that vastly favored the expansion of the Jewish element. Placed between two other elements, of which the one was enervated and the other in a state of barbarism, the Jews managed to push themselves imperceptibly forward and to strike firm root in the lands conquered by the barbarians. It is true that the Christian Church and the feudal power opposed hostile measures to their advance, and even checked their development; but the Jews did not allow themselves to be held back by any such obstacles, and contrived to cripple the hostility of both priests and nobles. There is only one hostility that the Jews fear: it is that which assumes the shape of competition, and attacks them on their own field—that is, the principle of material interests. So long as you allow the Jews to quietly accumulate money, they care about nothing else; on the contrary, they mocked behind their backs both the victors by force of arms and the victors by the spiritual principle.

While Europe during this time was separated into many nations and empires, the Jews scattered over all the trading places, taking up their abode there in order to carry on trade and usury. It is true that their riches, and especially the means by which they gathered them together, often drew upon them cruel persecutions; but these acts of violence were only temporary and not powerful enough to stem the rising tide of Jewish conquest that gained more territory daily.

Thus Jewish establishments penetrated into the chief commercial centers of Europe. One body of Jews settled in Venice, another in Genoa, while at the same time colonies arose in the chief cities of Spain, the Netherlands, Germany, and Poland. These bodies, although scattered over an extensive territory, formed a firmly connected, homogeneous union, exercising its activity under the impulse of a single motive power, the principle of material interests.

This assertion that the dispersed members of the Jewish race formed a united and fearful body is by no means an airy phrase, but a truth that can be proved with mathematical exactness.

As a first proof of this fact, I point out that even in the midst of the present civilization of the Western nations, the link of race union that chains Jew to Jew is much stronger than the link that connects a Jew with a Christian.

The second proof is the circumstance that the same religious and historical traditions, as well as the same race union, exists among all the Jews from one end of the world to the other, from Kamchatka to San Francisco, in the midst of civilized Europe as well as in the center of Asia. This whole scattered and yet united body is animated by a single idea, by a single faith: that its members are the "chosen people," and that the treasures of this world are their inheritance. Question, as I have often had occasion to do, the Jewish marauder who travels over the steppes of Tartary, or the refined stock broker, who strolls through the Leopoldt Street of Vienna, or Lombard Street of London, or Wall Street of New York, and you will find amongst all of them the same faith and confidence in their destination. Jewish solidarity is so great that if you attack one Jew in any particular place, all the Jews of the five continents arise as one man.

To illustrate this in a measure, I beg to refer to an incident of modern times. While [American] General Ulysses S. Grant was facing opposing forces in the State of Tennessee, he was so very much annoyed by the great number of Jews who followed his army, like the hound the deer, that he issued an order requiring the Jews forthwith to leave his lines.[8] An immense excitement was thus created among the Jews in all large cities of America, and committees of the faithful were formed who at once commenced their pilgrimage to Washington with the view to impress upon President Lincoln the supposed injustice of General Grant's order. The President listened attentively to the complaint of the committee, and in the goodness of his heart addressed a letter to General Grant in that he requested him to modify this order. General Grant replied, stating that he had complied with the wish of the President and rescinded the order in question, but added that the Jews in his opinion had not changed any to the better since they crucified Christ.

Wherever there are Jews, every Jew is sure of a lodging, of support, and assistance. At the same time, the Hebrew language, with its peculiar letters, serves the Jews of all countries as a bond of union, and connects the Jewish communities scattered over the whole surface of the world with each other.

The true Freemasonry is that of the Jews, in comparison wherewith our own Freemasonry is mere child's play.

In the Middle Ages, these Jewish adventurers stole in, in the most modest manner, without putting forth any pretension, as men who had to make their means of living. They submitted patiently, wrapped in rags, to fight with bitter misery; and yet their faith in their ultimate destination remained unshakeable.

In vain we look in history for a spectacle even approaching the self-abnegation to which the Jews submitted for centuries in order to accomplish their object, the conquest of the world. By the aid of this self-abnegation and this severe discipline, these conscripts of usury have remained true to their flag, the principle of material interests, and have changed themselves into sober, active, and powerful men. That principle became to the Jews a law that submitted them to a Spartan mode of living, keeping them from being corrupted through laziness or dissipation. This severe discipline and mode of living discloses the secret, how the Jews were enabled so successfully to fight the other races and to appropriate the plunder taken from them with

---

[8] *Ed.:* This was General Order number 11 of 1862, during the American Civil War.

such singular fortune. In this commercial and financial conflict, it often happens that the Jew beats hundreds of his opponents from the field, solely because the principle of material interests; the bait of gain makes him more sober, active, and powerful than hundreds of his opponents taken together.

Jewish Corruption

Few people will believe me if I tell them that the Jews nevertheless possess the quintessence of virtue. This assertion must appear all the more paradoxical since many people regard the Jews as the worst sort of men. But these persons will be still more astonished when I add that the Jews are *both*: that is, very virtuous, and abhorrently vicious; nay, the disseminators of vice. This apparent contradiction needs only a few explanations in order to make apparent its full meaning.

The Jew is virtuous because he experiences, so to say, a practical, and not, as we do, a platonic love for virtue. The Jew is virtuous because it is in his interest to be so; that is, on account of the material advantages that virtue procures to him. The exercise of virtue prolongs life and enables him to gain money; this suffices the Jew, and hence he venerates virtue. But if the principle of material interests compels him on the one side to embrace virtue, the same principle forces him on the other side to enter upon the path of vice.

The Jew who understands how to secure to himself the advantages of virtue, thereafter considers virtue his monopoly. "Virtue," he thinks, "is a very good thing, of that I must take good care. But it must not be in possession of everyone, for otherwise it would not be possible to make money out of it." Hence it is through calculation, or speculation, that he subjects even virtue to taxation, and uses vice as a tool or weapon of destruction.

Thus virtue and vice change in the hand of the Jews into powerful means, to be used as defensive or offensive weapons. With virtue, they brave losses and misfortune; with vice, they attack those whose fortunes they intend to devour.

If any further proof were needed to show that the Jews seek to enrich themselves by means of immorality, we need only point out some well-known facts. Benazet and Blanc, two Jews, were the founders of the gambling halls in Baden-Baden and Homburg.[9] Ibrahim Pasha, the son of the Viceroy of Egypt, had inherited a fabulous fortune, amounting to not less

---

[9] *Ed.:* The reference is to Jacques Benazet (1778-1848) and Francois Blanc (1806-1877).

than 150,000,000 francs. The Jew, Max von Oppenheim, in Alexandria, became his banker, and administered the affairs of the younger Pasha so mas-
terly that three years of his administration sufficed to make the prince a
bankrupt.[10]

Jewish Progress during the Middle Ages

Throughout the whole period of the Middle Ages, the commercial settlements of the Jews were simply so many separate encampments in the enemy's country, that could be taken down at any moment and put up again in
another place. Commerce was the great battlefield, so to speak, on that the
two enemies—the native-born on the one side, and the Jewish invaders on
the other—encountered each other and carried on their engagements; the
latter naturally coming off victorious in almost every case, and thus acquiring the hegemony of the whole commercial world; for commerce was most
specially adapted to the Jewish instincts.

It is characteristic of the Jewish disposition that not a single one of the
modes of living selected by the Jews serves to enrich the wealth of a nation
directly. The Jew, as is well known, does not engage in agriculture, in min-
ing, in the production of raw material, or even in the manufacture of things
from the raw material. He attends only to the circulation of values, and en-
riches himself by exchanging worthless articles for good money. I feel
obliged to call attention to this circumstance in order to establish the fact that
the Jews are, for the greater part, *unproductive parasites*; for what should
induce them to work by the sweat of their brows when they have in themselves the means to appropriate the productions of others? For this simple
reason, the Jews have always kept aloof from agriculture, and preferred a
changeful, nomadic life, that offers them the great advantage of leaving them
at all times free for any sort of movement. This mobility, by means of which
the Jews were always able to hunt up those places where the largest plunder
was to be expected, was evidently the result of their not being tied in the
least to the soil on which they lived. It harmonized, moreover, with their
cosmopolitan tendency and their aggressive system generally.

Thus, for instance, during the flourishing times of the Italian republics,
Venice, Genoa, and Florence were overrun with Jews. The downfall of these
republics compelled the Jews to pack up the treasures gathered in the South

---

[10] *Ed.:* The reference is to Ibrahim Pasha Milli (1843-1908) and German Jew Max
von Oppenheim (1860-1946).

and emigrate northward; settling in Germany, Poland, and the Netherlands, where, in the meanwhile, commerce, industry, and general prosperity had vastly increased. England was the last to suffer—not, indeed, until the close of the last century, when it had taken naval and commercial supremacy out of the hands of Holland, which had dominated until then. The Jews were least successful in Spain. In that country, the native-born people compelled them to emigrate, regarding them as foreign invaders and secret allies of the Moors.

*****

Jews will always be Jews

After this short review of the history of the Jews during the Middle Ages, it now becomes my duty to devote a special investigation to an isolated question, connected therewith, but that is even by itself a real miracle. I allude to the remarkable fact of the non-intermixture of the Jews. In spite of their own wide dispersion, in spite of centuries of continued intercourse with other races, the Jews are still today what they were 1800 years ago. We find in them the same characteristics, the same type; as if neither time, nor habit, nor the intercourse with foreign elements could have effected a change in them. This curious phenomenon is the result of the cooperation of different factors, the most prominent of which we here enumerate:

1. The tie of religious and historical traditions.
2. The tie of blood relationship.
3. The sentiment of a common solidarity.
4. The hatred of all other people.

It is due to the powerful cooperation of these factors that the Jews have remained Jews, although they have branched off into various countries and adopted the habits of those countries as times required. Their turning into Frenchmen, Germans, and Poles, or Americans, is merely superficial, and does not in the least affect their inner Jewish nature. Nay, this assumption of different nationalities has been, and is for them, nothing but a mask, undercover whereof they can all the more imperceptibly steal into the sheep-yard. We need not specify with what animal in the fable they have this characteristic in common.

One thing or the other! Let a man be either a Jew or a German, Frenchman, American, or Russian, etc. But no! The Jews maintain that they can combine both qualities; and while they flourish their "true," *par exemple*, French patriotism in the face of the world with special predilection, they have no scruple at the same time openly to boast of their pride in their Jewish nationality. Adolphe Cremieux and Armand Levy, two Israelite celebrities of our time, have unreservedly declared that they are "Jews to their fingers' ends," and since there is little room left beyond the fingers' ends, French nationality must fare rather poorly in these individuals.[11]

The Jews in Modern Times

Throughout the whole period of the Middle Ages, the Jews had quietly laid stone upon stone in the building up of their future power. Regardless of the movements of the rest of the world, they heaped treasures upon treasures in their hiding nooks and cleverly arranged the order of battle of usury from one end of Europe to another, and from there to the New World, awaiting the moment when they might issue forth from darkness into the light of day and climb to the top of their power.

At last, the long-expected day appeared. On that spring morning of liberty, when the old and rotten edifice of feudalism broke down with a crash, and all the previous political, civil, and ecclesiastical institutions of Europe received a shock from that they will never recover; when the rising tide of modern ideas swept everything before it, and unpityingly drowned every resisting object: on the day of the French Revolution, the hour of liberation sounded also for the Jews, when, freed from their chains, they could unfold the whole fullness of their power and enter upon a path that would lead them, in a short time, to the conquest of the world.

The sole obstacle that had hitherto kept the Jews in check now dropped away. Undermined by the doctrines of Voltaire and conquered by the power of liberalism, the national and religious limitations of the Middle Ages gradually crumbled into dust, and Europe, having broken with the past, was given over to a complete reconstruction. Going hand in hand with the Freethinkers, the Jacobins, the Carbonari—in short, with the revolutionaries of all shades—the Jews now undertook the reconstruction of Europe. Everywhere

---

[11] *Ed.:* Adolphe Cremieux (1796-1880) was a French-Jewish lawyer. Armand Levy (1827-1891) was a French-Jewish political activist.

they associated with those who cried out: "Long live Tolerance! Long live Fraternity! Down with Rank! Away with Privileges!"

But whilst these cries signified, in the mouth of other nations, a stern demand for measures of progress, recognized by them to be just and necessary, they were to the Jews nothing but a clever trick of war, wherewith to confuse the ranks of their enemies. How else can we explain the fact that these same Jews have not for a moment entertained the notion of turning their back on their own religion, their own traditions and principles?

With ranks closed, the Jews now opened attack on their enemies, and having overcome them on all points, erected their own standard on the ruins of ancient Europe. Since then we see the flag of Judaism unfurled on every watchtower of European power, and, indeed, over all the world, a flag that bears the inscription: "Materialism and Material Interests!" Significant words, the keys of Jewish world-supremacy.

The whole conquest has not cost the Jews one shot of powder. Apart from what the achievements of revolution and liberalism have caused to fall into their lap like ripe apples, they owe their present position in the main to the unprincipled intrigues with which they have successfully placed, one after the other, of their enemies *hors du combat*. Thus they have managed, by means of clever tactics, to secure for themselves the advantages of a central position, from which they can turn at pleasure now to the one and now to the other side. By alternating in this manner, stirring up revolutions today and tomorrow lending their support to legitimacy, assisting with one hand in the distribution of State-overthrowing Utopias, while with the other restoring Monarchies, and aiding to found new aristocracies, they connive to make both parties serviceable to them, and to derive immense advantages from whatever turn affairs may take. We all know that governments as well as revolutionary parties require money; and the men who lend it are Jews—of course, not without a corresponding percentage, both in cash and in concessions and privileges.

Financial Conquests

We have seen how the great religious and political revolutions that have shaken all Christendom, and divided it into various camps and parties, have been a special God-send to the Jews, since they enabled them, amongst all this confusion, to take a decided forward step in their work of conquest, and obtain hegemony in finances, in the State, and in society. This conquest, let us once more emphasize, is not on any account imaginary; it is a conquest in the word's widest sense. Nay, the Jews themselves, far from making a secret of it, confess it and call it "the main and distinctive problem of Judaism."

As early as the Middle Ages, the Jews had accumulated vast riches and obtained thereby a certain influence. But the cooperation of other causes was necessary to make it possible for their financial power to attain its present marvelous dimensions; nay, to grasp the lion's share of the various national properties and riches within their clutches. Amongst these causes we should like to enumerate, in the first instance, the dissemination of cosmopolitan ideas, the growth of greater equality in the morals and usages of the European nations, the multiplication of all means of public intercommunication, and the increase of international relations.

This growth of intercourse between the various members of the separate nations and between the remotest countries that was begun at the end of the 18ᵗʰ century, and has since steadily increased, has, in truth, contributed very materially to the marvelous development of Jewish financial power. The cause of this phenomenon is perhaps formulated in the best way by saying that the influence of that financial power has thus risen from a local to a universal power. The Jews, holding in their hands the financial condition of every single country, were better able than other people to derive advantages from the general growth of industry and the inventions of modern times. In the same ratio that financial enterprises began to flourish and become more universal, the sphere of Jewish activity extended also. As atoms are drawn towards large masses under the law of gravity, thus minor capitals drift towards the immeasurable riches of the Jews; and as, under the same law, the motion of the attracted bodies becomes more and more accelerated in time, thus the attractive power of Jewish capital grows greater daily. Nay, the iron girdle that that capital has at present drawn across the wealth of the nations, is already fixed so closely and unbreakable that we may say without exaggeration that the Jews hold even now in their hands the financial power from one end of the world to the other. It is a simple fact that in the present day, not a single important financial operation can be carried out unless the Jews participate in it and put the profits into their pockets.

In this way, the Jews have brought things to pass in such a short time that they are now the wealthiest and most influential class of men; and have attained a position of vast power, the likes of which we do not meet in all history. From the height of their immense capital, the weight whereof threatens to crush all other nations, they command the whole world of finance and industry. The most profitable and colossal enterprises of modern times, within and out of Europe, are simply Jewish monopolies; as, for instance, the Austrian Southern Railway—the main line of traffic for Central Europe—the mines of Brazil, the Union Pacific Railway in the United States, under the control of Jay Gould,[12] etc.

But we go further, and venture to assert, as we can do without great exaggeration that there is not a man amongst us who is not in some way tributary to Jewish power. We all, without exception, pay our tribute to the Jews, be it for our rents, our houses, the bread that we eat, or the clothes that we wear. You may count on your fingers even the kings and nobles who are not debtors to the Jews, and hence morally and in point of fact subject to them.

The Jewish financial power resembles thus, in a manner, an imp, who, without being visible, pokes his fingers into everybody's pockets. Like Care in Goethe's *Faust*, he knows how to enter through the keyhole, to be present everywhere, and yet to hide from the eyes of all.[13] He seems to be especially experienced in the role of a seducer; indeed, we have a notion that once upon a time he stole that role from the father of sin himself; for it is in the words of Satan that he speaks to us: "Worship me and I will lead you to happiness."

The Rothschild Dynasty

Hand in hand with the marvelous rise of Jewish financial power in general, or rather as a necessary condition and unavoidable basis thereof, we find rare individual progress amongst the single members of the Jewish people. The petty medieval usurers have changed everywhere into modern bankers or Stock Exchange brokers. Those wandering Jews of long ago have become crafty speculators, and the old clothes men and peddlers have opened elegant warehouses and industrial halls.

But there was for a time still lacking the crown of the edifice—that is, the embodiment of the motive principle in a concrete and tangible power that is inborn in every human enterprise. For, as the ecclesiastical or the military rule are ultimately incorporated into a Pope, or an Emperor, thus the Jewish money-supremacy must necessarily induce the formation of a dynasty that

---

[12] *Ed.:* Jay Gould (1836-1892) was an American railroad magnate known for his highly unethical business practices.
[13] *Ed.:* Along with Want, Debt, and Distress, Care was one of four spirits to confront Faust.

derived its origin and its permanent justification from the principle of material interests.

This crowning of the edifice was not long in being completed. The facts are these: At the close of the Napoleonic wars, a Frankfurt Jew by the name of Rothschild arose—more by the force of circumstances than in consequence of his own exertions—to the high and powerful position of a visible head of the Jewish supremacy.[14] All the Jews bowed down before this new ruler; and still bow down ever since his rule was recognized from one end of the world to the other. As the King of finances, Rothschild commands the rolling masses of Jewish capital as completely as the German or the Russian Emperor commands the moveable masses of his armies. The power of this "self-constituted Ruler of all the Jews" is not to be calculated, however, by the billions that he can call his own directly, but by that far greater, and really fabulous mass of gold, the circulation of which is dependent upon the orders issued by his cabinet. Each Jewish millionaire who carries on financial operations in Paris, Vienna, Berlin, or in the United States, is in so far a Lieutenant General of Rothschild, as it were, always governing his action by the indications of that financial barometer.

The wealth of the Rothschilds is something fabulous. Anselm Salomon von Rothschild (1803-1874), who died but recently in Vienna, has left a fortune of a billion francs. According to this statement, the wealth of the three branches of the family may be estimated at about three billion dollars. This is pretty nearly the amount that the French government was at some trouble to raise for the war indemnity. One family is, therefore, as wealthy as a whole nation! When one reflects that this immense wealth is the fruit of the labor of millions of unfortunates, one might doubt one's sanity! So long as the world exists, such an unnatural state of things has never before been known! The head of the Rothschild family is, therefore, a potentate, a ruler within the full meaning of the word; and his subjects are the millions of human beings who incessantly labor to support his power and his splendor!

The Rothschilds possess a dozen castles, truly royal residences, situated in the most magnificent and cultured countries. There, these rulers unfold a gorgeous splendor, and receive the adulations of the magnates of this earth, not excluding Emperors and Kings, and yet the head of the Rothschild family places little value on being *called* a King. His Jewish majesty is evidently

[14] *Ed.:* The reference is to Mayer Amschel Rothschild (1744-1812), founder of the dynasty.

content with *being* a King, and enjoying the power that his immense riches procure for him.

But in all other respects, Rothschild literally plays the role of a ruler and does not neglect the duties that this royal dignity imposes upon him. It is he who represents the Jewish people with splendor, as other rulers represent the power of their respective nations. The Jewish ruler, for instance, never shrinks from taking part in all subscriptions that fashion or report has invested with a certain importance. Rothschild also takes care always, when visiting any particular locality, to leave a memento of his presence, either by founding some philanthropic institution or by a princely donation. Besides this, the Rothschilds, as the visible head of the Jewish nationality, have in recent times made it their duty to lay the cornerstone whenever some benevolent institution, devoted exclusively to the Jews, is to be erected. Whatever other rulers do, the King of the Jews must do also, of course.

The power of this Jewish autocrat is so immeasurable and unlimited that it far outshines the power of all other kings and emperors. When but a few years ago, two great empires, France and Prussia, carried on a bloody war, each country putting forth many hundreds of thousands of soldiers, it was nevertheless necessary to call in a third potentate to establish quiet in Europe. This potentate was called 'Rothschild,' that king "By the Grace of God" whose signature was indispensable for the definite conclusion of the Treaty of Versailles.

Their power in the United States is well known and felt. It is stated on good authority that the demonetizing of the American silver dollar in 1873 was achieved by an agent from the Rothschilds and their confederates, by the name of Earnest Seagel, who went to Washington for that purpose, and it is believed by corrupt means succeeded in effecting the change. So cleverly was the matter done that some time elapsed before the change was generally known.

In connection with the above, we may state that by the untiring efforts of the Hon. Richard P. Bland, a member of Congress from Missouri, and his coworkers in both branches of Congress, the American silver dollar was again made a legal tender. And that contrary to the prophecies of those who were inimical to the restoration of bimetallic money, and who had predicted fearful results from its accomplishment, no change was observed in the general business of the country, other than that the premium on gold at once decreased, and the purchasing power of silver increased, the two metals becoming thus equalized.

*****

Social Conquests

The profits acquired by the Jews in the financial world necessarily placed in their hands the means to improve their condition also in a social and political respect. Recognizing full well the immense advantages of such progress, they never left them out of sight; and therefore, having crawled forth from their hiding places and Jew-quarters, tried hard to turn their commercial relations with the natives into social intercourse—until at last the doors of the whole Christian society were opened to them, and they succeeded in gaining entrance into the same families, intercourse with whom had until then been prohibited. But although having thus grown gradually into acquaintances, then from acquaintances into friends, and from friends into fellow-citizens, they yet remained inwardly the same Jews that they always had been.

When they had thus comfortably nestled into the bosom of the different nations of the world, they longed also for a monopoly of the liberal arts and sciences that are open only to the higher ranks of society. Knowing well that they could acquire honor, regard, and political power only by those means, they engaged in literature, medicine, and public education, and flooded the professions of law and especially journalism. To this latter sphere, they have devoted themselves always with special predilection, because they are better aware than other people of the rare advantages to be derived from a rolling and easily handled tool, by means of which one can make the world believe anything. These Jewish newspaper writers form in every State a closely connected and all-powerful consortium, composed of minds as clever and industrious as they are unscrupulous, and that have appropriated the right of intervention in all foreign affairs in order to levy tribute on the credulity of the public. It is very evident that a consortium, having such means at its disposal, far more powerful than church or Feudal State, is in possession of a vast and terrible power, in the hands of which we are nothing but abject slaves.

Political Conquests

The position that the Jews had attained within the Christian social world formed the key that was soon to open to them the doors of political equality. Ancient society, with its restrictions and limitations, having been overthrown, no further difficulties stood in their way. Going hand in hand with the advocates of liberty and equality, they had assisted at this overthrow; and thus those [non-Jewish] advocates, being now masters of the situations, could not refuse them a counter-service. In conformity with a program that promised equality on the broadest principles, they were bound to conquer all inward repugnance, and declare the Jews to be in all respects their full-blood fellow citizens. These renovating legislators said, therefore, openly that the Jews were men like all other men and deserved to be entitled to the same universal rights of men. Blinded by the existing, humane appearance of their theories, these men were incapable of perceiving the danger that threatened them from individuals, who, under the cover of national solidarity, had always in view only the object of a great, cosmopolitan, world-ruling consortium. Who, indeed, could have foreseen at that time that the same Jews, with whom political companionship was made, would make life so bitter to later generations? It should have been considered that however just and harmless the investure of equality may be to individuals, as such it may become all the more dangerous and generally productive of evil when it is conferred upon a whole, foreign race, scattered over all the countries of the world.

The consequences of Jewish emancipation were not slow to show themselves. As it would lead us too far to follow closely the path pursued by the Jews in their political conquest, we must content ourselves to show at least how far they have advanced up to today, and what position they now occupy in politics.

To begin with diplomacy, we note the fact that this field is overrun with Jews. The same fate is shared by the legislative assemblies of England, France, and Austria—the most influential members of which belong to the Jewish race. Jewish ministers and counsellors of State are also no rarities. Take for instance Disraeli, now Lord Beaconsfield, the leader of the Tories in the English Parliament.[15] Daniel O'Connell has said in one of his speeches, "that if his genealogy could be traced, he would no doubt be found to be the true heir-at-law of the impenitent thief on the cross".[16] Then there is George Goshen, lately First Lord of the British Admiralty.[17] And amongst

---

[15] *Ed.:* Benjamin Disraeli (1804-1881) was the first Jewish prime minister of the UK.

[16] The *Westminster Review* of the time when *Vivian Gray* was published [in 1826; it was Disraeli's first novel], thus speaks of Lord Beaconfield: "He has the flare of the livery, the flippancy of the shoulder-knot, the bustle, the pert smartness of those who stand, powdered and bare-headed, on the steps of great houses, and make sport of that part of the world below the peerage and above the servant's hall."

[17] *Ed.:* Goschen (1831-1907) long disputed any Jewish ancestry.

the English nobility we find such Jews as Sir Nathaniel Mayer de Rothschild (1840-1915), Sir Moses Montefiore (1784-1885), Sir Francis H. Goldsmith, and also Sir David Louis Salamons (1797-1873), Benjamin Samuel Phillips (1811-1889), Sir Albert David Sassoon (1818-1896), Sir Julius Vogel, Governor of New Zealand (1835-1899), Sir Borrow Herbert Ellis, George de Worms (1829-1902), Hermann de Stern (1815-1887), Baron Albert Grant, and a host of others too numerous to mention. Then there is the noisy Eduard Lasker (1829-1884) in the Prussian General Assembly, the elastic Arnim— all are Jews. Leon Gambetta (1838-1882) and Emilio Castelar (1832-1899), these two educators of France and Spain are of Jewish extraction; and both of these *"Rabagas"* try to play the role of Saviors of mankind.

If we consider further that in all these countries the Jews constitute only a small fraction of the population, we must admit that this small minority has already received too many advantages as against the majority of the people.

In order to gain this daily increasing advance on the field of politics, the Jews make use of a peculiar, sly system of tactics, the fundamental principles of which we may sum up as follows:

1. They endeavor to concentrate their influence, scattered as it is all over the world, at any given moment, at the point to be conquered in the most effective manner, in order to suppress all local opposition tendencies.

2. They endeavor at all times to derive advantage from our disunion. With this purpose in view, they place the power of their capital and their influence at the disposal now of this and now of the other party, while they take care at the same time to have representatives in every party. Thanks to this policy, the Jews are always on hand to turn every party victory to their advantage.

Such a distribution of power is like a good hand of cards, wherein all four colors are represented so that some points are always sure, no matter that color is turned up trumps. Thus for instance, we see in France Imperialistic, Republican, nay, even Socialistic Jews. If Imperialism gains the day, Messrs. Fould, Pereire and company are there to represent the Jewish interest. If, on the other hand the Republic, or perhaps even the Commune, chances to be victorious, there is Mr. Cremieux or Citizen Karl Marx at hand to change into the trump color, as it were, of the Jewish hand of cards. By the aid of this clever trick, the Jews preserve their prestige independently of all changes of government, and approach more and more their object, the conquest of the world, no matter how circumstances may change. They have discovered the secret of winning with all parties and losing with none.

This game that the Jews play so cleverly with every nation, they also play on a larger scale in international politics, on the Green Table of Diplomacy. Here the different nations serve them the same purpose as did in the former instance the different parties of a nation—that power being to them for the time the trump color that happens to be the director of the European concert. Let us illustrate this by an example:

So long as France and England were all powerful, Judaism leaned for support upon their influence—using the English and French as trumps, so to say. All the agents and emissaries that at that time directed the aggressive Jewish movement in Turkey, Russia, and Romania were English or French Jews. But the moment that the leaf was turned, and those two Great Powers were forced to cede the precedence to others, the Jewish trump colors changed, and the Israelite agents turned suddenly into full blooded Americans or Prussians. Now, if we recollect that the rise of the American and Prussian powers occurred just within these past few years, it is easily explained why the Jews should have wheeled around since 1867, abandoning the Tricolor as well as the Cross of St. George, and seeking their salvation meanwhile in the folds of the Star-Spangled Banner or under the wings of the One-Headed Eagle.

In the financial conflict that broke out a few years ago between the Romanians and the Jews, the latter have also acted strictly in accordance with the policy just pointed out, placing Dr. Strousberg, a Prussian Jew, as *Generalissimus* at their head; inducing the appointment of Mr. Benjamin Peixotto, an American Jew, as Consul of the United States; and finally ordering another Prussian Jew, a certain Dr. Von Levi, to the Danubian principalities and Servia, in order to maintain Jewish influence there, through all sorts of intrigues.

Peixotto (1834-1890), from the State of California, now represents the United States as Consul at Lyons, France. Ernest L. Oppenheimer, from the State of New York, represents, the Great Republic in the same capacity at Goettenburg. Henry S. Lasar, a citizen from St. Louis, Mo., has been appointed by the President, Consular agent at Haarburg, Germany. Another party, David Eckstein, has been nominated, but his case has not been passed upon by the US Senate. The above are American Jews, and more appointments of the same character will undoubtedly follow.

We may remark here, in passing that Prussian Jews were a rather scarce article before Sadowa, but since the Sedan victory, it would be very difficult to scare up a Jew who did not carry at all times a photograph of Bismarck in his pocket; for servility is also one of the noble traits of the Jewish people. And indeed, there is no reason why people should not contrive to unite both things: to kneel in awe-bound admiration before the strong, and at the same time to maltreat and swindle the weak unconscionably.

Whatever objection may be raised against this pliable and at the same time unscrupulous policy from a moral standpoint, one thing is certain: it is practical, and this is sufficient for the Jews. It is owing to this policy that the Jews gain ground daily at all points in Europe, Asia, and America, and occupy already amongst the various nations of the world a central position from that they can comfortably rule, control, nay, press down under the weight of their riches and their political influence all other peoples.

Let us glance first at France and Italy, and we shall see how in both countries Judaism carries its head high in the consciousness of its indispensability. Both countries are tributary to it; to both countries it has advanced money— to the former for the payment of its war indemnity, and to the latter for the achievement of its independence. Austria fares very little better. There Judaism has the upper hand in politics, and overshadows the influence of the nobility and of the large land-owners. In Germany it tries at least to keep militarism and Pan-Germanic ideas in check by the aid of its financial power. In Russia and in the countries of the orthodox religion, Jewish power has only to overcome the yet existing national and religious prejudices in order to also be master of the situation there.

But it is in Russia that Judaism has, for some time past, made the most appalling progress. Before the Crimean War [1853 to 1856], and the emancipation of the serfs, the Jewish population was limited to the kingdom of Poland and the region lying between the Austrian-Russian boundary and the Dnieper. The large cities in that district were at that time still safe from the invasion of the Jews; under the then-existing laws, Israelites were prohibited from settling down, or even taking up their abode for any length of time in them.

At present, all these checks have been overcome. The Jewish hordes have crossed the Dnieper and penetrated into the governments of Cherson, Pultawa, Charkow, Wornesch, Taganrok, etc. Of the two Russian capitals, Petersburg has been the first to allow the invasion of these financial locusts.

Moscow, the holy city, offers resistance as yet; but it is already encircled by a band of Jews who hold themselves concealed in the suburbs, and advance but gradually in their attacks upon the general riches. However, things have already come to such a pair in the greater part of Russia that it is impossible to carry on any kind of business without Jewish agency.

Such are the results and consequences of the present ruling liberalism. After so sad an experience, there is scarcely any other help than to return to such measures as were in use at the time of the Emperor Nicholas.[18] If we take exception to this alternative, the triumph of the Jews is unavoidable; and the triumph of the Jews means the ruin of all other races.

The Jews in Russia count now nearly four million souls; no other country in the world has so many. Yet the Jews hate the Russians because, so far, they have not succeeded in obtaining such a powerful influence in their country as they possess in England; and therefore the following cablegram, received in the United States, 29 March 1878, from abroad, will explain itself. Here it is:

Russia's pecuniary troubles increase every day. It is said that all the Hebrew bankers in London and on the continent have agreed not only to refuse to lend Russia any money, but to prevent the success of any loan she may put on the market. *England, on the contrary, can command practically endless supplies of the sinews of war!*

Judaism occupies a very peculiar position in England. There it is all-powerful; but its rule is not based on one-sided conquests, being rather the consequence of mutual concessions. A sort of friendly understanding had been arrived at on the basis of common interests between these two commercial powers, by virtue of which the British Empire lends its political influence and material assistance to Judaism, while the latter places it's financial influence at the disposal of England and supports British commerce. The English and the Jews both derive advantages from this tacit understanding; it enables the Britons to make use of the immense Jewish capital in disposing of their articles of commerce by means of Jewish middlemen, and to employ the Jews in case of necessity as spies and accomplices. These advantages explain the extravagant expressions of sympathy that the clergy and the press of England lavish on the "poor persecuted Jews." The Jews, on their part,

---

[18] *Ed.*: Czar Nicholas I ruled Russia from 1825 to 1855.

derive from this agreement the undeniable advantage of being thereby connected with a power that produces articles of commerce for them, and affords them generally successful protection.

Thus the English and the Jews go hand in hand together, and lend each other everywhere mutual support. Nothing, perhaps, can better illustrate the relation existing between these two parties than a simile that happens to strike me. The Jew is for the Englishman what a hunting dog is for the hunter. Whenever the Englishman lifts up his two-barreled gun—industry and commerce—the Jew is used as the hound, who must catch the game and bring it to his master. Now, it is true that the Jew is a vicious animal, for he never brings the game to his master without first having taken a bite out of it. But what is to be done? Without this commercial hound, hunting is impossible. Hence the Englishman must be content with whatever the other brings to him. Without the Jews, half of the productions of the English factories would rot in the docks and warehouses.

France plays the same game, and for the same purpose of getting consumers for her productions.

Thus the three allies have made it their object to provide mankind with all that makes life agreeable and comfortable. The English and the French have undertaken to manufacture all the things necessary for that purpose, while the Jews act as agents and brokers. This industrial and commercial union forms thus, a well and wisely-arranged structure that is plastered together by egoism so strongly as to render it next to indestructible. Everywhere the allies support each other and go hand in hand; and it is due to this united cooperation that the Occident has contrived to make all other countries tributary to itself.

Another result of this union is that the Jews, who possess neither country nor fixed habitations, have made Paris, London, New York, and San Francisco the headquarters in which Jewish power and Jewish influence have their support; London and Paris especially being the commercial and financial central points, where all the threads of Jewish pillage run together. For these are the places, whither tend all the yearning desires of Israel, and where its children dance, arm in arm with the natives, around the golden calf.

In all other countries, in Germany, in Russia, and in the Orient, the Jews form only hordes, ready for battle, or leeches, destined and longing to suck up the wealth of the people, and to effect connection with those two central basins of finances.

In America, finally, the Jews unfold almost as much power as in the Old World. Here as there, all the threads of wholesale and retail trade run through their hands. As regards their political activity, it is quite equal to that of the European Jews. As a proof of this latter assertion, we need only recall the fact that a Jew by the name of August Belmont (an agent of Rothschild and represented to be an illegitimate offspring of his Dynasty) has for a number of years been the chairman of the National Committee of a political party, and by his shrewd management has always succeeded in leading that party to defeat.[19] It is provable that the financial policy of the opposing party was the one under which his business was most prosperous. Why then should he desire a change?

Again, a few years ago, one of the scions of the Rothschild's Dynasty visited the United States, ostensibly for the benefit of his health, but in truth to review his lordly possessions. Traveling from New York to San Francisco, on his return East, he stopped at the Capital for the purpose of receiving the adulation of the then-Secretary of the Treasury, and for the further purpose of instructing the Secretary of the Treasury as to what additional legislation he deemed necessary in reference to the financial policy of the Great Republic. As soon as this Rothschild arrived in the City of Washington, the Secretary called upon him, received the instructions of the money Monarch, and subsequently had them carried out to the very letter.

*****

The Jewish Press

In the year 1840, an Israelite Council was called together at Krakow, Poland. This was a sort of an Ecumenical Council, wherein the most prominent men of the "chosen people" sat for consultation. The object of their meeting was to discover the proper means whereby to secure triumphs to Judaism in its extension from the North Pole to the South Pole.

As we will see, the program put forward by these gentlemen was very modest.

The subjects discussed in this Assembly were of a very varied character. Some belonged to the field of theology, others involved questions of political economy, while there were also some that belonged to politics pure and simple. A lively debate arose, amidst which suddenly a clear voice made

---

[19] *Ed.:* Belmont (1813-1890) was a Jewish-German-American politician who served as chair of the US Democratic National Committee from 1860 until 1872.

itself heard, and involuntarily imposed silence. It was the voice of a recognized authority, of a man of predominant mind, whose name is unfortunately unknown to us.

"What are you talking about?" said he to his colleagues in the gathering. "So long as we have not the press in our hands, all that you say is idle! In vain do you organize societies, loans, bankruptcies, and the like; so long as we have not got the press in our hands to deafen and deceive the world, we accomplish nothing, and our rule remains a phantom of our brain." These words produced a powerful effect on the minds of the Assembly. The hearers recognized that an oracle had spoken, that a new light had dawned on their minds to give a fixed direction to their exertions.

From that time, we may date the beginning of that work of the devil, which has for its object to turn the press into an engine of war, a sort of artillery, the fire of which can be directed against any kind of obstacle opposing itself to the financial and political conquest of the Jews. The plan, invented and adopted by the conspirators in order to bring the press under their control, consists in the following :

The press of all countries, without distinction, has been divided by the Jews into three classes, to-wit:

First class: Journals in the pay of the Jews.
Second class: Journals bearing the banner of some specific nationality.
Third class: Journals bearing the Jewish banner.

The first class is composed of all those journals that are supported by the Jews, either by subscription or shares purposely bought up by the Jews. Such are: *The London Times, Les Debats, L'Independance Belge, La Revue des deux Mondes, New York Tribune*, etc.

To be sure, there is no contract, no agreement between the editors of these journals and the Jews; the latter depend altogether on that partiality and sympathy that every editor must feel towards those men, who are always on hand to renew their subscriptions punctually at the expiration of every quarter. Of course, certain regards must be entertained toward such subscribers, and still more toward shareholders; and even if an editor should hesitate to do battle for them publicly, he must, at least, avoid everything that can be disagreeable to them, or expose them to any danger, in the columns of his journal. But this is sufficient for the Jews; and they are right; for it is, after all, not a small matter to have made journals of such influence as the *Times*, *Debats*, *New York Tribune*, etc., harmless.

The second class consists, as stated before, of such journals as raise the banner of any specific nationality, while being, in fact, Jewish organs. These journals are true wolves in sheep's clothing; for although they palm themselves off as English, French, American, or German journals, they are not the less Jewish, nay, arch-Jewish journals.

Now, these journals serve an excellent purpose under their mask, by effecting changes in public opinion; since their readers rarely perceive that the articles appearing in them conceal Jews disguised as Frenchmen or Englishmen. The public believe that these papers reflect the drift of opinion in this or that country; and yet they mirror only the reflection of the Jewish devil who tries to lead us astray at his pleasure, and to bewitch us with the doctrines and sophisms of the modern school.

In almost every country of Europe, we find an organ of this kind. In England, for instance, this organ is the *Daily Telegraph*, which has a circulation of 100,000 daily copies, and the exclusive proprietor of which is a Jew. The *Telegraph* was bought under foreclosure of a chattel mortgage some years ago by the Jew, Joseph Moses Levy, for £20,000. Two of the Levys have changed their name to that of Lawson, and the names of Mr. and Mrs. Lawson appear in the list of guests at the last ball of the Prince of Wales. The editor in chief, Edward Lawson, is a member of Parliament and expects a Baronetcy.[20]

France rejoices in two such journals, *La Patrie* and the *Paris Journal*, both the property of a Jew, the Baron Soubeyrand. Vienna has her *Neue Presse*,[21] and Italy her *Perseveranza*; both are Jewish journals. In Germany also, many such journals can be found; amongst others, let me mention the *Frankfurter Zeitung*.

The third class of Jewish journals proudly raises the Jewish flag. These journals show themselves without any mask, as their very names show: *Das Judenthum*; *Israelit*; *Israelitische Bibliothek*; *Jewish Cronicle*, Baltimore; *Jewish Messenger*, New Jersey; *American Israelite*, Cincinnati; *Jewish Record*, Philadelphia; *San Francisco Hebrew*, *Occident*, Chicago; *Independent Hebrew*, New Jersey; *Jewish Gazette*, etc., etc. The circulation of these and

---

[20] *Ed.:* The Jew Moses Levy acquired the *Telegraph* in 1855. His son, Edward Levy-Lawson (1833-1916) subsequently ran the paper for many years.

[21] *Ed.:* The Jew Eduard Bacher became editor-in-chief of *Neue Presse* in 1879.

many other periodicals extends amongst the community of Jews overall the world.

The role assigned to this press is to lead Israel in its aggressive movement upon the wealth of the heathens, or non-Jews. The press utters the war cry, and directs and leads the Jews onward. Without these journals, the Jewish movement would not form a whole, and its activity would necessarily lack inner force.

This exposition of the way and manner in which the Jews make use of the press unfolds before our eyes the existence of a secret, but fearful, power. In truth, the hundreds of journals that obey the orders of the Jews form an appalling battery, to fight against which appears next to impossible. Against the few journals that the victim may put forth to defend his cause, the Jews have ready at all times a bullet shower of scoff and calumny, vomited forth from the lying mouths of hundreds of journals.

When the Jews in 1868 came into a conflict with Romania, the Romanians had great trouble to find two or three journals ready to undertake the defense of their cause against public opinion. But the Jews at once put in motion against them such an overwhelming mass of journals that the unhappy Romanians found themselves excommunicated by the whole civilized world as fanatics. Every person who does not allow himself to be plundered by the Jews is a reactionary; and if he takes a cowhide in his hand, he is a barbarian.

We may add, in conclusion, that the pressure that Judaism exercises upon journalism is not limited to the tricks and artifices mentioned. Advancing from one success to another, they now stretch out their hands to grasp all the journals within their reach; and, to say the truth, they are successful, whether they act the role of editors, or correspondents, or peddlers of novels. Even the book trade has passed into the hands of the Jews; we meet them everywhere as book dealers and publishers. They alone can bring us enlightenment; but when we shall have been so enlightened, we shall be their slaves in a moral as well as material respect.

The "Alliance Israélite Universelle"

In consequence of the immense rise and universal spread of Jewish power in this century, the Jews have been awakened to the necessity of an organized central administration, by means of which the Jewish movement can be carried on in a more united spirit and with redoubled power. To fill up this lack in the system, an "Alliance Israélite Universelle" was formed in Paris about

30 years ago, and joined by the most prominent Jews of all countries.[22] It is true that, according to its official program, this Alliance is a purely philanthropic institution, having for its chief object to disseminate the benefits of civilization; but such fine words do not prevent carrying on politics at large in secret at the same time. Thus, for instance, there is at the disposal of this Alliance a large staff of officers, composed of newspaper writers, secret agents, spies, couriers, etc., all men of high intellectual gifts, speaking all languages and acquainted with all the countries of the world.

Probably no government is kept so well informed, and served so faithfully, as this Jewish Alliance. For its numerous servants combine with their devotion and reticence, the advantage that all of them together represent all the nationalities of the world; truly, a rare sort of human chameleon, as many colored in their scales as in their principles.

This Universal Alliance rejoices in an excellently regulated organism of administration. It has offices entrusted solely with its cosmopolitan correspondence that extends from Kamchatka to San Francisco. And it has also offices whose business it is to instruct the organs of the Jewish and of the subsidized press, so that these may at any time let loose their polemical batteries wherever any obstacle against the Jewish column of attack stands prominently in the way.

It is this same Israelite Alliance within whose bosom are resolved the secret rules of administration that become necessary wherever, as always happens, conflicts take place between the Jews and nations opposed to them. Sir Moses Montefiore and Cremieux, two prominent members of this Association, have repeatedly, in its name, exchanged communications with the Emperor of Russia, the Porte, the Viceroy of Egypt, the Emperor of Morocco, the Prince of Romania, etc., etc. In the year 1867, this Israelite Alliance undertook a money and paper war against the Danubian principalities, and, in order to be able to put on all the airs of a Great Power, it allowed the governing Princes of Romania a three months armistice at the very time when hostilities were in fine progress. It is but a short time ago since this same Association undertook a crusade in England, France, and America that had for its sole object to make Romania subject to its will.

But all these facts are cast far into the shade by the financial *salto mortale*, with which a few years ago Judaism, and its king, Rothschild, astonished the whole world. When this Jewish self-ruler and his political allies screwed up the French loan to the fabulous sum of $42 billion, they therewith

---

[22] *Ed.:* The AIU, founded in Paris in 1860, is still active today.

threw down the gauntlet to conquest-lusty Germany, as if saying: "Take care, Bismarck! Not a step further! For we are ready to sacrifice forty-two milliards in order to overthrow thy plans!" This antagonism between Jewish money-power and German military rule is, however, something quite natural. Both parties desire to rule, but each desires to build up its rule on a different principle: the former on the principle of material interests, the latter on that of armed supremacy. Now, as both of these principles mutually exclude each other, and have been so opposed from the beginning, it follows that, sooner or later, a rupture must ensue between those two parties.

Concluding Remarks

We have now arrived at the conclusion of our essay. I believe that the object I had in view, to give my readers a picture of the present position of the power of modern Judaism, has been fairly well attained. I have shown that it is no exaggeration to say that the Jews today trample underfoot the power of all the crowned heads and nations of the world.

In fact, the Conquest of the World by the Jews is henceforth a fixed fact, not to be disputed. What has materially assisted the Jews in this Conquest of the World is the pernicious habit, so prevalent of late, of issuing bonds on the part, not alone of nations, but also of municipalities, etc., thereby mortgaging the wealth of communities, as well as nations, all over the world. This has also materially contributed to producing the present business stagnation everywhere. The interest that these bonds bear goes on continually, by day as well as by night, without interruption. Its course sweeps like a tornado over fair fields, destroying everything in its path; or like the poisonous storms of the Sahara, bringing death and desolation wherever they touch. It is this secret power of compound interest that has enslaved mankind and that has been used as such an effectual weapon by the Jews for their Conquest of the World.

These facts stare everybody in the face. And while an individual may rid himself of his burden of debt by taking advantage of the bankrupt law, or by compromising with his creditors, whatever may be thought of such practice; as soon as a community or nation attempts a process of this kind, it is called repudiation. Where is the difference between the debt of an individual and that of a number of individuals? The question may well come up in this form: Can a father mortgage the prosperity of his children? He certainly cannot do so. What then is to be done? The only answer that can be made is this:

Keep out of debt! The welfare of individuals as well as of nations depends on this. The power of the usurer will be broken as soon as all debts are liquidated on a basis, both just and equitable.

The nations that once obeyed the behests of faith and honor are now condemned to bow down their heads before cunning and usury. The rule of such principles is a great misfortune for all mankind. For we may not conceal the fact that all modern society is brought to the verge of ruin by them, and now looks upon a terrible cataclysm that must undermine its very basis. The decisive conflict will be terrible; for the conquered and exhausted masses of the people will venture their all to shake off the yoke of Jewish slavery, and unarm the cosmopolitan thousand-headed hydra of Judaism.

Men have raised great opposition against the priest-craft that rests upon old Europe. But the rule of the priests is a very small matter in comparison with the power that the Jews and Jewish usurers exercise from day to day over the whole world. Rome has extended her power by a phalanx of priests, monks, and nuns, the number whereof exceed scarcely 400,000; and the Popes have been enabled to keep up their dominion with this comparatively small file of supporters. The Jews have now extended their net of money and financial power from one end of the world to the other; and this net is composed of *ten million* Jews, of which each one is more treacherous and rapacious than the other. Concealed behind their office desks and bank counters, these parasites uninterruptedly gnaw upon the wealth and the vitals of mankind.

The Popes slay their enemies with the ban, and expel them from the church. The Jews expel their enemies from the Stock Exchange and from social connections, and finally condemn us to starve without a roof to cover us. They have even made the priest-craft subservient to their power, as is clearly shown when it is asserted that the late Pope Pius IX had $20 million on deposit with the Rothschilds.[23] And why not? It is publicly stated that the Cardinal Cansolini had a good chance to be elected the successor of Pope Pius IX, but one thing stood in his way: this good man had had the audacity to write an essay, by which he conclusively proved that the grandfather of Pius the IX was a Jew.

Such are the excellent results of the emancipation of the nations and the so-called progress of our times. People consider themselves free and boast of high culture, and yet no one dares to rise against enemies who effect their conquest only by means of cheating and usury.

---

[23] *Ed.:* Pius IX held the papal title from 1846 to 1878.

Disraeli, some time ago, lifted up his voice against this cosmopolitanism that threatens to overthrow the whole present order of the world. This Israelite statesman may be altogether in the right; but in saying what he did, he made a distinction between two utterly opposite orders of cosmopolitanism—the Jewish cosmopolitanism and that of the social reaction. And while he—perhaps intentionally—brands the consequence instead of condemning the cause, he overlooks altogether the fact that the cosmopolitanism of the International Labor Associations is nothing but the logical consequence of the cosmopolitan tendencies first proclaimed by the Jews.

How is it possible that these statesmen allow themselves to fly into such a passion when they evidently tolerate and protect its cause? No, if they really intend to restore social equilibrium, they must take hold of the tree by the root, and direct their attacks against the cause of the cosmopolitan fundamental evil. Thus and only thus can they succeed in freeing mankind from the greatest plague under which it ever suffered. Let our motto be therefore:

Abolish Jewish Rule of the World!

— 3 —
THE JEWISH QUESTION

Fyodor Dostoyevsky
(1877)

Editor: The following is excerpted from Dostoyevsky's 1877 book *The Diary of a Writer* (vol. 2; B. Brasol, trans; pages 640-651)—also translated as *A Writer's Diary*. It is his honest and non-fictional assessment of the Jewish situation in Russia. It has been widely condemned as "anti-Semitic," but one could scarcely find a nicer bit of anti-Semitism in history; at every turn, Dostoyevsky takes pains to be polite and respectful toward the Jews. Clearly, for him, this is simply the *facts of the matter.* Moral judgements are left to others. The text here follows Brasol's translation, but with minor modifications.

True, it is very difficult to learn the 40-century-long history of a people such as the Jews; but, to start with, this much I know: That, in the whole world, there is certainly no other people who would be complaining as much about their lot, incessantly, after each step and word of theirs—about their humiliation, their suffering, their martyrdom. One might think that it is not they who are reigning in Europe, who are at least directing there the stock exchanges, and therefore politics, domestic affairs, and the morality of the states. Let noble Goldstein be dying for the Slavic idea. Even so, if the Jewish idea in the world had not been so strong, maybe, that very "Slavic" question [of 1876] would long ago have been settled in favor of the Slavs, and not of the Turks.

But let all this be merely verbalism on my part—light tone and light words. I concede. Nevertheless, I am unable fully to believe in the Jews' screams that they are so downtrodden, oppressed, and humiliated. In my opinion, the Russian peasant, and generally, the Russian commoner, virtually bears heavier burdens than the Jew.

[R]emember that at the time when the Jew "has been restricted in the free selection of the place of residence," 23 million of "the Russian toiling mass" have been enduring a serfdom that was, of course, more burdensome than merely "the selection of the place of residence." Now, did the Jews pity them then?—I don't think so; in the Western border region and in the South, you will get a comprehensive answer to this question. Nay, at that time, the Jews also vociferated about rights that the Russian people themselves did not have; they shouted and complained that they were downtrodden and martyrs, and that when they should be granted more rights, "then demand from us that we comply with the duties toward the state and the native population."

But then came the Liberator, and liberated the native people. And who was the first to fall upon them as on a victim? Who preeminently took advantage of their vices? Who tied them with that eternal gold pursuit of theirs? By whom—whenever possible—were the abolished landowners promptly replaced, with the difference that the latter, even though they did strongly exploit men, nevertheless endeavored— perhaps in their own interest—not to ruin the peasants in order to prevent the exhaustion of labor. Whereas the Jew is not concerned about the exhaustion of Russian labor; he grabs what's his, and off he goes.

I know that upon reading this, the Jews will forthwith start screaming that this is a lie; that this is a calumny; that I am lying; that I believe all this nonsense because I "do not know the 40-century-old history of these chaste angels who are incomparably purer morally not only than the other nationalities but also than the Russian people deified by me."

But let them be morally purer than all the peoples of the world. Nevertheless, I have just read in the March issue of *The Messenger of Europe* a news item to the effect that in America, in the Southern States, the Jews have already leaped *en masse* upon the millions of liberated Negroes, and have already taken a grip upon them in their, the Jews', own way, by means of their eternal "gold pursuit" and by taking advantage of the inexperience and vices of the exploited [black] tribe. Imagine, when I read this, I immediately recalled that the same thing came to my mind five years ago—specifically, that the Negroes have now been liberated from the slave owners, but that they will not last because the Jews, of whom there are so many in the world, will jump at this new little victim. This came to my mind, and I assure you that several times during this interim I was asking myself: "Well, why doesn't one hear anything about the Jews there; why don't newspapers write about them, because the Negroes are a treasure for the Jews; is it possible that they would miss it?" And at last my expectation came true: the newspapers have written it up—I read it.

Now, some ten days ago, I read in *The New Times* (No. 371) a most characteristic communication from Kovno [Kaunas, Lithuania] to the effect that "the Jews there have so assaulted the local Lithuanian population, that they almost ruined all of them with vodka, and only the Roman Catholic priests began to save the poor drunkards by threatening them with the tortures of hell and organizing temperance societies." True, the enlightened correspondent strongly blushes on behalf of his population, which still believes in its priests and in the tortures of hell. But he adds in this connection that following the example of the priests, enlightened local economists began to establish rural banks specifically with the object of saving the people from the Jew—the money lender. And they also established rural markets where "the destitute toiling mass" could buy articles of first necessity at real prices, and not at those set by the Jew.

Well, I have read all this, and I know that instantly people will start shouting that this proves nothing; that all this is caused by the fact that the Jews themselves are oppressed; that they are poor themselves; that all this is but a "struggle for existence"; that only a fool would fail to understand it, and that were the Jews not so destitute themselves, were they, contrariwise, to grow rich—they would instantly reveal themselves in a most humane light, so that the whole world would be astounded. First, however, it goes without saying that all those Negroes and Lithuanians are even poorer than the Jews who are squeezing the sap out of them, and yet, the former (so reads the correspondence) loathe the kind of trade for which the Jew is so eager.

Secondly, it isn't difficult to be humane and moral when one rolls in butter. But the moment "the struggle for existence" comes to play—don't you dare reproach me. To my way of thinking, this is not a very angelic trait.

Third, of course, I am not setting forth these two news items from *The Messenger of Europe* and *The New Times* as capital and decisive facts. If one should start writing the history of this universal tribe, it would at once be possible to discover a hundred thousand analogous and even more important facts, so that one or two additional facts would mean nothing in particular. However, it is curious in this connection that the moment you should require, say, in the course of an argument or in a minute of silent irresolution, information about the Jew and his doings, don't go to public libraries. Don't ransack old books or your own old notes; don't labor, don't search, don't exert your efforts. Instead, without leaving your chair, stretch out your hand to any newspaper at random that happens to be near you, and look at the second or third page; unfailingly, you will find something about Jews, and unfailingly—that which interests you. Unfailingly—that which is most characteristic, and unfailingly—one and the same thing, i.e., the same exploits!

Now, concede that this does mean something. It does indicate and reveal to you something, even though you be an absolute ignoramus in the 40-century-long history of this tribe. No question, I will be told that everybody is hatred-stricken, and therefore everybody is lying. Of course, it may happen that everyone to the last man is lying; but if this be so, there arises at once a new question: If everybody without exception is lying and hatred-stricken, *whence did this hatred arise?* This universal hatred does mean something; as Vissarion Belinsky exclaimed once: "indeed, the word *everybody* does mean something"![1]

"Free selection of the place of residence!" But is the "native" Russian absolutely free in the choice of the place of residence? Is it not true that also in the case of the Russian commoner, up to the present, the former restrictions in the complete freedom of the selection of the place of residence continue to persist—those undesirable restrictions which are survivals of the times of serfdom, and which have long been attracting the government's attention? And as far as Jews are concerned, it's apparent to everybody that in the last 20 years their rights in the selection of the place of residence have been very considerably expanded. At least, they have appeared throughout Russia in places where they have not been seen before. However, the Jews keep complaining of hatred and restrictions.

Let it be conceded that I am not firm in my knowledge of the Jewish modes of living. But one thing I do know for sure, and I am ready to argue about it with anyone, namely, that among our common people there is no preconceived, *a priori,* blunt religious hatred of the Jew, anything along the lines: "Judas sold out Christ." Even if one hears it from little children or drunkards, nevertheless our people as a whole look upon the Jew, I repeat, without a preconceived hatred. I have been observing this for 50 years. I even happened to live among the people, in their very midst, in one and the same barracks, sleeping with them on the same cots. There were several Jews there, and no one *despised* them, no one shunned them or persecuted them. When they said their prayers (and Jews pray with screams, donning a special garment) nobody found this strange, no one hindered them or scoffed at them—a fact that was to be expected from such a 'coarse people' as the Russians. On the contrary; when beholding them, they use to say: "such is their religion, and thus they pray"; and would pass by calmly, almost approvingly.

---

[1] Belinsky (1811-1848) was a Russian literary critic, born on the island of Suomenlinna, Finland.

And yet these same Jews, in many respects, shunned the Russians. They refused to take meals with them, looked upon them with haughtiness (and where?—in a prison!) and generally expressed squeamishness and aversion towards the Russian, towards the "native" people. The same is true in the case of soldiers' armories, and everywhere—all over Russia. Make inquiries, ask if a Jew, as a Jew as a Yiddisher, is being abused in armories because of his faith, or his customs. Nowhere is he being abused, and that is also true of the people at large. On the contrary, I assure you that in armories, as elsewhere, the Russian commoner perceives and understands only too well (besides, the Jews themselves do not conceal it) that the Jew does not want to take meals with him, that he has an aversion toward him, seeking as much as possible to avoid him and segregate himself from him. And yet, instead of feeling hurt, the Russian commoner calmly and clearly says: "such is his religion; it is because of his faith that he does not take meals with me and shuns me" (i.e., not because he is spiteful). And having comprehended this supreme cause, the Russian wholeheartedly forgives the Jew.

However, at times, I was thinking this: Now, how would it be if, in Russia, there were not three million Jews, but three million Russians, and there were 80 million Jews—what would they do with the Russians and how would they treat them? Would they permit them to acquire equal rights? Would they permit them to worship freely in their midst? Wouldn't they convert them into slaves? Worse than that: *Wouldn't they skin them altogether?* Wouldn't they *slaughter them to the last man,* to the point of complete extermination, as they used to do with alien peoples in ancient times, during their ancient history?

Nay, I assure you that in the Russian people there is no conceived hatred of the Jew, but perhaps there is a dislike of him, and especially in certain localities, maybe—a strong dislike. Oh, this cannot be avoided; this exists; but it arises not at all from fact that he is a Jew, not because of some racial or religious hate, but it comes from other causes, of which not the native people but the *Jew himself* is guilty. [...]

Hatred, and furthermore one caused by prejudice—this is what the Jews are accusing the native population of. However, if the point concerning prejudices has been raised, what do you think: Does the Jew have fewer prejudices against the Russian than the latter against the Jew? Hasn't he more of them? I have given you examples of the attitude of the Russian common people toward the Jew. And here I have before me letters from Jews, and not from common ones, but from educated Jews. And so much hatred in these matters against "the native population"! And the main thing is: they write without realizing it themselves.

You see, in order to exist 40 centuries on Earth, i.e., virtually the entire historical period of mankind, and besides, in such a close and unbroken unity; in order to lose so often one's territory, one's political independence, laws, almost one's religion—lose, and again to unite each time, to regenerate in the former idea, though in a different guise, to create anew laws and almost religion—nay, such a viable people, such an extraordinarily strong and energetic people, such an unprecedented people in the world, would not have existed without *status in statu*, i.e. 'a state within a state.' This, they have always and everywhere preserved at the time of their most dreadful, thousand, long dispersions and persecutions.

Speaking of 'a state within a state', I am by no means seeking to frame an accusation. Still, what is the meaning of this 'state within a state'? What is its eternal, immutable idea? Wherein is the essence of this idea?

It would be too long and impossible to expound this in a brief article; besides, it would be impossible for the same reason that, despite the 40 centuries, not all times and seasons have arrived, and mankind's last word on this great tribe is still to come. However, without fathoming the essence and depth of the subject, it's possible to outline, at least, certain symptoms of that 'state within a state'—be it only externally. These symptoms are: alienation and estrangement in the matter of religious dogma; the impossibility of fusion; belief that in the world there exists but one national entity—the Jew. And even though other entities exist, nevertheless it should be presumed that they are, as it were, nonexistent:

> "Step out of the family of nations, and form your own entity, and thou shalt know that henceforth thou art the only one before God; *exterminate the rest*, or make slaves of them, or exploit them. Have faith in the conquest of the whole world; adhere to the belief that everything will submit to thee. Loathe strictly everything, and do not have intercourse with anyone in thy mode of living. And even when thou shalt lose the land, thy political individuality, even when thou shalt be dispersed all over the face of the earth, amidst all nations—never mind, have faith in everything that has been promised thee, once and forever; believe that all this will come to pass, and meanwhile live, loathe, unite and exploit, and—wait, wait..."

Such is the essence of that 'state within a state,' and, in addition, there are, of course, inner and, perhaps, mysterious laws guarding this idea.

You say, gentlemen—educated Jews and opponents—that all this is certainly nonsense, and that even if there be a *status in statu* (i.e., there has been in the past, but at present, according to them, only the dimmest traces of it remain), it is solely because persecution has brought it about. Religious persecution since the Middle Ages, and even earlier, has generated it, and that this 'state within a state' came into existence merely from the instinct of self-preservation. However, if it continues, especially in Russia, it's because the Jew has not yet been given equal rights with the native population.

But this is how I feel: If the Jew were given equal rights, *under no circumstance* would he renounce his 'state within a state.' Moreover, to attribute it to nothing but persecution and the instinct of self-preservation is insufficient. Besides, there would not have been enough tenacity in store for self-preservation during 40 centuries; the people would have grown weary of preserving themselves for so long a time. Even the strongest civilizations in the world have failed to survive half of the 40 centuries, losing their political strength and racial countenance. Here it's not only self-preservation that constitutes the main cause, but *a certain compelling and luring idea*, something so universal and profound that on it, as stated above, mankind is perhaps still unable to utter its last word. That we are here dealing with something of a pre-eminently religious character—there can be no doubt. That their Providence, under the former, initial name of Jehovah, with his ideal and his covenant, continues to lead his people toward a firm goal—this much is clear. Besides, I repeat, it's impossible to conceive a Jew without God.

Moreover, I don't believe in the existence of atheists even among the educated Jews: they all are of the same substance, and God only knows what the world has to expect from the educated Jews! Even in my childhood, I have read and heard a legend about Jews to the effect that they are supposed to be undeviatingly awaiting the Messiah, all of them, both the lowest Yiddisher and the highest and most learned one—the philosopher and the Cabalist—rabbi. That they all believe that the Messiah will again unite them in Jerusalem and will bring by his sword all nations to their feet; that this is the reason why the overwhelming majority of the Jews have a predilection but for one profession—the trade in gold, and at the utmost—for goldsmithery. And all this, so it is alleged, in order that, when Messiah comes, they should not need to have a new Fatherland and to be tied to the land of aliens in their, the Jews,' possession, but to have everything converted into gold and jewels, so that it will be easier to carry them away when

> The ray of dawn begins to shine:
> Our flute, our tabor and the cymbal,
> Our riches and our holy symbol
> We will bring back to our old shrine,
> To our old home—to Palestine.

All this—I repeat—I heard as a legend, but I believe that the substance of the matter unfailingly is there, in the form of an instinctively irresistible tendency. But in order that such a substance of the matter might be preserved, it is, of course, necessary that the strictest 'state within a state' be preserved. And it *is* being preserved. Thus, not only persecution was and is its cause, but another idea…

If, however, among the Jews there exists in reality such an inner rigid organization as unites them into something solid and segregated, one almost may well give thought to the question whether equal rights with the native population should be granted to them.

It goes without saying that everything required by humaneness and justice, everything called for by compassion and the Christian law, must be done for the Jews. But should they, in full armor of their organization and their segregation, their racial and religious detachment; in complete armor of their regulations and principles utterly *opposed* to that idea abiding by which the whole European world, at least up to the present time, has been developing—should they demand complete equalization in *all possible rights* with the native population, wouldn't they then be granted something greater, something excessive, something sovereign, compared with the native population?

At this juncture, the Jews will, of course, point to other aliens:

"Now, these have been granted equal, or almost equal, rights, whereas we Jews have fewer rights than all other aliens; and this—because people are afraid of us, Jews: because we are supposedly more harmful than all other aliens. And yet in what sense is the Jew harmful? Even if there are bad qualities in the Jewish people, this is solely because these are being fostered by the Russian people themselves—by Russian ignorance, by the Russians' unfitness for independence, by their low economic development. The Russian people themselves demand a mediator, a leader, an economic warden in business, a creditor; they themselves are inviting him and surrendering themselves to him. On the contrary, look at things in Europe: there the nations are strong and independent in spirit; they are peoples with strong national sentiment, with a longstanding habit and skill for work, and there they are not afraid to grant all rights to the Jew! Does one hear in France anything about the harm resulting from 'a state within a state' of the local Jews?"

Apparently, this is a strong line of reasoning. However, in this connection there arises in one's mind a notion—in parentheses, namely: Thus, Jewry is thriving precisely there where the people are still ignorant, or not free, or economically backward. It is there that Jewry has a *champ libre* ('free rein')! And instead of raising, by its influence, the level of education, instead of increasing knowledge, generating economic fitness in the native population—instead of this, the Jew, wherever he has settled, has still more humiliated and debauched the people. There, humaneness was still more debased and the educational level fell still lower; there inescapable, inhuman misery, and with it despair, spread still more disgustingly. Ask the native population in our border regions: What is propelling the Jew—what has been propelling him for centuries? You will receive a unanimous answer: *mercilessness*. "He has been prompted for so many centuries only by pitilessness for us, only by the thirst for our sweat and blood."

And, in truth, the whole activity of the Jews in these border regions of ours consisted of rendering the native population as much as possible inescapably dependent on them, *taking advantage of the local laws*. They always managed to be on friendly terms with those upon whom the people were dependent, and, certainly, it's not for them to complain, at least in this respect, about their restricted rights compared with the native population. They have received from us enough of such rights over the native population. What, in the course of decades and centuries, has become of the Russian people where the Jews settled is attested by the history of our border regions. What, then? Point to any other tribe from among Russian aliens that could rival the Jew by his dreadful influence in this connection!

You will find no such tribe. In this respect, the Jew preserves all his originality as compared with other Russian aliens, and of course, the reason therefore is that the 'state within a state' of his—the spirit of which specifically breathes with pitilessness for everything that is not Jew, with disrespect for any people and tribe, for every human creature who is not a Jew.

And what kind of justification is it that, in Western Europe, the nations did not permit themselves to be overwhelmed, and that thus the Russian people themselves are at fault? Because the Russian people in the border regions of Russia proved weaker than the European nations (and exclusively as a result of their secular, cruel, political circumstances), for this sole reason should they be completely crushed by exploitation, instead of being helped?

And if reference is made to Europe, to France, for example—there too, hardly has their 'state within a state' been harmless. Of course, there, Christianity and its idea have been debased and are sinking not only because of the Jew's fault, but through their own fault; nevertheless, it's impossible not to note also in Europe the great triumph of Jewry, which has replaced many former ideas with its own.

Oh, it goes without saying that man always, at all times, has been worshipping materialism, and has been inclined to perceive and understand liberty only in the sense of making his life secure through money hoarded by the exertion of every effort, and accumulated by all possible means. However, at no time in the past have these tendencies been raised so cynically and so obviously to the level of a sublime principle as in our 19th century. "Everybody for himself, and only for himself, and every intercourse with man solely for one's self"—such is the ethical tenet of the majority of present-day people, even not bad people, but, on the contrary, laboring people who neither murder nor steal. And mercilessness for the lower masses, the decline of brotherhood, exploitation of the poor by the rich—oh, of course, all this existed also before and always. However, it had not been raised to the level of supreme truth and of science—it had been condemned by Christianity, whereas at present, on the contrary, it is being regarded as virtue.

Thus, it's not for nothing that, over there, the Jews are reigning everywhere over stock-exchanges; it's not for nothing that they control capital, that they are the masters of credit, and it's not for nothing—I repeat—that they are also the masters of international politics, and that what is going to happen in the future is known to the Jews themselves; their reign, their complete reign, is approaching! We are approaching the complete triumph of ideas before which sentiments of humanity, thirst for truth, Christian and national feelings, and even those of national dignity, must bow. On the contrary, we are approaching *materialism*, a blind, carnivorous craving for personal material welfare, a craving for personal accumulation of money by any means—this is all that has been proclaimed as the supreme aim, as the reasonable thing, as liberty, in lieu of the Christian idea of salvation only through the closest moral and brotherly fellowship of men.

People will laugh and say that this is not all brought about by the Jews. Of course, not only by them; but if the Jews have completely triumphed and thrived in Europe precisely at the time when these new principles have triumphed there, to the point of having been raised to the level of a moral principle, it is impossible not to infer that the Jews, too, have contributed their influence to this condition.

Our opponents point out that, on the contrary, the Jews are poor, poor even everywhere, especially in Russia; that only the very summit of the Jews is rich—bankers and kings of stock-exchanges—while the rest, virtually nine-tenths of the Jews, are literally beggars, running about for a piece of bread, offering commissions and anxiously looking for an opportunity to snatch somewhere a penny for bread. Yes, this seems to be so, but what does this signify? Does it not specifically mean that in the very toil of the Jews (i.e., at least, their overwhelming majority), in their very exploitation, there is something wrong, abnormal, something unnatural, bringing its own revenge. The Jew is offering his interposition, he is trading in another man's labor. Capital is accumulated labor; the Jew loves to trade in somebody else's labor! But, temporarily, this changes nothing.

As against this, the summit of the Jews is assuming stronger and firmer power over mankind, seeking to convey their image and substance to it. Jews keep vociferating that, among them, too, there are good people. Oh, God! Is this the point? Besides, we are speaking not about good or bad people. And aren't there good people among those? Wasn't the late James Rothschild of Paris a good man? We are speaking about *the whole* and its idea; we are speaking about *Judaism* and the *Jewish idea,* which is clasping the whole world instead of Christianity…

— 4 —
THE VICTORY OF JEWRY
OVER GERMANDOM

Wilhelm Marr
(1879)

Editor: Wilhelm Marr (1819-1904) was a German journalist, politician, and political activist. Well-read, intelligent, and a prolific writer, Marr was an ardent nationalist who worked for the unification of the various German states into a single, larger German nation—something which would happen in 1870. He could see that Jews had consistently resisted assimilation into any larger German state, preferring to maintain their own 'state within the state' (to quote Fichte from 1793). Worse, Jews were actively subverting German values and imposing their own social vision and own morality upon an unwilling German populace. By the late 1870s, Marr was ready to compose a small booklet on the dominance of German Jews: *Der Sieg des Judenthums über das Germanenthum*—The Victory of Jewry over Germandom. This was not an angry polemic; rather, it was simply a recognition of facts: Jewish culture had engaged in a struggle for social dominance with German culture, and the Jews had won, pure and simple. Marr saw it as his task to openly acknowledge reality. Clearly he had nothing personal against Jews; three of his four wives were Jewesses. He simply wanted to set the record straight. Of course, his many readers had other thoughts. For many of them, it was a rude awakening, and a call to arms.

The following translation draws from that of Rohringer (2009), but with significant changes for readability and clarity. All notes are the editor's, except where indicated.

In this booklet, I intend to accomplish less of a polemic against Jewry than a statement of facts regarding cultural history. Whenever circumstances cause me to use controversial speech, this can and must be understood as a "cry of pain" coming from the oppressed. Resigned pessimism flows from my pen. One thinks: "sure, there always will be odd characters such as this one," but rest assured that no one will be happier than I, should the facts that I touch upon are shown to be untrue.

Jews and Jewry have been attacked in literature many times. This however has almost always been done from the point of view of our non-Jewish, inflated opinion of ourselves—or may I say, in the arrogant style of retreat, such as Gambetta's.[1] Our conceit has not yet permitted us to admit that Israel has become a world power of the very first rank.[2] We have managed to understand the Jews, but we have failed to understand ourselves.

Regardless, this booklet can claim originality. Free of any and all religious bias, it will allow you to look into the mirror of historical-cultural facts, and it will not be the fault of the "pessimist" if what you see in this mirror are...slaves.

I want to achieve two things here:

1.) That Jewish critics will not silence it,
2.) That it will not be dismissed with the usual, smug commentary.

I declare, loudly and without any attempt at irony, that Jewry has triumphed on a worldwide historical basis. I bring the news of a lost battle and of the victory of the enemy; I do all of this without offering excuses for the defeated army. I would think that such honesty deserves the privilege to be treated with better than the usual, zealous journalistic drivel.

Section 1

When one people conquers another, one of the following two things may happen. First, it may be that the conqueror merges into the culture of the conquered and thus loses his identity. This fate befell the Tatars, for example, who conquered China under Genghis Khan and then turned into Chinese. The Lombards shared a similar fate, when their Germanism ended up

---

[1] Léon Gambetta (1838-1882) was a French politician who attempted to carrying on fighting after France had effectively lost the Franco-German War of 1870. He then fled to Spain.
[2] 'Israel' refers here to the Jewish people as a whole, and not to the modern nation-state, which was created only in 1947.

to be Italianized. On the other hand, the conqueror may succeed in impressing his culture upon the conquered. This is what happened with the Anglo-Saxon race in North America, and with Anglo influence in Central and South America.

As far-reaching as these developments may be in their various ramifications, they pale in comparison with the cultural history of Judaism. Here we are dealing with a completely new development. An entire Semitic tribe is repeatedly and forcibly taken away from its native country Palestine, led into captivity and finally "dispersed." Those who were taken into "Babylonian captivity" were let go, since the Babylonians seemingly soon tired of their Judaic captives. The majority returned to Palestine. The "bankers" and the wealthy stayed in Babylon, despite the ire and wrath of the elder Jewish prophets.

We now must point to the fact that Jews, from the very beginning, wherever they appear in history, were hated by all people—and that without exception.[3] This was not a consequence of their religion, because the Jews of antiquity, at least from what their prophets say, knew perfectly well how to join in the idolatry of other people, while "rigid Judaism" developed only during the time after the destruction of Jerusalem [in 70 AD].

The universal hostility against Jews had different roots. First is the loathing Jews demonstrate for real work; second is their codified enmity against all non-Jews. Anyone who has gone to the trouble to even superficially study the Mosaic law of the Bible will admit that a people adhering in war and peace to the codex of Moses will find it hard to elicit international sympathy. The relationship between Jews and Jehovah was unimaginative, calloused, purely contractual, businesslike, and rigidly formalistic. In everyday life, the most practical realism imaginable prevailed, and it was of brazen solidity. Even the Jehovah of the Old Testament was a rigid realist. He acknowledged the existence of "other deities" and was motivated by his hate for them.

Titus committed the most foolish act in all of world history, when, after the destruction of Jerusalem, he dragged some of the Jews into Roman captivity and forcibly dispersed the rest. At the time, there happened to be freedom of faith in Rome. It was said that "all Gods are welcome in Rome." But if people caused mischief in the name of deities that had found *salve hospes* (safe haven) in Rome and attempted to ruin Roman temples and committed other such mischief, then of course, the Romans re-established order. What

---

[3] This is a central theme of *Eternal Strangers* (Dalton, 2020).

caused the Jews to be hated in Rome as well, was the exclusive attitude, combined with haggling and profiteering which they had brought with them.

The Roman world of the day, as well as all of classical antiquity, was in the throes of disintegration at the time the Jews were imported. Semitism therefore encountered fertile ground for its realistic approach; and already in Constantine's days, the "new Jews" (Christians) were the power behind the money.[4] All the nations of antiquity, including the trading Phoenicians and Carthaginians, did not think well of engaging in what we now call speculation, profiteering, and usury. If in the Middle Ages we encounter a "Mr. Moneybag," he was certainly a Jew. Jews were used but despised. This attitude is similar to its modern form, in which traitors are met with contempt while their treason may be welcome.

The abstract realism of Judaism had thus been forcibly imported into Western society by the Romans. Times and circumstances proved favorable for Judaism's development and proliferation. Judaism had turned into the realistic helper in history and encountered a more fertile ground for its indolent and speculative realism in the West than it ever possessed in Palestine. This, of course, provoked envy among the peoples of the West, and since the mob has always preferred to use religion as a cover for its ends, so the spread of Christianity was accompanied by the spread of an (apparent) religious hatred of Jews in the West.

The nonsensical religious aspect of this hatred becomes obvious when one considers the fact that Jews were to be held responsible for the crucifixion of Christ—an event, known to have been set in motion by Roman authorities, which cowardly followed the clamor of a mob in Jerusalem. This Jewish mob at the time of Christ had not done any more or any less than any mob at any other time has done, is now doing, and will do in the future. Today they shout "hosannah" and tomorrow they will cry "crucify." Human nature calls upon providence and religion whenever a foolish act or some perfidy is about to be committed. It is rare that there has not been mutual annihilation without one side and the other calling upon the gods or our Lord and to plague them with the honor of an alliance. And this is how God and religion had to serve in each and every persecution of the Jews, while in reality, these events were nothing else but the struggle of nations and their response to the very real Judaization of society—that is, to a battle for survival.

---

[4] Most all early Christians were ethnic Jews, for at least the first few decades after the crucifixion.

Yes! If in reality during the Middle Ages some fanatical Jews had, during Passover, "slaughtered Christian children," and if such atrocious events had actually taken place—something which has no demonstrable basis in history[5]—then these would represent abominations which are nothing else but crimes and must not be used to justify general religious hatred. The same applies regarding the obscenities uttered by certain pietistic sects against Christianity. I therefore unconditionally *defend Jewry* against any and all religious persecution, and I think that it is hardly possible to express this more clearly than I have done here.

On the other hand, I emphasize the following indisputable truth: With the Jews, the Romans have forced a tribe upon the West, which as its history shows, was thoroughly hated by all the peoples of the Orient.

Section 2

So it is that the Jews did not come as conquerors with sword in hand. The Romans "interned" them as political prisoners into the West and they did this in a way that the Jews had the freedom to settle, and that in the cities, their domicile was subject to control—that is, it was limited to ghettos. Nothing is more natural than the hatred the Jews must have felt for those who enslaved them and abducted them from their homeland. Nothing is more natural than that this hatred had to grow during the course of oppression and persecution in the West over the span of almost 2,000 years. Nothing was more natural than the Jews becoming even more spiteful during their banishment and quasi-captivity than they had been in the Orient. Nothing is more natural than that they responded using their inborn gifts of craftiness and cleverness by forming, as "captives," *a state within a state*, a society within a society. The Jewish "state within a state" used guile to continue its war in the West, while it had used deadly weapons against the peoples in the Orient, where it had been the stronger party. This simply was a natural right for the Jews. One must not expect humility instead of defiance from the suppressed, and one certainly can't expect meekness from a people whose traditions do not know how to turn the other cheek.

"An eye for an eye, a tooth for a tooth," says Jehovism. If the practice of strict martial law against such a people was justified after the great political

---

[5] This is no longer true; we now have considerable evidence that Jews did indeed use human blood for ritualistic purposes. See, for example, *Passovers of Blood* (A. Toaff, 2020).

error had been made to forcibly introduce it into Western society, then the tough resistance offered by the Jews was equally justified. By the 19th century, the amazing toughness and endurance of the Semites had made them the leading power within Western society. As a result, and that particularly in Germany, Jewry has not been assimilated into Germanism, *but Germanism has been absorbed into Jewry.* This development advanced to such an extent that the leading voices of German patriotism, of the "Friends of the Reich" in our parliamentary and even religious strife, are those of the Jews.

Right at the start of the Jewish dispersion into the West, a remarkable historical-cultural event occurred: the Jews established themselves in the cities and showed themselves even less desiring to engage in agriculture and colonization than they had shown in Palestine and earlier in Egypt. One must not argue that in some countries Jews might have been prohibited from acquiring land and property. Until deep into the Middle Ages, the West comprised much uncultivated land. There was no reason to not "squat" on land and to lead a life like the cultural pioneers in the woods of North America. At that time, there was abundant unclaimed land in the West. It was, however, not claimed by the Jews, because they lacked the vigor of the old Anglo-Saxons, who, expelled on account of their faith, created states out of the wilderness in the Far West. It was not axe and plow, but the tricks and the crafts of the practical spirit of hagglers, which were the weapons by which the Jews conquered the West and created a New Palestine, particularly in Germany.

And, why in Germany, of all places? Romanism, the old Caesarean Rome, had itself turned towards political-cultural realism to such a degree that the Jews faced a political entity that could only be fragmented by the idealism of Christianity. With the introduction of the latter as the state religion, with the beginning of the papacy that had to maintain the juxtaposition of Christ and non-Christ in order to monopolize the world, the Jewish freedom of action in Rome and in Italy was limited. Jewry dispersed increasingly and retreated before the religionist Christian fanaticism. It diffused *en masse* to Spain and Portugal and into the Slavic countries, and then emigrated from there in large numbers by way of Holland into Germany—all the while able to continue with less hindrance in its socially-undermining activity among the Slavic barbarians. Next to Slavism, Germanism was least prepared to face foreigners. A sense of German nationality, not to speak of German national pride, did not exist in German lands. And it was exactly for this reason that Judaism found it easier to extend its roots in Germany than in other places.

But even here, the special character of the foreigners from the Orient caused offense. Within the agricultural Germanic lands, the Semitic craftiness and its practical business sense provoked a reaction against the Jews. This foreign tribe and its opportunism contrasted too much with the basic character of Germanism. Its rules, its articles of belief that allowed them to view all non-Jews as "unclean," provoked anger among the people, while on the other hand the Jews permitted themselves to be used by nobility in financial transactions carried out at the expense of the people. Highly gifted, with great flair for activities like these, the Jews dominated retail and wholesale trade as early as the Middle Ages and outwitted the hard-working common folk.

The common people realized that their own sense of ethics was not shared by the Jews, because these, rather than striving for emancipation, preferred to accumulate wealth. Where such accumulation was involved, they were ready to tolerate suffering. Openly suppressed from above, they were able to take advantage of those below. The common folk had no chance to grumble about being exploited by their nobles, an activity in which the Jews acted as brokers. For this reason, the people used religion as pretext. "The crucifiers of Christ are to exploit us?" they cried. "Hepp! Hepp!"[6] For those at the top of society, these occasional persecutions of Jews were not unwelcome. They had the effect of keeping the Jews dependent, willing to continue as brokers and not to think of demanding emancipation for their people as brokerage fee.

There is no way to deny that the abstract, money-oriented, haggling mind of the Jews has contributed much to the flourishing of commerce and industry in Germany. It is profits and not ideals that build a state, and if we liken profit to a person, then the means to an end are rarely pure and noble. Despotic princes in constant struggle with a despotic and predatory nobility, farmers that barely differed from black slaves except by the color of their skin, a middle class that, deep into the time of the Crusades, was poorly developed and lacked self-assurance—that is what German society was like, while in Italy, France, and Spain culture flourished.

Into this confused, clumsy Germanic element penetrated a smooth, crafty, pliable Jewry; with all of its gifts of realism, intellectually well-

---

[6] "Hepp! Hepp!" was the battle cry of populist anti-Jewish riots, which occurred in many Central European countries in the early 19th century. The meaning of these words is not clear. It was probably a derogatory variation on 'Hebrew' or 'Heeb.'

qualified as far as the gift of astuteness is concerned, to look down upon the Germans and to subdue the monarchical, knightly, lumbering German by enabling him in his vices.[7]

The Jew had no homeland. With each passing day, he became more estranged from his former native land and memories of it became merely symbolic. Nature had denied him the gift to blend with other people, to assimilate. He continued to reject their religion, and resisted their customs, traditions, and way of life. He was able to deceive his oppressors in everything, but not in his desire to be a Jew and to remain one. His charter was a lasting challenge of, and manifestation against, the "unclean" among whom he lived. He was a typical foreigner to them and remains one until today; and yes, his exclusive Judaism, as we shall demonstrate in what follows, shows itself even more today after his emancipation than it did in earlier times.[8]

We must therefore not be embarrassed to admit that *ab ovo* ['from the start'], an element had entered our society that surpassed our ancestors by far in guile and astuteness and fought with these weapons in the West, after the fire and sword of fanaticism and hatred against other people in the Orient had been wrenched from its hands. Ever since then, Jewry has, using these weapons, continued its struggle in the West against all that is not Jewish. It successfully resisted our own ideology and inoculated us from year to year with more of its own by making the line separating right from wrong so elastic; that, in the spheres of trade and exchange, the border is now found where brutal crime has its beginning and non-sanctioned crime has been turned into habitual practice. The mischievous remark that stock exchange brokers can be divided into "white" and "black" Jews has a ring of truth to it.

All of this demonstrates merely that Germanism did not possess sufficient spiritual endurance to protect itself from Judaization—and so Germany turned, step by step, into the new promised land for Semites which came flooding here from Spain, Portugal, and Poland to augment the already resident Jewry. This tribe, the Jews, possessed throughout its history by a theocratic fervor not found among any other people and whose theocratic code of behavior in war and peace was dreadful, transformed all of its destructive potential into new forms; and using these, vanquished the West—a victory it could not achieve in the Orient using fire and sword.

---

[7] Indeed—Jews trafficked frequently in illicit goods, including prostitution, alcohol, and stolen goods.

[8] Jews attained "emancipation"—that is, civil rights—in Germany beginning in 1848. They achieved rights throughout all Germany in 1870.

Such a historical-cultural event is not a bubble that can be burst with a cheap "Hepp, Hepp." Such an event is of demonic appearance, despite the "grotesque mask" it may show. This tribe, which drew laughter in Caesarean Rome, and covered with a filth heavier than one can see on them today in Russia and Poland, spread all over Europe.[9] This tribe, teased by the educated, abused by the mob, and persecuted by religious zealots, these people became "brokers" to the rulers and exacted tribute as early as the Middle Ages. Using the intelligence and flexibility with which it conducted its practical business, it exploited the masses, all the while maintaining its theocratic-Jahvistic rigidity. And so these people conquered the world with their Jewish soul!

This is not the power of the Jewish religious faith. The Jew has no real religion; he has a business contract with Jehovah, and pays his god with statutes and formulations and in return is charged with the pleasant task of exterminating all that is not Jewish. It is the powerful expression of a conscious, characteristic realism that we must admit exists in Judaism and which we encounter in its pathos and its satire. As far as the actual modalities of business and trade are concerned, we Germans hardly differ any more from the Jews; what we don't have is the drive of the Semitic people. On account of our tribal organization, we shall never be able to acquire such a drive, and because cultural development knows no pause, our future is none other than a time when we Germans will live as slaves under the legal and political feudalism of Judaism.

Section 3

One of our most respected citizens, one of our greatest thinkers, poets, and a sharp critical mind, Gotthold Ephraim Lessing, demonstrated in his drama "Nathan the Wise" what a fundamental error Germanism committed when it considered the Jewish Question as only of religious nature.[10] The 18th century

---

[9] The Eastern Jews were infamously filthy, rarely bathed, and smelled horrible.
[10] "Nathan the Wise" is a famous literary work by the German dramatist Gotthold Ephraim Lessing (1729-1781). It deals with the truthfulness of the three great religions, Christianity, Judaism, and Islam. Nathan, a Jew, presents the 'parable of the three rings' in which a father leaves one ring to each of his three sons. Two of the rings are copies of the one that bestows upon its wearer the gift to be loved by God and man. Unable to decide which is the true ring, the sons quarrel with each other and finally ask a judge for his decision. The

in which Lessing lived was a century of philosophical emancipation from prejudices of all kinds, in particular from religious ones. It is curious that, in that great epoch, English as well as French "freethinkers" more or less rejected Judaism. The great deist Voltaire took serious issue with the formalism of Judaism.[11] He and Mylord Bolingbrooke in England did not hide their dislike of Jewish tribalism and emphasized very clearly that the Jews could not lay claim to a true religion.[12] They treated Judaism as a spiritual matter of minor importance.

In Germany on the other hand, the great Lessing chose, with "Nathan the Wise," another, mistaken path. It is peculiar that this obviously mistaken approach of our immortal idol has encountered so little attention in our age of erosive and merciless literary criticism. The legend of the "three rings" is the most beautiful creation of poetic composition from the age of tolerance. But who is the character whom Lessing allows to speak this noble and exalting truth? It is a Jewish "Rothschild" under sultan Saladin! Was this choice essential for a drama of such noble purpose? Might Nathan not rather have been a Jewish scholar or a Baruch Spinoza speaking before his time? Where was the need to invoke the revolting element of an agent of mammon?

And yet, adopting the poet's frame of mind, for him, Jew and solicitor of money were subconsciously one and the same. One could not be separated from the other and the poet felt this instinctively. Nathan provides loans to finance the war against the crusaders. By doing so, he is financially taking the side of one of the three "rings." He offers Saladin money right after he told the wondrous story of these rings. Well, he did it without charging interest, but after all he supports the one "ring" which is not even Judaism. Though he also supports the "templar," the impartiality of the *Etre suprême* [Supreme Being] so beautifully illustrated by the legend of the three rings has now been undermined by Nathan himself. Lessing could not, in his subconscious, self-overcome the identity of Jew and servant of mammon. If a Jew had to be the protagonist of the drama, why then did Lessing not show him apart from precious metal? In this way Lessing glorified an exceptional

---

judge tells them, that since each of them received his ring from a loving father, each should believe that he is the wearer of the true ring. Lessing's drama contains additional symbolism regarding the equality of the three religions.

[11] Voltaire was deeply and profoundly anti-Semitic. See *Eternal Strangers*, pp. 70-72.

[12] St. John Bolingbroke (1678-1751) was a politician and widely-known philosophical deist who had the reputation of having been an anti-Semite.

Jew, who, however, as a servant of money, was a real Jew. Nathan is an individual, not a concept. He probably stands with his character above the Jew "Sheva" in the drama by Richard Cumberland.[13] The latter however is portrayed more believably and lifelike; Sheva is taken from life, Nathan is abstract, and enters the loftiest and most ideal poesy of humanism and tolerance as a banker.

The Jew Nathan would have represented 'monotheism' if Lessing had not portrayed him realistically as a servant of mammon. This only proves that even Lessing, against his will, has demonstrated the identity of Jew and the power of money. All the same, Lessing's Nathan became the real forerunner for the idea of Jewish emancipation among the Germans. German idealism was captivated by the legend of the ring, but missed that Lessing's Nathan could only be a character from a fable. If Nathan had been a Christian, there might have been others and not just Paul Lindau[14] to commit the act of "literary tactlessness" by putting Lessing on the dialectic dissection table.

It was a sign of the time. Truly: Jew and man of mammon were inseparable, even in the eyes of Lessing. The poet was unable to separate the latter attribute of his hero from the former. Only in this way did Nathan become a credible figure for the audience at large. And I don't wish to prove more with these statements than that not even our great Lessing was able to picture the "Jew" and "money" as separate. To anticipate Spinoza would have been too much to expect for this drama; this truly great Jewish non-Jew had been cursed by his own tribal associates all the way to attempted murderous assault! Baruch Spinoza! Philosophical messiah of the 17th century, "crucified" by the Jews, just like the Jew Christ had been crucified by the Romans.[15]

Baruch Spinoza! A fashionable Jewish example in the 19th century! But woe to the German who dares to show the Jewish masses who the great Spinoza was and what he stood for!! How despicable is humanity! How can any modern, run-of-the-mill Jew pretend any enthusiasm for Spinoza!

With Lessing's "Nathan" and Cumberland's "Jew" the idea of Jewish emancipation began to gain hold among the general public. The theater became its forum and the final theatrical chapter in this endeavor became

---

[13] Sheva is the Jewish protagonist in a play titled *Jew* by the famous English dramatist Richard Cumberland (1732-1811).

[14] Lindau (1839–1919) was a German journalist, dramatist, and novelist.

[15] Jesus—if he indeed existed—would have been an ethnic Jew.

Mosenthal's *Deborah*,[16] in which Jewish suffering and Jewish fury were shown in equal measure. After Lessing and the Jewish emancipation in France at the time of the first revolution, German Jewish emancipation developed a literature of its own.

Who can hold it against the Jews that they happily welcomed the revolutions of 1789 and 1848, and actively participated in them? "Jews, Poles, and writers" was the battle cry of the conservatives in 1848. Well, of course, three suppressed factions! The happy and content do not rise up in our world. It is understandable that the Jews were the loudest in this bacchanalian freedom frenzy in the press. Who can fault them for it? Finally, it again needs to be emphasized that philosophical self-deception had resulted in the view that the Jewish Question was one of religious freedom. In 1848, however, Jewry had long ago gotten to the stage where there was no longer a question of religious prejudice. Jewish "religion" represented nothing else but the constitution of a people, forming a state within a state, and this secondary or counter-state demanded certain material advantages for its members.

It was about political equality; because in civic life, Jewry had in fact long ago achieved a leading and dominating role—dominating to such an extent that Christian states bestowed baronage upon Jewish bankers, even though these Jewish barons could not be councilmen or hold similar office.

Nobody thought that the Jewish Question might be a social-political one. That with which we deceived ourselves for 1800 years—namely that we were dealing with a question of religious freedom and conscience—continued to be the subject of self-deception, and that is how the social-political inroads of Judaism into German society obtained their legal consecration. An already *de facto* existing foreign rule was legally recognized. A foreign rule, which, to express it in commonplace terms, had gotten so far as to have seized dictatorial control of the state's financial system—that is, of the *nervus rerum gerendarum* ['nerve center of business activity'], and had imbued it with the Jewish spirit of arranging and manipulating. What Jewry had secured long ago, the domination of Jewish realism at the expense of all idealism, was now not only to be safeguarded but expanded beyond all bounds. To this end, Jewry needed equal rights in creating laws and administrating the very same state that it negated on religious grounds.

---

[16] Salomon Hermann Mosenthal (1821-1877) was born and educated in Germany and later pursued a career as dramatist in Austria. In *Deborah* he addressed the problem of Jewish life within Christian society and of Jewish emancipation.

This and nothing else is the core content of Jewish emancipation, once all catchy phrases have been peeled away. Jewish foreign rule entered the sphere of Germanic statecraft in an absolute way. I am using repeatedly the word "foreign rule." But are they not a foreign people who, every year, repeats, among other things, the silly ritual phrase: "See you next year in Jerusalem!"? It bluntly affirms its foreign character, not to speak of its customs and persistent tribal characteristics, which, neither in spirit nor in substance, have been assimilated in an indistinguishable way into Germanism over a span of 1800 years. Can the Jews afford or really wish to diminish the image of their own power by faking the attempt not to appear as distinct aliens? The very "glory" of Judaism is precisely that it offered the West a most victorious resistance over a span of 1800 years. All other immigration into Germany (i.e. the French colonies) disappeared without a trace within Germanism; Wends and Slavs disappeared in the German element. The Semitic race, stronger and tougher, has survived them all. Truly! Were I a Jew, I would look upon this fact with greatest pride. No victor of antiquity or modern times can pride himself of such spiritual, historical-cultural successes as the humblest Jewish peddler (*Schacherjude*), who offers fabric from his cart at a streetcorner. Without a stroke of the sword, peacefully, despite political persecution over centuries, Jewry is today the political-social dictator in Germany.

Section 4

Only Germany? In the land of thinkers and philosophers, Jewish emancipation dates from 1848. At the same time began the Thirty Years War,[17] openly carried on by Jewry using the described weaponry. It was difficult to deny them these arms during a period of storm and stress[18] and after we had been more than half-conquered over the centuries by Jewish intelligence. Concerning elections, Jewry immediately entered a statistical contract with us. To be Jewish helped to gain a mandate with relative ease. In order to garner

---

[17] Here, 'Thirty Years War' is a metaphor used by Marr to describe the then-current strife, which had started 30 years earlier in 1848, for full Jewish participation in German political life. The real Thirty Years War of history took place between 1618 and 1648 and had, among others, religious roots.
[18] Storm and Stress (*Sturm und Drang*) was a prevalent movement in literature and music in Germany in the latter half of 18th century. It emphasized the emotional as opposed to the rational component of artistic expression.

the Jewish vote, the parties, when setting up lists of candidates, had to grant Jewry concessions, and this is what is going on to a greater or lesser extent until today.

Up to 1848, the Jews in Germany were predominantly of "democratic" conviction, or at least pretended to be. Later on, Jewry split into parliamentary parties—principally into "National Liberalism" because there the spirit of Judaization, the concepts of utility and practicality, and the lack of principles had progressed the most. So far only the ultramontane[19] party has remained free of Judaization. Conservative ruling parties however are teeming with Semitic elements because two-thirds of our semiofficial literature are represented by Jews. The same goal—disintegration of the Germanic state for the benefit of Jewish interests—is consistently pursued everywhere.

The daily press is predominantly in Jewish hands, which have transformed journalism into an object of speculation and industrial production, into a business with public opinion; critique of theater, and of art in general, is to three-quarters in the hands of Jews. Writing about politics and even religion is in Jewish hands.

Let us think about it for a moment. Once emancipation had been won, instinct demanded that it be consolidated and reinforced. This could only be achieved by using the press and unionism. Consequently, Jewry flooded into both like a high tide. It acted like it was extraordinarily intellectual and free of bias. It went as far as engaging in sarcastic irony of self; but while the highly gifted Ernst Dohm[20] offered the most precious jokes about Israel in *Kladdaradatsch*, it turned out that it was not advisable for a non-Jew to do the same. Using the word *Knoblauch* [garlic] sufficed to accuse us Teutons of being religious haters. Well, at least my name protects me from such reproaches.[21]

---

[19] Ultramontane refers to Ultramontanism, a tendency to look 'beyond the Alps' to Rome and the papacy for guidance in political and spiritual matters.
[20] Friedrich Wilhelm Ernst Dohm (1819–1883), a converted Jew, was an important contributor to a well-known, satirical weekly, known as *Kladderadatsch*.
[21] Marr adds this note: "Not being of any religious denomination has helped me but little. When at the beginning of the 1860s, upset about the consequences of Jewish emancipation, I fought in my *Judenspiegel* (Hamburg, Otto Meissner) passionately but impartially against the Judaizing of society, a gale against me arose, as though the band of Jericho had been reenforced by a thousand trumpets. An attempt was made to push me out of 'journalism' and even today I am unable to utter an independent thought on any question whatsoever in the Judaized press. I was put down as a common religious fanatic crying

From the very beginning of emancipation, Jewry had been declared a subject off-limits for us Germans. After Jewish hustle and bustle had reduced journalism to a trivial but commercially successful enterprise directed at the mob's liking of gossip and scandal, it had found the largest possible audience for its attempts at Judaizing. Centuries of a factual predominance of Jewish realism had done its preparatory work. Jewry dictated public opinion in the press.

But let us now look at the *non plus ultra* of arrogance of the Jewish victor! The 'culture struggle' had begun.[22] While we Germans had been banned and outlawed by the press since 1848 if we considered as much as criticism of anything Jewish, Jewry now involved itself in our religious and cultural struggles with Ultramontanism and, hard to believe, even did all the talking. While Jewry searched anxiously to find for its satirical journals anything which they might ridicule as a "Jewish witch-hunt," it unleashed its torrents upon Ultramontanism. Well! The latter opposed Judaism in the battle for world domination! Here one may certainly not speak of Judaic tactfulness, which in turn demands from us that we treat it like delicate glass or like a *Mimosa pudica*.[23]

And indeed, there were important newspapers in which we Germans were not even permitted to write about the "culture struggle" because we, in order to criticize the Roman fanaticism had called it an emanation of the

---

'Hepp-Hepp' even though every line in my *Judenspiegel* demonstrated the opposite. I had stirred up a hornet's nest.

"But let's not speak of myself. Where would Richard Wagner have been without the assistance of the King of Bavaria? Has there ever lived an artist who was more the object of attack by Jewry than Wagner? I am not referring to the musical experts who opposed him, but of the pack of scribblers and theater hounds who did not forgive him for his views of Judaism, even if these might have been mistaken. And from among the very same people in Israel who had complained about the 'lack of melody' in *Tannhäuser* and *Lohengrin*, a crowd rendered homage to him in Bayreuth—yes in Bayreuth—to play even there the first violin, just as it is 'the custom in Israel,' after Wagner had, in spite of it all forged his way. Even here there were two or three exceptions, Jews who had from the start shown friendly sentiments for the master's work, but it is the exception which makes the rule." [See, of course, Wagner's essay *Jewry in Music* in the present volume.]

[22] The culture struggle (*Kulturkampf*) refers to the heated political and ecclesiastical dispute between Protestant and Catholic factions in Germany during Bismarck's chancellorship.

[23] The mimosa is a "sensitive plant" that wilts when its leaves are touched.

Jahvistic fervor of the Old Testament. In books (such as by Johannes Scherr[24]) on the other hand Jewry could not stand in the way of such political-cultural deductions and analyses; but in its newspapers it even suppressed publications hostile to Ultramontanism if Israel was touched upon ever so slightly!

Just try to comment upon Jewish rituals and statutes. You will find that not even the Pope is more infallible and unimpeachable. To comment upon their rituals is "hatred," but if the Jew takes it upon himself to pronounce the last word in our religious and state affairs, then it is quite a different matter. Jewry is already calling *Vae Victis* ['woe to the vanquished'], while we are in the midst of our religious and political disputes.

At the beginning of the cultural struggle, I and several of my friends attempted to take part in it by expressing views from a sophisticated, historical-cultural point of view. In vain. We were only allowed to be heard provided we renounced the use of basic statements of fact and if we were, *ex abrupto*, willing to be abusive of 'clerics.' Not even with letters to the editor did we enjoy hospitality in the Jewish press—even there, where there might have been an opportunity to express opinions contrary to ours. And this is the way Jewry has monopolized free expression of opinion in the press.

It would be easy to hide our own impotence under cover of an abundant verbiage of Jew hatred. We Germans have officially resigned in favor of Judaism back in 1848. Check for yourself: in all aspects of life, the way to one's goal is subject to Jewish mediation. There is no "struggle for existence" without Jewry collecting its commission. Ask yourself, reader, whether I exaggerate!

This is the result of the Thirty Years War that Jewry has officially staged against us since 1848 and which does not even offer us the hope for a poor "Westphalian Peace".[25]

Section 5

There is no standing still. It is forward or back! Are there any signs that the Jewish twilight of gods is about to end? No, there are none. The social and

---

[24] Johannes Scherr (1817–1886) was a German social democrat who was forced to emigrate to Switzerland, where he became a successful historian.
[25] The "Westphalian Peace" concluded the Thirty Years War (1618-1648). Here Marr is again using his analogy to call the Jewish strife for political emancipation since 1848 a 'Thirty Years War.'

political dominance of Jewry as well as its religious and ecclesiastic pater-nalism are still full of youthful vigor and ready to achieve the Jahvist prom-ise ("I shall deliver all the nations to thee, etc"). A sudden reversal is impos-sible, if only for the reason that the entire social structure formed by Judaiza-tion would collapse and no concept exists to take its place and turn it into reality.

Neither can we look to the "Christian" state for assistance. The Jews are the "most perfect" citizens of this modern Christian state, which in turn perfectly matches their interests. They are—and this is said without a hint of irony—the best and truest *Reichsfreunde* because this Reich is quite ready to advance them to the highest office in the land.

May I direct a plea to my readers: Please save this booklet of mine, and provide in your will that it be passed from generation to generation. It is not a pretentious prophecy of mine, but a statement of my deepest conviction, that within less than four generations there will not be a single office in the land, including the highest, which will not have been usurped by the Jews. Yes, through Jewry, Germany will become a world power, a Palestine of the West. Not through violent revolutions, but by the voice of the people itself—just as soon as German society reaches the apogee of social bankruptcy, the apogee of helplessness towards which we are drifting. Let us not reproach the Jews on this account.

Jewry has fought the West for 1800 years. It has conquered and sub-jected it. We are the vanquished, and it is quite appropriate that the victor chants *Vae Victis!* Our Germanic element has shown itself to be impotent, to be powerless vis-a-vis foreign domination in a historical-cultural context. This is a fact, a bitter, inexorable fact. The state, the Church, Catholicism, Protestantism, credo, and dogma, must bow before Jewish judgment in the daily press.

But this by far is not all. Gambetta, Simon, and Crémieux were dicta-tors in France in 1870-1871 during the war and daily drove thousands upon thousands of Frenchmen needlessly to death. After Sedan,[26] everyone be-lieved peace would come. Not so! Bismarck would have been able to handle the phraseology of a Jules Favre,[27] but the frivolous, miserable fanaticism of

---

[26] Sedan was the location of the decisive battle in 1870 during the Franco-German War of 1870-1871. After this battle, the French emperor Napoleon III surrendered to the Germans.
[27] Julius Favre (1809-1880) was a French politician and staunch enemy of Germany in the Franco-German War.

action of the Semitic gentlemen in Tours[28] required more "Blood and Iron." Poor, Judaized France.

In England, a German hater, the Semite Benjamin Disraeli, *comme il faut* ['as is proper'], keeps the question of war and peace in his "waistcoat pocket." Who really gained at the Congress of Berlin[29] from the blood shed in the Orient? Jewry did. The "Association Israelite" was first in line. Romania was coerced to officially open floodgates to the corrosive influence of Semitism. As far as Russia is concerned, Jewry did not yet dare to make the same demand. This is yet to come.

And in Germany, who carried off the prize of raw, material advantage? Jewry, represented by a handful of Jewish bankers, Semitic brokers. We Germans got the abstract, imaginary result—to be "Friends of the Reich," to console us with the "Reich of Dreams."

Who headed, in numerically overwhelming fashion, the horrid, socially destructive *Gründerthum*[30] after the war? Jewry did.

Stop! Dear reader, don't gnash your teeth in anger. You have no right to. Foreign rule has been thrust upon us. The battle against Jewish domination lasted 1800 years, and hardly ever strayed from its biblical tradition. The Semitic people suffered unspeakably. You have abused it rudely, but rarely did you fight it spiritually. Starting from modest beginnings, it outgrew you, it corrupted society in all of its aspects, squeezed all idealism out of it; it occupies the most controlling influence in trade and daily life, penetrates ever more into public office, controls the theater, forms a social-political front, and has left almost nothing for you, except raw labor which it itself has always shunned. It has transformed talent into shiny virtuosity, pimpish advertising into the goddess of public opinion, and rules you today.

Or should Jewry not take advantage of its victory and triumph? The German people could have, because it had received permission 'from on-high' to get rid of French foreign rule in 1813-1814. Why has French domination

---

[28] Tours was the city in France where a provisional republican government was established after the battle of Sedan. It continued the Franco-German War unsuccessfully and with great sacrifice, until France's final surrender in early 1871. At its head stood Gambetta, Simon, and Crémieux—all Jews.

[29] The Congress of Berlin came at the end of the Russian-Turkish War of 1877-1878.

[30] *Gründerthum* describes the time late in the 19th century when the advent of large-scale industry brought about revolutionary changes in society and in the structure of cities.

not understood how to have its interests taken to heart 'from on-high' like Jewish domination has understood to accomplish this for itself? Of course, high-minded individuals such as Schill, Dörnberg, Stein[31] had been ostracized by Germanic monarchs, just as we might be ostracized for merely ascertaining the facts regarding Judaization.

Are we willing to sacrifice? Did we succeed in creating even a single, anti-Jewish leaning paper, which manages to be politically neutral? Are not even our homemakers and similar associations under patronage of Jewesses who combine 'the agreeable' with 'the profitable' and corner a little business on the side? Isn't every nook and cranny of our life subject to the flood of Jewry?

You rest yourself on Germanic bear hide. I marvel in admiration at this Semitic people which put its heel onto the nape of our necks. I gather the last remnant of my strength to die as peacefully as possible in Jewish bondage, but as one who has not surrendered and is not willing to ask for pardon.

Can we deny historical facts? We can't! The historical fact that Jewry has become the leading political-social great power of the 19th century is clearly before our eyes. We clearly lack physical and spiritual strength to de-Judaize ourselves. The raw, brute force—but completely subconscious—protest against the actual Judaization was Social Democracy, but this acted with and for the Jews, because Jewry had infiltrated its ranks as well. Just as the founder of German Social Democracy, Ferdinand Lasalle (1825-1864), was a Semite himself.

Why, therefore, should we now be surprised? We harbor a resilient, tough, intelligent, foreign tribe among us, one who knows how to take advantage of every form of abstract reality. It is not the individual Jew, it is Jewish *spirit* and Jewish *awareness* that have taken over the world. No longer can we speak of a persecution of Jews, when the howls of German persecution may be heard as soon as a non-Jew dares to rear his head. These are all historical-cultural facts, so unique in their aspects, so awesome, that it is impossible to dispute them using everyday polemics. The proud Roman Empire was unable to win such triumphs with all the might of its arms, as has typical Semitism won in the West, and particularly in Germany.

Among all the European states, only Russia is left to still resist the frank foreign invasion. The most recent example of coming action against this last bulwark was set by Jewry in the case of Romania. As current events and circumstances indicate, the final surrender of Russia is only a question of

---

[31] Schill, Dörnberg, Stein were three German heroes in the resistance against the Napoleonic occupation of Germany.

time. In this multifaceted, huge state, Jewry will find the cardinal point which it needs to completely unhinge the Western world. Jewish, resilient, fly-by-night attitude will plunge Russia into a revolution like the world might never have seen before. Social nihilism and abstract individualism will be conjured up in such a way that the only half-civilized Czarist Empire will be unable to resist.[32] The underdeveloped, still in swaddling clothes, living or already under Jewish influence, corrupted administration, will offer a suitable handle. Just look at the multinational Austria to see how solidly and irreversibly she is in Jewish hands today!

How could these partially primitive national elements in Russia be more resistant than we Germans are and were, when the exemplary, well-administrated and stalwart Prussia, with its honest and modest Hohenzollern, with its disciplined population, has already been breached by Jewry. Are we not witnessing today that, under the gentle and humane Czar Alexander, who has abolished serfdom, it is nihilism which flourishes?! And Russia is to offer resistance against the social nihilism that Jewry has imported into the West? This is impossible!

With Russia, Jewry will have captured the last strategic position from which it has to fear a possible attack on its rear, but once it has paralyzed Russia, its rear will be perfectly secure. After it has invaded Russia's offices and agencies the same way it did ours, then the collapse of our Western society will begin in earnest—openly and in Jewish fashion. The "last hour" of doomed Europa will strike, at the latest, in 100 to 150 years, since events develop more rapidly now than they did in past centuries.[33]

What Russia may expect from Jewry is clear. With exception of two or three platonically neutral Jewish papers, the entire Jewish daily press has frenziedly taken the side of Asia against Russia in the Russian-Turkish War.[34] Neither the religious aspect of this war—as secondary in importance as it may have been—nor, and this is the important point, the historical-

---

[32] This is a remarkable anticipation of the Judeo-Bolshevist revolution in Russia, which would come in 1917.

[33] Another remarkable prediction: this refers to the years 1980 to 2030. At present, we indeed see Europe, the USA, and much of Western civilization under the Jewish yoke. It is as Mahathir Mohamad stated back in 2003: "Today Jews rule the world by proxy"—referring to their dominant power in the United States, and indirectly, in Europe.

[34] The Russian-Turkish War was mentioned earlier. One of the results of the Russian-Turkish War was the liberation of Rumania, Bulgaria, Serbia, and Montenegro from Ottoman rule.

cultural idea, which stands above all diplomacy, the memory of the centuries, even millennia of struggle against Asia, not even the Hellenistic tradition, were able to convince the Jewish press to a adopt a more sophisticated attitude. Indeed! This press would have stood beside Russia if a Lasker or Bamberger had played politically the first fiddle on the shores of the river Neva,[35]or if Jewry had financially been even more important in Russia than in Turkey. But instead, a howling self-interest emerged from every anti-Russian newspaper article.

Á la guerre come á la guerre ['at war as at war,' or, 'keep a stiff upper lip']! It was a right for the Jews, because they are aliens and had been forced to wage war against us, and with that I only state a fact—*sine ira et studio* ['without anger or passion']. "Which side should I be on?" was and can be heard whenever Jews consider partisanship; they are more *toujours en vedette* ['on the lookout'] than the entire West is. Just as we fared in the question of the "culture struggle," we also fared in the Oriental question. Any opinion deviating from the Judaic position found no space in the Jewish dailies, which had almost completely taken sides for Jewish industrial interests. Securities speculation determined what public opinion should be.

In addition, Russia stumbled into the war without any spiritual preparation, without having sought even a shadow of public opinion for herself, and allowed the idea to take hold that she was driven by a titillating desire for conquest and not by its mission in the Orient. The thought that the insolence of the great sea-power England might be curbed, and that stating this idea would have yielded many friends for Russia, was never expressed, and so England became the ally of Judaism. It has always been a misfortune for the Slavs that they ignored the spirit of Germanism and judged it solely on the basis of Jewish newspaper reports. Good God, the German spirit is about to become a stranger even in the German press. It will not even be ten years and one will not be able to find a single journalist in all of Germany who has not been circumcised! At most, clerks for hire will be found rendering service in the industry of the Jewish press. And even that will be quite in order, because *á la guerre comme á la guerre* and prisoners of war must "dig trenches."

---

[35] Eduard Lasker (1829-1884) was a German-Jewish politician who opposed Bismarck's policies. Ludwig Bamberger (1823-1829) was a German-Jewish revolutionary in 1848, and later became a banker and finally a representative in the German Reichstag. He was a political supporter of Bismarck until 1878, but later opposed him.

I am not entitled to, and this is hardly the place, to criticize the domestic policies of Count Bismarck since 1866. Suffice it to say that since then, His Honor, the Count, is worshipped by Jewry like Constantine and that the national, liberal Jewish "opposition" quite openly pushes for power that the Count should grant it presently. I can't say that this Jewish expectation is ridiculous; the foundation of our domestic politics has, since the war with Austria[36] and even more so since the war with France, been such that the boldest Jewish aspirations can't be considered ridiculous. France had, within the last seven years, one Jewish dictator and one Jewish triumvirate, and England one Jewish premier; why should Germany, the social El Dorado of Jewry, not be able to swim with the tide? It would be rather laughable if Jewry would reduce its expectations by even half a tone.

If I as a German and one of the vanquished am not to criticize the domestic policies of Count Bismarck, then I would, if I were a Jew, say: "The Count understands his era as no other statesman before him. He has the clear historical-cultural insight that Germanism is bankrupt and in its last gasps, and he is casting about for elements with more vitality." How can men be of use to him, men like us, who can no longer be *Reichsfreunde*, because we don't have a "Reich" and don't ask the Count for more than approved space for a small and quiet community, which has not yet lost all ideals?

Section 6

The 1800 years of war with Jewry is nearing its end. Let us admit openly and without reserve: Germanism has suffered its Sedan. We have lost our armies and must not fight on like Gambetta wanted to, we must not carry on a war as *francs-tireurs*. We have been vanquished in open battle. Yes, in open battle; because Jewry has always shown its true face, and their little falsehood that we acted like religious fanatics when we offered resistance, must be forgiven. We are no longer a match for this foreign tribe.

Move on, and don't try to convince me otherwise! With the rude "Hepp, Hepp" of the mob, with the pyre and other similar ruses, nothing is accomplished. We never worked on liberating ourselves spiritually from unyielding Jewish realism. Intellectually we accomplished nothing because we were too sluggish and too miserly to battle the Jewish speculative spirit in the press. Don't complain, therefore, about a "scandal press," which is bought, read, and supported by your funds. Don't be disdainful of yourself if

---

[36] Reference to the Austrian-Prussian War of 1866 in which Prussia prevailed.

you see your image in a mirror. Stop being loud-mouths when you are the vanquished. The future and life belongs to Jewry; Germany is of the past and will die. This is the meaning of the historical-cultural development of our German people. There is no way to fight this iron law of world order.

From the very beginning, it was not a religious war; it was a battle for survival against the foreign rule of Jewry, of whose character we only now have become clearly aware. It is too late. We have been so thoroughly submerged in Jewry that all of modern society would have to be put in question if we wanted to forcefully emerge again.

In addition, we lack allies which might assist us in the peaceful and deliberate emancipation of Germanism; there are no allies among the nobility, none among the statesmen, and none even among the people itself. The historical-cultural bankruptcy of the West and of Germanism in particular appears to advance relentlessly. You may call it pessimism that speaks through me. Yet, it is, page for page, the entire history of culture that I adduce, which has led us with demonic logic into Judaization.

I repeat and believe that, in these days of easy suspicions against those of a different frame of mind, one can't repeat often enough: I do not harbor the least "hatred of Jews," and I do not hate the Jews for their religion. I have no hatred based on national origin or race. No people can be blamed for its special gifts. Events of world and culture history have hurled Jewry into the West. The latter encountered a foreign element in Jewry, just as it itself appeared alien to the newcomer. There started to be friction between the two people, and in the process, Jewry proved stronger than the West—and especially stronger than Germanism.

It would be a commendable task for a German scientist, provided he can spare the time, to expand this short but penetrating study of mine into a scientific work and to trace, step by step, the progress which Jewry has made in historical-political respects in Germany. This might be a task worthy of our greatest cultural historian, Johannes Scherr.

Now! I admit that at one time, I have fiercely polemicized against the Jews, but I recognize my error. My polemic was in error; it came centuries too late.[37] I do not harbor the least animosity towards "the Jews," provided they don't harm me; and if I harbor such hate, then of course only to personal enemies. That I, just as so many other writers and other fellow humans, have suffered on account of the Judaization of my profession, is in the nature of things. It is like war. How can I hate the soldier whose bullet happens to

---

[37] A reference to Marr's work *Der Judenspiegel*, of 1863.

hit me? Does one not offer one's hand as victor as well as a prisoner of war? Are we to be more barbaric than a soldier in war? In my eyes, it is an honest war that has been going on for 1800 years. Over there and over here, we did not want to admit this fact, because we had been doctrinaire on both sides and never grasped the essence of this historical-cultural battle.

The Jew—I am speaking in general here!—demonstrates quite admirable attributes towards his own. Some, within his family for example, allow for more intimacy than one finds among other people. He may be kind and agreeable with us, superficially. That he feels as belonging to "the chosen people," the fact that he hates us or views us as mere objects of exploitation, arises from the nature of his tribe and from his history in antiquity. It is understandable that he does not regard us with kindness, given the reception he has received in the West. He would not or he could not assimilate, and so he had to fight. Following his first decisive victory of 1848, he had to—whether he wanted to or not—pursue his success further, and must now attempt to ruin the Germanic world. The destructive mission of Jewry (which already existed in antiquity) will only come to a halt once it has reached its culmination—that is, after Jewish Caesarism has been installed.

From which quarters may one expect resistance? Certainly not from Germanism, because it lies in mortal agony. Perhaps—but only conditionally so!—the Slavs may come to the fore of the stage on which the great "tragic comedy" of world history is being playing out.

Section 7

It is easier to provide an illustration of what our current generation will likely have to experience. This, because, provided not all indications fail us, Jewry will have to face a final, desperate assault, particularly by Germanism, before it will achieve authoritarian dominance. The "Jewish Question" is of a political-social nature. The Judaization of the Germanic world has created concepts and theories of individual social "freedom" which can no longer be described as freedom but only as insolence. Its practical consequences have become intolerable to even Judaized Germanism.

The opposition against usury is the first, popular expression of the coming clash. One looks into an abyss of moral corruption, if one sees in the press the daily more numerous offers for investment bargains, invitations extended to people with a little capital to participate in "Lombard deals" guaranteed to yield 20-30% per month.[38] Some of these "fund negotiators" may be hidden agents of larger capitalists, others may be enticing lesser capitalists to lead a comfortable life as *rentiers* by turning them into leeches of poverty and misery. This is worse than graft because graft exploits only the stupid, while usury, by satanically enticing third parties to join, exploits poverty and misery.

In our parliaments, where the topic of usury is paraded about as of burning importance, one can as usual, only hear nonsense. The dogma of "individual freedom," which really stands for the impertinence and gall of the most unbridled avarice, has become such a basic tenet of society that our valiant representatives—what a despicable picture they offer—attempt to make an omelet without breaking any eggs. Well! One might also have to curb the unbridled manipulations of big industry and of big capital, and this is the reason why the question of usury remains without practical response and does not advance beyond theoretical resolutions.

The doctrinairism of our Judaized society is an aid in getting around the cliff of usury. The impoverished members of every layer of our society remain victims of usury and of its corrupted German helpers, who, with the help of Jews, would love to make 20-30% per month from the hardship and misery of the poor! "It may be possible, but it won't work!" That will be the end of the parliamentary filibuster regarding the problem of usury.

In the meantime, the cancer of usury spreads ever farther in society. The inner bitterness "against Jews" increases from hour to hour (exactly as in the Middle Ages under similar, but less grandiose circumstances) and an explosion is inevitable.[39]

One must also keep in mind that Count Bismarck, with his custom and tax initiatives, has alienated the better part of his most faithful Jews, because the golden International[40] knows no Fatherland, just as the black and red Internationals do not. The seven "meager years" that the German Reich has had for us Germans since 1871 threaten Jewry now as well, and his Excellency will soon find out how quickly in matters of money the patience of his

---

[38] Lombard deals (*Lombardgeschäfte*) describe the granting of short-term credit secured by easily marketable securities, such as precious metals or shares. These yielded huge returns, at least in the short run.

[39] Yet another remarkable anticipation of the coming of a deeply anti-Semitic National Socialism movement.

[40] Golden, black, and red International seem to refer to international associations of financial, Catholic, and socialist interests.

Semitic proteges will run short. The German state is disintegrating in the most rapid fashion, and once the explosion which we foresee occurs, then the state will have no good reason to protect the Jews from the *ardor civicum*. How so often before in history the violent "Hepp, Hepp" will become the safety valve for the state. Perhaps the time is not far away when we, the "Jew haters" par excellence, will have to *protect* the Semitic aliens who have vanquished us from the outrage of indignant popular passion.

Such a catastrophe lies ahead because the indignation against the Judaization of society is intensified by the fact that it can't be ventilated in the press without showing itself as a most abstruse religious hatred, such as it surfaces in the ultramontane and generally in the reactionary press. We have been silenced to such an extent that we can't, even in the press, appeal to the human-ethical sentiment of the Jews. We may rail against Rome and crack jokes about it. The same applies to Protestantism. All of this is received with hospitality in the Judaized press. The cause of humanitarianism vis-a-vis abstract individualism must not be presented. Germanic indolence, Germanic stinginess, and convenient Teutonic disdainfulness of expression are responsible, now that the agile and clever Israel decides what one shall say and what not.

I ask of you, do not berate the Jews! *You* vote for their foreign rule in your parliaments, *you* make them into legislators and judges, *you* elevate them to become dictators of your state's finances. *You* have turned the press over to them, because you find brilliant frivolity more to your liking than moral fortitude; what is it that you rather want? The Jewish people thrive because of their talents, and you have been vanquished, as you should have been and as you have deserved a thousandfold.

Neither must you say that "the Jews spoil the price." They seize dizzyingly large-scale industrial overproduction, sell at "rock-bottom prices," make money, and use it in usury. Is this not entirely in "good order" and in agreement with the dogma of "abstract individualism" that you have accepted with enthusiasm from the hands of Jewry?

We are so stuck in Judaization that nothing will be able to save us, and that a violent anti-Jewish explosion will only delay, but not avert, the disintegration of Judaized society. You will no longer be able to halt the great Jewish mission. Jewish Caesarism is only—and I repeat this from deep inner conviction—a question of time. Only after this Caesarism has reached its apogee may we perhaps be saved by a "nameless God," in whose honor the

Caesarean Roman Empire had built altars, in a semi-ironical, semi-foreboding mood.

Epilogue

I have come to the end of my draft of historical-cultural history. Those of fair judgment will forgive the expression of pain that I feel when I face the Judaization of my Fatherland and acknowledge at the same time that I have only adduced facts fairly and truthfully, and not have flattered the German people at the expense of Jewry. Should I have offended "the Jews" by showing them as well where the logic of Judaization has led us and still is about to lead us, let me say that I had no choice. The victor can't demand from the vanquished that he humbly offer incense.

It is exclusively a historical-cultural process of friction that took place between two different tribes, as I have described it. I should think that this one time, the Jewish press ought to make an exception and without loss of face, treat a pamphlet, which is not to their liking, fairly.

I am aware that my journalist friends and I stand defenseless before Jewry. We have no patronage among the nobility or the middle-class. Our German people are too Judaized to have the will for self-preservation. It is therefore time to finally state *sans phrase* the fact that we are the vanquished and are now subservient. I make this admission to definitively lift the fog of abstraction and partisanship from the Jewish Question. Yes, I am sure that I have said what millions of Jews are quietly thinking. World power belongs to Semitism.

Speak therefore openly as well, you Jews. Be open and sincere in your thinking. You do have the power to do so! And we shall no longer complain. No hypocrisy between us. A world-historic "destiny," that is what I would call it, has placed us like gladiators into the arena of cultural history. The battle had to be fought without hatred against the individual combatant, who was forced into the role of attacker or defender. Tougher and more persistent than we, you became victorious in this battle between people, which you fought without the sword, while we massacred and burned you, but did not muster the moral strength to tell you to live and deal among your own. In our medieval mentality, we thought we could "manipulate" you and we were "manipulated" instead.

May it be that your realistic view of world and life is the true one. May it be that "destiny" intends to make us your helots. We are already on our way. Possibly the spirit that you brought with you to the West, and to which high and low genuflects socially and politically, is the only true one that will assure Germany hegemony forever. An individual Teuton can't answer these questions today with a yes or a no. But you may look down upon us with justifiable pride.

Don't dare to think of my words as irony! I solemnly protest. I have torn the veil from the Semitic "image of Sais"[41] and I am firmly looking at awesome "Isis" because I don't deny her power. The unveiled image offers no new message. Admit that no enemy has more decently, more approvingly treated you than I have done—I who personally have lived a life full of reasons to hate you, as so many, many among you know.

But one no longer hates, if one has become aware. *Beaucoup savoir, c'est beaucoup pardoner* ['to know much is to forgive much'] says Voltaire, and I know that you are the victors. Am I asking your "clemency"? No, I am not! I wish nothing of you, but respect for my convictions. I may have erred. It might be that Semitism and Germanism will enter a political-social peace. I just don't believe in such a peace. I only believe what I see: our social, political subjugation by you. But instead of boastfully rattling the chains as is done by many, I admit that we have been fettered "hand and foot," "heart and soul," from palace to hovel.

In place of the passion of battle, I have adopted stoic resignation. If you can't help it, take it out on me, the stoic, and do it cheaply. But don't speak of religious or race hate. It is the sorrow of a subjugated people which speaks through my writing, of a people who grieves under your reign just as you have grieved under our reign—a reign that you have abolished, step by step, with time. The twilight of the gods has come upon us, you are the masters, we are the slaves.

What is there left to us? Are we to surrender to Rome?[42] Are we to "go to Canossa"[43] and put all of our science at the disposal of the papacy? That

---

[41] The Image of Sais (*Das verschleierte Bild zu Sais*) is a poem by poet Friedrich Schiller (1759-1805). It describes a youth, who, in search of truth, travels to Sais in Egypt. There he finds a giant veiled statue of the goddess Isis who is the guardian of truth. He is warned never to remove the veil, but is finally overcome by his desire to see the statue and thus learn the truth. Upon removing the veil, he falls lifeless before the statue, then awakens not to speak of what he has seen, forfeits happiness forever, and dies an early death.
[42] By 'Rome,' Marr refers to the ultramontane party, which looks to the Pope for guidance and leadership in political and spiritual affairs.

would mean even greater humiliation than Luther suffered in Worms.[44] Are we to ally ourselves with "fawning" Protestants and feign religious hatred on one side or the other? That is out of the question as well. The "liberal" daily press is also off-limits because you knew how to monopolize it. Yes, holy freedom itself has become a Jewish monopoly! Freedom has to adhere to political-social Jewish dogma. And I think it is my duty to absolve even my publisher of any moral responsibility for this booklet, and for this pronouncement of resignation, to save him from the vindictiveness of the Jewish victor.

"A voice in the desert" has been raised and has merely stated facts—incontrovertible facts. Let us accept the inescapable, since we can't change it. Its name is:

Finis Germaniae.

---

[43] Canossa was a castle in Italy to which the German Emperor Henry IV had to travel in 1077 to beg forgiveness from his opponent Pope Gregory VII. Bismarck during the culture struggle stated that Germany would not go to Canossa again.

[44] Martin Luther in 1521 had to appear before the German Diet (Reichstag) in Worms to defend his theses which were inimical to the papacy. He did not recant his views.

— 5 —
JEWISH FRANCE

Edouard Drumont
(1886)

Editor: Edouard Drumont (1844-1917) was a French journalist, writer, and politician. Over his lifetime, he wrote some two
dozen books and founded a right-wing political newspaper, *Le
Libre Parole* ('Free Speech'). His early books, including a historical study of Louis XIV, were followed in 1886 by a monumental analysis of Jews in France, titled *La France Juive*—
Jewish France. It was a huge undertaking, covering two volumes and around 1200 pages. But the book was well-received
and popular, bringing much fame to the author. Other anti-
Jewish works followed, including *Testament of an Anti-Semite*
(1891), *The Masonic Tyranny* (1899), and *The Jewish People*
(1900). The following essay is taken from chapter one of Volume One of *Jewish France*. The translation follows Phillip-
son, but with substantial revisions for readability and clarity.
All notes are by the editor.

At the beginning of this study, we must try to analyze this particular being—
so lively, so completely different from other beings: the Jew. The task, at
first glance, seems easy. No one else has a more energetically characterized
physiognomy, no one else has preserved more faithfully the sharpness of his
first incarnation. The difficulty is that our own preconceptions prevent us
from understanding and describing the Jew truthfully; our point of view and
his are absolutely distinct.

"The Jew is a coward," says the common man. But 1800 years of persecution, borne with a force of incredible endurance, testify that, even if the
Jew does not have the combativeness, he has this other form of courage,
namely, resistance. When we see rich men who once had honored names
serve a government that offends all their beliefs, can we seriously treat people
who have suffered everything as cowards, rather than to renounce their faith?

"The Jew worships money." This assertion of an obvious fact is still just a rhetorical phrase in the mouths of most of those who pronounce it. There are great lords, pious women, regulars of St. Clotilde and St. Thomas Aquinas, who leave the church to go and make *salaams* with a Rothschild who considers the Christ they adore as the basest of impostors. Who forces them to go there? Does the host who attracts them have an extraordinary spirit? Is he an incomparable conversationalist? Did he render services to France? Not at all. He's a foreigner, a little Germanic talker, who is often rude to the aristocratic guests that he is vain enough to invite to his house.

What brings these representatives of the nobility under his roof? Respect for money. What will they do there? Kneel before the Golden Calf.

The remark made about the Duke of La Rochefoucauld-Bisaccia is also true of the Duke of Aumale. When he arrives, looking humble, to pay his respects to Rothschild, who calls him 'the old sergeant-major,' one cannot avoid the conclusion that, by not staying at home in comfort to re-read the glorious history of his race, the descendant of the Condé is admitting that earning a lot of money by more or less honest speculation is equivalent to winning the Battle of Rocroi [in 1643]. After all, one only visits one's equals, and he calls on these people.

At heart, all those people who despise money are quite happy when people who have plenty are prepared to share its fruits with them. After their fall from grace, they are the first to poke a little fun at themselves. "Do you want to see how blood speaks?" a French duke once asked his friends. He had married a Rothschild from Frankfurt, despite his mother's tears. He called his little son, pulled a golden coin from his pocket, and showed it to him. The child's eyes lit up. "You see," continued the duke, "the Semitic instinct reveals itself straight away."

Semites and Aryans

So let's leave these commonplaces aside. Let us take a more serious examination of the essential features that differentiate the Jew from other men. Let us begin our work through the ethnographical, physiological, and psychological comparison of the Semite and the Aryan. These two personifications of distinct races are irretrievably hostile to each other, and their antagonism has filled the world in the past, and will trouble it even more in the future.

The generic name of *Aryans* or *Aryas*, from a Sanskrit word that means 'noble,' 'illustrious,' and 'high-minded,' is commonly applied to the superior branch of the White race—the Indo-European family that had its cradle in the vast plains of Iran. The Aryan race spread out across the world in successive waves of migration. The Ario-Pelasgians (the Greeks and Romans) had as their frontier the shores of the Hellespont and the Mediterranean, but the Celts, the Ario-Slavs and the Ario-Germans, headed west, bypassing the Caspian Sea and crossing the Danube. To quote from Littré:[1]

> All the evidence points to the fact that the Romans were Aryans. The Latin they spoke is clear proof of this. It was a complete surprise when Latin and Greek were authoritatively shown to be related and were classed with Persian and Sanskrit as members of one and the same family.
>
> The Christians of Western Europe are the direct descendants of the Romans, and by virtue of this, they hold all the rights of their progenitors. But that is not all: When their credentials are examined in the light of linguistics, then Christians are seen to be Aryans in their own right. The Italians are Latins, and as such, are obviously Aryans. So too are the Celts of Gaul and Albion: Celtic is a dialect of a language spoken by many tribes, some of which dispersed to the far ends of the West. It was from one of these emigrant tribes that Germany took its language, and hence can be called 'Aryan' like the others. The only doubtful case is that of Spain. Its people are Iberians who are not indebted to the Aryans either for their language or their race. However, the government of Rome, by dint of long occupation and their superior civilization, obliged them to speak Latin, and despite early divergences, it is no longer possible to separate Iberians from the Gauls and the Italians, who are all brothers by education.

Thus it can be seen that all the nations of Europe are very closely linked to the Aryan race, from which have sprung all the great civilizations.

The Semitic race consists of diverse essences—the Aramaic, the Hebrews, and the Arab—that seem to have come originally from the plains of Mesopotamia. Doubtless Tyre, Sidon, and Carthage did, for a time, achieve a high degree of commercial prosperity. Later on, the Arab Empire knew a

---

[1] Emile Littre (1801-1881) wrote the definitive *Dictionary of the French Language* (1863).

fleeting glory, but nothing about those ephemeral states was comparable to the fertile, durable civilizations of Greece and Rome, and the admirable Christian society of the Middle Ages. The Aryan or Indo-European race is the only one to uphold the principles of justice, to experience freedom, and to value beauty.

Eugene Gellion-Danglar (1827-1882) states in *The Semites and Semitism* (1882):

> The Semitic civilizations, however brilliant they might appear, are only vain images, more or less coarse parodies, painted cardboard pictures which some people are gullible enough to take as works of marble and bronze. In these artificial societies, whims and pleasure are everything; the word 'justice' had been prostituted as a cover for them, and means nothing. The bizarre and the monstrous are what they consider beautiful, and superabundance has banished taste and decency from their art. The Semite is not suitable for civilization and the sedentary life. In his tent in the desert, he has his beauty and his own grandeur. There he leads his own life. He is in harmony with the rest of humanity. Elsewhere he is out of place: all his qualities disappear, his vices show their face. The Semite, a man of prey in the Arabian sands, not without a certain heroism, becomes, in society, a man of vile intrigues.

Ever since the dawn of history, the Aryan has been at odds with the Semite. Ancient Troy was a completely Semitic town, and the Trojan War was particularly momentous because it was a duel between two races. This conflict has continued over the ages, and it was almost invariably the Semite who sparked off the clash, only to be repulsed.

In fact the Semite has dreamt constantly, obsessively, of reducing the Aryan into a state of slavery, and tying him to the land. He tried to achieve this through war. Littré, with his customary clarity, has revealed the true nature of the great invasions that almost gave the Semite world hegemony. Hannibal was very near to it when he camped outside the walls of Rome.[2] Abd al-Rahman I conquered Spain, going as far north as Poitiers, with some

---

[2] Hannibal (247-182 BC) was a North-African military leader of the city of Carthage (present-day Tunisia).

grounds for hoping Europe would be his.[3] The ruins of Carthage, and the bones of Saracens [Muslims] that the plow sometimes throws up in the fields of Charles Martel's triumph, are testimony to the lesson such presumption had to learn.[4]

Today the Semites believe their victory is certain. It is no longer the Carthaginian or the Saracen who is in the vanguard, it is the Jew—and he has replaced *violence* with *cunning*. Dangerous invasion has given way to silent, progressive, and slow encroachment. The noisy armed hordes have been replaced by single individuals, gradually forming little groups, advancing sporadically, unobtrusively occupying all the jobs, from the lowest of all to the highest in the land. Instead of making a frontal assault, the Semites have attacked Europe from behind. They have outflanked it. In the country around Vilna—the *Vagina Judaeorum*—a succession of exoduses were organized; Germany was occupied, the Vosges Mountains were crossed, and France conquered. No violence has been used—and I stress this point—but there has been a sort of gentle takeover, an insinuating process of hounding the indigenous people from their houses and jobs, of gently stripping them, first, of their property, then of their traditions and customs, and finally of their religion. I believe this last element will prove to be a stumbling-block.

The two races are doomed to come into conflict because of both their qualities and their shortcomings. The Semite is mercantile, covetous, scheming, subtle, and cunning. The Aryan is enthusiastic, heroic, chivalrous, disinterested, frank, and trusting to the point of naivety. The Semite is earthbound, with scarcely any concern for the afterlife; the Aryan is a child of heaven who is constantly preoccupied by higher aspirations. One lives in the material world, the other in the world of the ideal.

The Semite is a businessman by instinct; he is a born trader, dealing in everything imaginable, seizing every opportunity to get the better of the next man. The Aryan on the other hand is a peasant, a poet, a monk and, above all, a soldier. On the battlefield he is really in his element, and happily affronts danger and braves death. The Semite has no creative ability, whereas the Aryan is an inventor. Not a single major invention has been the work of a

[3] Al-Rahman (731-788) was the founder of the Umayyad Dynasty, which ruled over much of present-day Spain for over 200 years. Poitiers is a city in west-central France.
[4] Martel (688-741) was an early French/Frankish military leader who struck a blow against the Muslims at the Battle of Tours in 732. He was the grandfather of Charlemagne.

Semite. He exploits, organizes, and produces whatever the creative Aryan has invented, and, needless to say, retains the profits for himself.

The Aryan is an adventurer, and discovered America. The Semite then had an admirable opportunity to leave Europe behind and escape persecution, and in so doing, to show he was capable of doing something on his own. But he waited until all the pioneer exploration had been accomplished, until the land was under cultivation, before going off to get rich at the expense of others.

To sum up, anything that takes man on to unfamiliar paths, anything that involves an effort to extend man's knowledge of this earthly sphere, is quite beyond the Semite, and above all, the Jew. He can live only at the common expense, within a society that he did not help to build. What is unfortunate for the Semite—and this crucial observation should be remembered—is that he always goes just a little bit too far for the Aryan.

The Aryan is a good-natured giant. He is happy whenever the needs of his romantic imagination are satisfied by a recital of one of the old legends. He is not amused by such stories as the Semitic *Thousand and One Nights*, in which singers find hoards of treasure, or fishermen throw their nets into the sea and draw them in full of diamonds. For him to be moved, he needs to be able to see a noble figure standing out from the backcloth of fantasy, like Parsifal meeting a thousand dangers in his conquest of the Holy Grail, his cup filled with the blood of God.

The Aryan has remained as ingenuous as he was in the Middle Ages, swooning over the *Chansons de geste,* or the adventures of Garin le Lorrain, Olivier de Béthune, or Gilbert de Roussillon,[5] who, after refusing to marry the daughter of a sultan, ran through 5,000 infidels with a single blow from his lance. The legend of 1789 is listened to attentively, as though it was the account of a cycle from the days of chivalry. The editors of the *République française* might almost make him believe that the members of the Government of National Defense, mounted on fiery steeds like knights of old, had braved the most terrible dangers in order to win the battle for a Morgan loan.[6] And while the Aryan takes a naive interest in such acts of valor, nothing is easier than to deprive him of his purse or even to remove his books, on the pretext that they might impede his advance on the path of progress.

---

[5] The *Chansons* are a series of some 100 French epic poems, dating to around 1000 AD. The named individuals are heroes in those poems.

[6] A reference to American industrialist JP Morgan.

The Aryan, I repeat, will allow anything to be done to him; only he must not be unduly provoked. He can be stripped of all his possessions, but then suddenly fly into a rage over a cherished trifle, such as a rose. Then he jerks out of his stupor, understands the situation at once, seizes the sword that was collecting dust in a corner, lashes out, and inflicts a terrible vengeance on the Semite, who was exploiting, pillaging, and tricking him, but who will bear the marks of this punishment for three centuries.

Moreover, this in no way surprises the Semite. He is by nature an oppressor and is familiar with punishment. There is almost a certain satisfaction in things returning to normal. He then disappears, fades into the mist, digs his heels in somewhere else, and plots how to start all over again in a few centuries' time. By contrast, when he is at peace and happy, he experiences what a witty member of the Académie called '*la nostalgie du sanbenito.*' The Semite, though shrewd and nimble-witted, is in fact of limited intelligence. He has no foresight, he cannot see beyond the end of his hooked nose, and is unable to grasp any of the subtleties that give life its meaning.

Into the Present Day

It is the Semite's faults that are responsible for the natural antipathy between him and the Aryan continuing over the centuries. If you want to understand the Middle Ages, take a look at what is happening in our own country at the present day.

France, thanks to the principles of [the French Revolution of] 1789 that the Jews had cleverly exploited, was disintegrating. Jews had taken control of the public purse, and invaded all sectors except the army. The representatives of the old families of the aristocracy and the bourgeoisie were split into two classes: one led a life of pleasure, had Jewish mistresses who corrupted or ruined them, and Jewish horse merchants and usurers, who were in league with the girls; the other was drawn by the attraction the Aryan race feels for the Hindu nirvana, the paradise of Odin. The latter took little interest in contemporary developments, and were lost in ecstasy. They barely had a foothold in real life.

If the Jews had been patient for a little longer, they would have been near their aim. One of the few really wise men of their race, Jules Simon,[7] a disciple of Philo and a representative of the Jewish school of Alexandria,

---

[7] Jules Simon (1814-1896), Jewish professor of philosophy at the Sorbonne, politician of the left center and Minister of Education.

was to give them good advice: occupy the earth quietly and leave the Aryans to emigrate to heaven. However, the Jews never wanted to listen to such counsel. They preferred the Semite Gambetta[8] to the Semite Simon. Under the pretense that this charlatan had made the French swallow the most incredible nonsense, they supported, financed, and sustained him. The Jews believed he was going to rid them of the Christ they hated as much as on the day of his crucifixion. The Freemasons contributed, the Jewish newspapers inflamed general opinion, gold was squandered, and large sums were paid to police commissioners, who right until the last moment had refused to cooperate in any crime.

What did happen? Exactly what was described earlier. The Aryan, provoked and worried, his innate feelings of nobility and honor wounded, felt the blood rush to his head when he saw helpless old men being dragged from their rooms by thugs. He needed a little time for reflection to gather his thoughts and collect himself. "But what is the guiding principle behind these acts?" he asked. "The principle of *liberty*," the newspapers of Porgès, Reinach, Dreyfus, Eugène Mayer, Camille Sée, and Naquet answered in chorus. "What does this principle consist of?" "Of this: a Jew leaves Hamburg, Frankfurt, or Vilna, or anywhere else for that matter, amasses a few million at the expense of the *goyim* and then he is universally accepted, and his house inviolable, because he would naturally never be called upon to explain his actions in a court of law. A native-born Frenchman, on the other hand— or to use Saint-Simon's term, a natural Frenchman—divests himself of all his possessions, to give to the poor; he walks barefoot, and lives in a cramped, whitewashed room that Rothschild's servant's servant would object to; he is outside the law and can be thrown into the street like a dog."

Once the Aryan had awoken from his slumber, he judged, not incorrectly, that since his tolerance, of which so much had been made over the past century, had been interpreted in this way, it would be preferable to start *giving blows* rather than just receiving them. He felt it was high time to wrest the country from such testy masters. "Since your rough monk's habit gets in the way of your frock-coat, we will replace them with yellow rags, old Semite." This was the conclusion his meditations led him to. The first anti-Semitic, or to be more precise, anti-Jewish committee, was set up at this period.

---

[8] Leon Gambetta (1838-1882), Jewish organizer of the resistance to Prussia after the French military defeat in 1870, and a leader of the republican left in the Third Republic.

The French experience is similar to what has taken place in Germany. The Jews helped the *Kulturkampf* as much as they could, and strove with all their energy to harass the Catholics. The *Kulturkampf* is over and the anti-Semitic war is just beginning. A perusal of the present work would reveal that the same thing has happened in almost identical circumstances in all ages and in all countries.

It appears that the Jew is, in reality, obeying an irresistible impulse. The idea of conforming to other people's habits, traditions, and religions never occurs to him. *You* are the ones who have to submit to the Jew, adapt to his customs, and suppress everything he dislikes. Nonetheless, they are quite happy to accept anything from this society of the past that flatters their vanity. They are grotesquely hasty in seeking for the military titles 'baron' and 'count,' which are about as suitable for these financial manipulators as a woman's hat is for a monkey. Even the most abject speculator or nut-and-bolt merchant with close or distant ties with Israel is at least a knight of the Legion of Honor.[9] But there his condescension is at an end; any of our customs that shock him must go.

The Jew's right to oppress other people is rooted in his religion. For him it is an article of faith. It is proclaimed in every line of the Bible and the Talmud. The Psalms of David (Psalm 2:8): "Ask of me, and I will make the nations your heritage, and the ends of the earth your possession. You shall break them with a rod of iron, and dash them in pieces like a potter's vessel." Deuteronomy 7:22: "The Lord your God will clear away these nations before you little by little; you will not be able to make a quick end of them, otherwise the wild animals would become too numerous for you. But the Lord your God will give them over to you, and throw them into great panic, until they are destroyed."

Against the Christian, the Gentile, the *goy* (singular *goy*, plural *goyim*), all means are good. The Talmud contains some assertions that our legislative deputies, who are so touchy on theological matters, would do well not to bring up in parliament; otherwise they might be refused service in the Jewish banks where they draw their salaries:

- One can and one must kill the best of the *goyim.*
- The money of the *goyim* devolves from the Jew. Thus it is permitted to rob them and deceive them.

---

[9] "Israel" refers to the collective Jewish people, not to the modern nation-state, which would not come into existence for another 55 years.

The Jew's social evolution itself is totally different from ours. The typical Aryan family lives in civilization and in the Romans *gens,* which became the feudal family. For many generations, the life force, the genius, lies dormant; and then the tree whose roots sink into the earth brings to the summit an illustrious man who seems to represent all the qualities of his fellow men. This predestined being sometimes takes a century to develop, but from the humblest origins springs forth a figure who is complete, charming, and valiant, a hero and a scholar. In the pages of our history, many such men can be found.

With the Semitic race, matters are different. In the orient, a camel-driver, a water-carrier, or a barber is singled out by his sovereign. He suddenly becomes a pasha, a vizier, the prince's right-hand man—like, for instance, Mustapha Ben Ismail, who found his way into the Bardo by selling cakes and who, to borrow M. Dauphin's ribald comment, "was of service to his master day and night".[10] As a result, our government, dishonest as we know it to be, rewarded him with the cross of grand officer of the Legion of Honor.

It is the same with the Jew. Apart from the priestly class, which constitutes a real aristocracy, there is no nobility. There are no illustrious families. Though some transmit credit from father to son, there is never a legacy of glory.

In less than 20 years, if he strikes it lucky, the Jew achieves his full development. He is born at the bottom of a ghetto, his first venture brings him in a few dollars, he sets up shop in Paris, obtains a decoration thanks to the mediation of some Dreyfus or other, buys a baronetcy, introduces himself boldly to a wide circle, and acts as though he has always been rich. His transformation is more or less instantaneous; this does not surprise him in the least, and he has absolutely no timidity.

Take a Russian Jew, with his filthy *thouloupe* and his corkscrew curls and carriage, and after a month's bathing, he will take his seat in a box at the opera with the aplomb of a Stern or a Gunzburg. By contrast, take a good French building contractor, who has amassed his wealth honorably. He will always have a slightly unnatural, awkward air about him, and will shun the more elegant circles. His son, born in better circumstances and initiated into the refinements of life, will be quite different. The grandson, if the family continues to rise and remain honest and Christian, will be a true gentleman; he will possess a subtlety of thought and a nobility of feeling which the yid will never have.

---

[10] Ben Ismail (1850-1887) was a half-Jewish Tunisian barber who managed, somehow, to rise to "Grand Vizier" in the court of the King of Tunisia.

On the other hand, though the Jew may achieve aplomb straight away, he never achieves distinction. With the exception of a few Portuguese Jews who, when young, have beautiful eyes, and when old, a certain oriental majesty, you will never find in them the kind of calm, leisured, courteous dignity that makes it easy to recognize an authentic French lord, a pure-bred Frenchman, wherever he may be. The Jew is insolent and never proud. He can never rise above the basic level of life, which admittedly he achieves very easily. The Rothschilds, in spite of their billions, look like hawkers of second-hand clothes; their wives, with all the diamonds of Golconda, will always look like haberdashers, dressed up not for Sunday, but for the Sabbath. Vis-à-vis the Christian, the Jew will always lack the chief attraction of social relations, *equality*. The Jew—and pay close attention to this observation—will never be the equal of a man of the Christian race. He either grovels at your feet, or crushes you under his heel; he is either on top or beneath, never beside.

There is a further reason for Jews not being suited for intercourse where gain is not the sole motive, and that is their *uniformity*: there is a total absence of the refined culture and free-ranging intellect that are essential as the spice of all conversation. One seldom hears from them the brilliant, imaginative theories, the sharp insights or the amusing paradoxes with which some talkers sprinkle their discourse. If such ideas did ever occur to the Jew, he would take good care not to waste them on his friends, he would try to make money out of them. But the reality is otherwise: he lives off other people. He plays a single tune, and the lengthiest conversation never presents any surprises.

Whereas the Aryan race counts an infinite variety of organizations and temperaments, a Jew always resembles any other Jew; he does not have a variety of gifts, but one single aptitude, which is used for everything: this is the *Thebouna* ("groveling"), the practical subtlety so highly praised in the Talmudic *Moschlim*, the marvelous, unanalyzable gift which is the same for the politician as for the courtier and which serves him admirably in life.

The truth is that the Jew is incapable of rising above a certain level. The Semites have no man of genius of the stature of Dante, Shakespeare, Bossuet, Victor Hugo, Raphael, Michelangelo, or Newton, and it is difficult to imagine how they could. The true genius is almost always unrecognized and persecuted, a superior being who gives something to humanity; now the very essence of the Jew is that he does not give anything. It is not surprising that what they cherish is a talent for which there is a ready market. Their Pierre Corneille is Adolphe d'Ennery, their Raphael is Jules Worms.

In art they have created no original, powerful, or touching statues, no masterpieces. The criterion is whether the work will sell; the sublime is 'commissioned to order'—a false sublime, of course. They prefer to concentrate on the real, as it enables them both to get rich by flattering the coarse appetites of the masses, and to serve their cause by making a mockery of the enthusiasm, the pious memories, and the august traditions of the people who are the source of their wealth.

The Jesuit is the exact opposite of the Jew. Ignatius Loyola is a pure Aryan. The hero of the siege of Pamplona, knight of the Holy Virgin, is the last of the Paladins. There is something of the Don Quixote about this saint, a very modern one, of course, who went to Paris late in life, to sit on the benches of the university. He was the personification of the movement that was spreading across the world, when henceforth the pen would take the place of the sword.

It is certain that Benjamin Disraeli knew the Jews better than the Jesuits, and the English statesman is worth consulting. In *Endymion,* Disraeli considers the occult diplomacy that, over the previous century, had turned the world upside down:

> But the Semites now exercise a vast influence over affairs by their smallest though most peculiar family, the Jews. There is no race gifted with so much tenacity, and such skill in organisation. These qualities have given them an unprecedented hold over property and illimitable credit. As you advance in life, and get experience in affairs, the Jews will cross you everywhere. They have long been stealing into our secret diplomacy, which they have almost appropriated; in another quarter of a century they will claim their share of open government. Well, these are races; men and bodies of men influenced in their conduct by their particular organisation, and which must enter into all the calculations of a statesman.

It is easy to appreciate that Jews who are not distinguished by their clothing are all the more effective because they are less visible. In the civil service, in diplomacy, in the offices of conservative newspapers, even in the priest's cassock, they live unsuspected.

The Jewish army thus disposes of three regiments: firstly, the true Jews, the 'notorious Jews' as they are called in the Archives, who officially venerate

Abraham and Jacob, and are satisfied with claiming the chance to make their fortune while remaining faithful to their God. Secondly, the Jews disguised as free-thinkers (like Gambetta, Dreyfus, and Raynal) who conceal the fact that they are Jews, and persecute Christians in the name of the glorious principles of tolerance and the sacred rights of liberty. Thirdly, the conservative Jews who pretend to be Christians but whom the closest links unite with the first two classes, and who pass to their friends any secrets that might be useful. In these circumstances, the incredible success of the Jew, however improbable it may appear, and the unheard-of way he multiplies, are easily comprehensible.

Modern Characteristics of the Jew

The strength of the Jews lies in their solidarity. They all feel a common bond with one another, as is proclaimed in the *Alliance Israelite,* whose emblem is two hands clasped together beneath a halo. This principle is strictly observed from one end of the universe to the other, in a truly touching manner. It is obvious what advantages, from the human point of view, this principle of solidarity gives the Jew over the Christian, who esteems charity and to whom any feeling of solidarity is foreign. Believe me, no one could admire more than I do the sublime flower that Christianity has set in the human heart—indefatigable, inexhaustible, ardent charity, which always gives, gives unceasingly, which gives not money alone, but the heart itself, time, and understanding. What I would like to indicate in this work, which is one of rigorous analysis, is the difference between the *solidarity* of the Jew and the *charity* of the Christian.

Christians welcome every disaster with open arms; they answer every appeal, but they do not club together. As they are accustomed to feeling at home, which is most natural in a country belonging to them, they never even consider the idea of forming serried ranks in order to resist the Jews.

It is thus only to be expected that the Jew strikes in one place at a time. One day it is a merchant whose capital is coveted by the Jew; Israeli traders agree quietly to reduce him to bankruptcy. The next day it is an irritating writer whom the Jews reduce to despair and push into drunkenness or madness. Another time it is a noble lord, with a beautiful name, who treated a baron of doubtful origins somewhat brusquely at the races; it is arranged for the unfortunate man to acquire a Jewish mistress, a broker affiliated to the band recommends an advantageous investment, sometimes the victim is led on by an initial gain, but in the end he finds himself both misused and shamed. If the merchant, the writer, and the lord had pooled their interests and united, they would have escaped—they would have joined in each other's defense. They would all have brought mutual help, but, and I repeat it, they succumb without seeing one another, without even suspecting who their real enemy was.

Thanks to their solidarity, everything that happens to a Jew, even in the most remote corner of the desert, takes on the dimensions of "an event." The Jew has indeed an incomparable way of squeaking; as they were told, "Croak and multiply, sons of Abraham, without number."

The term 'mother country,' as we use it, has no meaning for the Jew. The Jew—and here I am borrowing the forceful expression of the *Alliance Israelite*—is an inexorable universalist. I do not see how the Jews can be reproached for thinking in these terms. What does 'country' mean? The land of one's fathers. The feeling of the mother country is engraved in the heart as names carved on a tree, which each passing year hollows and deepens into the bark as the tree grows older, so that the tree and the name become one. Patriots cannot be improvised; it is in the blood and the bones. The Semite, however, is perpetually nomadic; can he experience such durable impressions?

It is certainly possible to change country, as some Italians did when Catherine de Medici arrived in France, and as the French Protestants did at the time of the revocation of the Edict of Nantes. But for these transplantations to succeed, the moral soil must be more or less the same in the new country as in the old, and beneath the surface humus, there must be a Christian foundation. Moreover, the first condition of adopting a new country is to give up the old. Now, the Jew has a home that he will never renounce: Jerusalem, the holy, mysterious city. Jerusalem, triumphant or persecuted, joyful or sad, is a bond uniting all its children, who say each year at Rosh Hashanah, "Next year in Jerusalem." Outside Jerusalem, any country, whether it is France, Germany, or England, is simply a dwelling-place, much like anywhere else, a social agglomeration in which he can live well. It may even be profitable for him to serve the interests of that country for a while, but he participates only as a free associate, a temporary member.

French Attitudes

Here I must examine a point that I have already raised and that I shall have to refer to later. This is the incontestable degeneration of the French spirit, a partial softening that can be seen in a vague sympathy resulting in *people liking everyone*, and at the same time in an envious note that makes us detest our fellows. This is the case of a number of insane people who disinherit their children and shower civilities on foreigners. If our fellow citizens' brains were functioning in their regular, normal manner, as in their fathers' time, they would quickly appreciate that the Jew can have no possible motive for being a patriot. Reflect for a moment and ask yourself why a Raynal, a Bischoffsheim, or a Leven should be attached to the France of the crusades, of Bouvines, Marignano, Fontenoy, St. Louis, Henry IV, and Louis XIV. By virtue of its traditions, beliefs, and memories, this France is an absolute negation of the Jewish character itself. This France, when it was not actually burning Jews, stubbornly closed its gate to them, covered them with scorn, and used their name as the cruelest of insults.

I am aware that the Jews believe a new France was born in the September massacres, that its old glories were purified by the blood flowing from the heads of old men and women, and that the Revolution was, to adopt the Jew Salvador's expression, "a new Sinai." These words are sonorous but quite meaningless. A country remains as it was when it was born, just as a growing child retains its early nature. France, Germany, and England will never be mother countries for the Jews, who are quite right in my opinion not to feel at home anywhere and to follow a distinct, characteristic policy in every location—namely, a Jewish policy.

Our ancestors, who were sensible people, knew this perfectly well, and defended themselves. Let us do the same, if there is still time, and not be surprised by anything. Victor Hugo, who had to entrust his grandchildren to the care of a Jew, should not be the only one to indulge in the indignant tirades against Deutz.

Uniquely Jewish Qualities

Again, Jews must not be judged by our standards. It is indisputable that every Jew betrays his employer. Cavour said of his secretary, the Jew Isaac Artom: "This man is invaluable to us in publicizing what I have to say: I don't know how he goes about it, but after I have uttered only a word, he has twisted it before he has even left my office." And Prince Bismarck is quoted as saying, "Why else should God have created the Jew, if they were not to be spies?"

From these facts, which it would be simple to multiply an infinite number of times, it is apparent that what we are dealing with is not an isolated case, one that would prove nothing against a community, but with the special calling of a particular race, the vocation of Abraham. Do such acts constitute spying or treachery for the Jew? Not in the least. It is not their mother country that they are betraying; they are merely making capital out of diplomacy and politics. The real traitors to their country are the native-born people who allow foreigners to interfere with matters that are not their business. Not content with making Henri Opper de Blowitz—a German by birth and a second-hand Englishman—an officer of Legion of Honor, the republican ministers take him into their confidence and hand over military secrets; this is despicable. But what right would you have to prevent a Jew who was vacillating between two countries from passing their information to whichever country paid better?

It is thus extremely difficult to study the criminality of the Jew. As the excellent Crémieux says, the intention is paramount. The evil that Jews perpetrate—terrible, unfathomable, unknown evil—falls into the category of crimes committed for reasons of state. To assassinate, ruin, and despoil Christians counts as a crime that is pleasing to God. As Eisenmenger explains in his *Judaism Unmasked*, that is what they call a 'Korban' [sacrificial offering].

Furthermore, it is a fact: the Jew smells bad. Even the smartest of them give off an odor, *foetor Judaicus,* or as Zola would say, a 'whiff,' which reveals the race and helps them to recognize one another. The most charming woman, because of the very perfumes she covers herself with, justifies what Martial said [circa 100 AD]: *Qui bene olet male olet* ("one who wears perfume does not smell good"). This fact has been noted a hundred times. "The Jews all stink," said Victor Hugo, and he died surrounded by Jews. He recounted that, in 1266, a memorable encounter took place before the King and Queen of Aragon between the learned Rabbi Zeckhiel and a very erudite Dominican father, Paul Cyriagne. After the Jewish doctor had quoted the Toldus Jechut, the Targum, the Archives of Sanhedrin, the Nissachon, and the Talmud, the Queen was prompted to ask him why the Jews stank.

The question of understanding why Jews stink has long preoccupied a number of well-intentioned people. In the Middle Ages it was felt that they could be purified of this odor by baptizing them. Bail claims that this feature is due to natural causes, and that there are still black men in Guinea who emit an unbearable odor. Banazzini, in his *Traité des Artisans,* attributes the evil smell of Jews to their lack of hygiene and their immoderate taste for goat's meat and geese.

A disease that implacably attacks Jews is neurosis. This people was for a long time persecuted, always living in an atmosphere of constant fear and ceaseless plotting; later they were shaken by the fever of speculation. In addition, their work was almost invariably of a cerebral kind, and their nervous system has finally been affected. In Prussia, the proportion of lunatics is much higher among Israelites than among Christians. Whereas there are 24.1 per 10,000 Protestants, and 23.7 for the same number of Catholics, per 10,000 Jews there are 38.9. In Italy the ratio is one lunatic per 384 Jews and one per 778 Catholics.

Dr. Charcot made the most bizarre revelations about Russian Jews, and these are the only ones that can be discussed, because the others take great care to conceal their diseases behind their palace doors. The *Archives Israelites,* while taking note of this terrible state of affairs, say that there is no need to comment upon it, and that it increases, if that were possible, the pity people feel for the unfortunate Israelites of Russia. Yes, indeed, let us hope all the Jews who are mentally sick will be treated. But why should they inflict the troubles of their own mind on peoples who were living quietly and happily so long as the Jewish race was not actively interfering with their way of life? With Hertzen in Russia, Karl Marx and Lassalle in Germany, everywhere one looks, there is, as in France, a Jew preaching communism or socialism, and demanding that the wealth of the old inhabitants be shared, while their co-religionists arrive barefoot, make their fortune, and do not show the least inclination to share anything.

The Jews are always well-informed about what is going on, in the world of facts, and in the world of ideas. They are therefore very concerned about the anti-Semitic movement that has been spreading over the whole of Europe. Their fury was unimaginable when *L'Anti-Sémitique*, a gallant little newspaper, very modern and well versed in financial jobbery, was launched in Paris. Whenever people think it has vanished, it reappears on the stalls. To put it bluntly, the Jews have a vague premonition of what is coming to them. They went through a period of delirious pride between 1870 and 1879. The Jew Wolff used to write in the *National-Zeitung,* "What joy to be born in such an age!," "*Es ist eine Lust zu leben!,*" while on the banks of the Spree River, the Laskers, Bleichroeders, and Hansemanns were skinning the Prussians of their millions. "What joy indeed!" the cosmopolitan band in France echoed, when they saw that the squares, money, hotels, carriages of the nobility, hunts, boxes at the opera, everything was theirs, and the good people's reaction was merely sincere comments on the 'new classes.' But they have moderated their tone a little now, and they recognize that concerted action is being taken by Christians everywhere, and that this could be stronger than the universal Israelite alliance.

The Psychology of the Jew

The Jew is essentially a sad man. If he becomes rich, he is insolent but remains gloomy; he is morosely arrogant, with the *tristis arrogantia* of Pallus in Tacitus. Hypochondria, only one of the manifestations of neurosis, is the only present they have made to France, which was formerly cheerful and blithe, blooming with robust, healthy gaiety.

"The Jew is somber," said Shaftesbury in his *Characteristics*.[11] It is a strong adjective, and his comment is deeper than would first appear. It is a mistake to believe the Jew enjoys himself with his fellows, even a mistake to believe that he loves them. Christians do not coordinate their activities, but they love one another, and enjoy being in company. Jews, on the other hand, support each other till their dying day, but they do not feel for their fellows—in fact they detest them, and when business does not bring them together, they avoid each other like the plague. They are scarcely more content in the company of Christians. If someone praises Christ, they at once feel sick; a little joke about Judas produces a sickly laugh, but quite puts them out. Fundamentally, the inscription that one can read on the walls of Italian ghettos is still applicable: *Ne populo regni coelestis hoeredi usus cum exhoerede sit* ("May the people who inherit the kingdom of heaven have nothing to do with those who are excluded").

There is occasionally a sly smile to be detected when they think of how they have tricked the Christians. Indeed, the allegorical representation of the Jew is the fox; the *Meschabot Schualim* ('Tales of the Fox') is the first book the young Hebrew child meets. As an adult, he is happy to underline how he has got the better of the Aryan. For example, Bleichroeder organized the Tunisian campaign, which cost France a number of lives and a lot of money, and resulted in the rupture of the Italian alliance. He then goes on to ridicule his victim by getting an ignominious minister to appoint him commander of the Legion of Honor.

These moods of evil joy can sometimes give way to more naive pleasures. But, you will retort, how on earth can a Jew be naive? Well, he does have a childish side to him. This representation of civilization in its most

---

[11] Lord Shaftesbury was an English philosopher. He published *Characteristics of Men, Manners, Opinion, and Times* in 1711.

advanced, refined, and morbid form, has the wiliness, and at the same time the naive vanity, of the savage. When his success brings him a little cheap publicity, his mouth gapes open with pleasure, just as an African's eyes and teeth light up when he has a trinket or a shred of gaudy material in his hands.

When Louis Blanc was buried [in 1882], I watched the Jewish delegates line up in the Rue de Rivoli. It made an incredible impression on me to see how all those people with yellowish, dirty beards swaggered past, wearing the blue sash of a Freemason. These mean-looking people were experiencing a puerile pleasure in being there, opposite the Tuileries, respectfully treated by the policemen, in having a certain importance, a role to play in a semi-official ceremony, and in wearing something that distinguished them from other people. The Jew is more often like this than is commonly believed. When he tells you that he has been awarded some sort of a distinction, or that he has won a chocolate medal at an exhibition, he looks at you closely to make sure you are not laughing at him (which is his constant fear); reassured, his pale, bloodless face lights up with happiness, just like a child's.

There is one feeling that these corrupt, puffed-up people still possess, and that is *hatred*: of the Church, of priests, and above all of monks. On reflection, this hatred appears quite natural. If a man is born intelligent and rich, with a name that rings differently from all the noble Gerolsteins, and renounces everything in order to become just like the poor, does not such an act deny and suppress everything the Jew stands for—namely, money? Is not the monk's vow of poverty a permanent mockery of the Jew's vow of wealth? The woman who prefers a simple frieze garment, who does not want servants dressed in silk and lace, is not she, in spite of the gentleness of her angelic physiognomy, a living and perpetual insult to the Jew, who is quite incapable, with all his money, of buying what this indigent possesses: faith, hope, and charity? She is quite indifferent to death, and a coffin, even one in whitewood, does not frighten her.

Simon Lockroy insults the monks and says they should be chased out of their cells. Dreyfus suggests that our honest republicans should deprive the Sisters of Charity of the bread that keeps starvation at bay. Nevertheless they will never be stripped of the crucifix they wear round their necks; it is in copper, and the Jewish barons like only whatever bears the stamp of the mint. The very fact that such sublime virtues, such indifference to everything material, and such proud self-denial can exist, reacts on the Jew like a thorn in a crude sybarite's bed; he thinks he is master over all things, yet he cannot influence these souls.

Closing Thoughts

Another useful source when considering the mentality of the Jew is the scholar Ernest Renan. His portrait of the modern Jew in *Ecclesiastes* (1882) is priceless. In his work, one can detect that the artist has a mysterious sympathy for Judas: when the truth is a little stark, he softens the blow; a comment that would wound is followed by a complimentary adjective. He admires this parasite, "who quickly left dynastic prejudice behind him, knows how to get the best out of a world he did not make, and to harvest the fruits of a field he did not plow, to replace the idler by whom he is persecuted, and to make himself indispensable to the foolish man who scorns him."

You would think that it was *for him* that Clovis and his Franks struck such mighty blows with their swords [in 500 AD], that the race of the Capets shaped policy over a thousand years, and that Philip Augustus was victorious at Bouvines [in 1214] and Louis Condé at Rocroi [in 1643]. Vanity of vanities! The best way to obtain the joys of this earth is to proclaim that they are vain. We have all known these worldly-wise men, who are not distracted by any supernatural chimeras, who would surrender every dream of another world for a single hour of the realities of this one. The Jew is strongly opposed to injustice, but is as undemocratic as possible. He is both flexible and proud in wielding his power. His delicate skin, his nervous sensitivity, and the impression he gives of being someone who does not indulge in tiring work make him an aristocrat. His low opinion of the bravery of the warrior and an age-old feeling of being an underdog, which his distinction cannot eradicate, make him a bourgeois. His faith in the kingdom of God once shook the world, but now he believes only in wealth. This is because wealth is indeed his true reward. He knows only how to work and to enjoy. Nothing in the annals of chivalry would make him prefer hard-won glory to his luxurious home; no stoic asceticism will induce him to abandon his prey for obscurity. To his mind, everything life has to offer is material. He has come to the perfect truth: to enjoy the fruits of his labor in peace, surrounded by works of a delicate art and the images of a pleasure that has been exhausted.

This is a surprising confirmation of the philosophy of vanity. Go and trouble the world, put God to death on the cross, endure every torture, burn your country three or four times, insult all the tyrants, smash all the idols, and end up dying of a disease of the spinal cord in a comfortable hotel off the Champs-Élysées, regretting that life was so short and pleasure so elusive. Vanity of vanities!

No, dilettante, it was not so that a Jew should die of a spinal disease in a hotel off the Champs-Élysées that Clovis fought at Tolbiac and Philip Augustus at Bouvines. If our fathers were courageous, if they fell on the battle field, it was so that there should be a France, just as there is an England and a Germany; so that our children should pray as their fathers prayed, with their faith as a staff in life.

The Semites, those restless people, were happy to destroy the foundation of the old society, and to use the money they extorted from it to found a new one. They have created a social problem, and it will be solved at their expense. The property that they have wrongfully acquired will be distributed to all those who take part in the great struggle that is getting under way, just as, in days gone by, land and fiefs were distributed to the most valiant.

In Germany, in Russia, in Austria-Hungary, in Romania, and in France itself where the movement is still dormant, the nobility, the middle classes, and intelligent workers—in a word, everyone with a Christian background (often without being practicing Christians)—are in agreement on this point: *the Universal Anti-Semitic Alliance has been created, and the Universal Israelite Alliance will not prevail against it.*

The committees may be more active in some countries than others, propaganda may be more or less protracted, but before the end of this century there will be yet another repetition of the following sequence of events: the Jew takes advantage of the divisions he has created, and his cunning makes him master of the whole country; he attempts to transform the ideas, the customs, and traditional beliefs of the country, and, as a result of his provocation and insolence, people who quarreled with one another are reconciled overnight, and set upon the Jew with prodigious determination.

My own role is merely to announce modestly the curious events that will shortly take place. It is possible that I may die, insulted, defamed, and misunderstood, without witnessing the things that I have predicted so confidently; but I do not think so. Either way, it is really of small importance, because I shall have done my duty and accomplished my task. Everything in the future will confirm my forecasts.[12] As Bossuet wrote, "Events are prepared, fostered, and realized by different causes. The true science of history lies in observing what were the hidden factors that paved the way for great changes, and the important circumstances that brought them about."

---

[12] This is a remarkable anticipation of the Holocaust, which would occur some five decades later.

THE JEWISH QUESTION IN EUROPE

La Civilta Cattolica
(1890)

Editor: The *Civilta Cattolica* ("Catholic Civilization") is one of the longest-running journals in existence today, having been published continuously since 1850; all issues are in Italian. As a formal organ of the Catholic Church, it serves as an official mouthpiece of Catholic views on contemporary issues. Prior to the "reconciliation" with Jewry in the 1960s, the Church was generally very skeptical toward Jewish intentions, and at times quite hostile. For most of its existence, the Church was willing to respond very harshly to Jewish threats to its parishioners—there being, for most of that time, little in the way of an organized Jewish opposition. Beginning in the mid-1800s, though, Jewish wealth and power began to push back against Catholic interests and ideology. Hence the present essay, originally published as a 3-part series in late 1890, under the title *Della questione giudaica in Europa.*

The anonymous author of this series (many pieces at the time had no byline) is highly incensed at Jewish power and its growing ability to morally corrupt Christian society; as a result, he has written a stunning indictment of Jewry. The essay is well-written, on point, and well-researched. It has a high level of scholarship. The author clearly knew his topic very well, and held nothing back in his criticism. It stands as one of the strongest and most potent Catholic critiques of the past two centuries. The contrast to contemporary Church views is notable, and telling.

There is, of course, a large irony in such Catholic critiques: Christianity itself was born in a fully Jewish milieu, as a Jewish project, suffused with Jewish characters, and constructed in Jewish interests. Jesus, Mary, Joseph, the 12 Apostles, and all the New Testament writers would have been ethnic Jews, as was, most significantly, Paul of Tarsus (born Saul). Christianity emerged in the context of an invasion of Palestine by the Roman Empire, which captured the territory in 63 BC. The formerly-reigning Jewish elite would have been outraged at the takeover by Roman heathens, and thus sought all means to undermine their base of power.

On the most plausible thesis, Paul undertook a reconstruction of the life (and death) of an agitating rabbi, Jesus of Nazareth, in order to create a new religion from whole cloth—the purpose of which was to pull the masses away from the Roman worldview and more toward a Jewish-friendly, and yet morally corrupting, outlook. For millennia, Jews held foreigners and non-Jews in great contempt, and Paul and friends would have not hesitated to confuse and corrupt the Gentile masses as a way of eroding support for the hated Romans. Paul's "Christianity" played one group of detested people against another, with no regard for truth, integrity, or moral consequences. And though it took more than 300 years, in the end, he prevailed; Rome first converted to the new religion, and then collapsed, and then was replaced by its usurper. Western civilization has paid a price ever since. And the long-standing "conflict" between Jews and Christians is thus properly seen as a struggle between two Judeo-centric ideologies—Jews hating Christians not for their views but simply because they are a White, Gentile competitor in the battle for wealth and power.

In any case, the present essay serves to accurately document the state of Jewish power in the late 19th century. There is much valid and useful insight expressed here. But the proposed "remedy" is both interesting and wholly inadequate: to prohibit Jews (and all foreigners) from owning rural land. "Universal banishment" would be preferable, says the author, but this is simply "not practical." Seizing Jewish wealth also has its merits, but evidently this too is impractical. Only the mildest of actions seems feasible. In the end, though, the curse of the Jews is *God's curse*; the European nations have fallen away from the true faith—as through Protestantism, among other things—and thus are being punished by God. The Jews are divine punishment, something like a plague of locust, for a wayward people. Only a return to the true faith, says our Catholic author, can fundamentally solve the Jewish Question in Europe.

Part I : The Causes

Preamble

The 19th century will soon close upon Europe. It leaves behind a very sad question, because of which, in the 20th century, there will perhaps result such calamitous consequences that it will be definitively resolved and brought to a conclusion. We allude to the badly phrased "Semitic Question," or more strictly speaking, the Jewish Question, which is intimately linked to economic, moral, political, and religious matters in Christian Europe.

The fervor presently surrounding this situation is demonstrated by the collective outcry against the influence of the Israelites over every sector of public and social life. In order to stop this invasion, laws have been passed in France, Austria, Germany, England, Russia, Romania, and elsewhere; also, Parliaments are discussing stringent immigration quotas. As well, this question has been and continues to be treated in a great number of newspapers, in books and in pamphlets, whose purpose is to demonstrate the necessity of reducing and combating this plague, as well as to provide evidence of its most pernicious damage.

Here, too, we attempt to reflect upon and pose questions of a more critical, historical, scientific, and social nature, in order to identify the true cause of the lamentable effects that are now increasingly deplored. Thus, for our purposes here, we wish to review and compile, in a few pages, material that we hope Italians will consider. Already in Italy, where Judaism rules over the middle class, there is as yet not much available, and still no complete volume, such as that by Edouard Drumont of France, which we think would find an enthused reception here.[1]

---

[1] Here is a list of the main works, published in the past few years, especially in France: *La France juive* ("Jewish France"), 2 volumes; and *La fin d'un monde* ("The End of a World"), by Edouard Drumont; *Le juif* ("The Jew"), by G. des Mousseaux; *Études historiques* ("Historical Studies"), by Van der Ilaeghen; *L'entrée des Israelites dans la société française* ("The Entry of the Israelites into French Society"); *Les juifs nos maitres* ("The Jews, Our Masters"), by Father Chabautey; *Rome et les juifs* ("Rome and the Jews"), by Lémann; *La question juive*

Historical Background

The Jewish Question in our times does not differ greatly from the one aroused in Christian people of the Middle Ages. Mosaicism in itself is unable to be argued as being hateful toward Christians, since, until the coming of Christ, it was the only true religion, prefiguring and preparing the way for Christianity, which, according to God's law, was its successor. But the Judaism over the centuries turned its back on the Mosaic law, replacing it with the Talmud, a fifth of which is pharisaical and which in great part fulminates against Christ, the Redemption, and the Messiah. And since Talmudism enters greatly into the Jewish Question, it cannot be said that this disapproval of Judaism is expressed in an intrinsically religious form, because in Talmudism, the Christian nations are despised, but not primarily from a theological standpoint. Rather, Christians are reduced to a kind of *moral nothingness*, which contradicts the basic principles of natural law.

Nor does the question originate in the loathing of the race, as implied by the improperly applied adjective, Semitic. In the first place, the Israelite family is not the only one in the world which carries the noble blood of

("The Jewish Question"), by R. P. Ratisbonne; *Les juifs, rois de l'époque* ("The Jews, Kings of the Epoque"), by Toussenal; *La France n'est pas juive* ("France Is Not Jewish"), Reynaud; *Le juif* ("The Jew"), by Kraszewki; *Pavore Moshko* ("Poor Moscow"), by Franzos; *Il sangue christiano nei riti ebraici della moderna Sinagoga* ("Christian Blood, or the Christian Race in the Hebraic Rites of the Synagogue"), by Floro; *La juiverie* ("Judaism"), by G. de Pascal; *La piaga ebrea* ("The Jewish Plague"), by Prof. Giov. De Stampa; *Le juif, voila l'ennemi* ("The Jews: Behold the Enemy"), by Martinez; *La prépondérance juive* ("Jewish Preponderance"), by Father Joseph Lémann; *La politique israelite* ("Israelite Politics"), by Kimon; *Socialismo, discussioni* ("Socialism: Discussions"), by Professor Sebastiano Nicotra; *La haute Basque et les Révolutions* ("The Proud Basques and the Revolutions"), by Auguste Chirac; *La Russio juive* ("Jewish Russia"), by Kalixt Wolski; *L'Algérie juive* ("Jewish Algeria") by Georges Meynié; *Le mystère du sang chez les juifs* ("The Mysteries of Blood, or, Race Among the Jews"), by Desportes.

For these and other similar volumes, we would like to suggest to Italian writers that they might perform a great service to Italy, by doing a review of the very fine volume of Professor Martinez, *Behold the Enemy, The Jews: A Call to Catholics*. This contains the best selections of the most recent and celebrated authors; it is argued with rare doctrine and logic. Doing so would be a notable opportunity for Italy, and we are convinced that it would have a wide circulation and would be a very great help in opening the eyes regarding the revolution that is subverting, perverting, and worrying our unfortunate peninsula. We also pray that it might arouse the valiant Italian and inspire him to salutary action.

Shem. Nor can one understand the reason why the Aryans, who derived from Japheth, harbored a generational hatred for the tribe of Shem, in whose tabernacle, however, the solemn profession of Noah was carried out, through which they were destined to live in fraternal peace.[2] Thus we do not irrationally respect the designation Semitic, when treating the Jewish Question. And Semitism, when applied to Judaism, overloads its meaning, substituting the whole for a part, and consequently, succeeds in conveying a false concept.

Nevertheless, the aversion to the Jews based on race is involved in the question, and constitutes one of its primary aspects, i.e., how a different element is introduced through the religious codex of the Talmud. Yet, the Jewish race, in which there is also a nation, although one without a fixed fatherland and without a political organism, lives dispersed among nations, mixed among them. Although sheltered within the whole, the Jews still form a social union. They view their hosts as enemies, and they greedily prey upon them, even as they sit at their tables. Thus it is that the great Israelite family, dispersed among the Gentile people of the world, form a foreign nation within the nations in which they reside, and are their sworn enemy, since the cardinal point of Talmudism is the oppression and spoliation of the very people who extend hospitality to their disciples. On this, St. Paul, at the end of his days, said that the Jews were God's displeasure and repulsive to all men, *Deo non placent, et omnibus hominibus adversantur* ("…who please not God and are adversaries to all men"; 1 Thess. 2:14).[3]

The rules of the secretive codex of the Talmud prescribes an execrable morality, one that demands hatred of all men who don't have Jewish blood, and especially Christians. The Talmud makes it permissible to deprecate and beat them as noxious brutes. These are only some of the doctrinal points that can't be denied. Thus, not only the work of Rohling, the Roman author and collector of whimsical quotations, but also the more sensible and serious studies of Mischnah and Gemarah, including many rabbis, among them the more notable ones of yesterday and today, leave one with no doubts. It would be enough to consult the work of Achille Laurent, which the Hebrews have taken out of circulation because it revealed the secrets of Talmudism in terms of exterminating Christian civilization, and which is thus able to persuade

---

[2] *Ed.:* In the Bible, Shem and Japheth were two sons of Noah; Ham was the third.
[3] *Ed.:* Long before and since the Bible, Jews have been condemned as enemies of mankind. For a more detailed account, see *Eternal Strangers* (T. Dalton, 2020).

even the most doubtful.[4] We could add to this unimpeachable list, but it would be superfluous.

Portalis on Civil Status

Let us refer to two documents which clearly establish the true condition of the Israelite in the countries extending him refuge; and the powerful reason for the ills that befall him; and therefore the malevolence he carries out wherever he goes. The first document is that of the famous legal consultant, Portalis, written at the beginning of this century, when Napoleon I considered recommending the full civil equality of the Jews—equal, that is, to the French.[5] At that time Portalis extended his observations into the future, with *meminisse iuvabit* ("it will be good to remember").[6] On the subject of the Hebrews, he observed that it was not necessary to confuse religious tolerance with granting them civil status:

> Jews are not simply a sect, but a people. This people, who in ancient times had its own land and government, was dispersed, but did not meld. They went all over the world, in order to find refuge and not a homeland; one finds them in all the nations, yet not melded with any; they live as strangers in a strange land. This is due to the nature of Jewish institutions. As conquest was the specialty of the Roman power, and war of the Spartan republic, culture for the state of Athens, commerce the domain of the Carthaginians, so religion is the specialty of the Hebrew race, for whom religion is everything—the basis and law of their society. It should, then, be clearly understood that the Jews everywhere form a nation within a nation; and that, although they live in France, in Germany, in England, they nevertheless do not ever become French or German or English. Rather, they remain Jews and nothing but Jews.

---

[4] *Rélation des affaires de Syrie* ("Report from Syria"), 1846.
[5] *Ed.:* Jean-Étienne-Marie Portalis (1746-1807) was a prominent French attorney during the Napoleonic Empire.
[6] *Ed.:* A reference to a famous line from Virgil: *forsan et haec olim meminisse iuvabit* (Aeneid 1.203)—"someday we will remember this and smile."

Later, this same reality was more crudely and frankly asserted in public by Crémieux, the main publicist of the Jewish inner council, and also prominent in the Jewish Alliance, and its periodical of the same name. In the latter, he defined the Hebrew as the man of an inexorable universalism.

Thus concluded Portalis, when explaining and supporting his views regarding civil laws treating this heterogeneity which, by virtue of its vigorous institutions and its principles, remains both separate, yet always part of the common society.

The other document is the manifesto of 31 members of the legislative body of Romania, where in 1868, attempts were made to pass a law granting civil equality to the Hebrews:

> The Jews, who, in substance, say they are members of the nation, are necessarily constrained to ostensibly obey the authority of the non-Jewish State. But they are never able to consent to become an integral part of it, because they are unable to shed themselves of the idea of their own State. Thus, they do not form a religious sect, but an indelibly racial complex with a set belief that they maintain within the mixture of other peoples, and which is always Jewish. Because of this, it is impossible for them to unite in blood with other peoples, and impossible to partake of their sentiments, which are directly opposed in all things to those of Christians. And the strongest obstacle is in the area of religion, which is at once legislated by them to be both religious and civil, thus constituting a political and social cult and organism. Because of this, wherever they settle, by necessity, Judaism establishes a State within a State.

As to the gratitude shown to the people who extend them hospitality, the Israelites regard them as enemies, since they believe they will usurp them. To avoid this, they use every sort of means, in order to gain supremacy over them, which they think can be accomplished by conversion. They pass their time in the breast of other people, which for them is a time of expiation, of trial and exile. Soon, the inhabitants of the countries that harbor them are given a bill of account, which now is making good on the promise of a universal Jewish people in the world, who will finally subjugate them.

The corollary of this situation is that the Jews have no fatherland anywhere. Therefore, their ultimate imposture is their continual boast of patriotism, by which they pretend to be loyalists and followers, in order to extend the scope of their ruination and devouring of those nations which have accorded them the right of citizenship. Out of such a situation emerges their most innate, most hateful trade, that of traitor and spy. As Bismarck noted, "God created the Hebrew in order to serve those who need spies." And his Count Cavour said of his Hebrew confidant, "He is useful to me, in order to tell the public what I want. As soon as I finish speaking with him, he has already betrayed me." In July, the *Gazzetta della Croce* of Berlin published this account of an army official:

> During the war of 1870, I was assigned to the 10th Regiment, commanded by General Voigts-Rhetz. He was given 100,000 talleri to pay spies. But he returned to Berlin with all of the money, because he found no Frenchmen willing to be a spy. However, in 1866, in the fight against Austria, the situation was quite different. The Jews showed up in great numbers, and for a price they sold news of the movements of the imperial army. These Jews were Austrian subjects, and thus, voluntary spies.

Moreover, history is full of treason committed by Hebrews for both public and private powers. The Jew, Goldsmit, stole and sold Prussian state secrets. The Jew, Klotz, betrayed the English general, Hicks, and his troops, who were killed by the Mahdi barbarians in the Sudan. The Jew, Adler, abused the trust of his employ by Krajewski, in order to hand him over to the Prussians. The Jew, Deutz, betrayed the Duchess of Berry for 500,000 francs. And in the last century, the Jew, Sedecia, poisoned Carlo il Calvo, who was betrayed by the Jewess, Païva. Earlier, in Paris, it was she who managed to sell the battle plans of the French army.[7]

The Talmud

Another element that makes the Jewish organism in Christian countries so dangerous, and a hundred-fold abominably so, is the innately superstitious

---

[7] *Ed.:* The references here are uncertain. The Jew Gustav Klotz indeed betrayed William Hicks (or Hicks Pasha) in 1883 in the Battle of Sheikan. The Jew Simon Deutz indeed betrayed Marie-Caroline of Bourbon-Two Sicilies, Duchess of Berry, in 1883; she spent a year in prison.

faith of the Talmud. It holds that the Jews not only form a superior race of human beings, all others being comprised of races inferior to them, but which, by a completely divine right, entitles them to the entire universe, which shall one day be theirs. Because of this insane belief, Judaism insinuates itself everywhere; thus this is the utmost expression of what they call their religion. This is what comprises the depraved doctrine of messianism that they have professed from the 3rd century of the Christian era, when the Babylonian Talmud was compiled. Over time, commentaries were added by the most revered rabbis, always with the same import—as the Jew Benjamin Disraeli, who became Lord Beaconsfield and head of the British government, exposed in our time. In order to rise to power by converting to Anglicanism, in his famous novel, *Coningsby*, Disraeli had the following expressed by the novel's main Jewish protagonist:

> No penal laws, no physical tortures, can effect that a superior race should be absorbed in an inferior, or be destroyed by it. The mixed persecuting races disappear; the pure persecuted race remains. And at this moment, in spite of centuries, of tens of centuries, of degradation, the Jewish mind exercises a vast influence on the affairs of Europe. (Book 4, chapter 15)

Disraeli emphasized that "The modern world is governed by persons far different than is assumed; they are unseen and stay behind the scenes." By this he meant to say the Jews, who run everything from the shadows. We could accumulate proofs of this proud declamation, culled from the centuries. In fact, this would result in much evidence, even excessively so.

The falsification of the prophetic tradition regarding the Messiah and his reign over the people, which is the Church that rose up from the time of the destruction of Jerusalem, resulted in the Jewish people being scattered or reduced to slaves by the Roman conquerors. In his *Lives of the 12 Caesars* (circa 119 AD), Suetonius wrote: *Percrebuerat Oriente toto vetus et constans opinio, esse in fatis, ut eo tempore Iudaea profecti rerum potirentur* ("Over all the Orient, there had spread an old and established belief, that it was fated at that time for men coming from Judaea to rule the world"; *Life of Vespasian*, 4.5). Also, in his *Histories* (circa 100 AD), Tacitus corroborated this: *Pluribus persuasio inerat, antiquis sacerdotum literis contineri eo ipso tempore fore ut valesceret Oriens, profectique Iudaea rerum potirentur* ("The majority were convinced that the ancient scriptures of their priests alluded to the present as the very time when the Orient would triumph, and men from Judaea would come forth, destined to rule the world"; 5.13). Similarly, St. Jerome also treated true and false matters regarding the Jews.

Drach, a convert to Christianity,[8] and deeply knowledgeable of the Talmud and the Jewish mysteries, explained the doctrine of ancient and modern Israel:

> The Messiah had to be a great conqueror who subjugated the nations to a state of slavery by the Jews. They would return to the Holy Land as vanquishers, and take the riches from the infidels. The purpose of the coming of this Messiah would be to liberate the dispersed Jews, assembling them in the Holy Land, and establishing a temporal kingdom there, lasting to the end of the world. Then all the people will be subjects of the Jews, and they will pay tribute to them with their persons and their goods. The learned rabbis of the synagogue routinely end their discourse by invoking this triumph, as well as all of the blessings promised with the coming of the one who is heralded as the Messiah. Among these promised blessings is the much awaited and longed-for moment of the slaughter of the Christians, and of the complete end of the sect of the Nazarene.[9]

The same concept, although slightly changed, pays lip service to modernized Jews, who give no weight to this rancid interpretation of the Talmud. The actual Messiah is replaced by a messianic people, that is, the Israelites, predestined—although how or why is not mentioned—to rule all future human generations. Such a concept, among other recent ones, comes from the apostle Adolphe Crémieux, one of the principal founders of current Jewish power.[10] He said, "The Jews will have no end. The little family (remnant) is the greatness of God. A messianism for the new age will be born and unfold. A Jerusalem of a new order, situated between the East and the West, will be greater than the cities of the Caesars and the Popes."

Stann, a German Hebrew, published his book which announced to the world that, "The reign of universal liberty over all the world will be instituted

---

[8] David Paul Drach (1791-1868) worked as a librarian in Rome.

[9] *L'Église et la Sinagogue* (The Church and the Synagogue), pages 18, 19.

[10] *Ed.:* Crémieux (1796-1880) was a wealthy French politician and attorney.

by the Jews." And we have seen the face of this liberty, which these insane ones dream of for Christians. Another man, a native of Frankfurt, in late 1858, wrote: "Rome, which ground the Jews under its feet 1800 years ago, will fall, ruined. The work of the Jews will spread its light over the universe and will bring the greatest advantage to the human species."

Thus it is always the same: Judaism is always an alien and inimical force in countries where it takes root, and is also a force that tends to overpower the inhabitants and to predominate, by virtue of their dogmatic and civil, juridical, and national constitutions. And they do so by every evil art, and by faithlessness.

More on Talmud

There is no lack of theories, which manifest themselves more and more each day. For instance, there are some important doctrinal religious principles set out in and inculcated by the Talmud, which is the supreme codex of this entire race. The first principle of Jewish morals, contained in the laws treating rules of conduct toward one's neighbor, states that other men, in relation to the Hebrew, are no more than animal beasts. "O seed of Abraham," exclaims the Talmud, "The Lord has surely chosen you, as spoken by Ezekiel; you are my sheepfold; I mean that you are men, whereas the other peoples of this world are not men, but beasts".[11] The Jew who insults a non-Jewish woman and assaults her is absolved of all judgment, because he has done evil "to a mare".[12] Maimonides, who is considered infallible in the ghettoes, wrote a passage on an Israelite who kills a Goy; the Jew, he said, cannot be punished, precisely because the Goy is not a Jew.

What else? One of the authoritative Jewish books seriously asserts that "non-Jews are black animals," who are also described as boars.[13] Thus it is that the race is outside the nation by virtue of its refusal to be assimilated, and so the Jews were disgusting to the Romans of the Caesars; or as Tacitus wrote, *proiectissima ad libidinem gens*.[14]

Enough? No: The Talmud elevates the Jew above all humankind. It teaches that an Israelite is more pleasing to God than the angels of paradise;

---

[11] Treatise, Baba-Metsigna, f. 114. f.
[12] Treatise, Barakout, f. 88. f.
[13] Salkutro-Ubéni, f. 10.3.
[14] Tacitus, *Histories* V.5: "as a nation, they are singularly prone to lust."

that to strike a Jew is to strike Him; that the non-Hebrew is actually worthy of death.

Another book of Jewish morals is one that concerns the law. The Jews who sit on the Tribunals have the power to dissolve or nullify all judicial decisions, and to grant release from signed contracts. Drach explains this protocol very well, which is called Kol-Nidre. The Talmud affirms that the three men who compose the Tribunal possess the same authority as the Tribunal of Moses.[15]

Aside from this, the Hebrews have varied their external practices and their words so as to invalidate the law, which they also make. All of this amounts to malfeasance, which they and their loyalists have calumniously set in opposition to the followers of Jesus, and have done so with unscrupulous religiosity. Better still, the night before the feast of Kippur, they absolve themselves, through their ceremonies and oaths, of all bonds of conscience to all negotiations they have entered into, and which are formally binding. Thus, for them, all obligations of conscience, present and future, are dissolved; i.e., those already undertaken and those not yet undertaken, all for their advantage, and to please themselves. Moreover, according to the Talmud, in a case between a Christian and a Hebrew, the Jewish judge must always give the advantage to his fellow Jew.

On average, the codices of this morality allow, and even make obligatory, that the Jew appropriate to himself the lost property of non-Jews. And behold the incredible reason: "to make the non-Jew shameful in the sight of the mercy of God".[16] And as a matter of strict obligation, Maimonides avers that the dirty trick is a strict obligation: "Whoever pays [the Goyim] back," he wrote, "commits a sin, because he strengthens the hand of the impious".[17]

The legitimization of theft from Christians is impudently professed by the rabbinical schools. "Since the life of the idolaters [this is what Jews call Christians] was given to the Jews to decide, it is for the Israelites to decide how much or how little is due them." This is taught by Rabbi Giusseppe Albo.[18] "The possessions of Christians, according to Bova-Baria, are, or ought to be, thrown into the desert or the sea; the first one in will be the

[15] Treatise, Rosch-Ilaschshaun, f. 25. f.
[16] Treatise, Baba-Koummah, fol. 29, 50; and Treatise, Sanhedra, fol. 76, 5.
[17] In his treatise, *Della rapina e delle cose perduto* ("Regarding plunder and lost property"), chap. IX, art. 3, 4.
[18] *Fondamento della fede* ("Fundamentals of the Faith"), Part III, c. 25.

owner, because the first one will be an Israelite." This is the teaching of Rabbi Pfefferkorn.[19]

"It is permissible, whenever possible, to cheat a Christian. Usury imposed on a Christian is not only permissible; rather, it is a good; and it is lawful to impose it even on holy days. So much so that you ought to cheat a Christian in such a way as to ensure that he remains ruined".[20] These examples are from Rabbinical documents that are considered holy.

Thus are the moral doctrinal flowers, embracing all turpitude, in which our pens are steeped, and that are foisted on the people of any country infected by this race. The illustrious Maxime du Camp, of the prosperous Jews of Paris, published a monograph that merits being published in every language.[21] Colonel Cerfbeer, a Jew by birth, in an 1847 French study of Jews convicted of robbery, found their numbers to be double that of French convicted of the same crime. He added this warning:

> That which differentiates the Hebrew delinquents from the others is that their crimes stem from a more malignant perversity because they are the result of premeditation. These crimes include sponging, lying, usury, theft, premeditated bankruptcy, contraband, counterfeiting, extortion, theft, and all forms of deception and every sort of aggression.[22]

So it is that 40 years later, the Talmudic ethic has made progress, and the price of it, thanks to the civil equality that Judaism now has in all of Europe, is the great number of crimes committed by Jews which, one way or another, go unpunished. Instead, the Jews have been regaled with ribbons, knights' crosses, and baronial titles.

Aversion to Judaism

Anyone having dispassionately investigated the facts and documents, cannot but conclude that there has never been ambition madder and more tenacious, and none more frankly stated, than that of the Jews. They arrogate to themselves the conquest of the world, of reigning over all the nations by over-

---

[19] Ph.D dissertation, p. 11
[20] *Shulchan Aruch*, Chshen Mispat. F. 48, n. I jore d'cáss. 159 n. i.
[21] *V. fleuve des deux mondes* ("Currents of Two Worlds"), 1 June 1869.
[22] *Les Juifs* ("The Jews").

throwing them, of subjugating all the peoples to themselves. And they appropriate the right to stake their claim on all of the blessings of the universe, as their legitimate birthright given them by God. It is amazing to read and hear about this terrible challenge by a handful of men, about 8 million, who work among 500 million others, and who seriously wish to enslave them, and dream of doing so!

There is no end to the persecutions of the Jews that have been carried out before, still, and everywhere. But these persecutions were and are a consequence of their mad wickedness. All of this is manifested by the avidity of their ambition; by its legitimization by virtue of their supposed superiority; and by their sense of privilege over the people they live among. They have demonstrated themselves to be intractable and hostile evildoers toward the nations that have tolerated them, bestowing upon them, above all, the blessing of the right of citizenship.

Universal effect always corresponds to an equal cause. The aversion to Judaism was not begun by Christians, because of the Jews' killing Christ on Calvary. This aversion existed and was recorded by the Muslims, Arabs, Persians, the Greeks, Egyptians, and Romans.[23]

The famous Marie-Theodor Ratisbonne, a Jew by birth, who converted, becoming a fervent servant of Christ, analyzed the persecutions of Jews that occurred in every age and place:

> The evil of the Jews is that they don't want to open their eyes, in order to recognize the true cause of their persecution, carried out in all the centuries and without equal in history. Throughout the centuries, many people were persecuted by others. These tortures, however, came to an end. However, the persecution of the Jews is marked by its perpetuity and its universality. Thus it is a unique case, which cannot be humanly explained.[24]

Because of these facts, commentators have attributed the ongoing persecution of the Jews to the design of God's justice, which, through their persecution, re-enacts on Earth the satanic rebellion inexorably manifested against heaven. The human causes of this fact, unique in history, are witnessed by

---

[23] *Ed.:* Again, for the full story, see the book *Eternal Strangers* (T. Dalton, 2020).
[24] *La Question juive* (The Jewish Question, 1868).

the Jews' insatiable appetite for usury to gain power through betrayal in order to dominate, and whenever possible, to take over and overthrow the State.

In every country, this immutable law of Hebrew prosperity in every country is always to the detriment of the well-being and liberty of the inhabitants. Many years before Rome fell into the claws of history, the famous Lemann brothers, Joseph and Augustin, who converted from Judaism and became priests of the Catholic Church, wrote in one of their works:

> O Israelites of Rome, we understand the attitude of our people.
> If you are conceded the right of possession which you invoke,
> we wager that, within 30 to 50 years from now, Rome will be
> in your hands.[25]

And so the prophecy came to pass. The city of Rome fell quickly into the abyss, and was economically and materially subjugated to the Jews, as were all of the major cities of the great nations of Europe. And commensurate with this subjugation, which continues to fester in the moral, political, and economic spheres, the European people see in it the kernel of the Jewish Question in our time.

1869 Leipzig Synod

In the last century, in all nations, revolutions have upset the lives of average ordinary Christians. Who has brought us to this state of affairs? Not the people who have been oppressed by it; not the monarchy who have been displaced by it. Everyone knows that it was done solely by Judaism. By virtue of the lying principles of liberty, fraternity, and equality, they have attempted to color over, with the outstretched hand, their willful lust to predominate, to an extent never before attained, and because of which, the sword of the wrath of God dispersed their followers over the entire Earth. Or as the jurists have it: *Is fecit cui prodest* ("done by the one who profits from it").

On 29 June 1869, a synod of Jews was held in Leipzig. Participants came from all over Europe, and it was presided over by Lazarus of Berlin. Although some were more traditional, others more modernist, they agreed on rationalism, as well as on their hatred of Christians, a subject they discussed extensively. Finally, they unanimously approved the proposal put forward by

---

[25] *Rome et les juives* (Rome and the Jews).

Professor Philipson of Bonn, and strongly supported by Astrue, the High Rabbi of Belgium:

> The Synod recognizes that the choice and practice of modernist principles offers the most solid security for the present and future of Judaism and its followers. These principles contain the most efficacious seeds for a fruitful life and for the broadest expansion.

And in effect, the modernist principles—that is, those called the rights of man—were invented by Jews in order to divest the people and their governments of their defenses against Judaism, and in order to multiply the advantage of this faction, which forms the offensive force. Having acquired absolute civil liberty and equality in every sphere with Christian nationalities, the dam was opened, and so, a devastating torrent let loose. In a short time, they penetrated everything, took over everything: gold, business, the public purse [or stock market], the highest appointments in political administrations, the army and the diplomatic corps. Public education, the press, everything fell into their hands, so that everything came to depend upon them. The result is that our Christian society encounters major impediments from giving them access to the same laws and to state constitutional rights, and is thrown over the precipice of impotence, brought about by Hebrew audacity, under the guise of liberty.

Prince Metternich described the method by which the audacity of Judaism advances: "The revolutionaries of the first phase assured their final triumph over Christianity." In Paris, Stern, a Jew, leveled this warning: "Within ten years, I don't know how a Christian will be able to live." And consider that Croesus, who among the prominent Israelites is Hirsch,[26] standing at the top of the staircase of his regal palace, watching the elect nobles of France come up the steps for a party, said to his daughter, "Do you see these people? In 20 years, they will be our servants. And I am not exaggerating."

In sum, such are the causes of the Jewish Question. Next, we shall demonstrate the principal effects.

---

[26] *Ed.:* Maurice de Hirsch (1831-1896) was a German-born Jew who resided in Paris. Croesus was an ancient king of Lydia, circa 550 BC, renowned for his ostentatious wealth. Hirsch was clearly the 'Croesus' of the Jews at that time.

Part II: The Effects

Source of Power

That series of proverbs that culminated in the synthesis of the rights of man in 1780, in fact amounted to the anointing of the rights of *Jews*, to the detriment of the people in whose breast the practice of these rights was introduced. These rights were the door to the palace of power, through which, in our century, Judaism entered and laid siege to Christian society, assaulted it, upset it, and to a great extent, overtook it. What is today manifesting itself, amid the universal stupor in which Europe finds itself, is that the diffusion of political-irreligious ideas is now sweeping the nations. This is almost totally due to the power of the Jews. So much so that Chabany was able to publish a book truthfully titled, *The Jews: Our Masters*, which no one has challenged.

In late 1847, Cerfbeer, president of the central Jewish Consistory in France, thus described the success of his fellow Jews in that country:

> The Jews, in proportion to their numbers, occupy more posts than the Catholics and Protestants combined. Their ruinous influence is at work more than ever in that they are responsible for deals which greatly aggravate the patrimony of the nation. There are hardly any businesses in which they do not participate, nor public loans which are not held by them, nor disastrous crashes which they have not prepared, and from which they have not profited. Many complain, as with each day they enjoy the best of the favors, and gain the advantage over all the others.[27]

Later, the convert Ratisbonne emphasized:

> Because of their dexterity and ingenuity, and because of their desire to dominate, step by step, the Jews have occupied all of the areas that lead to wealth, to dignity, to power. Modern society is imbued with their spirit. They regulate the stock exchange, the press, the theater, literature, the upper rungs of commerce, on land and sea; and through the possession of the

---

[27] *Les juifs* (The Jews), page 9.

capitals, and through shrewdness, they have at present taken, as in a hidden snare, all of Christian society.[28]

And so it is, not only in central Europe, but everywhere, except in Russia. As in the time of Arianism—a time in which the Christian world, without realizing it, found itself Arianized[29]—thus today, Europe finds itself mired, and to a great extent no longer Christian, but Jewish or Judaized. From this emerges the question of what ought to be done to protect the rights of Christianity?

Usury, Weapon for Subjugation

Sebastian Nicotra quotes a passage from an old manuscript, only lately discovered, in which a Jew describes the key of Jewish power in our day. He said to his brothers:

> My sons, Jehovah is with us in his mercy and has reserved to us a powerful weapon—or better said, an invincible virtue, which we ought to launch into the midst of the nations of Christ in order to subject them to our domination. This virtue is named in the holy book, and it is called 'usury.' The holy book, you know it, prohibits usury among brothers, against the tribe, against ourselves; but it doesn't prohibit using it against the foreigner, against the infidel, against the enemy, since it is a weapon of war and an instrument of victory. Usury then remains to us, and better than the faith and morals of Christ, usury is the little stone that fell from the mountain, which must cover the world; the mustard seed that grows into a superb tree, which will dominate the world.[30]

Nine years ago, a great rabbi, speaking in Paris to his faithful, said:

> Using the pretext of aiding the masses of workers, we can overtake the world by taxing the majority of landowners. And

---

[28] *Question juive* (*The Jewish Question*), page 9.
[29] *Ed.:* Arius (256-336 AD) was an early Christian from Egypt who held somewhat unconventional views of the divinity of Jesus, and thus of the Trinity. (Note that 'Arian' is completely unrelated to the term 'Aryan'.)
[30] *Socialismo* ("Socialism") pages 339-40.

when their property (through usury) shall be transferred to our power, the labor of the Christian proletariat will fall to our advantage. "Poverty enslaved," said the poet. The proletariat are the lowest servants of the speculators (usurers), but oppression and outrage humbly serve the cunning. Who can deny the cunning, prudence, and shrewdness of the Israelites?[31]

This flower of Talmudic doctrine has permeated the spirit of contemporary Judaism, mindful of the Bible's words, *Pecuniae obedium omnia* ("all things obey money"; Eccl. 10:19). On the freedom to practice usury, Michelet wrote: "The Jews have resolved the problem of volatizing money; they were granted the freedom to lend, and they are now freemen, owners; from transaction to transaction, they have ascended to the throne of the world."

In March, the editor of *Pall Mall Gazette* in London sent one of his correspondents to Berlin to interview the preachers of the Stoecker faction, one of whom is the very zealous leader of the anti-Semitic league of Germany. Pastor Stoecker was quoted as saying:

> I do not hate the Jews, nor do I wish them evil through religious hatred. But as I serve God, as a Lutheran pastor, and as a representative of the nation, I cannot remain quiet, having heard and seen the infinite evil that the Jews have done and still do in my country and especially in Berlin. Here the Jew has all of the gold in his hands, and consequently he also holds in his hands all of the power. I do not detest the Hebrews because they are rich, but because they accumulate wealth dishonestly. In the countryside, they cheat the businessmen, and in the city, they make money by dirty means. I maintain what I have said earlier: that from the viewpoints of trade, of social interests, of politics and morality, the Jews are leading Germany to the precipice.

The situation in Germany has reached such a point, that in September Mr. Hermann Ahlwardt was able to publish in Berlin his book titled *The Desperate Struggle between the Aryan People and Judaism* (1890)—which, because of its fearful evidence, the government believed it was necessary to suppress.

---

[31] *V. La Contemporain* (*The Contemporary*), 1 July 1881.

The same month, the German parliament echoed the Austrians' warnings against the rampant financial domination of Judaism. The Jews were
bandits ten times over in their domination of the House of Austria; and took
firm hold under Ferdinand I, brother of the Emperor Carlo Quinto. In Austria, they were permitted entry; and they remained there as servants of the
Holy Emperor, up to the time of Tersa who favored them, and permitted
them to go into various provinces. In the German countries, there was an
interdict on their entry, except in Vienna; they were permitted entry in the
reign of Wenceslas, on the condition that they did not exceed a fixed number
of families. They were more tolerated in the reign of Stefan, remaining there
because of other countries' laws forbidding them to immigrate. However, the
greatest amount of liberty was accorded them in Trieste. From the ghettos of
the Duchy of Mantova, from the Republic of Venice, from the Papal States,
and from the Levant, they were able to come into Trieste, because of which
today they feign a fondness for Trieste, professing a kind of hyper-
patriotism, that is actually ridiculous. They have also gone into Poland,
where the Jews of Galicia and other Polish regions gained the same privileges. Finally, from 1848 to 1869, all of the defensive restrictions of the Empire
were repealed, and the Jews were free to enter, and to insinuate themselves
there. This has been done, and is being done at present.

During the discussion in the Viennese Reichsrath, regarding the Jewish
Question, the valiant orator, Lueger, said, amid the approval of the majority
of deputies:

> Is the universal domination of the Hebrews a fairy tale?
> Look at France, look at Hungary. In the latter country, the
> basest Hebrew has more power than the Cardinal Primate.
> And who, in Austria, in terms of evidence of the predomi-
> nance of the Jews, can deny that they own the ironmaking
> industry of the North, and the oil concerns, and the coal; and
> that everything cedes to their advantage? And is it not a seri-
> ous argument in favor of their predominance, that the presi-
> dent of the Reichsrath intends to ask our colleague, Pattaï,
> not to speak here of Rothschild, for fear that he might cut
> down our public funding?

Property Extortion

Something similar also enlivens the example of Austria-Hungary, so cor-rupted by Judaism, worse than a vine fallen prey to caterpillars. An explana-tion is required.

The progeny of Abraham has increased by 1.8 percent annually: from 1,154,000 in 1869, now to 1,648,708. The legal limit on the possession of property by the Hebrews was lifted after 1848 in Hungary, and after 1862 in the rest of the Empire. In such a brief interval, the Rothschild family, in Bo-hemia alone, acquired a quarter of the land, as well as possession of 60 of the oldest homes in the realm; and now they possess seven times more than the imperial family. Today, in the realm of Saint Stefan, the Jews have in their power so many nobles, that they enjoy more than a quarter of the electoral votes in the elections for the highest positions; and they have begun to pluck the titles and the names of the most illustrious lineages of that region. Half of the County of Nyitra now belongs to a single Hebrew, Baron Poppel.

The Hungarian public debt, which in 1873 was $221 million, rose in 1885 to $1,461 million, and now is more than $1,600 million. And the Min-ister, Tisza, the great patron of the Jews, three years ago proposed giving a seat of honor in the court to Alberto Rothschild and his wife, in recognition of his merits in sponging off the national credit. This only adds to the mockery.

But the most desolate example is Galicia. The Jews, in just a little more than 20 years, have assumed ownership of 80 percent of its territory, fol-lowed by gaining ever more power and holdings, and auctioning off all lands failing to pay taxes.

The arrogance of this race in the Hapsburg Empire has come to such, that not long ago a Jewish municipal lawyer from Vienna publicly responded to a Christian, who was complaining of the great amount of power being ceded to the Jews: "If the Christians are unable to tolerate this state of affairs, the remedy is clear: leave the Empire, emigrate somewhere else more hospi-table." Many will take this advice, since 2 million foreign usurers have ap-propriated the patrimony of 40 million Austro-Hungarians, who have ex-tended hospitality and civil equality to them. And throughout the Empire, cultivation of land by slaves will return, who make money for the new own-ers. The descendants of the old princes and magnates will dig the gardens and the fields of the emancipated rag dealers of Vienna, of Presburg, of Bu-da; and their children will wash the feet of Sara and Guiditte.

We could also cite the example of the Balkans, especially Romania, upon which the Congress of Berlin of 1878, dominated by hidden Jewish power, imposed the obligation of making the Jews fully equal both on the national and civic levels. We are also able to state that, in Russia, the land owned by the nobility is more than two-thirds mortgaged to German bankers who are mostly Jews, and farm lands fall daily into the hands of the usurers.

But let us also cast a glance at our Italy, where Judaism has been both boss and plunderer for 30 years. In Italy, there are approximately 50,000 Jews who have burrowed into the peninsula, and who have their headquarters in Venice, in Mantovano, in the ancient Extended States, and in Ferrara. In this region, which can be called Jewish Italy, they rule over everything. No one spends a lira without benefiting them. Commerce, industry, currency exchange, wholesale, country and city real estate are in their hands. It is enough to note that a quarter of the provincial territory of Padova is owned by Hebrews, and a fifth more of the mortgages are in their hands. Ancona, Livorno, and Florence live under the yoke of the usury of the Israelites. Among them, many already look forward to the day when the most sumptuous villas, the biggest land holdings, and the most famous patrician palaces will fall into their baskets, so as to be, by these acquisitions, powerful over the discouraged or imbecile owners, who are unable to free themselves from them. Two years ago, one of these Hebrews, who perhaps not long ago was selling matches somewhere in Florence, died, leaving to his children the blessing of $18 million in cash, accumulated as God ordained.

And how can we speak of Rome, which is caught in the noose of the great Jewish snare, that binds it by every sort of petty and grand theft. Rome is swallowed by a succession of troubles, of weeping, of misery moving one to pity. Usury in this capital is due more to the Jews than the Italians; the Jews reign supreme; and through usury they make their sumptuous way to smuggling, graft, and plunder. And they also penetrated into the recesses of that purse called 'the public works,' the monopolies and the various companies that serve the state. It is horrible to see the millions swallowed up by that same lack of concern with which the Grand Master of Italian Masonry earned his fame: through the national tobacco concession. In August 1887, a Jew from Rome wrote these noteworthy words to his German-Jewish son:

> The honorable [prime minister] Francesco Crispi is the best
> friend of the Hebrews and he protects their interests with all
> his soul. Because of this, we Jews in Italy have great influence

in the government. He makes us so happy, because we are able to hope for sufficient power to be able to prosper and to reap the fruit of our labor, without being bothered.[32]

The French Revolution

Above all other countries, France merits treatment here. Drumont's revelations clarified the accumulation of money made by the Hebrews, under the aegis of the rights of man, which was disseminated a hundred years earlier. Let us follow up on this. In 1791 the Jews there were few, only a few thousand; more often than not, they were stealing from the realm, an evil plague on the nation. Today there are perhaps 60,000 to 100,000, all with looks, language, and names that show that they have come from Frankfurt, Hamburg, Poland, and Portugal. The French Revolution of 1793—bloody and practically wiping out the goods of the nobility and the clergy—attracted them, like a pack of rapacious vultures. A century later they have also become, perhaps even more so than in the Austrian Empire and in Italy, dominant in every area.

Recent figures show that the *Jews own half the total capital in circulation in the world*, and in France alone possess 80 billion francs. In the French capital, they handle between 150 and 200 billion francs! In order to get an idea of the monstrous fortune accumulated there by the Jews, it is convenient to compare their number with those of the nationals. Here is the comparison: on average, each Jew possesses between 800,000 to 1,200,000 francs; whereas, each Frenchman, using the same data, only has no more than 6,000 francs. The house of Rothschild, on its own, notoriously possesses a fortune of 300 billion francs. The Prince of Bismarck affirmed that when old Giacomo, the founder of that house, died, he left his beneficiaries 100 million, accumulated in about fifty years. But when he came to France, his fortune was no more than 10 million!

Everyone in Paris knows the palaces of this family of Hebrew Croesuses. These homes are valued at 30 million, and the lavish interior decoration at another 30 million. An equal sum is reckoned for the castles and factories they own. There is another 120 million of worth that this one house enjoys, that they dangle in broad daylight right under the eyes of the French, who are not ignorant of their billions in liquid capital. But that isn't all. The main banks are all held among Jews and not Frenchmen, and they possess inestimable

---

[32] *Judische Press* (Jewish Press), 8 August 1887.

wealth. The litany of the princes of Israel is long; and all have last names that do not sound French, like those of Arabs or Zulus: Dreyfus, Bichoffsheim, Oppenheim, Erlanger, Hottinguer, and on and on. They form a banking Sanhedrin, one that possesses a total of at least 10 billion francs, all extracted from the veins of the French, thanks to 'the rights of man,' invented by them and granted to this cosmopolitan and voracious race.

Among over 600 bankers, most of them in Paris, at least 300 are provably Jews, another 100 are probably so. The trade and the profession, then, of high finance is a quick route to hegemony, and almost everything is snatched up by it. Half of the gold smithing, of the jeweler, the antiquarian, the fur and diamond trades are dominated by the Hebrews. The best is monopolized and captured by them, and usury is flaunted, ostentatiously and without restraint.

And they know the ways, worse than by usury, with which to aggrandize themselves with the safes full of French money. There are the innumerable bankruptcies; there are the famous swindles of hundreds and hundreds of millions, cynically carried out with feigned lending and tricks, such as was done in Honduras and Panama by the General Union, that controlled the metal resources, and by the *Comptoir d'escompte* [discount bank], which are remembered by all.

In the colony of Algeria, which was bled by the Hebrews like a body in the tentacles of an octopus, by the Jew, Crémieux, during the war of 1870. This was a masterpiece of perfidy; they gave themselves a share in the rights of the French and of the Arabs. In the Parisian newspaper *La France*, certainly not hostile to Judaism, Mr. Hugonnet wrote on 3 July 1884 that this race of usurious thieves loaned soldiers one franc, in order to gain two the next day; that the rate of usury was 3,650 francs per 100. Maupassant, describing the Algerian ghettoes where filthy Hebrews in Arab dress would loan a man a silver shield, making the man sign a note to give him back four in six months, or 20 per year. If the poor man could not do it, the greedy Jew, with his coupon in his hand, made him give him a handful of land, if he possessed that much; or a camel, or a horse, or some beans that he had in his hovel. Through this artful method, eventually all of southern Algeria came under the power of the Israelites.

Professor Ratzinger has legitimately observed that the expropriation of French society by means of liquid capital proceeds as though by a rule, like a law of nature. If nothing is done to check its course, in 50, or at most, in 100 years, all of European society will be abandoned to the discretion of a handful of Jewish bankers. If they continue to enjoy the full security that they now have, in terms of civil equality, they will increase two and threefold. If, in France, in a century, the Jews have been able to take over the magnificent sum of nearly 80 billion francs, in another century the entire national patrimony will be in their grip. Sixty thousand people comprise a financial feudal bloc, which will have for its servants and slaves, 36 million Frenchmen. And this will be the well-deserved crown on the overall work, having arrived at that point through the promulgation of 'the rights of man.'

Since today one cannot negotiate a loan in Europe without the good will of the Rothschilds, in a short amount of time, no one will be able to do any business at all without the consent of the international Jewish league. Judaism brings with itself a barbarous world, because of its adoration of the golden calf, which represents its power. Pietro Ellero exclaimed, "There is no virtue on Earth but work, no religion other than money, no priesthood other than the businessman, no rite other than money-changing, no God but money".[33] Hence, the crystal-clear effect of Hebrew hegemony!

Journalism and Education

Because of their financial predominance, the Israelite race controls that which directly subdues the spirit: we mean the domain of the public press and of the academy. In 1848, at the Jewish Congress in Krakow, attended by the world's richest Hebrews, it was decreed that all over Europe, Jews should become the owners of the most powerful newspapers in Europe. "By means of this," said the statute that was approved, "the Hebrew Star will spread its light over all the world." And only those most out of touch would be unable to concede that this decree was indeed carried out.

Journalism and higher education are the two wings of the Israelite dragon, as it goes plundering and corrupting everything in Europe. Pastor Stoecker, mentioned here earlier, told London's *Pall Mall Gazette*, "The Jews buy the press, so that half of the newspapers are in their power, and they use it to broadcast their ideas." In the Berlin Parliament, they have denounced Jewish influence over the schools because it is the wellspring of indescribable depravity. Recent German reports cite that out of more than 1,000 students who are enrolled in higher studies in Germany, 830 are Israelites.

In the Viennese Parliament, Deputy Lueger, in March of this year, told his colleagues:

---

[33] *Questione sociale* (The social question).

Remember, Sirs, that our schools are in the hands of the Hebrews, that our Christian teachers are being suddenly put on trial, and not the least of the accusations against them are made by Hebrews; that our employees are unable to say that they are Christians, if they wish to evade persecution; that our newspapers that publish Christian writings are continually suppressed.

He also remarked that the Empire's universities are running over with Jewish teachers; and that especially in the Catholic university of Vienna, there are no longer any baptized professors, except those in the theology faculty; all of the others, without exception, are circumcised. At present even the prestigious rector is Jewish. What else? Trying to choose a teacher for the unfortunate Archduke Rodolfo, they found that they could do no better than the Hebrew journalist, Weil, who then converted to Christianity, and took the name of the knights of Weilen; he proceeded to destroy the piety and the innocence of the young and most unfortunate prince.[34]

The same has befallen Italy. One can truthfully say that almost all of liberal journalism of every type is directly or indirectly manipulated by Jews. Milan, Turin, Venice, Modena, Bologna, and Florence live by public opinion created in the ghettoes and in the synagogue. The so-called official newspapers are all, more or less, Jewish goods sold to the government. In Rome, it is the same. The most widely read newspapers, such as *La Riforma, La Tribuna, L'Opinione, Il Diritto, Il Messagero, La Capitale, Il Capitan Francesca*, all issue from out of the brain of the sons of Jacob.

What can one say about public education? We are surrounded by Hebrews in the university, by Hebrews in the lycée, in the gymnasium, by Hebrews in the elementary schools. It is enough to report that in a count made in 1885, a quarter of the students in our universities were Jews.

Now let's return to France. In general, all of the republican newspapers there are forged in the Jewish crucible. Drumont exposed this incredible situation to public view. But what is worse, all of the irreligious and pornographic press is Jewish-owned.[35] It sullies the country and has no equal in

---

[34] *Ed.:* Rudolf, Prince of Austria, would later commit suicide, dying in 1889 at the age of 30.

[35] *Ed.:* This is a striking parallel to the present day, where Jews have long dominated the print and Internet pornography business.

any barbarian place. And as Judaism controls the domains of the daily press, and of books, thus it also controls education; the majority of the texts employed in the public schools are compiled by Hebrews.

In sum, then, in Christian Europe, the Jews enjoy civil equality, and through it, they also monopolize journalism, publishing, and education. As a result, these areas suffer under the maleficent influence of their anti-Christian spirit.

Parliamentary Power

But these are only the means to the primary goal: of effectively predominating over the affairs of State, and to lead the states to their end. Since the Jews are singularly shrewd servants of the rights of equality, they have used this to influence public policy, the army, the Parliament, and the Council of Ministers, just as they have taken over the schools. It can be asserted that the Austrian empire is governed, in part secretly and in part openly, by the Hebrews. When this story becomes well known to everyone, it will be demonstrated that the great military disasters of Austria—in Magenta, in Solferino, and in Sadova—occurred because of the crimes of the Jews, and were not due to the strategies employed by the French and Prussian armies.

Italy proves the point: In 1859, it became a reign of Hebrews, who knew how to cheat the great multitude of fools, passing themselves off as great patriots. The valiant Professor Giovanni DeStampa exclaimed:

> What a disgrace for Italy, a nation known for its strength and freedom, to have a parliament which seems more like a synagogue! Italy has 30 million inhabitants and 50,000 of them are Jews. Thus, Parliament should not be half Hebrew. Yet one finds them there and in great and terrible numbers. Venice has the honor of being represented in Parliament almost completely by Jews.[36]

---

[36] *La piaga ebrea* (The Hebrew Plague), page 17. *Ed.:* This is a truly remarkable statement. If Italy is dominated by 50,000 Jews out of 30 million, this represents just 0.16%. Clearly, any nation wishing to be free of Jews must restrict the Jewish percentage to well below 0.1%. This marks a notable contrast with present-day America, which has almost 2% Jews (6 million out of some 330 million).

Since then, they reign in Parliament. Thus they hold the majority of public offices, as well as most of the posts in banking, in the ministries, and in diplomacy. No matter where one goes, one runs into a Jewish inspector, a commission president, a magistrate, secretary, or lawyer. And what about in the municipalities? In most of them, the Jews exercise despotic authority. And haven't we seen Rome taken over, in the most jealously guarded areas, by Hebrews, who do not even have Italian names, but who are held in great esteem by everyone in our city? In a hundred Italian cities, this can be proven, just by observing the signs over the stores in the most populated areas.

The same can be said of France. In the Senate and in the Camera of Paris there are 20; and these represent no more than 60,000 of their own people. If the Christians were represented at this rate, Parliament would count no less than 40,000 representatives, divided between deputies and senators. A few years ago, 42 departments were governed by Jewish Prefects; and among Prefects, Sub-Prefects and general receivers, the number of Jews amounted to more than 200.

The revolution of 4 September 1870 catapulted the Jews to the apex of power;[37] and the ferocious governor of the Paris Commune was one of them. And his chiefs and primary assistants number nine more. Among them, there was Gustave Dacosta, who threw out the priests; Lisbonne who donned a biretta, served by a prostitute in a nun's habit; and Simone Mayer, who presided over the destruction of the columns of the Vendome. They settled into the Republic, appointing ministers, among them not only Crémieux, Raynal, Magnin, and Lockroy; but also Say, Ferry, and Floquet, all married to Jewish women.

As in Italy, so also in Austria-Hungary and in Germany. These bigwigs took over the financial and political sectors, in service of their own interests and their power. They are supported by a journalism that confuses, swindles, deceives, and frightens off whoever does not wish to be molded by Judaism. Thus the cry: "The Jews are the bosses, they crush us under their feet, they reduce us to nothing."

---

[37] *Ed.:* The French government collapsed in 1870 after defeat in the Franco-Prussian war.

World Jewish Alliance

But the crowning achievement is the World Jewish Alliance. With the help of the Masonic sects, this group has increased modern Jewish power a hundredfold. It was founded in Paris by Crémieux, and then fanned out all over the world, conferring on various groups of Jews everywhere the vigor of the entire body of Israel. Its founder was therefore correct in describing it as "the most beautiful and fertile institution that has ever been created in modern times, and an instrument of domination so powerful that it governs the world." In fact, it is a type of *government*, the official representative of the Hebraic nation, one that grants the right to speak in its name.[38]

It is simple in its organization. Every Jew can take part, on the condition that he pays a tax of ten francs per year. It is ruled by a 60-member Sanhedrin, called the Central Committee, which resides in Paris and represents the various locales. These directors are elected by universal suffrage, and remain in power for nine years, with a third of them replaced every three years. Additionally, there are ten members who form a local commission, who are in turn able to set up a regional commission. This interdependent structure treats the issues which are important for the entire association. The number of members, or adepts, is more than 30,000, with a million francs in capital; however, the exact amount has not been exactly disclosed, because the Croesuses of the brotherhood carefully withhold the actual amount.

Numerous other organizations are clustered around this center, from every country. Through the influential press outlets that form the beak of the Alliance, other periodicals and papers are also part of the Jewish-owned press. "The Alliance is neither French, nor German, nor English; it is Jewish, it is universal. The felicitous success and prosperity it has obtained is due to this same universality."

Whoever might wish to understand this Alliance need only read the infamous novel *The Wandering Jew*, written by Eugene Sue against the Society of Jesus. This calumny against the Jesuits is actually the story of this Alliance; and the same Jews act as though they are astonished by any such comparison.

---

[38] *Ed.:* Today this group is known as Alliance Israélite Universelle; it is still a leading advocate of Jewish interests in France.

One of their spokesmen in the general assembly of February 1870, who addressed Sue's comparison between this organization and the Society of Jesus, said:

> The comparison between the two societies is true in terms of both being worldwide; but no further. But the difference between the two is enormous! One (the Jesuits), uses its power to oppress; the other (Judaism), to liberate. The Jesuits fan out in order to suffocate freedom; Judaism to bring it; the Jesuits bring the coldness of death, Judaism the warmth of life.

It is always the language of Satan, their father ("you are of your father, the devil," John 8:44), who is the prince of turning lies into truth and life into death.

It is not difficult to argue that through this Alliance, this group, that is now in the bosom of many nations, forms an army of stateless men who pledge obedience to the commands that come from a single center. The Israeli Alliance works through the power of Freemasonry, and its union is held together by the lodges that rule over the barbarous underworld.

Whence Freemasonry?

Let us now assert, along with various other authors, that the sect of Freemasonry was, in its first instance, created by Jews. This assertion is now proven, although it is contrary to what the more cautious historians say. It is certainly true that Judaism in past centuries was the one to introduce Masonry; and using its diabolic talents, Judaism imbued it with its spirit, directing it toward its goals, incorporating itself into it and making it part of its living power, in order to lead it wherever it wished.

In order to arrive at this perfect model of domination—which was always and still is the ultimate superstition of Talmudism—the Jewish genius understood that there was a formidable obstacle in its way, one that barred them from the baptized world, consequently making it impossible to gain access to the much-coveted gentile domain. That is to say, this obstacle was the Christian religion—the basis of all of the institutions and laws, and from which, over the centuries, flowed the regulation of civil order. But in order to gain access to the structure of the Christian religion, and especially of Catholicism, it occurred to the Hebrews that the best method would be to work 'under water' by deceptively sending out their representatives to run ahead of them, and hiding themselves behind; this, in order to hide the Jewish claw from all blame. In sum, they needed to make their assault through soldiers not their own, so as to capture the fort in the name of liberty. It was therefore necessary to scale this stony foundation in order to overturn the entire edifice of Christianity. And in service of this, they have joined hands with the head of the occult world, by means of Freemasonry, which is subject to them.

Thus, the bonds that unite modern Judaism to Freemasonry are now evident, and ought to put to rest any doubts. The study of the so-called Semitic Question in France, in Germany, in Italy, and elsewhere, once inscrutable and only able to be seen in the shadows, has now come out into the light. It is now known how the Talmudic Cabala was introduced into the rites, mysteries, symbols, and allegories of the Masonic degrees. It is also known that the Jews have not only intermingled with all of the lodges, and so increased their numbers, but they have also then filled the lodges with their own advocates. Through them, they reign over and direct the others, and anyone who gets entry must be approved by the Jews, who rule by blood and by cult. It can be said with complete confidence that everything in Freemasonry is ordained by a Jewish Sanhedrin, and no other power can obtain except that which comes through this nefarious sect. Thus it is that one of the most qualified of the French periodicals has legitimately written that "Judaism and Freemasonry seem today to be able to be explained as an identical entity. It necessarily follows that for Judaism to govern the world, Freemasonry was made Jewish and Judaism made Freemasonic".[39]

Among the many authors who have published books, all enlivened by documents and various argumentation that have demonstrated this intimate connection, the best is by the illustrious Professor Martinez, whose work we have quoted. It would be a great benefit to Italy if it were translated.[40]

Liberty and Judeo-Masonry

In sum, Judaism is comprised of love and hate: the insatiable love of money, *auri sacra fames*, and the insatiable hatred of Christ. The love serves the hate; and the hatred and the love drive them on to the *apogée* of power, which is the Satanic delirium of degenerate Israel. To know the history of

---

[39] *Revue des questions historiques* I (Review of Historical Questions), 1 April 1882.
[40] *Le juif, viola l'ennemi* (Behold the Enemy, the Jew), Vol. 1.

Masonry is to see, from previous centuries all the way up to our own, that their concerted gaze was fixed on accumulating wealth and fighting to the death against Christ and His Church. All of the power, both overt and covert, of Freemasonry was pressed into service by the avaricious Jew, and by the Jewish anger that was bent on felling Christian power, in order to attempt to set up its own empire on its ashes. From 1 May 1789, the day when the 'rights of man' were devised purely on behalf of the Jews, until 20 September 1870, when Rome was conquered with bombs and the Pope was made a prisoner, the conspiracies, uproars, rebellions, assassinations, massacres, and wars, in fact everything associated with revolutionaries, always emerged from and moved toward the same end: greater wealth and opulence accruing to the Jews, and of depriving and oppressing Christian civilization.[41]

Freedom—which is the pretext for ascending the throne, in hatred of the true God and Christ—*was always used by the Jews.* Through it, they have acquired complete power in service of overcoming nations, and of ordaining that the few must tyrannize all. And they tyrannize them through legal imposture over their possessions, conscience, faith, and family. Out of the spasm of 'liberty, equality, and fraternity' emerged the despotism of this tyrannical oligarchy, who have formed the modernist States, and to whom the modern States are subjugated. They are the Jewish oligarchy, or the Masonic oligarchy, the interweaving capillaries of the Jews. Catholic religious freedom was forbidden; this is the 'freedom' of Judeo-Masonry. The liberty of bestiality and of sacrilege was converted into a public right; this is its 'equality.' Brutal hatred against whoever professes faithfulness to God and his fathers was applauded as love of country; this is its 'fraternity.' In Rome of the Popes, when they held processions, the Cross of Christ was debased; but the bust of Giordano Bruno, votary of Satan, was carried aloft, and paid noble homage. Thus it is a simple and practical fact that Judaism and Masonry are identical, like the gun in the hand of the assassin who shoots it, like the torch in the fist of the arsonist who clutches it.

Thus the Jews fatten themselves on everything, and satiate themselves on the blood of the people and the Church; but the Freemasons are always claiming an empty stomach. Look at Italy. Most of the Freemasons rise up from beggary to opulence. Our Freemasons aspire to the glory of dying

---

[41] *Ed.:* 1 May 1789 was the date of the "Estates General," a general assembly that effectively marked the beginning of the French Revolution. On 20 September 1870, Italian civil authorities finally defeated the political power of the Papal States, ending a 1,000-year Catholic reign of power.

'poor'; but poor with villas, poor with palaces, poor with holdings, poor with the millions they leave to their beneficiaries. We see matriculated sectarians who collect huge pensions, accumulated without scruples; we see the venerable of the lodges who fix the laws in the public administration and smell of millions of dollars' worth of tobacco. We see heroes of that sect who don't know how to resist the temptation of a bribe of two million, in order to be immortalized with statues in all of the cities. We see the children of these heroes who sell Caprera twice over and pocket huge sums, while deploring the prevailing misery. Our Freemasons have not perfected the art of making quadruple profits, like the Hebrews; but both together have perfected the art of snatching up everything, for love of Italy.

Whoever then hurts Masonry actually pokes Judaism in the eye; and whoever offends Judaism, wounds the heart of Masonry. They have in common gluttony of money and of arrogance, and they also co-exist because of their shared program against Christianity. For instance, there is the French example. The war cry "Clericalism is the enemy" was conceived among the overflowing jewel cases of the Jew, Rothschild, and broadcast by way of Cousin, Grand Master of Masonry, to Gambetta, who taught it to his bandits. The fiercest chiefs of the crusade against clericalism—that is, against the Catholic Christian religion—were Dreyfus, the Herolds, the Mayers, the Naquets, the Spullers, the Lockroys, the Ollendorfs, all foreign Jews. Among the more pitiless persecutors of Catholicism, the prize goes to the Jews Hendlé, Schnerb, and Levaillant. The Jew, Sée, invented the young girls' lycée, in order to dechristianize French girls as much as possible. The Jew Giedroye mutilated the great classics, in order to purge the holy name of God, so that young scholars would never read it.

The Jew, Lyon-Alemand, ruined a teacher, because he had dared, in a book submitted for publication, to praise the beneficial influence of Christianity on civilization. The Jew, Naquet, proposed and saw to it that the laws promoting divorce were approved. The Jews tore down crucifixes in the Paris schools, breaking them and throwing them into the sewers; and they doggedly defend the mandatory secular primary school, which is against the Christian God. The Jews demanded that the church of the Pantheon be consecrated; and all of these things were allowed. The Jews wanted to disband the religious orders and throw the male religious out of their houses and likewise dispatch the nuns; and immediately it was done. The Jews glutted France with the most lurid, outrageous, and nauseating journalism imaginable; and the Masons happily promoted it. In substance, the Jews oversee the work of destroying Christianity and every noble national tradition; and the renegade Masons promoted it among the people there.

We have emphasized France as an example. But we are able to trace the same situation in all of the other countries in which the Jew has been granted complete freedom through civil rights. Everywhere, holding hands with the Freemasons, they insidiously reach for the money and unveil themselves as being against the Christianity of the people. In the United States of America, abusing the freedom conceded them by the Republic of Washington, the Hebrews are already champions of the neutral public school, out of hatred of the Catholics, who wish to have free and Catholic schools for their children.

The same is true here in Italy. Aside from journalism, which the Jews openly operate, for the rest they operate more discreetly, quickly extending their hands from behind the rocks. The ruins that were amassed over 30 years of the Masonic revolution have only become more extensive, to the great loss of Christianity and Italy. Through this, Judaism took over so many sectors, all of which now belong to them. Mazzini plotted with the synagogue; the fruits of their mutual affection was made clear at the Campidoglio of Rome; Garibaldi plotted with the synagogue, and so did Cavour, Farini, and Depretis. And the humble servants of the synagogue were heralded as great, and a credulous public erected busts and monuments of them, so as to glorify the love of liberty and of country.

If it is not superfluous to continue in service of proving a fact, brighter than the noonday sun, then we shall discuss the ultimate prize in the eyes of Judaism—something to be gained by means of its anti-Christian and depraved program, by means of Masonry.

Global Power Objective

This prize is universal domination: the power of the world, taken to be article of faith by the degenerate Cabbalists of Israel. An authoritative author, in one of his books of 1859, wrote:

> About 30 years ago, around 1859, a well-known Viennese diplomat recounted the story of his voyage from a South American capital city to Europe. Traveling with him was a Brazilian minister, who at that time was in charge of foreign affairs, and who was also the Grand Master of the Masonic

lodge of Brazil. The long and tedious sea journey caused the two statesmen to strike up a bit of a friendship. "You shall see," the Grand Master said one day to the other, "that three great monarchies will be formed in Europe: the Roman one, under the House of Savoy, the German monarchy under the Hohenzollern, and the Slavic, under the Romanoff-Gottorf. These three Monarchies shall serve as paths to three great European republics, from which then shall be born the great republic of all humanity, which is the project of all of the initiated brotherhood".[42]

Through this Republic, Judaism intends to assert its power over all, as it already has done in France.

Celebrating the first 100-year anniversary of the French Revolution, the Grand Orient Lodge of Paris held a Congress composed of representatives from two hemispheres—which is to say, a worldwide Congress. The acts of this combined council have come to light through the speeches and toasts that were made there. On what point did most of the speakers dwell upon for their prophecies? Here it is: That the Christian world, 100 years after the revolution of 1789, will be at death's door; and by the year 2000 will be finished; that the destruction of the Monarchy and of religion, in the countries still immune to the benefits of the joy of 1789, will be near; that finally that great universal Republic will arise—an event they look forward to administering with passionate enthusiasm.[43]

The goods of the monarchy will be auctioned off, along with the dynastic tradition, the moral and civil patrimony of the various nations. The religious communities that had been protected by the Monarchy, by force of the states, will then be overpowered in every country by Masonry. Thus do they plot ruin in order to replace the solidity of the thrones with the fragility of "government by the people," and all of this is simply an instrument toward the purposes of a race that has neither country, nor public cult, nor its own armies, but lives dispersed everywhere, in order to subject everyone.

It is also good to note that, in Europe, the political, religious, and economic disorder, mainly derived from the Jewish Question, established a *socialism* that enlivens the vein and pulse of the Jew. Thus it seems that there

---

[42] *Interessante Eushüllungen der Freimauerei* (Interesting Packages of Freemasonry).
[43] See *L'Univers* (The Universe), 5 August 1890.

ought to be, in our times, a just scourging, to crush the Judaic pride and to make them pay the price of their Luciferian arrogance.

Part III : The Remedies

Revolution

Some years ago, a French writer completed a sharp work on the Jewish invasion of his country, using a rationale that, in substance, can be summarized as follows.

French Christians have never forgotten that these Jews—by name and birth *barbarians*, most of whom are not pure—have become their overlords in less than a century. Their influence occurred in three phases: in 1791, when all of the national institutions collapsed; in 1815, when France fell prostrate; and in 1870, when the German armies mutilated France.

In 1789, when the era of revolution against the hegemony of the nobility and clergy began, what militated against these two ranks of our civilization? Their ownership of two-thirds of French soil. Taine recently justified the basis for this ownership. The nobility was formed in order to defend the nation against external enemies, and thus procure security and glory for the nation. The clergy have well-merited credit for civilizing the nation, of having sweetened our customs, of enriching us through knowledge and churches, and through many thousands of expressions of charity.

Before the Revolution, the clergy's combined capital was estimated at about 4 billion francs. In 1789 there were at least 130,090 priests and religious; that comes to 30,000 francs for each. But after the Revolution, this was reduced to an income of 1,500 francs. To understand the magnitude of this, one need only look at the great number of people who cashed in on this reduction of capital to the clergy, and at the privileges that were passed around everywhere. Who can deny that a legitimate ancestry was subjected to an enormous abuse; and essentially confiscated?

A hundred years later, there are no longer 130,000 priests and religious, but 60,000 foreign, non-French Jews, who head a social order that is not marked by distinguished service toward the nation. Rather, they are a voracious mob of worldly superfluities, who, 100 years later, have snatched up in our house, not a sum of 4,000, but 90 billion francs.

And now, lords as they are over the public trust, they ardently inflame the common people, goading them against the clergy. The wicked popular passions they arouse form a screen for their monstrous wealth. At the time of the first Revolution, they reproved the clergy for their 4 billion francs. Yet, today isn't it amazing to see the fortune of just one family of Jews—the Rothschilds—who have amassed it by bleeding the nation from behind the scenes, in less than 70 years? And what's more, this race was not content with bleeding us. They also made haste to kidnap the faith of Christ and all that is most beautiful in our culture!

Thus did the passionate French writer end by exclaiming: "Christian Frenchmen, let us join together to thwart the wicked tricksters. Let us form a defense league against these enemies of the name, race, belief, and fatherland of our traditions."

A similar cry is heard in other countries. It might even reach those where there is, as of yet, no outcry—but which may soon reach the boiling point.

How to Defend?

But will such defense leagues, made up of many hopefuls, be one of the effective remedies for resolving the Question of the Jews—who, with each passing day, inflict their greed upon the people, through their oppressive and suffocating power?

Whoever knows their history is aware that the question of the power of the Jews who live among the Christians is as old as Christianity itself. There is no nation whose history does not include a record of rescinding permission for Jews to stay in their country, banishing them with solemnity, because of the abuse and disorder they inflicted. But, today, at the end of our century, the Hebrew race is no longer merely tolerated in our Christian countries, and (as in the past) viewed with suspicion as enemies, foreigners, and malefactors, and regulated by the laws of exception, which constituted the common defense against their residing in those countries. At present, this is no longer the case. Thanks to the principles of the Revolution that prevail now everywhere, the Jew was admitted and treated to equal rights. The laws proclaim that he is "fully equal" to everyone else, and accord him equal protection. Thus the politics of the defense of Christian society has been abolished, and the Jew has been granted the complete freedom to destroy the same countries that have given him refuge.

Such is the highly principled conquest won through 'liberty,' which Judaism, allied with Freemasonry, underwrote, and because of which they united to obtain.

But in order to make themselves secure, they strove to deplete many national institutions of their intrinsic history and national identity. More or less, they succeeded in this—except in Russia, whose form of government assures that real power, direct and indirect, rests with the oligarchy. Modern parliaments, by contrast, pretend to govern in the name of national sovereignty, but in fact, exist for the few, who practice legal tyranny over all the others.

The principles of universal equality in all things were thus enshrined. Based on that right of equality, the prevailing parties have ruled the nations; *but the right of equality has no basis in religion.* Judaism, along with the instrument of Masonry, has been able to attain complete power, and has the Christian people at their mercy, plundering, corrupting, and trampling them, as is now occurring all over Europe.

The most legitimate weapon of defense against oppressive Judaism, is, however outside the grasp of Christians. Rather, because the insidious 'rights of man' are at their popular apex, promulgated in 1789, and by the parliamentary statutes in force today, there is no human hope for Christian liberation from the Judaic-Masonic yoke—something that prostitutes and perverts the populations.

The earlier quoted writer justifiably invites Christians to band together in a defense league; he demonstrates the necessity of doing so with these completely true words:

> The Jews, still barbarians in the 19th century, are also still the ancient offensive force, which today is a hundredfold stronger because they advanced through the breach opened to them by the Revolution. Secure in their triumph, they are pushing us over the precipice. You have lost the right to defend yourselves. Faced with a half-victorious enemy, you remain disarmed. Here is the danger that increased a hundred times over the risks of the past in our conflict with overarching Judaism. Which principles or rights are ever going to be able to repel the invasion? The State is atheistic, or if not atheistic, then religiously neutral, and so leaves the field open—not to *the best*, but to the most audacious in trickery. Additionally, Judaism has extracted absolute equality, unrestricted liberty, from all

citizens, and so society has been transformed into a struggle between diverse and opposing forces, in which the most powerful will have the upper hand. And this, unfortunately, is always the most unfair, regardless of dishonesty in the choice of weapons.

Defense Proposals

Having established this, we refer now to some proposals by certain publicists who, being both motivated against Jewish wealth and also by religious or patriotic zeal, seek something more than a moderate form of justice.

In Germany, Austria, and France, there is a school of thought which advances the most radical solution of liberation from the Jewish plague, but one which does not conform to the Christian spirit; and which is, at present, practically speaking, impossible. After proving, with hundreds of facts and documents, that, in general, the Hebrews are a plague on Christian society, and a scourge on the Church of Jesus Christ, they argue that the right of *making war against them*, as a public enemy, has thus been demonstrated. But they do not agree to resort to bloodshed. Rather, they propose two more restrained solutions: (1) That the Jews return what has been stolen; and (2) that they be banished from the nations. Through the confiscation of their property, and through exile, the great evil done by them in countries that have given them the legal right of equality would be undone, and they would be punished for their wrongdoing.

Who can doubt that such confiscation would be just? The majority of the money possessed by the Jews was gotten by evil methods, accumulated by fraud, usury, and thievery. If no end is imposed on their scandalous accumulation, then in a few more decades, almost all of the fixed and liquid capital of the Christians will fall prey to them.   To take the ill-gotten gain from the thieves is most legitimate, if not by particular individuals, then by the nation so robbed.

What else? Another aspect is not agreed upon: that the goods accumulated by the Jews would be legitimately seized through the principle of the just war, with expropriation certainly being the lesser of two evils. Since the accumulation of wealth is the most powerful weapon employed by the Jews, and used toward the goal of exterminating religion and of oppressing the people, then, to say the least, in terms of a necessary defense, there is the right to take the money out of their clutches.

And another argument flows from that one, namely, that there is a right to *compensation* for the inestimable material and moral damage done to the Christian peoples.

This is echoed in the memorable sentence of the great Peter the Venerable: *Serviant populis christianis, etiam invitis ipsis, divitiae Judaeorum* ("Let the wealth of the Jews serve Christian people, even against their will").[44] Although greatly to their displeasure, the plenty harvested from the Jews is in the interest of the Christians.

That the first part of the remedy would result in a decrease in anti-Semitism is expressed by the vow: "Apply the laws to the Jews, the same Jews who have, with the sanction and approval of Freemasonry, ruled against the Church in Catholic countries." Through a two-pronged decree, we call for the seizure, without exception, of all Jewish goods. This would have the effect of immediately paying off the national debt.

Now we turn our attention to a critical examination of what has been proposed. We note that such an idea has many examples in history. But in order to be legitimate, such a confiscation must first of all be decreed by those who, in the various nations, have legally constituted authority; and secondly, that such be carried out according to the norms of Christian justice and charity.

Not all of the Jews are thieves, dissemblers, cheats, usurers, Freemasons, scoundrels, and corrupters of customs. Everywhere, one can count among them a certain number who are not complicit in the racketeering and knavery of the others. Should the innocent be included in the punishment of the others?

Supporters of the heroic remedy answer that, in war, even in the most just and holy wars, great numbers of innocents perish; that without distinction, the Hebrews act in solidarity with each other; that in all of their hearts, they nurture mortal hatred of the Christians; that all, under one guise or another, agree on the Christians' destruction; and finally, that the experience of former centuries has demonstrated this, since the Hebrew has always abused the mercy and charity of Christians in order to undermine them all over again. And that because of this, and not out of any vendetta, but because of the laws of necessary self-defense, the most radical position should be taken: *Salus populi, suprema lex esto* ("The people's welfare is the highest law").

At present, this idea is only a sketch, its details not filled in, and so we shall leave it for now. However, we emphasize that justice and charity ought,

---

[44] *Ed.:* Peter was a French abbot, circa 1100 AD.

always, to be upheld, and should win out over the crudity of overly draconian ideas.

Defense by Expulsion

According to the proponents of that remedy, confiscation would not be enough; they would also want the public enemy to be exiled. They do not say: "Death to the Jews!" Rather, they say: "Out with the Jews! Live, but far from us."

One French author claims that more than ten centuries of history have proven that our race is totally incompatible with the Jews. We are never able to live together, never immune from great risks. During the Renaissance, Bishop Simone Majoli, in his famous essay *On the Perfidy of the Jews*, told Christians that the only choice that they had for remaining free from these implacable enemies of their families, country, faith, peace, goods, was to recognize them as: traitors, the most wicked knaves of the human race, an army of harpies, devils, the scourge of decent men, unworthy of being tolerated. To concede to them, as did the Revolution, the right of citizenship, was to unleash vampires on the nation; it was to open, through human sentiment, the doors of a cage of ferocious beasts. This race has no right to be given shelter on our soil. Whenever this happens, it results in damage to the Christian faith. To entertain such an enemy is to give entry to those who want to expunge us from the Earth and deprive us of heaven.

We limit ourselves to observing that the banishment of Jews by empires and states has many examples: but banishment was legitimate because it was done by legitimate authorities. Additionally, if this remedy would be universally carried out in all of the civilized countries, where would more than 8 million Jews go? Once dispersed, how could they hide from everyone?

In certain circumstances and in particular countries, this mass banishment, as is today suggested, was justified; as a purely practical matter, it would not generally be possible. Additionally, it was always the attitude of the Church, the Popes, and the Catholic princes that, for almost twenty centuries, the Jews were cursed by deicide: "His blood be upon us and upon our children" (Matt 27:25). And yet:

> The Popes, citing the two Lemann brothers who converted
> from Judaism, always kindly permitted the Jews to sojourn in

their city. This exiled and errant people were permitted to go there, and in gratitude, they called Rome a Jewish Paradise.[45]

And the kings imitated the Popes. They tolerated the presence of the Jews in their countries; but through legal provisions, they also protected the sustenance and the faith of their Christian subjects. Thus, while admitting that the remedy of universal banishment of the Hebrews is not practical, it would also not be in keeping with the sentiment and the work of the Roman Church.

The Foreigner Concept

The followers of a more moderate school will, out of concern for the preponderance of Jewish power, offer suggestions of various types and measure, but which are nevertheless difficult to carry out in our time. Further, there are those who are concerned with moral arguments, with the relation of the Christians to the Hebrews, and with the politics regarding the freedom of the press, which is the main force of Jewish power, and with the tolerance of the Masonic sects. They also introduce arguments from social or economic viewpoints, especially those which refer to the ownership of land and to what is called capitalism.

It is clear that the usurious prices set by the Jews via real estate mortgages, year by year, facilitate the transfer of national land out of Christian hands and into Jewish ones. Through this vehicle, in Austria, 10,000 farms have fallen into Jewish hands; and in France and in Italy and elsewhere, much the same has happened. Eventually this will result in the arable land of these various countries being turned into vast estates, enjoyed by a handful of foreign Croesuses, to whom the people will be enslaved.

Thus, here is a simple remedy for such a great evil as this: a law composed of two articles: 1. All ownership of rural land in the country is forbidden to foreigners, and 2. Jews are included in the definition of 'foreigner.'

The first article would be a defensive and completely just form of national caution. If carried out, the prohibition would be restricted to rural property. Foreigners would still be able to own urban property. The second article's proposal would be based on the fact that the Jew is a cosmopolitan, and thus always and forever a Jew—never German, English, or Italian, no matter whether born in Germany, England, or Italy. Such cosmopolitanism

---

[45] *Rome et les Juifs* (Rome and the Jews).

of their race is even admitted by the Jews. As Pascal warned, it is folly to resort to equality and equal rights. A great statesman said that fairness is the necessity of having equal respect for those possessing different rights. This suited our ancestors quite well, and after all, resulted in a beautiful harmony—and not in anarchy, which we see all about us and deplore today.[46]

Thus a wise internal regulation of rural property, which would also result in protecting the minority and the weak, would be a good internal defense against the effects of a rapacious usury. Where not stabilized, it is certain that the proletariat of the cities will be overrun by those of the country; that is, the common people, who, loosed from their ties to the land, will be essentially expatriated, left without bed or roof, and made prey to whoever cares to use them to rebel against society.

No small measure of redress could be won through a complex series of good laws—such as against the abuses of capitalism, the vital center of today's Jewish power in Europe. Thus, what is termed 'money commerce,' beneath which the Hebrews sequester the most execrable infamy of usury, is tantamount to the ruin of the economic order of nations. In the same way, freedom of press is ruinous to the political and religious order. Professor Ratzinger judiciously advises:

> The expropriation of society, by means of fluid capital, is carried out with exactly the same precision as the laws of nature. If nothing is done to stop it, in 50 or 100 more years, all of European society will fall, bound wrists and foot, into the basket of a few score of Jewish bankers.

It is superfluous to our purpose here to treat the particulars of the many reforms expounded and illustrated by various proponents of this type of thinking. Such men are wise, motivated by the best intentions, as well as concerned for the rights of the Christian people, and who, in charity and justice toward the Hebrews, seek to free Christianity from the oppression of Judaism.

If Christianity cannot be saved from being flung over the political precipice of Masonry, then it will be vain to propose and discuss alternatives for liberation. The single most important thing is to turn back and retake the road badly chosen. If the Hebrews are not stopped with humane and Christian laws—except civil equality, to which they have no right, and which is just as pernicious for them as it is for Christians—then no remedy, great or

---

[46] *La Juiverie* (Jewry), page 107.

small, will matter. *Given* the reality of their presence in various countries; *given* the immutable nature of their being strangers in every country, and of their being enemies of the people in every country that supports their presence; *given* that they always are a separate society within the nations; *given* their Talmudic morality; *given* the fundamental tenet of their religion which impels them to seize, by any means, the goods of all, because they believe that the possessions and the power of the world belong to them; *given* the experience of many centuries; *and given* what they have done today and in the past—then, the equal rights conceded to them by Christians in Christian countries has resulted in the oppression of the Christians. From this emerges the point that the only way of allowing Jews to stay among Christians is to regulate them with such laws that at once impede the Hebrews from offending the rights of Christians, and by the same laws, impede the Christians from offending the rights of the Hebrews.

This is then what, by perfect or imperfect means, ought to happen because of what the Hebrews, over many centuries, have done. By force or by love, this will result in redress. And perhaps the Hebrews themselves will be constrained to ask that this be initiated. For the overpowering force set in motion by that revolutionary right has today resulted in the Jews constructing an abyss, as wide as it is deep, into which all will go. And at the first outburst of the whirlwind that they provoke, the nations that have foolishly exalted them will hurl them over the precipice—an unprecedented audacity in modern times.

Conversion to Christianity?

There is no dearth of writers who believe that the Jewish Question's resolution is to be found in the conversion of Israel to Christianity. They believe that this would be a triumph for the Church, one which will announce the end of the world—the conversion of the Jews being one of the prophesied signs precursing the return of the Hebrews to the God they forsook on the Cross of Calvary. But we see no sign of this conversion, which would have the advantage of returning to the Church the immense wealth seized by Judaism, and would also end the unlimited influence that Jewish material power exercises over all.

It is certainly true that the entry of the Jewish apostates into the breast of Christ is one of the signs given in sacred scripture as being the forerunner of the consummation of history. But since there is no sign of any such conversion, we are not persuaded. The errant and dispersed state of the Jewish people—which, according to the scriptures is their inherent condition—is living proof of the faith of Our Lord God, Jesus. After the destruction of Jerusalem, they have been without a king, without a priesthood, without a temple, without a nation, without a home, and the bitter enemy of the Church of Our Lord, Jesus—who was crucified by them. We discern no clear or subtle allusion to any change for the better; or that they intend to embrace as their savior the Jesus whom they killed.

What we do discern is the right of civil equality, which they enjoy everywhere today. There are some who think that this means that many Jews are in fact atheists and profess no religion except that of the golden calf. Other Christians, who have been influenced by Masonic liberalism, believe that they are moving toward the Church, in whose lap, without much of a fuss or uproar, they will climb in great numbers.

As we have seen and as we have proven at length, we can say that equality extended to the Jews by the anti-Christian party has everywhere usurped the governments of the people, and has had the effect of uniting Judaism with Masonry in the persecution of the Catholic Church. The effect has also been to elevate the Jewish race over the Christians, through occult power and manifest wealth. As is well known, some Jews have become Protestants; or rather, they have feigned converting to the rationalistic Christianity of the Lutherans, Calvinists, and the Anglicans. But it is also well known that these feigned conversions are motivated by something quite different than religion. Some do go from the synagogue to Catholicism. This is true, but it is done secretly. And exactly because it is done secretly is why such conversions are insufficient.

In every century, God has taken Jews into his Church in some measure—sometimes many, sometimes few. It would not be easy to compare today's numbers of Jewish converts with those of prior centuries. But certainly it can be said that at present, Judaism, taken as a whole, displays an unparalleled hatred and oppression of Christianity. And the satanic wave of anti-Catholic Masonry was shrewdly fed by the pen, the managers, the suggestions, and the money of the Israelites.

Unless the resolution of the Jewish Question in Europe will have a different resolution from that of the apostolate of Enoch and of Elias, we think that there will be a time when we shall see Europe become, after centuries, a huge plantation, exploited by Jews, worked with the sweat of Christians reduced to slavery. Consequently, there is no remedy that we can adopt that is, on the one hand, too harsh, and on the other, not harsh enough.

Apostasy and Punishment

We have clearly demonstrated the nature of a true solution to the problem, and a radical cure for the Jewish disease in Europe. If it has been proven that it is now a practical impossibility that the nations return to the Commandments as the basis of government—which are now usurped by the principles articulated by the French Revolution—then Christian society shall wait in vain for its liberation from the iron grip of the Jews. As long as sin endures, so shall the punishment also endure.

The apostasy of the Greeks was punished by the Mohammedans who annihilated their empire. The instrument of Heaven's chosen anger at today's degenerate Christianity is the Jews. Their power over Christianity is increasing because of the increase, throughout Christianity, of the replacement in the souls of Christians of the laws of God by the wicked spirit of 'the rights of man.' The justice of Eternity is being served up to an apostate and cursed people in order to scourge the apostasy of the nations by the most preferred mercy of this same justice.

France is our example of this. It just celebrated the first centenary of that Revolution which separated France from God, from the Church, and from her kings. But how did France celebrate? Prostrated in the dust before the Masonic temple of Solomon, humiliated under the feet of the Talmudic synagogue, in the clutch of a pack of foreign vultures who have already sucked out three-fifths of the patrimony of their ancestors. And thus, the Revolution of 1780 had the glorious advantage of moving from a noble respect of its most Christian kings, to ignoble servitude of the kings of mammon.

And from France we move on to Italy, where, in 30 years, Masonry, more so than in any other nation, has injected its poison of liberty, which has already murdered France. And the effects are most deplorable—not only in the political, economic, and moral realms, but also in terms of the slavery to the ghetto, which, by means of Masonry, oppresses Italy more each year.

Yet, laws are being formulated by Christians who wish to shore up the bursting floodgates of Judaism, which, loosed from all restraints, devastates the most precious treasury of the Faith and of our civilization. These laws propose the idea of the necessity of shutting off this flood at its source. Thus the proponents of those laws write, publish, speak, and work toward such a solution, and always within the confines of what the Gospel teaches as permissible. But anyone possessing genuine love of religion and of country never tires of reiterating this one great truth: that with respect to the nations that are in a state of apostasy from the Church because they have followed Masonic impostors, *the Hebrews are the scourge of God's justice*. And all of the sweet lies of liberalism will result in their being snared in the trap of the voracious octopus of Judaism.

Tousle, Proudhon, Lafargue, and a hundred others predicted what would be the resolution of the Jewish Question in Europe. As the barbarians from outside loosed their corruption on the Roman world, thus the barbarians inside will resolve the Question of the Jews. We refer to the so-called ruling class, or bourgeoisie, who have been seduced, inebriated, and ground into bits between the bones of Judaism. Haven't they refused, out of hatred of Christ, every proposed social reform? Thus, a new Attila will be unleashed upon their republics, their monarchies, their institutions, their treasuries, their theaters, their bureaus, their places of recreation and delight. And they will all wind up ruined by Jews.

Haven't they all repudiated Christ God? They cry for Barabbas. And when Barabbas has had his way with them, as he must, they shall return Christ to their homes—illuminating again the truth, that whoever raises his horns against Him will end up defeated, kissing the dust of His feet; *pulverem pedum tuorum lingent* ("they shall lick the dust of thy feet"; Isaiah 49:23).[47]

---

[47] *Ed.:* The author's proposed remedy—prohibiting Jews from owning rural land—is both tepid and surely insufficient. This Catholic resolution to the Jewish Question makes a notable contrast with the famous proposal of the Protestant Martin Luther in 1543: destroy the synagogues, ban Judaic teaching, confiscate Jewish wealth, put Jews to hard labor, and ultimately drive them out. For details, see Luther's work *On the Jews and Their Lies* (2020; T. Dalton, ed.).

— 7 —
QUESTIONS AND ANSWERS

Theodor Fritsch
(1893)

Editor: By the early 1890s, the anti-Semitic movement in Germany, especially, was gaining real momentum. Advocates were increasingly attempting to turn ideas and principles into action, and to make abstract theorizing about Jews into something concrete. A prominent position in this movement was held by Theodor Fritsch (1852-1933). Born in Saxony and trained as a machinist, Fritsch became politically active by his late 20s, and quickly sought to unify anti-Jewish individuals into a coherent organization. He also became a writer and journalist, and would eventually found a publishing house, Hammer Verlag, in 1902.

In 1887, at the age of 35, Fritsch published what would become his most famous book: *Anti-Semitic Catechism*. A 'catechism' is a kind of educational or instruction manual, typically in the form of questions and answers. And indeed, the first 30 pages of the book are a series of questions and answers on the Jewish Question; this portion is reproduced below, drawing from the 1893 edition. The remainder of the book includes a large section of anti-Jewish quotations from famous men in history, a look at Jews in Russia, Poland, and Hungary, an extensive list of "Jewish statistics" (naming famous Jews in contemporary society), a history of the anti-Semitic movement, and a variety of related topics. The book proved extremely popular, and went through many editions and revisions. In 1907, Fritsch retitled the book as *The Handbook on the Jewish Question*. It continued to be updated and republished, even after Fritsch's death in 1933; the final edition was released in 1944.

What follows here, as mentioned, is the introductory Questions and Answers section of the early editions of the book. This text was intended as an overview of the main issues surrounding the Jewish Question, and as a reply to critics and defenders of Jews. Footnotes are those of the translator and editor, except where noted.

What does one mean by anti-Semitism?

'Anti' means 'against' and 'Semitism' means the character of the Semitic race. Antisemitism therefore means the combating of the Semitic race. Since the Semite race in Europe is represented almost exclusively by the Jews, we mean 'Semites' in the narrower sense, i.e. the Jews. An 'anti-Semite' therefore means, in our case, 'an opponent of the Jews.'

How can the Jews be still persecuted in our enlightened age on account of their religion?

It does not occur to anyone to combat the Jews on account of their religion. No one is trying to destroy their religious cult; it enjoys careful protection on the part of all classes of people—even anti-Semites. The tracing of anti-Semitism to religious hatred is a crude distortion of the facts. The most determined anti-Semites can be found among free thinkers (Giordano Bruno, Voltaire, Schopenhauer, Feuerbach, Johannes Scherr,[1] Dühring, etc.).

As already the name indicates, anti-Semitism is directed against the 'Semites,' that is, against a race, not a religion. If the anti-Semites combat the religion of the Jews, they must call themselves 'anti-Israelites.' It therefore betrays a deficient linguistic knowledge if anybody conflates anti-Semitism with the religion. Furthermore, this falsification of concepts is intentionally cultivated by a certain party in order to deceive the people about the real nature of the Jewish Question.

But were the Jews not persecuted in the Middle Ages on account of their religion?

That too is not relevant. The cause of the popular anger against the Jews in the Middle Ages, as in all ages, was Jewish usury and the exploitation of all classes of the people by Jewish schemes and ruses. This is clearly proven by numerous complaints that were made by the citizens of different cities to the governments at that time; these are still available today. Only, in those times,

---

[1] Johannes Scherr (1817-1886) was a German novelist and cultural historian.

people were not sure that, in the Jew, one was dealing with a foreign nation and a foreign race and therefore the 'religion' had to serve as the differentiating mark.

What do the anti-Semites really want?

They want to see the Jewish influence in different fields restricted through legal means because they consider them as deleterious. They strive therefore for a change of legislation in such a way that the Jews have certain restrictions. Furthermore, they wish to work in a way that is enlightening regarding the true nature of Jewry, warn people of their wiles and schemes, and support all reforms that lead to the economic, intellectual, and moral recovery of our people.

But why should the Jews not have the same rights as the other citizens?

First, because they do not deserve them; second, because they misuse them! Every nation has obtained the right to its land and soil through the fact that it made these fruitful and cultivated them through centuries of steady industriousness, or won them through superior military strength and thus earned them with their blood. The Jews have not obtained native rights in our country in either way. They took no part in the cultural work of our people and as little in the bloody battles that our forefathers had to go through for the altar and the hearth.

The equal rights that the Jews possess today are a merciful favor that they were given in 1848. Up to then, however, they did not show themselves worthy of these because they form, even today—politically, socially, and commercially—a separate community that searches for its advantage at the cost of the other citizens.

Are the Jews not good Germans?

They would like to present themselves as if they really were that, but they themselves do not believe it! There are numerous declarations from authoritative Jewish men that constitute proof that the Jews even today consider themselves as a separate nationality and do not want to be absorbed into the other nations. Their arrogance itself does not tolerate that idea, since they have attributed to themselves the name of the 'chosen people.'

Haven't many Jews also spilt their blood for the Fatherland in the last war?

It's not so bad! Of course, the Jews, after they were granted full citizen rights, had to adopt also the citizens' duties, and one of these is military service. But in truth, they do not take part gladly. In well-informed circles, it is well known how the young Jews employ all means to get out of military service. (In the military 'liberation process' that took place some years ago in Alsace, and in which about 70 individuals were involved, it was almost all Jews!)

The Jew, however, is naturally little-suited to military service, since a heroic physique is not one of the advantages of the Jewish race. That is why the percentage of the Jews in the army is an extraordinarily small one. In addition, on the field, many of these Jewish soldiers reported sick and lay in military hospitals during the war campaign. If one or two had to face actual fire, that is certainly not on account of a thirst for battle but only through the unavoidable pressure of circumstances. A Jew who voluntarily rushes into a battle where it may cost him his life can only rarely be found. It was certainly not an enthusiasm for the Fatherland that allowed individual Jews to take part in our battles.

But the Jews are also men, and they too wish to live!

Granted that the Jews are men; it is however a curious procedure to present this fact as an excuse, as it were, for their conduct. One who wishes to live as a man must also feel and act in a human way and fulfil his duties towards his fellowmen in a human way. The Jew very rarely does this. He bases his progress on the ruin of others, and his entire thought and action is a continuous hostile battle against mankind. And in this he employs mostly the basest means: lies, deception, and betrayal.

But is it not rather simplistic to want to excuse the misdeeds of somebody by pointing to his humanity? Should one not also say then, in the defense of a robber and murderer: "He is also a man, he too wishes to live!" Precisely this sentence proves the enormous brainlessness of many people; it proves also how badly the Jews' conscience must be constituted that they cannot present any other justification of existence for themselves than their biped nature and that they consider their dishonest dealings as excused through a reference to this biological characteristic.

Don't the Jews lead an exemplary family life?

In certain respects, this is true, but the use of this exemplariness does not benefit us but only the Jews themselves. Not all the characteristics of the Jews are reprehensible; I admit, on the contrary, that our people can learn from them in many respects. In general, however, the good characteristics of the Jews are only such as benefit themselves. The Jew seldom exhibits virtues that operate externally.

The much talked of 'exemplary family life' of the Jews is explained through the following circumstances:

1) The hostile attitude towards the humanity surrounding him and the subsequent external animosity force the Jew to seek an ever-closer attachment to his fellow Jews. He requires the 'inner unity' in the family for a more successful hostility towards outsiders.

2) The great self-mastery of the Jewish disposition and the malleability of character bound to it facilitate communal life and harmony within a narrow circle. True passions are foreign to the Jew and so he is, with his cool calculation, always able to maintain peace among his people for the sake of an all-round advantage. The natural disposition towards hypocrisy and flattery facilitates the game among all fellow-Jews.

3) The Jewish woman is aware that, according to Talmudic law, she must blindly subordinate herself to the man like a slave or worse, and that, within the Jewish community, she does not have any rights vis-à-vis the man. She therefore seldom dares to act authoritatively against the man, and that is an essential reason for domestic peace.

4) The Jew considers marriage essentially from a utilitarian point of view; he sees in the woman an object of convenience and pleasure, guarding it from damages through cleverness and thriftiness.

Finally, there is the fact that, in the Jewish marriage, all spheres of higher interest are excluded; the conversation turns mostly around commercial matters, in which the man possesses a natural superiority, or the uniformity of character quickly leads to agreement. Without deeper passions, without any higher striving, without essential differences in intellectual and moral character, the Jewish married couple lacks almost any occasion for deeper quarrels.

What have the Jews really done wrong?

More than one can describe in 10 heavy volumes. The crimes against mankind imputed to the Jews constitute already a special literature of several hundred writings, and only the circumstance that the public press in the hands of the Jews has silenced all those announcements explains the fact that, even today, someone can pose such a naïve question.

The Jewish register of sins is briefly as follows: The Jews constitute, under the guise of a 'religion,' a political, social, and commercial fraternity that, directed by similar instincts and in a secret agreement within itself, operates towards the exploitation and subjugation of the non-Jewish peoples. The Jews of all countries and all languages are united in this goal and cooperate among themselves towards it. That is why it is also impossible for the Jew, in the country where he happens to live, to have any honest share in the fate of his non-Jewish countrymen. In short: he can never foster honest patriotism; he feels always and everywhere only as a member of the 'chosen' nation of Judah and, if he seeks to play the German, Frenchman, or Englishman, it is mostly only well-calculated hypocrisy.

In his separate community, the Jew considers all non-Jews as his enemies whom he has to combat with cunning and treachery. Through his special moral laws, the Talmud and the Shulchan Aruch,[2] the Jew considers himself as standing outside all other legal prescriptions and considers himself justified in violating all national laws—but always in such a way that this abuse cannot be proven in him. On the basis of the Talmudic view of life that grants the name of 'man' only to the Jew and counts the other peoples as animals, the Jew is exempted from every feeling of duty and any conscience with regard to the other peoples. Talmudic moral doctrine justifies him to commit every lie and deception towards mankind—although he is required to do so in such a way as to avoid any retribution via the letter of the public law. One must understand this principle of Jewish 'morality' to find what follows comprehensible.

Another spur to Jewish efforts is found in the superstitious 'promises' of the ancient Jewish scriptures: "All nations shall serve you and you shall be a lord above all thy brothers," "You shall consume all nations," etc. The Jews, in their arrogance, consider themselves the 'natural aristocracy' of mankind and think that they must, as such, actually strive for the mastery of

[2] The Shulchan Aruch is a codification of Jewish law made by Joseph Karo in 1563. It is much more concise than the Talmud.

the world. But since they cannot do this at all through bravery and truly superior strength, they attempt it through lies and deception—and money. Jewry thinks that it has recognized as the final wisdom of the world the fact that
"money rules the world." Jewry thinks that one who has money is the natural
ruler of the world. The Jews therefore do not reject any means and ways to
amass money. Every deception and treachery that leads to enrichment seems
therefore to be, in their eyes, not only permissible but commanded and
blessed! In this way, usury, robbery, false bankruptcy, etc. seem to them to
be harmless activities. They consider every lie, every betrayal, every perjury
as justified if they lead to an advantage for themselves.

With the help of these unconscionable principles, they have now,
through the decades and centuries, perpetrated the following against our nation—and others:

• They have, through profiteering, fully ruined many peasants, trades-
men, officials, officers, etc. and exposed them not only to material but also to
moral collapse.

• They have, through dishonest conduct and secret conspiracy, undermined the sound trading and industrial class and brought many commercial
branches so fully under their control that the honest non-Jewish businessman
can hardly exist anymore beside them.

• They have almost fully destroyed honorable handicraft, so that the formerly independent master has today become a wage-slave of the Jewish
shopkeeper and works for the same for a starvation wage.

• They have lowered the work-wages and the prices of all products so
much that it is becoming increasingly impossible to feed oneself through
honest work. The social misery and the social discontent are thereby becoming ever greater, and the danger of bloody popular rebellion grows ever more
imminent.

• They have taken over the public press and make use of it to deceive the
people of the true causes of general distress and to redirect people's discontent
in a false direction (to the government, against 'priests,' 'Junkers', the police,
bureaucracy, etc.). Even here they foment, through the undermining of all authority, social revolution; in this way, they hope to reap dishonest profits.

•   They promote moral confusion through their newspapers by entertaining people with all sorts of 'piquant' scandal- and crime-stories, and thereby seek to dull the moral consciousness. They poison the way of thought of our people through the Semitic mentality spreading in the press, and force the entire public life to a low intellectual level by cultivating the basest taste and pampering the lowest passions in art, literature, theater, etc.

•   They have, through the press, stolen from the people billions in the 1870s, destroyed many lives thereby, and got such enormous wealth in their hands that they can exercise the strongest pressure on all matters. The companies and persons trading in the stock-exchanges during the period of the incorporation fraud[3] were 90% Jewish.

•   They have, through Jewish parliamentarians (Lasker, Bamberger, et al.), as well as non-Jewish paid subjects in the parliament, influenced legislation in such a way that maximum leeway was given to the Jewish desires— for example, to fraudulent bankruptcies, stock-exchange tricks, incorporation fraud, etc., as well as through unrestricted freedom of trade, liberalization, etc. Indeed, they helped to create legislation that protects a scoundrel more than an honest man!

•   They are to blame, through their financial influence and their unscrupulous desires, for the loosening of society in every respect. *They sell everything*: offices, titles, names, honor, love, and so forth. They institute, especially among the female youth of our people, an unprecedented moral devastation. The base sensual disposition of the Jews and their lack of shame and conscience makes them the most daring seducers. Girls who go to Jews in a service capacity in big cities mostly fall victim to prostitution. One will scarcely be exaggerating when one says that the majority of unfortunate girls who constitute metropolitan prostitution have fallen through Jewish seduction. Even the infamous 'trafficking of girls' is conducted almost exclusively by Jews.

---

[3] The *"Gründungs-Schwindel"* was a stock exchange crash of 1873 brought about in the first years of German unification by speculative company incorporations. Fritsch adds this: See Germanicus, *Die Frankfurter Juden und die Aufsaugung des Volks-Wohlstandes*; and Glagau, *Der Gründungs-Schwindel in Deutschland*.

- They have been able to attract many persons into prominent places in their networks and, through their financial influence, made them serviceable to them, or at least, ensured their silence. The few men of strong character who resist these temptations and step up as accusers of Jewry are rendered suspicious and publicly reviled in an unheard-of manner through the Jewish press.

- They have thrown even governments into their chains through cunning financial operations and made them dependent on the mercy of Jewry, so that hardly any help can be obtained for the people even from these quarters. Through their international relations, the Jews influence all state cabinets and hold the governments mutually in check so that no individual state can dare to proceed against Jewry without having the neighboring states incited against them immediately.

Wouldn't we have heard of these surprising facts already, if they were based on the truth?

From whom should the people hear these things? The largest part of the public derives all their knowledge from the newspapers. The latter, however, are almost exclusively under Jewish direction and Jewish financial influence. Jewry has recognized the importance of the public press and, for that reason, taken control of them in time. As Major Osman Bey reports in his book, *The Conquest of the World by the Jews,*[4] a prominent Jew is supposed to have said in a meeting of the Jewish supreme council in Krakow in 1840: "As long as we do not have the newspapers of the world in our hands in order to deceive and anaesthetize the peoples, our rule remains a phantom of the brain."

And the goal that the Jews set for themselves at that time has been reached. The major part of the public newspapers in all the countries of the world is in the hands of the Jews, conducting the 'deception and anaesthetizing' of the nations with surprising success.

---

[4] Major Osman Bey was the pseudonym of the British author Frederick Millingen, who was born in Istanbul, the son of a British surgeon attached to the Greek army. His book *Die Eroberung der Welt durch die Juden* was published in German in 1873 and translated into several European languages. See chapter two of the present book.

Are the Jews not men, just like us?

They are indeed men, but not "like us." That the Jews have another religion is incidental; more important is the fact that they belong to a quite different type of men, to another race, and consequently are essentially differentiated from us, not only in their physical and intellectual qualities but also with respect to their character, their view of life, their customs and moral concepts. If the Jews were not strikingly different from the rest of mankind, how does it happen that one immediately recognizes the Jew from out of all the peoples?

In what does this 'racial difference' consist?

Nearly all of the European peoples belong to the Aryan or Indo-Germanic race, but the Jews, to the Semitic. The Aryan peoples are of a more settled nature; they perform agriculture, trade, art and science; they found states, are courageous and brave; the basic feature of their character is uprightness, honesty, loyalty, and dedication. They are the truly cultured peoples. The genuine Semites, on the other hand, are naturally nomads; they have no real lasting settlement, no real Fatherland. They go where the best booty beckons. They do not build or cultivate anything themselves, they look for the best cultural sites created by foreign industriousness, exploit the already present favorable conditions, graze, as it were, the pasture grounds and leave them plundered and deserted. Agriculture, technology, and art are foreign to them, just as is every creative work. They give themselves the appearance of despising manual work, but in truth they lack the capacity for it.

The Semitic nomads of the desert (Bedouins) conduct even today robbery and plunder in the most open and vigorous manner. The Jew, however, is, as it were, a 'cultured Bedouin'; he conducts the same business in a rather civilized form. His domain is 'trade,' which for him covers a very broad concept; in the Jewish language, the word *Massematte*[5] means equally a trading company and theft. The plundering traits of the cultured Bedouins emerge in the form of peddling, itinerant sales, pawn-brokerage, installment sales, 50 cent bazaars, usury, fraudulent bankruptcy, stock-exchange speculation, etc. Some of these branches are exclusively represented by Jews. But even as a 'doctor' of sexual diseases, fraudulent lawyer, Social Democratic

---

[5] The word is of Yiddish origin, from the Hebrew *massa u'matan* (= negotiations).

agitator, etc., the cultured Bedouin knows how to undertake very profitable raids into the pockets of his fellow citizens.

But were the Jews not forced into dishonest trade because they were excluded from the legal professional branches?

This pretext was formerly justified for a long time, but no more. Besides, the question remains still open: Why were they earlier excluded from honest manual labor? Clearly because they introduced all sorts of abuses into it, exploited it, and subverted its sound foundations. Furthermore, the Jews have never longed for honest manual work. Haggling and usury were for them not just a temporary remedy but, as we have seen above, it constitutes from the past the foundation of their Semitic nature. For decades, all professional branches have stood open to the Jews but we do not see that they become masons, carpenters, thatchers, joiners, smiths, locksmiths, machine builders, watchmakers, typesetters, etc. And if one tried to place all Jewish youths in workshops with free training and free expenses, they would however run from them at the first opportunity—in order to haggle. The Semite does not wish to, and cannot, work and produce but only effortlessly grab and plunder.

Hence guile, slyness, hypocrisy, and lies constitute the main features of the Semitic character, to which we may add harassment, insolent assertiveness, unrestricted egoism, ruthless cruelty, and excessive sexual desire. Our German concepts of loyalty, modesty, devotion, and sacrifice for a cause, are incomprehensible to the Jew and elicit his contempt. To him, only that which promises personal advantage or enjoyment appears as a virtue.

What then should happen to the Jews?

This is actually not our concern. The Jew who has exploited a peasant up to his last shirt and driven him from his house and yard also does not ask what should become of the peasant. He leaves him on the highway and does not worry whether he starves, becomes a thief, takes his own life, or dies in a lunatic asylum. He insists on his payment, demands his 'right,' and considers himself thereby exempted from all duties towards his fellow men.

But it is a good trait in the German that, even where he makes a right judgement, he still offers a defense of the accused. Indeed, even though the Jew has committed an outrage against the German people in the most arrant way and deserves the most merciless damnation, the German still, in his end-less patience, breaks his head over the Jew and asks: 'What should become of him?'

Now, this concern is superfluous. The majority of the Jews possess great wealth and, if one leaves them just a part of it, we really have no reason to fear for their future. They can live more comfortably with it than we. But even if that were not true: Do we then do an injustice when we demand that the Jews should sustain themselves on their own strength? Let them indeed obtain a colonial land somewhere, create a culture themselves, and thereby enter into an honest competition with the other nations! Indeed, we demand that of every people, why should we not demand it also of the Jews?

How then should the Jewish Question be solved?

Without doing injustice to the Jews in the least, the Jewish Question can be solved in the following manner:

• Either the Jews have to acquire somewhere—best if outside Europe—their own national territory (they do not lack the means to do that!) and emi-grate before a legally established date (in my opinion, within 10 years). Or if, through pure obsession, you wish to maintain them here, I propose the fol-lowing conditions:

• Jews may conduct only agriculture or productive manual labor and, indeed, only with Jewish assistants and workers.

• They are to be excluded from every other activity, and—with penalties for both parties—it should be prohibited that any non-Jew work for a Jew. This demand would be quite fair and well-intentioned for, if there were gen-erally a way of making something useful of the Jewish race, it is only that one should force them to honest productive work.

• Baptized Jews and their descendants should be placed under the same law as circumcised ones—and miscegenation [i.e. inter-breeding] with Jews should be declared impermissible.

The haggling and profiteering activity of Judah is ineradicably grounded in its racial character, and since, for this reason, there can be no question of any education and improvement, our most decisive demand for the protection of our people should be that:

- The emancipation of the Jews is to be revoked, and they must be placed under a special foreigners' law (Jewry law).

Further, with time, through private initiative, they will become commercially and socially isolated. With increasing education, everyone will learn to feel it as shameful to stand in any relationship with Jews. The seclusion and separation that Jewry has sought from the beginning will then be granted in fullest measure.

But surely there are also respectable Jews?

That may be. But the fact that one emphasizes this so often is itself an admission that the Jew in general is *not* respectable and, through the exception, only the rule will be confirmed. Moreover, every Jew strives naturally to play the part of a respectable, indeed a selfless and magnanimous, person, and thereby win trust and misuse it badly.

One always waits in vain for the time when one may evaluate a Jew as good and noble. We have, in recent years, repeatedly experienced that 'respectable' Jews who have enjoyed universal trust through the years and occupy honorary positions of all sorts, etc., suddenly turn out to be great crooks. We recall only the Bernstein brothers in Königsberg, Pauli in Eberswalde, Wolf and Sommerfeld in Berlin, and similar cases.

Are there not also bad Christians?

There are mangy sheep also in every large herd, and among the non-Jewish or Aryan peoples, individual wayward and depraved subjects can be found. Among the German people, however, the situation is still that the scoundrel is the exception and the upright person the rule, whereas one can maintain the opposite of the Jewish nation. One must bear in mind always that, in the German Reich, only every 80th person is a Jew and that, accordingly, it is not to be wondered at that there are apparently more German than Jewish criminals. It is not a question of whether there are also good Jews and bad Germans but the numerical proportion of the good to the bad that clinches the matter. One may compare the crime statistics, and one will conclude therefrom that crimes are more numerous among Judah than among our people!

One should also finally bear in mind that 'Christian faith' is not a decisive indicator, for there are very many baptized Jews who conduct their unhealthy life under mock-Christianity and help to damage the Christian and German name. And if in fact a moral deterioration of our people is to be ascertained in the last decades, one must not forget that Jewish example and Jewish seduction are responsible for much in this. When a nation has, for decades, been overwhelmed with the loose mentality of the Jewish press, it is no wonder if it is morally coarsened and sinks to Jewish characterlessness. Yes, one must wonder that our people, in spite of these corrupting intellectual influences, has still maintained its relative moral health.

But we have many famous men among the Jews!

Indeed, strikingly many! But that is due to the fact that it is ten times easier for a Jew to become famous than for a German. As soon as a Jew shows just a trace of talent, the Jewish press of the entire world sets to work for him and trumpets his reputation in all the corners of the Earth. But the most gifted German who does not stick to the Jews is ignored with silence and does not succeed. In the theaters, for example, nothing can be achieved today without the intervention of Jewish agents, and the latter protect by preference Jewish 'artists,' male and female. One must indeed consider it a miracle that German actors and singers can still generally go on stage.

It is exactly the same in the case of the 'fine literature,' where Jewish scribes mass-produce the reading fodder for the 'dear clueless plebs' and fill all the illustrated and non-illustrated newspapers and tabloids with them. Indeed, one needs to be a Jew today to 'accomplish' anything and to become famous.

Haven't Spinoza, Mendelssohn, and Heine accomplished significant things?

The reputation of these Jewish greats has been similarly exaggerated inordinately by Jewish publicity. If they had not existed, German science and art would not miss anything essential. Besides, it is characteristic among the three mentioned that they more or less turned away from Judaism and displayed some better characteristics that seem to confirm the conjecture that they were not of pure Jewish blood. That which is appreciable in them as valuable could therefore be possibly attributable to some drops of foreign blood.

For Spinoza's philosophical thought, the Jews had, as we know, so little sympathy that they sought to reject the isolated philosopher through banishment and murder. In Heine there contests a striking duality. It is as if, in him, a piece of the Germanic spirit wished to rise at times to idealistic heights—until the Jew in his bones suddenly drags him down again to the swamp, where he wallows with pleasure and scorns all ideals.

But we owe it to the memory of Lessing to avoid hostility towards the Jews.

This pious thought is normally the last refuge of those who are unable to bring forward anything more objectively against the justification of anti-Semitism. When one cannot defend the actual and living Jew any more, one resorts to an imaginary character. Isn't the bankruptcy declaration of the Jewish defenders already evident here?

Nathan the Wise[6] never lived: he is the imaginative creation of a poet who, out of a falsely understood 'tolerance' and 'friendliness towards men,' wrote a tendentious play that wears on its sleeve its intention of whitewashing the Jews. The 'wise Nathan' is a shady idealizing image that lacks all characteristic traits of the Jewish race; he is therefore not a Jew at all. I won't expound on the notion that Lessing was financially very dependent on Jews and wrote the play possibly as a 'commission', and the same goes for the suspicion of Dühring,[7] who sought to demonstrate that Lessing himself was of Jewish origin. The fact that one's only reply to anti-Semitism is no real Jew but only a theatrical character with a Jewish mask characterizes—I emphasize again—the intellectual bankruptcy of the Jewish and Jewish-friendly gentlemen.

---

[6] *Nathan der Weise* is a play written by German playwright Gotthold Ephraim Lessing (1729-1781) in 1779, championing religious tolerance.
[7] Eugen Dühring (1833-1921) was a German economist who wrote a work on the Jewish Question, *Die Judenfrage als Racen-, Sitten- und Kulturfrage* (1881) in which he maintained that Lessing was most probably of Jewish origin. See Dühring, *The Jewish Question as a Racial, Moral and Cultural Question*, Alexander Jacob, trans., 2017, chapter 3.

FIRST LETTER ON THE JEWS

Adolf Hitler
(1919)

Editor: Hitler was 30 years of age at the time of this writing, having survived injury in World War One and having witnessed the Jewish role in the German Revolution of November 1918. This letter, dated 16 September 1919, seems to be his first written statement on the Jews. At this time, Hitler was working in a military intelligence unit and was assigned to follow and report on a little-known political group called the *Deutsche Arbeiterpartei* (German Workers' Party), or DAP. He soon joined the small group and quickly assumed a position of leadership. Within a few months, he would refashion the party as the National Socialist DAP—the NSDAP, or the 'Nazi' party.

The letter is addressed to a fellow soldier, Adolf Gemlich, and was prompted by Hitler's superior, Karl Mayr. For background details, see W. Maser, *Hitler's Letters and Notes* (1974).

Dear Herr Gemlich,

If the threat with which Jewry faces our people has given rise to undeniable hostility on the part of a large section of our people, the cause of this hostility must be sought in the clear recognition that Jewry as such is deliberately or unwittingly having a pernicious effect on our nation, but mostly in personal intercourse, in the poor impression the Jew makes as an individual. As a result, anti-Semitism far too readily assumes a purely emotional character. But this is not the correct response. Anti-Semitism as a political movement may not and cannot be molded by emotional factors but only by recognition of the facts. Now the facts are these:

To begin with, the Jews are unquestionably a race, not a religious community. The Jew himself never describes himself as a Jewish German, a Jewish Pole, or a Jewish American, but always as a German, Polish, or

American Jew. Jews have never adopted more than the language of the foreign nations in whose midst they live. A German who is forced to make use of the French language in France, Italian in Italy, Chinese in China does not thereby become a Frenchman, Italian, or Chinaman, nor can we call a Jew who happens to live amongst us and who is therefore forced to use the German language, a German. Neither does the Mosaic faith, however great its importance for the preservation of that race, be the sole criterion for deciding who is a Jew and who is not. There is hardly a race in the world whose members all belong to a single religion.

Through inbreeding for thousands of years, often in very small circles, the Jew has been able to preserve his race and his racial characteristics much more successfully than most of the numerous people among whom he has lived. As a result, a non-German, alien race lives amongst us, unwilling and indeed unable to shed its racial characteristics, its particular feelings, thoughts, and ambitions and nevertheless enjoying the same political rights as we ourselves do. And since even the Jew's feelings are limited to the purely material realm, his thoughts and ambitions are bound to be so even more strongly. Their dance around the golden calf becomes a ruthless struggle for all the possessions that we feel deep down are not the highest and not the only ones worth striving for on this Earth.

The value of an individual is no longer determined by his character or by the significance of his achievements for the community, but solely by the size of his fortune, his wealth. The greatness of a nation is no longer measured by the sum of its moral and spiritual resources, but only by the wealth of its material possessions.

All this results in that mental attitude and that quest for money and the power to protect it that allow the Jew to become so unscrupulous in his choice of means, so merciless in his use of his own ends. In autocratic states he cringes before the 'majesty' of the princes and misuses their favors to become a leech on their people. In democracies he vies for the favor of the masses, cringes before 'the majesty of the people,' but only recognizes the majesty of money.

He saps the prince's character with Byzantine flattery; national pride and the strength of the nation with ridicule and shameless seduction to vice. His method of battle is that public opinion which is never expressed in the press but which is nonetheless managed and falsified by it. His power is the power of the money, which multiplies in his hands effortlessly and endlessly through interest, and with which he imposes a yoke upon the nation that is

the more pernicious in that its glitter disguises its ultimately tragic consequences. Everything that makes the people strive for higher goals, be it religion, socialism, or democracy, is to the Jew merely a means to an end, the
way to satisfy his greed and thirst for power.

The result of his works is racial tuberculosis of the nation.

And this has the following consequences: purely emotional anti-
Semitism finds its final expression in the form of pogroms. Rational anti-
Semitism, by contrast, must lead to a systematic and legal struggle against,
and eradication of, the privileges the Jews enjoy over the other foreigners
living among us (Alien Laws). Its final objective, however, must be the total
removal of all Jews from our midst.[1] Both objectives can only be achieved
by a government of national strength and not one of national impotence.

The German [Weimar] Republic owes its birth not to the united national will of our people, but to the underhanded exploitation of a series of circumstances that, taken together, express themselves in a deep, universal dis-
satisfaction. These circumstances, however, arose independently of the political structure and are at work even today. Indeed, more so than ever before.
Hence, a large part of our people recognizes that changing the structure of
the state cannot in itself improve our position, but that this can only be
achieved by the rebirth of the nation's moral and spiritual forces.

And this rebirth cannot be prepared by the leadership of an irrespon-
sibly majority influenced by party dogmas or by the internationalist catch-
phrases and slogans of an irresponsible press, but only by determined
acts on the part of nationally-minded leadership with an inner sense of
responsibility.

This very fact serves to deprive the Republic of the inner support of the
spiritual forces any nation needs very badly. Hence the present leaders of the
nation are forced to seek support from those who alone have benefited and
continue to benefit from changing the form of the German state, and who
for that very reason became the driving force of the Revolution—the Jews.
Disregarding the Jewish threat, which is undoubtedly recognized even by
today's leaders (as various statement from prominent personalities reveal),
these men are forced to accept Jewish favors to their private advantage and

---

[1] An important statement: Hitler calls not for the deaths or imprisonment of
the Jews, but simply for their removal from Germany. Despite common belief,
this seems to have been his intention right through the end of WW2.

Classic Essays on the Jewish Question

to repay these favors.[2] And the repayment does not merely involve satisfying every possible Jewish demand, but above all preventing the struggle of the betrayed people against its defrauders, by sabotaging the anti-Semitic movement.

Yours truly,
Adolf Hitler

---

[2] The parallels to the present government of the United States are striking.

THE CORE OF THE JEWISH QUESTION

Theodor Fritsch
(1923)

Editor: As noted in chapter 7, Theodor Fritsch retitled his famous book *Anti-Semitic Catechism* in 1907, preferring now
the title *The Handbook on the Jewish Question*. The following
section is taken from the 1923 edition to that book. All notes are
those of the translator and editor, unless otherwise specified.

The favorite means of the Jews to ensure the sympathy of weaker souls for
themselves was always the appeal to compassion. The Jews played, in all
ages, the role of those persecuted unjustly and never tire of singing their song
of complaint about oppression. In fact, they are the persecutors and oppressors. Untrue also is the pretense that they were persecuted on account of their
faith, and that hatred of the Jew arises from narrow (medieval) religious
prejudices. We, however, stand outside narrow ecclesiastical doctrinal concept and revere a free idealistic concept of life that cannot be forced into rigid dogmas and religious formulae. Thus we would be the last people who
could "persecute" anybody on account of deviating religious ideas.

From a close understanding of rabbinical doctrines, though, we know at
the same time that there are Jewish moral conceptions that offend not only
the "Christian" concept of life but human morality in general. They arise
from the idea of the special and "chosen" status of the Jewish tribe through
which the Jews feel superior to all other men and reject an inward common-
alty with them. The Talmudic doctrines are rooted especially in the concept
that the believing Jew may not bestow full human value on a non-Jewish
person. He considers non-Jews as subhuman creatures and concludes therefrom that he is exempted from moral obligations towards them.

But these religious and moral matters are not the most striking in the
Jewish Question. What we have to expose is the following:

Even though scattered through all countries, the Jews form, up to the
present day, a firmly-linked community that is bound not only through the
bond of religion but at the same time pursues common material and political

goals. As easily as the Jews may externally adapt to a foreign people—in language, clothes, and life customs—they never forget for a moment their membership in an association that feels that it stands outside the rest of mankind and sets its interests inimically against those of all other peoples. One may recall that, already from ancient times, the lunacy of "chosenness" rules all Jewish minds and that this small people, at a time when it lived in total insignificance alongside peoples of great culture, was already possessed of the delusion of subjugating all peoples to themselves and to eventually achieve world supremacy ("All peoples should serve you"; "You should be a master among your brothers"; "Kings should be your care givers and princesses your wet nurses"...).[1] If one adds to this the fact that their priests have promised them the possession of all the world's wealth, if only they would cling tenaciously to the statutes and superstitious promises of their rabbis, one begins to understand how such a people, enticed by these bold promises, holds unshakably to its tribal community and shows no inclination to merge with any foreign people.

No other people in the world presumes to make its members such high-strung promises. How therefore should anyone leave a flourishing international company—to speak in the Jewish way of thought—and abandon the prospect of enormous gain in order to join another company that, in the Jewish conception, marches towards certain bankruptcy? The Jewish faith promises the Jew not only rule over all nations and all the wealth of the world, it announces to him at the same time the downfall and the destruction of all other nations—through Judaism! In the rough Lutheran translation, the Jewish national and special god Yahweh says to his people: "And you shall destroy all the peoples that the Lord your God will give over to you" (Deut 7:16).

A people with such goals and hopes does not think to be absorbed into other peoples and to merge with them. Indeed, the Jews would be unfaithful to their own mission if they were to lose themselves in other nations—for their mission is indeed to be the enemy, a threat, and instigator of the other

---

[1] Fritsch is paraphrasing here, but accurately. The more complete passages read as follows: "Let peoples serve you, and nations bow down to you. Be lord over your brothers..." (Gen 27:29); "The Lord God says: Look, I will raise my hand to the nations, and to the peoples I will lift up my signal. They will bring your sons in their arms, and will carry your daughters on their shoulders. Kings will be your attendants, and their queens your nursemaids. With faces to the ground, they will bow down to you; they will lick the dust from your feet." (Isa 49:22-23).

nations. Nature offers examples of how individual animal species represent the instigators and stimulators of other creatures in order to preserve the latter from sinking into listlessness and debility. Thus the bold scholar Adolf Wahrmund[2] aptly says: "The Jews are the spur that fate presses into the bleeding points of nations to stir them to the utmost development of their forces."

In such a state of affairs, it is clear that it is a foolish delusion if non-Jewish people respect the idea that the Jews living among them could remove their Jewish nature, live as loyal, good state citizens in closest community with the others, and pursue common life goals with them. There is nothing in common between the Jews and other peoples. It is a question here of an opposition willed by God. Jewry is built on a hatred of all of mankind.[3]

Thus the Jews are something alien, hostile, and unassimilable among all nations. It would be a lack of knowledge of their nature to devote oneself to the hope that one could make of them men of a normal sort. The Jews themselves cannot, understandably, admit this fact; they would thereby cut off the branch on which they sit and defeat all their goals; they are required to wear a mask. They will therefore continue to assert, with glowing eagerness, that they are as good state citizens and patriots as the others and are attached to the Fatherland (which many of them, to be sure, often change) with devotion. That is a necessary pretense that is produced from their situation and that they cannot dispense with. One who knows their secret writings knows what to expect of such assurances.

The truth is: The Jews form, in spite of their dispersal through all countries, a special nation, indeed a special state, a "state within a state," as Fichte said [see below]. They are unwilling to give up this special political community since it assures them enormous advantages. While they enjoy all the rights of state citizens along with the others, they possess, further, the protection of their Jewish special state; and in this way, they attain a greater possibility of operating for their international Jewish secret state and obtain all sorts of advantages. It is manifest to every businessman how useful it is to

---

[2] Wahrmund (1827-1913) was a German Orientalist and anti-Semite who wrote a work entitled *Das Gesetz des Nomadenthums und die heutige Judenherrschaft* (The Nomad's Law and Today's Jewish Dominion, 1887).

[3] This Jewish misanthropy has been well-documented for literally thousands of years. See *Eternal Strangers* (T. Dalton, ed., 2020).

obtain, as a member, all insights into a business enterprise and at the same time to be secretly also a co-owner of a rival business.

The philosopher Fichte described the situation concisely and trenchantly more than 100 years ago when he says:

> Throughout almost all the countries of Europe there is spreading a mighty hostile state that is at perpetual war with all other states, and in many of them imposes fearful burdens on the citizens: it is Jewry. I do not think, as I hope to show subsequently, that this state is fearful—not because it forms a separate and solidly united state but because this state is founded on the hatred of the whole human race... In a state where the absolute monarch cannot take from me my paternal hut and where I can defend my rights against the all-powerful minister, the first Jew who likes can plunder me with impunity. This you see and cannot deny, and you utter sugary words of tolerance and of the rights of man and civil rights, all the time wounding in us the *primary* rights of man. ... Do you not remember the state within the State? Does the thought not occur to you that if you give to the Jews, who are citizens of a state more solid and more powerful than any of yours, civil rights in your states, they will utterly crush the remainder of your citizens?[4]

It is one of the great irresponsibilities of our public life that such judgements and warnings by our best men a century ago were suppressed—for there are similar judgements also from Herder, Goethe, Arndt, Kant and others. Of course, that happened through the operation of the Jews themselves; they surely knew what they were doing when they separated the German people from their intellectual leaders; except that our teachers of philosophy, politics, and history also share in the guilt for that.

Fichte was right: Since the time the Jews have had full civil rights among us, they are dual citizens and we only single; they are at the same time citizens of two different states and can sell and betray one to the other, and they have attended to this business unsparingly. They have raised the Jewish state up at the cost of the German state.

---

[4] Johann G. Fichte, *Beiträge zur Berechtigung der Urtheile des Publicums über die französische Revolution* (Contributions to the Correction of the Public's Judgment concerning the French Revolution, 1793).

But their treason extends at the same time to all the other states of the Earth—with the exception of England, which has entered into a "corporate merger" with the Jewish state. England's world-rule therefore signifies at the same time the world-rule of Jewry. (In England, the Jews have spread the fairytale that the English emerged from the lost ten tribes of Israel—an idea of which many educated Englishmen are proud!)

But the Jews are more than a foreign nation and religious community: They are not only a separate state but a race that is closed within itself. In order to be acknowledged in the Jewish state as a fully entitled member, one must be of Jewish blood, Jewish origin. Jewry does not allow any foreigner into its community but also none of its own to leave it. The *Archives Israelites* (1864) says:

> Israel is a nationality. We are Jews because we are born Jews. A child that stems from Israelite parents is an Israelite... The seal of the Israelite is stamped on us through our birth and this seal we can never lose, never discard. Even the Israelite who denies his religion, who is baptized, does not stop being an Israelite, and all the duties of an Israelite apply to him always.

The baptized Jew therefore remains a secret member of the large blood-brotherhood of Hebrews and has the duty to take care of Jewish special interests.

In this form, Jewry constitutes a strongly closed community that hardly has anything like it on Earth. It indeed possesses the character of a *conspiracy*. The Talmud also threatens betrayal of the Jewish business with death. Apart from the common blood and spirit, the Jews are bound by a common hatred of everything non-Jewish. As certain as conciliatory Love forms the fundamental feature of the Christian doctrine, so certainly does intransigent hatred constitute the essential character of Jewry.[5] From that is produced an

---

[5] Nietzsche made precisely this point, and with great force: "Out of the trunk of that tree of vengeance and hatred, Jewish hatred—the deepest and most sublime hatred, that is, a hatred which creates ideals and transforms values, something whose like has never existed on Earth—from that grew something just as incomparable, a *new love*, the deepest and most sublime of all the forms of love: —from what other trunk could it have grown?

However, one should not assume that this love arose essentially as the denial of that thirst for vengeance, as the opposite of Jewish hatred! No: the reverse is the

opposition to all other peoples; this must urge the latter to the utmost caution and resistance.

It is therefore a superficial and misleading conception when the opposition to Jewry is represented as a mere religious and racial hatred when, in reality, it deals with a selfless defense borne by the highest ideals against an enemy of mankind, civilization, and culture.

*****

Tacitus already recognized that, at the basis of Jewry, lies a hatred of the entire human race, and on this hatred is based the self-exclusion of the Jewish people from the human community.[6] The constant complaint of the Jews about their suppression and persecution among other peoples is one of the customary distortions in which Jewish dialectics is so rich. The Jew is the born enemy and persecutor of honest men. He is filled with an irreconcilable hatred against everything that stands outside his tribe. The ancient Jewish scriptures produce enough evidence of that; and yet the Jewish people are constantly reminded by their rabbis that the peoples living beside them, the Hittites, the Amorites, Perizzites, and whatever else they were called, were given to them for exploitation, subjugation, and extermination.

They hold to such a view, up to the present day. Today we are, to them, the Amalekites and Edomites, and are called that even in their writings. They view the non-Jewish peoples not only as objects of exploitation but aim—consciously or unconsciously—at their economic, moral, and racial destruction.

---

truth! This love grew out of that hatred, as its crown, as the victorious crown unfolding itself wider and wider in the purest brightness and sunshine, which, so to speak, was seeking for the kingdom of light and height, the goal of that hate, aiming for victory, trophies, seduction, with the same urgency with which the roots of that hatred were sinking down ever deeper and more greedily into everything that was evil and possessed depth. This Jesus of Nazareth, the living evangelist of love, the "Savior" bringing holiness and victory to the poor, to the sick, to the sinners— was he not that very seduction in its most terrible and most irresistible form, the seduction and detour to exactly those *Jewish* values and innovations in ideals?" (*On the Genealogy of Morals*, First Essay, sec. 8).

[6] Tacitus (56-120 AD) was one of the greatest historians of ancient Rome, and wrote extensively against the Jews. For a discussion of his writings, see *Eternal Strangers* (2020), pp. 30-33.

Prof. Wahrmund says: "The path of the Jews over the Earth is a campaign for its conquest. They lie in wait among the enemy, covered by false flags, ever ready for attack and ambush."

The constant awareness of seeing other men as enemies who are to be feared, hated, and duped lends to the Jew that shamefaced alertness of the senses that always lurks, eavesdrops, spies, and speculates; it does not for a moment give itself to careless communion with others. Whereas the guileless German opens his heart to everyone, the Jew never betrays his innermost aims. Even when he seems to give himself up to harmless distraction along with others, he stands constantly in wait to discover foreign weaknesses and to detect his advantages. This uninterrupted distrustful tracking and observing has, in the course of generations, cultivated that sharpness of senses that lends the Jew a certain superiority in all sorts of day-to-day matters, but especially in business affairs. Through an opposite disposition, through a blind trust of all men, the German allows his senses to slumber and appears therefore only too often as obtuse and weak and thus quite suited to being duped at every turn by his cunning opponent. Thus: the spur of Jewish cleverness and activity is mistrust and hatred. The restless drive to harm his neighbor, wherever it may be, which the Jew feels virtually as an obligation, does not allow him to rest even a moment.

Honest Jews frequently admit this. The Zionist Cheskel Zwi-Klötzel[7] wrote in the newspaper *Janus* (1912/1913, no. 2) an essay titled "The great hatred" in which he says, among other things:

> Against anti-Semitism, against Jew-hatred stands, on the Jewish side, a great hatred of everything that is non-Jewish. Just as we Jews know about every non-Jew that he, somewhere in a corner of his heart, is and must be an anti-Semite, so every Jew is, in the depths of his being, a hater of everything that is non-Jewish.
>
> This great Jewish hatred once found a truly brilliant artistic evaluation in world literature, in Shakespeare's Shylock... Before us stands a Jew, and more than that, a Jew who hates![8]

---

[7] Zwi-Klötzel (1891-1951) was a German Jewish journalist who served as editor of the Zionist *Jüdische Rundschau* from 1922 to 1929. On the accession of the National Socialists to power, he emigrated to Palestine.

[8] See the chapter "Jewish self-awareness" in Fritsch's book *Anti-Semitic Catechism*.

Given such a situation, the Jews form a hostile element in the state; they are everything that cannot be tolerated in an orderly society.

Everything that they cite in justification of themselves is a masquerade. In recent times, they have to deflect all complaints by pointing out that they participated in battles during the war and did their duty for the defense of the country. It must seem strange that this fact is raised as a special service whereas it must be true for a state citizen who enjoys the rights of membership in the state as something obvious. Germans, feeling themselves nationalists, rushed to arms with enthusiasm when treacherous foes threatened us; but from the declamations of the Jews there constantly sounds an undertone that says: *Even though your battle did not have anything to do with us at all, we agreed nevertheless to play the soldier too.* Besides, it is sufficiently well-known that the military service of the Jews was mostly restricted to the garrisons, communications, and battalion writing rooms. All Germans who were at the battlefront can confirm that Jews were only rarely seen in the battle line.

On the other hand, they developed an uncanny wartime activity in the interior. They were the most important army suppliers, ones who were able to charge the state, in its distress, huge amounts of money; they were predominantly the racketeers, chain retailers, and price gougers who mercilessly exploited the distress of the nation. The four issues of *Hammer* from 1914-1918 are full of factual material that confirms this opinion.[9] A few people will be found who may collect these and then provide a clear picture of the "service" of the Jews during the war.

The fateful activity of the more than 100 war societies that did everything to hinder our success will also find its recorder. They were founded by the Jews Rathenau and Ballin, and filled by Jews in their leading offices.[10] Eighty percent of the officials in the war societies were Jews—mostly young people who thereby also avoided service on the Front. These war societies, which lent their functionaries a bureaucratic character, were very useful to

---

[9] Fritsch founded the publisher Hammer Verlag in 1902 and edited its principal journal, *Hammer*.

[10] Walther Rathenau (1867-1922) was a German Jewish industrialist and politician who directed the German war economy during the First World War. Albert Ballin (1857-1918) was a German Jewish shipping magnate who sought to mediate between the German Empire and Great Britain before the outbreak of the First World War.

the Jews, particularly to get a glimpse into the undertakings and books of their rivals and to explore all business secrets. They gave the Jews an opportunity to build up internal and external trade into a Jewish monopoly. The German big businessman and industrialist strives in vain to shake off this leech. A Jewish business monopoly arises in many fields.

The moral injuries that Judah imposed on us during the war [WWI] look worse. It cannot escape one who has eyes to see that large Jewish circles during the entire war stood with their sympathies on the side of our enemies. One may recall how many Jews born in Germany but living during the outbreak of the war in England immediately became naturalized [British citizens], changed their names, and published hateful declarations against their former Fatherland. Also, credible eye-witnesses assure us that the "Alsatian women" who greeted the incoming French with great spectacle were mostly Jewesses made up as native Alsatian girls. In America, the Jewish bankers with German names, Loeb, Kuhn and Co., Speyer, Ladenburg, Kahn, etc. constituted the worst warmongers.[11]

What the Jewish *Frankurter Zeitung* and the no less Jewish *Berliner Tageblatt*, the favorite newspapers of all Jews, conducted during the war often bordered on treason. To this day, they have not been convicted of what they did to encourage our enemies and weaken our will to win.

And the 'stab in the back' of our fighting front was performed by Jewish hands. One may recall the words of a Jewish soldier in the *Hammer*, no. 399, p. 66: "Germany will not win, for, before the end of the war approaches, we (!) will make our revolution."

And they did it. The directors were Jewish Bolshevists from Russia whom the Jewish ambassador Joffe[12] allowed to come over the border in hundreds as "couriers." Jewish millions from Russia had to recruit the necessarily dubious elements... And Jewish men took the new government in their hands. A full disclosure of the effect of Jewish influences on the misconduct of our government businesses and the false advising of our princes—before and during the war—must wait for a later time. Everything was conducted exactly as the ancient rabbinical prescription states it: "The princes shall be your caregivers and the princesses your wet nurses."

---

[11] For details on the extensive Jewish role in the war, see *The Jewish Hand in the World Wars* (T. Dalton, 2019).

[12] Adolph Joffe (1883-1927) was a Russian Jewish Bolshevist diplomat who served as the Soviet representative in Berlin from April to November 1918.

But the complete internal collapse of Germany is the fruit of a long burrowing activity. Jewry had been working for decades with unceasing eagerness in the internal demoralization of the German people. It was able to find really demonic means and ways to dupe and to corrupt the guileless people. Everything that constituted the core and the character of our strength, the Jew has burrowed and gnawed through, slowly and secretly. The essential armor of our nation—the peasantry and the bourgeois middle-class—he wore down economically, threw the provincial and urban properties into debt; through the monopolizing of banks and stock-exchanges, he was able to make trade and industry dependent on him. Above all, however, the press in Jewish hands gave a suitable means to radically falsify German thought and feeling and to disseminate among the masses all sorts of erroneous ideas. Even the strongest and healthiest nation cannot bear 50 years of Jewish press.[13] Everything that a nefarious destructive spirit could conceive in order to undermine German morality, to confuse the economy, to unsettle trust, to destroy all authority, to make the German contemptible in front of foreign nations and to himself, to incite the individual classes and estates against one another, and to divide through internal strife—all that was accomplished with incomparable refinement. German guilelessness supported the plan.

In this way, the German nation was worn down to its bones, divided within itself, misled and falsified in its thought and aspiration. It will be a miracle if it could be strong and capable of life once again.[14]

Rightly indeed does Richard Wagner characterize the Jew as the "plastic demon of decay of humanity".[15]

*****

And the German workforce finds itself in the talons of this demon. It has become its instrument without a will of its own, because it was able to give the appearance of being a champion of freedom and of the interests of the proletariat. One has to wonder about the unequal couple. How should a people

---

[13] In America, the *New York Times* has been Jewish-owned and -operated since Adolph Ochs bought the paper in 1896. Thus, the USA has experienced a "Jewish press" for 126 years—and counting.

[14] Fritsch was unaware that Hitler and his NSDAP party were rapidly gaining power at the time of this writing. They would rise to power in just 10 years.

[15] From Wagner's 1881 essay "Know thyself." For a short discussion of this seminal passage, see *Eternal Strangers*, p. 91.

who never worked and indeed disregards all physical work as something degrading and whose entire thought is directed to cunning and effortless acquisition, ever have an honest share in the flourishing of productive work? How then does this foreigner come to play the role of leader of the German proletariat?

Like everything about the Jew, this is also a clever disguise and a prudent precaution. It was foreseeable decades ago that the grabbing of all the treasures of the Earth conducted with ardent avarice by the Jews would create ever-more dispossessed and disinherited people. In this way, the day had to come when the indignation of the dispossessed masses rose against the owners of the golden billions. That had to be prevented. Therefore the Jews Marx and Lassalle founded an organization of the proletariat, Social Democracy. They took the leadership of their natural opponent even into their hands in order to deter the latter from a reasonable use of his power. They taught him how to combat capital, but focused all attention solely on visible property, on productive and immobile capital, which is active in industry and agriculture and actually helps to produce something.

They did not tell the worker, however, that there is another capital that hides cunningly behind the scenes and is generally not perceived by the normal state citizen: *speculative or mobile capital* which, fully unproductive, leads a parasitical life on the back of nations and, unobserved by the mere senses, skims the cream off all national economy. It works in banks and stock-exchanges, operates through artificial price shifts and inflations, and plunders entire nations—without the people betrayed knowing exactly what happened.[16] One never heard people speak of these things in workers' conferences. Nothing is ever written about it in the Social Democratic newspapers. There, people incite only against the "chimney barons" and the "German Junkers," but never do they speak of the thieves of millions at the stock-exchange.

In this way, the masses of the nation are fully in the hands of clever directors of foreign origin who use them for quite other goals than the "liberation of the peoples." They are much rather intent on binding the peoples under another yoke, under one that is harsher than anything they have ever borne. Confusion and entanglement have proceeded so far that there is hardly an escape anymore. The only rescue can be found by opening the workers' eyes so that they may perceive whom they actually serve.

---

[16] In Fritsch's book *Das Rätsel des jüdischen Volkes* (The Enigma of the Jewish People; published under the pseudonym 'Stoltheim'), these matters have been presented in an easily comprehensible way.

All those who are concerned with the national welfare, truth, freedom, culture, and civilization should immediately proceed to this task.

We do not wish to strike the Jews dead or offer them any sort of violence; we only want to see them removed from our national life—because they disturb us, and we them, in the naturally determined development of our own life. Let them establish their own national state somewhere, as is the desire of the Zionists. We indeed wish to be helpful to them in this. The present-day demand voiced so loudly for the self-determination right of peoples should be guaranteed as much to the Hebrews as to us. Our right of self-determination tells us: The Hebrew is a foreigner, of different blood and spirit, whose character can never fuse with ours. As a foreign body, he is a thorn in our side that hinders the fulfilment of our striving for German ideals; therefore we wish to peacefully and amicably separate ourselves from him.

May Judah develop its best powers in a free competition of nations, and may it demonstrate to the world that the high characteristics of which it boasts are capable of maintaining its particular character and of raising it into a useful member of human society.

A REAL CASE AGAINST THE JEWS
AND
COMMISSARY TO THE GENTILES

Marcus Eli Ravage
(1928)

Editor: Little-known Jewish writer Marcus Ravage (1884-1965) was born Marcus Revici in Vaslui, Romania. He migrated to the US in 1900 at age 16, staying several years. He attended the University of Missouri, majoring in English. But his life after this is largely a mystery; at some point, he returned to Europe, eventually settling in southern France, where he died at age 81.

Ravage wrote some eight books, but he is perhaps best known for two articles published in *Century Magazine* in January and February of 1928. Using remarkably blunt language, he first admits (perhaps sarcastically) that Jews have been detrimental to Gentile society. But he castigates anti-Semites for emphasizing relatively petty issues and missing the truly dominant matter: the pervasiveness of a Judeo-Christianity over Western society. Jews, he rightly says, invented Christianity, with its Jewish God, Jewish savior (Jesus), Jewish mother (Virgin Mary), and Jewish apostles. The Jew Paul then took a nascent movement and turned it into a weapon against Rome and against the pagan masses. Calling this Christianity a "subversive Jewish conspiracy," Ravage shows how a malicious group of early Jewish Christians spread a toxic ideology, ultimately subverting the Roman Empire itself.

In these essays, Savage is almost certainly drawing on Nietzsche—in particular, his *On the Genealogy of Morals* and *Antichrist*—though he gives the German philosopher no credit. Furthermore, both men lacked the anthropological data we have today; had they known what we know, they would have pressed the case even harder. For example, we have no corrobo-

rating data of any kind for the years 0 to 70 AD (Jesus allegedly lived from roughly 0 to 30 AD)—but this is almost inconceivable if indeed he was the Son of God. Second, the four
Gospels were written between the years 70 and 95 AD, which
of course is decades after the alleged events; they can hardly
be considered accurate. Third, the first outside sources to
comment on the 'miracle' of Christianity do not appear until
93 AD (Josephus) and 115 AD (Pliny the Younger)—which
again seems impossible if the alleged events were true. In
sum, the facts and the data support Nietzsche's and Ravage's
view: Christianity was a Jewish conspiracy, a Jewish hoax,
and Western civilization has suffered at its hands ever since.

A Real Case Against the Jews

Of course, you do resent us. It is no good telling me you don't. So let us not
waste any time on denials and alibis. You know you do, and I know it, and
we understand each other. To be sure, some of your best friends are Jews,
and all that. I have heard that before once or twice, I think.

And I know too, that you do not include me personally—"me" being
any particular individual Jew—when you fling out at us in your wholesale
fashion, because I am, well, so different, don't you know, almost as good as
one of yourselves. That little exemption does not, somehow, move me to
gratitude; but never mind that now. It is the aggressive, climbing, pushing,
materialistic sort you dislike—those, in a word, who remind you so much of
your own up-and-coming brethren. We understand each other perfectly. I
don't hold it against you.

Bless my soul, I do not blame anybody for disliking anybody. The
thing that intrigues me about this anti-Jewish business, as you play at it, you
make such fantastic and transparent excuses, you seem to be suffering from
self-consciousness so horribly, that if the performance were not so grotesque
it would be irritating.

It is not as if you were amateurs: you have been at it for over fifteen
centuries. Yet watching you and hearing your childish pretexts, one might
get the impression that you did not know yourselves what it is all about. You
resent us, but you cannot clearly say why. You think up a new excuse—a
"reason" is what you call it—every other day. You have been piling up

justification for yourself these many hundreds of years and each new invention is more laughable than the last, and each new excuse contradicts and annihilates the last.

Not so many years ago, I used to hear that we were money-grubbers and commercial materialists; now the complaint is being whispered around that no art and no profession is safe against Jewish invasion.

We are, if you are to be believed, at once clannish and exclusive, and unassimilable because we won't intermarry with you, and we are also climbers and pushers and a menace to your racial integrity.

Our standard of living is so low that we create your slums and sweat industries, and so high that we crowd you out of your best residential sections. We shirk our patriotic duty in wartime because we are pacifists by nature and tradition, and we are the arch-plotters of universal wars and the chief beneficiaries of those wars (see "The Protocols of the Learned Elders of Zion".) We are at once the founders and leading adherents of capitalism and the chief perpetrators of the rebellion against capitalism.

Surely, history has nothing like us for versatility!

And oh! I almost forgot the reason of reasons. We are the stiff-necked people who never accepted Christianity, and we are the criminal people who crucified its founder.

But I tell you, you are self-deceivers. You lack either the self-knowledge or the mettle to face the facts squarely and own up to the truth. You resent the Jew not because, as some of you seem to think, we crucified Jesus but because we gave him birth. Your real quarrel with us is not that we have rejected Christianity but that we have imposed it upon you!

Your loose, contradictory charges against us are not a patch on the blackness of our proved historic offense. You accuse us of stirring up revolution in Moscow. Suppose we admit the charge. What of it? Compared with what Paul the Jew of Tarsus accomplished in Rome, the Russian upheavals were a mere street brawl.

You make much noise and fury about the undue Jewish influence in your theaters and movie palaces. Very good; granted your complaint is well-founded. But what is that compared to our staggering influence in your churches, your schools, your laws and your governments, and the very thoughts you think every day?

A clumsy Russian forges a set of papers and publishes them in a book called "The Protocols of the Elders of Zion" which shows that we plotted to bring on the late World War. You believe that book. All right. For the sake of argument, we will underwrite every word of it. It is genuine and authentic. But what is that besides the unquestionable historical conspiracy which we have carried out, which we never have denied because you never had the courage to charge us with it, and of which the full record is extant for any-body to read?

*****

If you really are serious when you talk of Jewish plots, may I not direct your attention to one worth talking about? What use is it wasting words on the alleged control of your public opinion by Jewish financiers, newspaper own-ers, and movie magnates, when you might as well justly accuse us of the proved control of your whole civilization by the Jewish Gospels?

You have not begun to appreciate the real depth of our guilt. We are intruders. We are disturbers. We are subverters. We have taken your natural world, your ideals, your destiny, and played havoc with them. We have been at the bottom of not merely the latest Great War but of nearly all your wars, not only of the Russian but of nearly every other major revolution in your history. We have brought discord and confusion and frustration into your personal and public life. We are still doing it. No one can tell how long we shall go on doing it.

Look back a little and see what has happened. Nineteen hundred years ago, you were an innocent, care-free pagan race. You worshipped countless Gods and Goddesses, the spirits of the air, of the running streams and of the woodland. You took unblushing pride in the glory of your naked bodies. You carved images of your gods and of the tantalizing human figure. You delighted in the combats of the field, the arena and the battle-ground. War and slavery were fixed institutions in your systems. Disporting yourselves on the hillsides and in the valleys of the great outdoors, you took to speculating on the wonder and mystery of life and laid the foundations of natural science and philosophy. Yours was a noble, sensual culture, unirked by the prickings of the social conscience or by any sentimental questionings about human equality. Who knows what great and glorious destiny might have been yours, if we had left you alone?

But we did not leave you alone. We took you in hand and pulled down the beautiful and generous structure you had reared, and changed the whole course of your history. We conquered you as no empire of yours ever subju-gated Africa or Asia. And we did it all without bullets, without blood or turmoil, without force of any kind. We did it solely by the irresistible might of our spirit, with ideas, with propaganda.

We made you the willing and unconscious bearers of our mission to the whole world, to the barbarous races of the world, to the countless unborn generations. Without fully understanding what we were doing to you, you became the agents at large of our racial tradition, carrying our gospel to un-explored ends of the earth.

Our tribal customs have become the core of your moral code. Our tribal laws have furnished the basic groundwork of all your august constitutions and legal systems. Our legends and our folk-tales are the sacred lore which you croon to your infants. Our poets have filled your hymnals and your prayer-books. Our national history has become an indispensable part of the learning of your pastors and priests and scholars. Our Kings, our statesmen, our prophets, our warriors are your heroes. Our ancient little country is your Holy Land. Our national literature is your Holy Bible. What our people thought and taught has become inextricable woven into your very speech and tradition, until no one among you can be called educated who is not fa-miliar with our racial heritage.

Jewish artisans and Jewish fishermen are your teachers and your saints, with countless statues carved in their image and innumerable cathedrals raised to their memories. A Jewish maiden [the Virgin Mary] is your ideal of motherhood and womanhood. A Jewish rebel-prophet [Jesus] is the central figure in your religious worship. We have pulled down your idols, cast aside your racial inheritance, and substituted for them our God and our traditions. No conquest in history can even remotely compare with this clean sweep of our conquest over you.

How did we do it? Almost by accident. Nearly two thousand years ago in far-off Palestine, our religion had fallen into decay and materialism. Mon-ey-changers were in possession of the temple. Degenerate, selfish priests grew fat. Then a young patriot-idealist arose and went about the land, calling for a revival of the faith. He had no thought of setting up a new church. Like all the prophets before him, his only aim was to purify and revitalize the old creed. He attacked the priests and drove the money-changers from the tem-ple. This brought him into conflict with the established order and its support-ing pillars. The Roman authorities, who were in occupation of the country, fearing his revolutionary agitation as a political effort to oust them, arrested him, tried him and condemned him to death by crucifixion, a common form of execution at that time.

The followers of Jesus of Nazareth, mainly slaves and poor workmen, in their bereavement and disappointment, turned away from the world and formed themselves into a brotherhood of pacifists non-resisters, sharing their memory of their crucified leader and living together communistically. They were merely a new sect in Judea, without power or consequence, neither the first nor the last.

Only after the destruction of Jerusalem by the Romans did the new creed come into prominence.[1] Then a patriotic Jew named Paul or Saul conceived the idea of humbling the Roman power by destroying the morale of its soldiery with the doctrines of love and non-resistance preached by the little sect of Jewish Christians. He became the Apostle to the Gentiles, he who hitherto had been one of the most active persecutors of the band.[2] And so well did Paul do his work that within four centuries, the great empire which had subjugated Palestine along with half of the world, was a heap of ruins. And the law which went forth from Zion became the official religion of Rome.

This was the beginning of our dominance in your world. But it was only a beginning. From this time forth, your history is little more than a struggle for mastery between your own old pagan spirit and our Jewish spirit. Half your wars, great and little, are religious wars, fought over the interpretation of one thing or another in our teachings. You no sooner broke free from your primitive religious simplicity and attempted the practice of the pagan Roman learning, than Luther, armed with our Gospel, arose to down you and re-enthrone our heritage. Take the three principal revolutions in modern times—the French, the American, and the Russian. What are they but the triumphs of the Jewish idea of social, political, and economic justice?

*****

And the end is still a long way off. We still dominate you. At this very moment your churches are torn asunder by a civil war between Fundamentalists and Modernists, that is to say between those who cling to our teachings and traditions literally and those who are striving, by slow steps, to dispossess us. Again and again the Puritan heritage of Judea breaks out in waves of stage

---

[1] This seems to be incorrect. According to modern estimates, Paul did all of his proselytizing and writing before the fall of Jerusalem in 70 AD, and in fact he likely died before that momentous event. But the Gospels did come after.

[2] "I am speaking to you Gentiles. Inasmuch as I am the apostle to the Gentiles, I magnify my ministry" (Rom 11:13).

censorship, Sunday blue laws, and national prohibition acts. And while these things are happening, you twaddle about Jewish influence in the movies.

Is it any wonder you resent us? We have put a clog upon your progress. We have imposed upon you an alien book and an alien faith which you cannot digest, which is at cross-purposes with your native spirit, which keeps you everlasting ill-at-ease, and which you lack the spirit to either reject or accept in full.

In full, of course, you never have accepted our Christian teachings. In your hearts you still are pagans. You still take pride in the glory of the nude human figure. Your social conscience, in spite of all democracy and all your social revolution, is still a pitifully imperfect thing. We have merely divided your soul, confused your impulses, and paralyzed your desires. In the midst of the battle, you are obliged to kneel down to him who commanded you to turn the other cheek, who said "Resist not evil" and "Blessed are the peacemakers". In your lust for gain you are suddenly disturbed by a memory from your Sunday school days about taking no thought for the morrow. In your industrial struggles, when you would smash a strike without compunction, you are suddenly reminded that the poor are blessed and that men are brothers in the Fatherhood of the Lord. As you are about to yield to temptation, your Jewish training puts a deterrent hand on your shoulder and dashes the brimming cup from your lips. You Christians have never become Christianized. To that extent, we have failed with you. But we have forever spoiled the fun of paganism for you.

So why should you not resent us? If we were in your place, we should probably dislike you more cordially than you do us. But we should make no bones about telling you why. We should not resort to subterfuges and transparent pretext. With millions of painfully respectable Jewish shopkeepers all about us, we should not insult your intelligence and your own honesty by talking about communism as a Jewish philosophy. And with millions of hard-working impecunious Jewish peddlers and laborers, we should make ourselves ridiculous by talking about international capitalism as a Jewish monopoly. No, we should go straight to the point. We should contemplate this confused ineffectual muddle which we call civilization, this half-Christian half-pagan medley, and—we should say to you point-blank: "For this mess, thanks to you, to your prophets, and your Bible."

Commissary to the Gentiles

You Christians worry and complain about the Jew's influence in your civilization. We are, you say, an international people, a compact minority in your midst, with traditions, interests, aspirations and objectives distinct from your own. And you declare that this state of affairs is a menace to your orderly development; it confuses your impulses; it defeats your purposes; it muddles up your destiny. I do not altogether see the danger. Your world has always been ruled by minorities; and it seems to me a matter of indifference what the remote origin and professed creed of the governing clique is. The influence, on the other hand, is certainly there, and it is vastly greater and more insidious than you appear to realize.

That is what puzzles and amuses and sometimes exasperates us about your game of Jew-baiting. It sounds so portentous. You go about whispering terrifyingly of the Jew in this and that and the other thing. It makes us quake. We are conscious of the injury we did you when we imposed upon you our alien faith and traditions. Suppose, we say trembling, you should wake up to the fact that your religion, your education, your morals, your social, governmental and legal systems are fundamentally of our making! And then you specify, and talk vaguely of Jewish financiers and Jewish motion-picture promoters, and our terror dissolves in laughter. The Goy, we see with relief, will never know the real blackness of our crimes.

We cannot make it out. Either you do not know, or you have not the courage to charge us with those deeds for which there is at least a shadow of evidence and which an intelligent judge and jury could examine without impatience. Why bandy about unconvincing trifles when you might so easily indict us for serious and provable offenses? Why throw up to us a patent and a clumsy forgery such as the Protocols of the Elders of Zion when you might as well confront us with the Revelation of St. John? Why talk about Marx and Trotsky when you have Jesus of Nazareth and Paul of Tarsus to confound us with?

You call us subverters, agitators, revolution-mongers. It is the truth, and I cower at your discovery. It could be shown with only the slightest straining and juggling of the facts that we have been at the bottom of all the major revolutions in your history. We undoubtedly had a sizeable finger in the Lutheran Rebellion [i.e. the Reformation], and it is simply a fact that we were the prime movers in the bourgeois democratic revolutions of the century before the last, both in France and America. If we were not, we did not know our own interests. But do you point your accusing finger at us and charge us with these heinous and recorded crimes? Not at all! You fantastically lay at our door the recent great War and the upheaval in Russia, which have done not only the most injury to the Jews themselves but which a school-boy could have foreseen would have that result.

*****

But even these plots and revolutions are as nothing compared with the great conspiracy which we engineered at the beginning of this era and which was destined to make the creed of a Jewish sect the religion of the Western world. The Reformation was not designed in malice purely. It squared us with an ancient enemy and restored our Bible to its place of honor in Christendom. The Republican revolutions of the Eighteenth century freed us of our age-long political and social disabilities. They benefited us, but they did you no harm. On the contrary, they prospered and expanded you. You owe your pre-eminence in the world to them. But the upheaval which brought Christianity into Europe was—or at least may easily be shown to have been—planned and executed by Jews as an act of revenge against a great Gentile state. And when you talk about Jewish conspiracies, I cannot for the world understand why you do not mention the destruction of Rome and the whole civilization of antiquity concentrated under her banners, at the hands of Jewish Christianity.

It is unbelievable, but you Christians do not seem to know where your religion came from, nor how, nor why. Your historians, with one great exception, do not tell you. The documents in these cases, which are part of your Bible, you chant over but do not read. We have done our work too thoroughly; you believe our propaganda too implicitly. The coming of Christianity is to you not an ordinary historical event growing out of other events of the time, it is the fulfilment of a divine Jewish prophecy—with suitable amendments of your own. It did not, as you see it, destroy a great Gentile civilization and a great Gentile empire with which Jewry was at war; it did not plunge mankind into barbarism and darkness for a thousand years; it came to bring salvation to the Gentile world!

Yet here, if ever, was a great subversive movement, hatched in Palestine, spread by Jewish agitators, financed by Jewish money, taught in Jewish pamphlets and broadsides, at a time when Jewry and Rome were in a death struggle, and ending in the collapse of the great Gentile empire. You do not even see it, though an intelligent child, unfuddled by theological magic, could tell you what it is all about after a hasty reading of the simple record. And then you go on prattling of Jewish conspiracies and cite as instances the Great War and the Russian Revolution! Can you wonder that we Jews have always taken your anti-Semites rather lightly, as long as they did not resort to violence?

And mind you, no less an authority than [Edward] Gibbon long ago tried to enlighten you. It is now a century and a half since *The Decline and Fall of the Roman Empire* (1776) let the cat out of the bag. Gibbon, not being a parson dabbling in history, did not try to account for the end of a great era by inventing fatuous nonsense about the vice and degradation of Rome, about the decay of morals and faith in an empire which was at that very time in the midst of its most glorious creative period. How could he? He was living in the Augustan Age in London which—in spite of nearly two thousand years since the coming of Christian salvation—was as good a replica of Augustan Rome in the matter of refined lewdness as the foggy islanders could make it. No, Gibbon was a race-conscious Gentile and an admirer of the culture of the pagan West, as well as an historian with brains and eyes. Therefore he had no difficulty laying his finger on the malady that had rotted and wasted away the noble edifice of antique civilization. He put Christianity down—the law which went forth from Zion and the word of God from Jerusalem—as the central cause of the decline and fall of Rome and all she represented.

So far so good. But Gibbon did not go far enough. He was born and died, you see, a century before the invention of scientific anti-Semitism. He left wholly out of account the element of deliberation. He saw an alien creed sweeping out of the East and overwhelming the fair lands of the West. It never occurred to him that the whole scheme of salvation was dedicated. Yet the facts are as plain as you please.

Let me, in very brief, recount the tale, unembroidered by miracle, prophecy or magic.

For a good perspective, I shall have to go back a space. The action conveniently falls into four parts, rising to a climax in the third. The time when the first curtain rises is roughly 65 BC. Dramatis personae are, minor parts aside, Judea and Rome. Judea is a tiny kingdom off the Eastern Mediterranean. For five centuries it has been hardly more than a geographical expression. Again and again, it has been overrun and destroyed and its population carried into exile or slavery by its powerful neighbors. Nominally independent, it is now as unstable as ever and on the edge of civil war. The empire of the West, with her nucleus in the City Republic of Rome, while not yet mistress of the world, is speedily heading that way. She is acknowledged the one great military power of the time, as well as the heir of Greece and the center of civilization.

Up to the present, the two states have had little or no contact with one another. Then without solicitation on her part, Rome was suddenly asked to take a hand in Judean affairs. A dispute had arisen between two brothers over the succession to the petty throne, and the Roman general Pompey, who happened to be in Damascus winding up bigger matters, was called upon to arbitrate between the claimants. With the simple directness of a republican soldier, Pompey exiled one of the brothers, tossed the chief priesthood to his rival, and abolished the kingly dignity altogether. Not to put too fine a point on it, Pompey's mediation amounted in effect to making Judea a Roman dependency.

The Jews, not unnaturally, objected; and Rome, to conciliate them and to conform to local prejudice, restored the royal office. She appointed, that is, a king of her own choosing. He was the son of an excise-man, an Idumean by race, named Herod [in 37 BC]. But the Jews were not placated, and continued making trouble. Rome thought it very ungrateful of them.

All this is merely a prelude, and is introduced into the action to make clear what follows. Jewish discontent grew to disaffection and open revolt when their Gentile masters began importing into Jerusalem the blessings of Western culture. Graven images, athletic games, Greek drama, and gladiatorial shows were not to the Jewish taste. The pious resented them as an offence in the nostrils of Jehovah, even though the resident officials patiently explained they were meant for the entertainment and edification of the non-Jewish garrison. The Judeans resisted with especial strenuousness the advent of the efficient Roman tax-gatherer. Above all, they wanted back a king of their own royal line.

Among the masses, the rebellion took the form of a revival of the old belief in a Messiah, a divinely appointed savior who was to redeem his people from the foreign yoke and make Judea supreme among the nations. Claimants to the mission were not wanting. In Galilee, one Judas led a rather formidable insurrection, which enlisted much popular support. John, called the Baptist, operated in the Jordan country. He was followed by another north-country man, Jesus of Nazareth. All three were masters of the technique of couching incendiary political sedition in harmless theological phrases. All three used the same signal of revolt—"the time is at hand." And all three were speedily apprehended and executed, both Galileans by crucifixion.

Personal qualities aside, Jesus of Nazareth was, like his predecessors, a political agitator engaged in liberating his country from the foreign oppressor. There is even considerable evidence that he entertained an ambition to become king of an independent Judea. He claimed, or his biographers later claimed for him, descent from the ancient royal line of David. But his paternity is somewhat confused. The same writers who traced the origin of his mother's husband back to the psalmist-king also pictured Jesus as the son of Jehovah, and admitted that Joseph was not his father.

It seems, however, that Jesus before long realized the hopelessness of his political mission and turned his oratorical gifts and his great popularity with masses in quite another direction. He began preaching a primitive form of populism, socialism, and pacificism. The effect of this change in his program was to gain him the hostility of the substantial, propertied classes, the priest and patriots generally, and to reduce his following to the poor, laboring mass and the slaves.

After his death, these lowly disciples formed themselves into a communistic brotherhood. A sermon their late leader had once delivered upon a hillside summed up for them the essence of his teachings, and they made it their rule of life. It was a philosophy calculated to appeal profoundly to humble people. It comforted those who suffered here on Earth with promised rewards beyond the grave. It made virtues of necessities of the weak. Men without hope in the future were admonished to take no thought for the morrow. Men too helpless to resent insult or injury were taught to resist not evil. Men condemned to lifelong drudgery and indigence were assured of the dignity of labor and of poverty. The meek, the despised, the disinherited, the downtrodden, were—in the hereafter—to be the elect and favored of God. The worldly, the ambitious, the rich and powerful, were to be denied admission to heaven.

*****

The upshot, then, of Jesus' mission was a new sect in Judea. It was neither the first nor the last. Judea, like modern America, was a fertile soil for strange creeds. The Ebionim—the paupers, as they called themselves—did not regard their beliefs as a new religion. Jews they had been born, and Jews they remained. The teachings of their master were rather in nature of a social philosophy, an ethic of conduct, a way of life. To modern Christians, who never tire of asking why the Jews did not accept Jesus and his teachings, I can only answer that for a long time none but the Jews did. To be surprised that the whole Jewish people did not turn Ebionim is about as intelligent as to expect all Americans to join the Unitarians or the Baptists or the Christian Scientists.

In ordinary times, little attention would been paid to the ragged brotherhood. Slaves and laborers for the most part, their meekness might even have been encouraged by the soldier class. But with the country in the midst of a struggle with a foreign foe, the unworldly philosophy took on a dangerous aspect. It was a creed of disillusion, resignation, and defeat. It threatened to undermine the morale of the nation's fighting men in time of war. This blessing of the peacemakers, this turning of the other cheek, this non-resistance, this love your enemy, looked like a deliberate attempt to paralyze the national will in a crisis and assure victory to the foe.

So it is not surprising that the Jewish authorities began persecuting the Ebionim. Their meetings were invaded and dispersed, their leaders were clapped into jail, their doctrines were proscribed. It looked for a while as if the sect would be speedily wiped out. Then, unexpected, the curtain rose on act three, and events took a sudden new turn.

*****

Perhaps the bitterest foe of the sectaries was one Saul, a maker of tents. A native of Tarsus and thus a man of some education in Greek culture, he despised the new teachings for their unworldliness and their remoteness from life. A patriotic Jew, he dreaded their effect on the national cause. A travelled man, versed in several languages, he was ideally suited for the task of going about among the scattered Jewish communities to counteract the spread of their socialistic pacifistic doctrines. The leaders in Jerusalem appointed him chief persecutor to the Ebionim.

He was on his way to Damascus one day to arrest a group of the sectaries when a novel idea came to him. In the quaint phrase of the book of Acts, he saw a vision.[3] He saw as a matter of fact, two. He perceived, to begin with, how utterly hopeless were the chances of little Judea winning out in an armed conflict against the greatest military power in the world. Second, and more important, it came to him that the vagabond creed which he had been repressing might be forged into an irresistible weapon against the

---

[3] See Acts 9:3-6 ("As Saul drew near to Damascus on his journey, suddenly a light from heaven flashed around him. He fell to the ground and heard a voice say to him, "Saul, Saul, why do you persecute Me?"…)

formidable foe. Pacifism, non-resistance, resignation, love, were dangerous teachings at home. Spread among the enemy's legions, they might break down their discipline and thus yet bring victory to Jerusalem. Saul, in a word, was probably the first man to see the possibilities of conducting war by propaganda.

He journeyed on to Damascus, and there, to the amazement alike of his friends and of those he had gone to suppress, he announced his conversion to the faith and applied for admission to the brotherhood. On his return to Jerusalem he laid his new strategy before the startled Elders of Zion. After much debate and searching of souls, it was adopted. More resistance was offered by the leaders Ebionim of the capital. They were mistrustful of his motives, and they feared that his proposal to strip the faith of its ancient Jewish observances and practices so as to make it acceptable to Gentiles would fill the fraternity with alien half- converts, and dilute its strength. But in the end he won them over, too. And so Saul, the fiercest persecutor of Jesus' followers, became Paul, the Apostle to the Gentiles. And so, incidentally, began the spread into pagan lands of the West, of an entirely new Oriental religion.

Unfortunately for Paul's plan, the new strategy worked much too well. His revamped and rather alluring theology made converts faster than he had dared hope, or than he even wished. His idea, it should be kept in mind, was at this stage purely defensive. He had as yet no thought of evangelizing the world; he only hoped to discourage the enemy. With that accomplished, and the Roman garrisons out of Palestine, he was prepared to call a truce. But the slaves and oppressed of the Empire, the wretched conscripts, and the starving proletariat of the capital itself, found as much solace in the adapted Pauline version of the creed as the poor Jews before them had found in the original teachings of their crucified master. The result of this unforeseen success was to open the enemy's eyes to what was going on. Disturbing reports of insubordination among the troops began pouring into Rome from the army chiefs in Palestine and elsewhere. Instead of giving the imperial authorities pause, the new tactics only stiffened their determination.

Rome swooped down upon Jerusalem with fire and sword, and after a fierce siege which lasted four years, she destroyed the nest of the agitation (in 70 AD). At least she thought she had destroyed it.

The historians of the time leave us in no doubt as to the aims of Rome. They tell us that Nero sent Vespasian and his son Titus with definite and explicit orders to annihilate Palestine and Christianity together. To the Romans, Christianity meant nothing more than Judaism militant, anyhow, an interpretation which does not seem far from the facts. As to Nero's wish, he had at least half of it realized for him. Palestine was so thoroughly annihilated that it has remained a political ruin to this day. But Christianity was not so easily destroyed.

Indeed, it was only after the fall of Jerusalem that Paul's program developed to the full. Hitherto, as I have said, his tactic had merely been to frighten the conqueror, in the manner of Moses plaguing the Pharaohs. He had gone along cautious and hesitantly, taking care not to arouse the powerful foe. He was willing to dangle his novel weapon before the foe's nose, and let him feel it's edge, but he shrank from thrusting it in full force. Now that the worst had happened and Judea had nothing further to lose, he flung scruples to the wind and carried the war into the enemy's country. The goal now was nothing less than to humble Rome as she had humbled Jerusalem, to wipe her off the map, just as she had wiped out Judea.

*****

If Paul's own writings fail to convince you of this interpretation of his activities, I invite your attention to his more candid associate John. Where Paul, operating within the shadow of the imperial palace and half the time a prisoner in Roman jails, is obliged to deal in parable and veiled hints, John, addressing himself to disaffected Asiatics, can afford the luxury of plain speaking. At any rate, his pamphlet entitled "Revelation" is, in truth, a revelation of what the whole astonishing business is about.

Rome, fancifully called Babylon, is minutely described in the language of sputtering hate, as the mother of harlots and abominations of the Earth, as the woman drunken with the blood of the saints (Christians and Jews), as the oppressor of "peoples and multitudes and nations and tongues" and—to remove all doubt of her identity—as "that great city which reigned over the Kings of the Earth." An Angel triumphantly cries, "Babylon the great is fallen." Then follows an orgiastic picture of ruin. Commerce and industry and maritime trade are at an end. Art and music and "the voice of the bridegroom and of the bride" are silenced. The gentle Christian conquerors wallow in blood up to the bridles of their horses. "Rejoice over her, thou heaven, and ye holy apostles and prophets; for God hath avenged you on her."

And what is the end and purpose of all this chaos and devastation? John is not too reticent to tell us. For he closes his pious prophecy with a vision of the glories of the new—that is, the restored—Jerusalem: not any allegorical fantasy, I pray you, but literally Jerusalem, the capital of a great reunited kingdom of "the twelve tribes of the children of Israel."

Could anyone ask for anything plainer?

Of course, no civilization could forever hold out against this kind of assault. By the year 200 the efforts of Paul and John and their successors had made such headway among all classes of Roman society that Christianity had become the dominant cult throughout the empire.

Meantime, as Paul had shrewdly foreseen, Roman morale and discipline had quite broken down, so that more and more the imperial legions, once the terror of the world and the backbone of Western culture, went down to defeat before barbarian invaders. In the year 326 the emperor Constantine, hoping to check the insidious malady, submitted to conversion and proclaimed Christianity the official religion. It was too late. After him the emperor Julian tried to resort once more to suppression. But neither resistance nor concession were of any use. The Roman body politic has become thoroughly worm-eaten with Palestinian propaganda. Paul had triumphed.

This at least is how, were I an anti-Semite in search of a credible sample of subversive Jewish conspiracy, I would interpret the event of a modified Jewish creed into the Western world.

THE SCHUTZSTAFFEL AS ANTI-BOLSHEVIST COMBAT ORGANIZATION

Heinrich Himmler
(1936)

Editor: Apart from Hitler, Himmler (1900-1945) was one of the highest-ranking leaders in National Socialist Germany, and the head of the Schutzstaffel, or SS. During his lifetime, he published a number of small booklets and collections of speeches and essays. This text—*Die Schutzstaffel als antibols-chewistische Kampforganisation*—contains several interesting comments on Jews and the Jewish Question, within a historical context. It closes with some thoughts on the core values of the SS, values which stand in marked contrast to Judeo-Bolshevist ones. (All notes are those of the translator and editor.)

I. BOLSHEVISM

People speak a lot about Bolshevism today, and most are of the opinion that this Bolshevism is a phenomenon that arises only in our modern age. Many even believe that this Bolshevism, this battle of the sub-human organized and conducted by the Jew, has become a problem for the first time in the history of the world as something totally new.

Against that, we consider it right to maintain that, so long as there are men on the Earth, the battle between man and the sub-human is a historical rule, that this battle conducted by the Jew against the nations, as far into the past as we can look, belongs to the natural course of life on our planet. One can safely come to the conviction that this life-and-death struggle is perhaps even as much a natural law as the battle of man against any epidemic, as the battle of the plague bacillus against the healthy body.

It is therefore necessary to study the methods of this battle in the past through our present day, in some clearly manifest examples, in order to apprehend the tactics of our Jewish-Bolshevist opponent.

Purim Festival

One of these historical examples of the radical destruction of an Aryan people through Bolshevist-Jewish methods is given to us by the Bible. Just read with perceptive eyes that part of Jewish history in which it is explained how the Jews stand divided among the Persian people in all cities, in all villages, and in the capital Susa; how among this Persian, Aryan people, the knowledge of the danger of these Jews is present; how the will to solve this Jewish Question in Persia—embodied in the minister Haman—emerges. It explains, further, how the monarch, who is called Ahasuerus in the Bible and was Xerxes, through extraordinarily cleverly spun intrigues of his court Jews, is separated from his Persian wife Vashti; and how the Jew in many shapes—in this case, through Jewish girls and especially through the Jewish whore Esther—ensnares the king.[1]

We hear then how, against the will of the racially-related and racially-conscious minister Haman, the game of intrigues is played out with all possible Jewish refinement. It ends in such a way that the minister Haman, faithful to his people and king, is delivered to the Jew Mordecai and to the gallows by his monarch made senseless by his blindness—a disgraceful process that we can ascertain not for the last time in the history of nations. It shows how this Jew Mordecai was made vizier and now, with that cold-blooded, unemotional, and ruthless calculation characteristic of all Bolshevism, gives his order, on the basis of which the noblest of Persians in all cities and villages, all enemies of the Jews, are killed on a day fixed previously in writing by the Jew protected by a royal decree. The Bible reports that 75,000 Persians were killed at that time.[2] And to crown it all, through a decree of this Aryan king, it was determined that the 14th and 15th of the month of Adar were made a legal holiday and yearly celebrated as the great feast-day of the victory of the Jews, as the Purim Festival, up to the present day.

It is obvious that the ancient Persian people could never again recover from this blow. And you may perceive the entire tragedy of this people, struck to the core and destroyed by Jewish Bolshevism, in the fact that not

---

[1] See the Old Testament 'Book of Esther.'
[2] Esther (9:16).

only the lofty, pure, divine doctrine of Zarathustra of this Aryan people, but also its mother tongue, were relegated to oblivion. Only after more than 2,000 years have German scholars been able to translate, through painstaking labor, the books of Zarathustra from the ancient Persian language into German.

For Bolshevism proceeds always in this manner: The heads of the leaders of a people are bloodily cut off, and then it turns into political, economic, scientific, cultural, intellectual, spiritual, and corporeal slavery. The remainder of the people—robbed of their own worth through countless blood mixtures—degenerate. And in the historically short course of centuries, all one knows is that there was once such a people.

Other Examples

We cannot declare with absolute accuracy how many such tragedies—complete or incomplete—have taken place on Earth. We can, in many cases, only guess that here the eternal enemy of all of us, the Jew, had, in some disguise, or through one of his organizations, his hand in the game. We see, in the course of ages, the tireless executioner's sword of Canstatt and Verden shining.[3] We see how the funeral pyres blaze on which, in uncounted tens of thousands, the tortured and mangled bodies of the mothers and daughters of our peoples burned to ashes in the witch-trials.[4] We see in our mind's eye the judge's seats of the Inquisition that emptied Spain of its men exactly like the Thirty Years' War, which, in one generation, reduced our flourishing German people of 24 million to a half-starved remnant of four million.[5]

The French Freemasonic Revolution

I now jump to the modern age. Here I touch lightly, only for a certain European comprehensiveness, on the methods of the Reign of Terror of the French Revolution. This represents, in Jacobinism and in the times of the 'law for the removal of suspects,' the most complete Bolshevism—the

---

[3] Canstatt, in Stuttgart, was the seat of a court held by Charlemagne to try the rebellious dukes of Alemannia and Bavaria. Verden in Lower Saxony was the scene of a massacre of 4,500 Saxons by Charlemagne in 782.

[4] By some estimates, up to 500,000 people in Europe, mostly young women, were executed as witches.

[5] The Thirty Years' War lasted from 1618 to 1648, when it was ended by the Peace of Westphalia. Modern casualty estimates range from 5 million to 8 million.

246

246

systematic murder of the blond and blue-eyed, of the best sons of the French people. For the sake of the truth, let it be mentioned here: the French Revolution and its Reign of Terror was solely a revolution of the Freemasonic Order, this outstanding Jewish organization. Freemasonry not only acknowledged its 'glorious' revolution but praised it in every Lodge of the globe, including the most harmless German Lodges, as their triumph and their deed of the liberation of mankind.

Russian Revolution

I come now to the Russian Revolution. It is not my task to repeat once again often-enumerated dates, but I see that the most important thing in this context is an indication of the method.

At first, the discontent of the socially-depressed people of Russia was exploited according to plan and used for revolutionary propaganda. A number of Russian leaders who wished to repeal serfdom, especially the minister Stolypin,[6] were replaced by the Jewish-anarchist side before they could implement their reforms for the benefit of Russia. Russia was incited to the war against Germany with all conceivable means.[7] Even here, we may recall, in just a few words, the Jewish-Freemasonic activity in the launching of the [first] world war.

Then came the next chapter of the Bolshevist Revolution in Russia. Freemasonry calls this the change from the 'system of the yellow flag' to the 'system of the red flag.' In parliamentary jargon it meant: rule passes from the democratic-bourgeois parties to the moderate socialist party—in our case, the Social Democrats, there, the Mensheviks. At its head was the Jew Kerensky,[8] a man whose actions are a textbook example of Aryan good-naturedness. His Jewish mother—I may insert here this instructive episode—was sentenced to death for participation in anarchist attacks, and her life was pardoned by the father of the last czar because she was pregnant with Keren-

---

[6] Pyotr Stolypin (1862-1911) was the monarchist Prime Minister of Russia from 1906 to 1911. The agrarian reforms he introduced were called the Stolypin Reform. He was a rabid anti-Semite, and was ultimately assassinated by a Jew in 1911.

[7] For details, see *The Jewish Hand in the World Wars* (2019; T. Dalton).

[8] Alexander Kerensky (1881-1970) was Minister-Chairman of the Russian Provisional Government of early 1917. His relatively moderate Menshevik Marxists were contrasted with the more violent Bolshevik Marxists. Kerensky's government was overthrown by Lenin's Bolshevik Party in the October Revolution of 1917.

sky. And this Kerensky, who was born only through Aryan good-naturedness, deposed the last czar and was the one who prepared the way for Bolshevism.

But there were still many forces of resistance in Russia. Cold-bloodedly, these people were once again incited to take the offensive, and once again the Aryan Russian people had to go to the slaughterhouse. The final solution was effected. Now the 'system of the red flag' was turned, to speak again in Masonic language, to the 'system of the black flag'; or to adopt a parliamentary expression, rule passed from the moderate socialist party to the hands of the radical socialist party, the Bolshevists. Nothing stood in the way any longer. With all political violence, the Jews accomplished the radical massacre of all blood opposed to them, and all others bowed down in fear and terror. One could also use here the sentence from the Book of Esther in which it says: "and many Persians became Jews through fear of the Jews".[9] In this system of the black flag, then, all the non-Jews who were of weak character crossed over to the Jew and became his henchmen and thus serviceable minds, informers, and spies against their own racial comrades.

The tactics of the State Political Directorate (SPD) show how completely sophisticated this method of extermination was.[10] It was organized to plan resistances repeatedly against their own regime with *agents provocateur*, in order to find the leaders who would still participate in such a resistance. In this way, every head of resistance, every person who was still capable among this tormented Aryan people even of thinking of being a leader against the Bolshevists and the Jews, would fall. If you observe the Russian Revolution, you can draw innumerable parallels with the German Revolution of 1918.[11] The only difference here was that a merciful God and good fate set up a blockage against Jewry and called forth resistance forces which, at the right time, in 1919, brought forth Adolf Hitler to the task.

All things considered, through these examples that have been hastily offered and only outlined, you can complete the picture yourself; you will perhaps be able to collect innumerable small and major evidences of this bloody canvas of Bolshevism in the history of nations.

---

[9] Esther (8:17).

[10] The SPD was the intelligence service and secret police of the Russian Republic, and later the Soviet Union, from February 1922 to November 1923.

[11] The German Revolution, or November Revolution, lasted from November 1918 until the establishment of the Weimar Republic in August 1919. It caused Germany to lose World War One.

I think you will find yourself in agreement with me. I ask you not to consider, in exaggerated Aryan and German objectivity, minor details but to apprehend the entire line. Then you may conclude that, in the Jew, in the sub-human, and in his assistant organizations, there stand shrewd opponents—clever, competent in the organization of destruction, in the application of every opportunity and every possibility; on the floor of the salon and in the antechamber of ministers and monarchs; in assassinations; in the mixture of poisons; in consciously directed murder weapon; in the starving of entire undesired ethnicities; in intriguing; in the defamation of individual leaders; in the setting of leading personalities in opposition to each other—who would otherwise have been friends in life and death; in the battles on the street as well in the tricks of bureaucracy; and in the uprooting of the peasantry, as well as in the misuse of religion and religiosity. Indeed, the peasants have recognized better than us that there are no truces in these battles but only victors or defeated, and that to be defeated in this battle means for a nation to die.

You may also determine that this opponent could inscribe on his bloody flag of destruction a not inconsiderable number of victories that cannot be denied him—the names of destroyed and eliminated peoples.

These are some observations on Bolshevism of the past, present, and—never forget this—also in the future.[12]

II. THE PATH TO OBEDIENCE

The Service of the Church and the Knightly Orders

At the beginning of our millennium, almost all the younger sons of the best German families, following the rule of the Church, entered into the service of the Church as their priests and church leaders. A great number took up the cross and went on a Germanic crusade to the distant east, to deserts and sands. Some of these crusading knights were incorporated as knightly priests in the different knightly orders, who brought with themselves German bravery, German leadership, and German incorruptibility. Within the order of the Roman Church, they entered the school of obedience, subordination, and state authority—a school that was, indeed, older than the Church itself.

---

[12] At this point, the original essay continues with a section titled "Our People"; it has been deleted here, both for reasons of space and the fact that it has little bearing on the Jewish Question.

The Sicilian State of Friedrich II

And in this way did this knightly order participate in the creation of the first modern state of Friedrich in Sicily,[13] built according to the principles of state authority and authoritarian obedience. Filled with this knowledge, the Order was transplanted, through the political astuteness of the priestly noble Hermann von Salza,[14] to the German east in the first half of the 13th century. It established there the German state of the Order in the eastern territories that is perhaps well-known to you.

At that time, it was easy to introduce obedience in the German territory; for, alongside rule of the Christian religion, there operated the circumstance that a knightly order of the noblest families, selected racially from the best German blood, through battle, raised itself above peoples and miscegenated folk who did not equal our people in racial worth. Thus there arose, alongside the ecclesiastical obedience, a hierarchy of *performance* and *personality*.

The Prussian Army

From this East Prussia, which the electors of Brandenburg took over as kings of Prussia, the principles of the organization of administration, cleanliness, and above all of unconditional obedience to Prussia, were adopted. The Prussian Army, with its mercenaries, became, within the German interior, the first great school of absolute discipline. This discipline was at that time not only based on the noblest impulses of the human soul but indeed, in many cases, on the strength of the stronger entity, the state, on salary and livelihood, and on the fear of the broadsword of the corporal.

The Prussia of Old Fritz

This lasted until a heroic spirit, the greatest Prussian king, Old Fritz,[15] led this disciplined army himself in three great wars. It is perhaps right that, even

---

[13] Friedrich II (1194-1250) of the Hohenstaufen dynasty was King of Sicily from 1198 and Holy Roman Emperor from 1220.
[14] Hermann von Salza (ca.1165-1239) was a Grand Master of the Teutonic Knights, an order founded during the Siege of Acre in 1190. He was a friend of Friedrich II and led the campaign to Christianize Prussia in 1230.
[15] Friedrich II [Frederick the Great] (1712-1786) was the Hohenzollern ruler of Prussia from 1740 until his death.

in the last battles of the Third Silesian War,[16] the Prussian officer with his pike, who had been trained to obedience equally mercilessly in the cadet corps, stood behind the musketeer. And nevertheless, this obedience was already ennobled by the love of the leader, the love of the developing Fatherland Prussia, and by the honor of being not only a mercenary but a hero of this heroic Prussian Army. And for the first time, this unconditional obedience sang the melody 'Let us be brave countrymen'.[17]

Wars of Liberation

The next step led, through a frightful defeat, to the popular army of the Wars of Liberation[18] from 1812 to 1815, in which the bourgeois son and student already considered it an honor to be territorial army men and soldiers of the Prussian popular army, in voluntary obedience. And history then proceeded in quicker steps. More and more people began to draw closer to the concepts of freedom and honor, as well as of obedience.

1864, 1866

With such a spirited army, Prussia could, in 1864 and 1866,[19] not only conquer and defeat but also inwardly win over the freedom-loving Schleswig-Holsteiners, Bavarians, Württembergers, and other South Germans. These were people who were in many points related but had not followed such a straight path, and Prussia could incorporate them into the order and obedience of the German Reich through inner conviction.

---

[16] The Third Silesian War (1756-1763) was one of three wars between Prussia and Habsburg Austria for the control of Silesia.

[17] "*Lasst uns zeigen, dass wir brave Landeskinder sein*" ('Let us show that we are brave countrymen') is a line from the military march *Fridericus Rex* composed in honor of Frederick the Great.

[18] The German campaign conducted in Germany by Prussia, Austria, Russia, and Sweden against Napoleon. The campaign ended in Napoleon's defeat in the Battle of Leipzig in 1813.

[19] The Second Schleswig War was fought in 1864 between Denmark and the forces of Prussia and Austria for control of Schleswig-Holstein and Saxe-Lauenburg. The Austro-Prussian War of 1866 was concluded by the victory of Prussia over Austria in the Battle of Königgratz/Sadowa. It resulted in the dissolution of the German Confederation of 1815 and the replacement of the latter, in 1867, by a North German Confederation that excluded Austria.

The World War

And once again history moved, half a century later, into our own times, into the world war. Honor, freedom, and obedience were molded more closely together. And two million of the best Germans volunteered not only for the war for freedom but equally willingly for incorporation into the order of the best organization, the German Army.

For four and a half years, we burned. And once again, destiny showed us that we had not yet learned fully. Destiny showed those who had to command and who, in many positions, forgot that the final obedience in the time of the final, hardest test—when everything related to crowns, symbols, and external insignia of political authority was obliterated in distress, in mire and misery—is offered by people of the same blood only to leaders. And it does so only when honor, freedom, and obedience sound as a single unadulterated chord. It showed those who had to obey that every disobedience—even when it seemed to be justified through supposedly hurt honor and supposedly injured freedom—constantly strikes one's own masters and, as a violation of loyalty, as the original sin of the ancestors, throws one's own people and thus every disobedient person into the depths.

The Führer and National Socialism

The German people, who had been fully disintegrated, thus began the last school—we hope—on our path to obedience. Fate sent us the Führer.

Himself an obedient soldier of the great German Army, he bore the entire knowledge of freedom, honor, and the value of the blood of our people in himself, and took us into his school. Henceforth, in 15 years of battle and victory, he educated at first few people, then more and more of the persons most enamored of freedom, the select soldierly German blood, into National Socialists. Let me interpret this concept in this way: into men who are conscious bearers of the value of our race and blood, knowing that blood is the most necessary precondition for culture and greatness. At the same time, he spurred the will to freedom and honor, even of the most fanatic, to even stronger energy, to even more unbending will. He bound, as a third element, those strengths—of the same blood, unrestricted will to freedom, and the most sharply felt concept of honor—into an obedience arising from blood, honor, and will to freedom that was voluntary. For that reason, it was so much more motivating.

I think that one can look at German history and the self-afflicted course of suffering of our people with these eyes and believe that it reveals a significance according to the eternal benevolent law of this universe. It thus becomes, at the same time, an indication and obligation that our nation does not stand at the end but at the beginning of the mission and task given to it among the nations of this Earth.

III. THE SCHUTZSTAFFEL

I come now to the Schutzstaffel[20] itself, which is one part of this National Socialist German Workers' Party created and trained by Adolf Hitler. It has received from the Führer, within the scope of the movement, its special task of the internal security of the Reich.

Establishment of the Schutzstaffel

When the order came from the Führer years ago, in 1925, for the establishment of the Schutzstaffel and then, in 1929, when the order for the greater organization of this association was given, it was clear to us in 1929 that this Schutzstaffel could fulfill its task only if would be established to the highest degree according to the knowledge and the guidelines established by the leader of the movement and according to the virtues instilled in it.

Knowledge of the Value of Blood and Selection

The first guideline was, and is, important for us: knowledge of the value of blood and selection. This precondition was true in 1929 and will be so, as long as there is a Schutzstaffel.

We proceeded like a seed grower who has to cultivate anew purely an old, good species which has become mixed and degraded, who first goes through the field to the so-called selection of shrubs. We then sifted out the men whom we thought we could not use—regarding external aspects—for the building up of the Schutzstaffel.

The manner of selection was concentrated on the choice of those who approximated most, physically, to the desired ideal, the Nordic type of man. External indicators like height and the racially corresponding appearance played a role here.

---

[20] 'Protection Squadron,' or SS for short.

I not need remind you that this principle was, in the course of years, built up better and more sharply, as we became more experienced. Likewise, I ask you to be convinced that, among us, there exists the fullest certainty that, in this selection, there can never be a standstill. From year to year, our demands become sharper as—through the operation of the German racial laws and the ever-growing understanding of blood and breeding—the emergence of the Germanic man begins.

It must be in such a way that the conditions that are placed by our successors, in a hundred years or more, will demand much more from an individual than can be the case today.

Likewise, we know that the first selection that followed external points of view—today, according to ancestral tables and many researches—can only be the first, and only just the very first, principle of selection. A selection process spreads out through all the years of life in the Schutzstaffel; consequently, a sifting out of those not fit for us in character, will, heart, and therefore blood, must follow.

Through laws that we give ourselves, we wish to state for the future, that not every son of an SS family inscribed in an SS *Sippenbuch*[21] is entitled, or indeed has the right, to become an SS man in his turn. But we must ensure that always only one part of the sons of these families be accepted and acknowledged by us as SS men, and will further take care that always the selection and the bloodstream of the best German blood of the entire nation may be admitted into the Schutzstaffel. This is the first principle of selection.

Will to Freedom and the Fighting Spirit

The second guideline and virtue that we strove to inculcate in the Schutzstaffel, and to instill in it as its innate indelible characteristic for all time, is the will to freedom and the fighting spirit.

Tests of Performance

We have always had the ambition to be the best in every battle and in every position. And we are proud here of every man and every association that, with its accomplishments and fighting spirit, matches our own or even exceeds

---

[21] The *Sippenbuch* (clan book) was a genealogical record carried by every SS member to prove that his lineage, from 1750 on, was fully Aryan. This was a custom initiated by Himmler.

us. For everyone who matches us is a gain for Germany and is proof that we ourselves had too little strength in ourselves and that we had to double our efforts, refine our will to battle, and toughen our hardness against ourselves further.

Through an extremely hard schooling that each of us has to go through all our lives, through tests of performance that are replaced every year, we ensure that the courage and fighting spirit of every individual, especially of the *Führerkorps*,[22] is tested repeatedly. We shall, at the same time, through these performances demanded annually by us, see that the complacency that has already so often become a deadly danger to the German people, will never enter our ranks. Furthermore, a community from which—at regular intervals until old age—physical and will-focused performances are demanded will remain simple and, in the long run, discard from itself things that may indeed be fine for a sedate life but that may weaken our strength for Germany and cause the fighting spirit to slacken.

Loyalty and Honor

As the third guideline and virtue that is necessary for the establishment and system of this Schutzstaffel, the concepts of loyalty and honor may be mentioned. The two cannot be separated from each other. They are set down in the principle that the Führer has given us, 'My honor is loyalty' and in the motto of the old German law, 'All honor comes from loyalty.'

Many things can be pardoned on this Earth—so we teach the SS man—but one thing never: *infidelity*. One who damages fidelity is excluded from our society. For, fidelity is a matter of the heart, never of the understanding. The understanding may falter. That is often harmful, but is never incorrigible. But the heart has to always strike the same pulse, and if it stops, the man dies, exactly like a nation when it violates loyalty. We mean thereby loyalty of every sort: loyalty to the Führer and thus to the German people, its will and its type, loyalty to the blood, to our ancestors and grandchildren, loyalty to our customs, loyalty to comrades and loyalty to the irrevocable laws of decency, cleanliness, and chivalrousness. One does not sin against loyalty and honor only when one passively lets one's honor or that of the Schutzstaffel be damaged, but especially when one does not consider the honor of others, scorns things that are sacred to others, or when one does not intervene in

---

[22] The officer elite of the SS.

a manly and decent manner on behalf of those who are absent, weak, and defenseless.

Obedience

The fourth guideline and virtue that is valid for us is obedience. This is an obedience that comes unconditionally from highest voluntariness, from a service to our worldview, one that is ready to offer every sacrifice of pride, of external honors, and everything that is personally dear and valuable to us; of obedience that does not hesitate even once but unconditionally follows every order that comes from the Führer or is legitimately given by one's superiors; of obedience that is silent in the time of political battle when the will to freedom may think that it has to rage—that, with the most alert concentration and the most intent observation of the enemy, does not move a finger if that has been forbidden, that as unconditionally obeys and goes on the attack even if it may believe deep down that it will not be able to prevail.

We are honest enough not to maintain that all these laws have already been comprehended by every man with the fullest, deepest understanding. But we believe that, in six years, the Schutzstaffel has emerged and was built up largely according to these guidelines and lives according to them. We know that we accept, from year to year, more and more of these virtues in ourselves and they become more and more the obvious possession of every SS man. We are convinced that when, after some years—whenever fate determines it, sooner or later—we are no longer there as the first generation of this Schutzstaffel, we can hand down these virtues as the full legacy, the best tradition, to those who are SS men after us.

Marriage law

Corresponding to these guidelines and virtues, we have given ourselves laws and established the life of our community and laid out the path for a distant future.

The first law in 1931 decreed the order that prescribed the marriage and engagement authorization for every SS man. We have drawn the conclusion from a knowledge of the value of blood. We realized that it would be senseless to undertake an attempt to gather together racially-elite men and not think of tradition. We did not wish, and do not wish, to make the mistake of the soldierly and male associations of the past that perhaps existed for centuries and then, because their breeding lacked blood and the group lacked tradition, declined into nothing.

We indeed know, through deepest and innermost conviction, that a community can go forward on the path to the future only when, convinced of the eternal origin of its people, it lives with respect for the ancestors of the most distant and dimmest past. We know that only when the knowledge of blood is understood as an obligation, as a sacred legacy that is to be inherited further in a racially pure clan, do a race and a people have an eternal life. We are infused with the conviction that only the generation that is embedded between ancestors and grandchildren adopts the right yardstick for the greatness of its task and obligation.

The Triumph of the Child

We have experienced that only the man of this conviction learns to humble himself even in times of success and to avoid the mistake of presumption, of arrogance. Similarly, only such men bear the times of hardest oppression with the same iron calm as they live through times of good fortune, humbly and in a simple Spartan way. We therefore teach our SS men, beyond the law of marriage, beyond the training for the choice of the right woman racially, that all our battles—the death of two million in the world war, the political battle of our last 15 years, the establishment of our army for the protection of our borders—would be in vain and purposeless if the victory of the German spirit was not followed by the victory of the German child.

We have set it as one of our tasks to proceed even here not with speeches and words but through deeds and examples in our own ranks. We shall impress on our men today and throughout the future that every mother of our blood, conscious of the sanctity of her duty, is the most sacred and valuable person among our people, and that the most precious wealth is the German child.

Law of Honor of the SS Man

As a further law, it was established on 9 November 1935 that every SS man has the right and the duty to defend his honor with weapons. It was at the same time established in the order that every member of the SS who, after the completion of 1½ years as a candidate, after the completion of his SS oath to the Führer, after honorable completion of his work service and army service, receives the SS dagger—thus at the age of 21 is an SS man in the sense of the Order of the SS, and is accepted into the Order.

Each of us, whether a man of service rank or Reichsführer, is an SS man. We have given ourselves this law of honor because we are of the conviction that only the man who knows that he is made responsible for every one of his acts and his words in any position will understand the deep significance of our community; only he learns to serve his people as an impeccably pure soldier of life. For this law of honor obliges him equally to the preservation of his own honor as it demands from him the respect of others, and as it—with all strictness of principle—imposes on us as a duty, goodness and magnanimity towards one's comrades, one's compatriots, and one's fellowmen.

Now I must state my views on a couple of problems. First, in a booklet that is entitled *50 Questions and Answers for the SS Man*, the first question is 'What is your oath?' The answer is,

> We swear to you, Adolf Hitler, as Führer and Chancellor of the German Reich, loyalty and bravery. We pledge to you, and the superiors determined by you, obedience until death. So help us God!

The second question is: 'Do you believe in a God?' The answer is: 'Yes, I believe in a God.' The third question is: 'What do you think of a man who does not believe in any God?' The answer is: 'I think he is arrogant, delusional, and stupid; he is not suited to us'.[23]

I have shared these three questions and answers with you to set forth unequivocally our position towards religion. You must be convinced that we would not be able to be this sworn body if we did not have the conviction and the belief in a God who stands above us, who has created us and our Fatherland, our people, and this Earth, and has sent to us our Führer.

We are fully convinced of the fact that we have to be responsible for every action, every word, and every thought according to the eternal laws of this world. Everything that our mind conceives, that our tongue speaks, and that our hand executes, is not finished with the event but is a cause that will have its effect, which recoils in blessing or curse on ourselves and on our people. Believe that men with this conviction are completely different from

---

[23] This is a remarkable statement of the religious beliefs within the SS. It is a far cry from that which is commonly presumed.

atheists. But for that reason, we refuse to tolerate that, because we do not as a community profess any religion, any dogma, or even demand this of any of our men. We, through misuse of the word 'heathen,' may be decried as atheists. However, we assume the right and the freedom to draw a sharp and clean line between church or religious activity and political and worldview battles; we will defend ourselves sharply against any encroachment, just as we teach our men, in spite of many justified furies and bad experiences that our people had in the past, that all that which is sacred to any racial comrade—according to his education and conviction—should be respected by us without any insult through words or deeds.

Blood and Soil

The second observation that I would like to make to you, German peasants, as the SS Reichsführer—who am myself in origin, blood and being, a peasant—is this: The idea of blood represented from the beginning in the Schutzstaffel would be condemned to death if it were not bound inextricably to the conviction of the worth and the sanctity of the soil. From the beginning, the Race and Settlement Head Office[24] established the concept 'blood and soil' within its name, in different words but in the same sense. I may assure you that it is no coincidence that the Reichsbauernführer[25] of the German Reich has for years belonged as a leader to the SS and, as Obergruppenführer, is the leader of this Race and Settlement Head Office, just as it is no coincidence that I am a peasant and belong to the Reichsbauernrat.[26]

Both peasants and SS men do not belong to the type of men who say many superfluous, pleasant, and friendly words. But it may be expressed in a clearly understandable way that, as it was until now, so will it be also in the future according to our will. For, where the peasants of Adolf Hitler stand, they will always have the Schutzstaffel as their truest friend at their side, just as we know that where Adolf Hitler's Schutzstaffel stands, the German peasant stands beside it as its best comrade and friend. That is how it is today and so may it always be in the future.

---

[24] *Rasse- und Siedlungshauptamt* (RSHA).
[25] Farmers' Leader of the Reich.
[26] Peasants' Council of the Reich.

Security Service and Secret State Police[27]

I know that there are many people in Germany who are uncomfortable when they see this black uniform. We understand that, and do not expect that we will be loved by very many. All to whom Germany lies in their heart will respect us; and those who may somehow and at some time have a bad conscience with regard to the Führer and the nation should fear us. For these men, we have built an organization that is called the Security Service and similarly we, as the SS, employ men for service in the Secret State-Police.

We shall ceaselessly fulfil our duty of being the guarantors of the internal security of Germany, just as the German Army guarantees the protection of the honor and greatness and peace of the Reich externally. We shall take care that never again—in Germany, the heart of Europe, from within, or through emissaries from outside—will the Jewish-Bolshevist Revolution of sub-humans be allowed to be kindled. We shall be pitiless; for all these forces whose existence and activity we know, a merciless executioner's sword awaits on the day when there is even the slightest attempt to act—whether today, or in decades, or in centuries.

Bolshevism is Not an Ephemeral Phenomenon

I thus return to the beginning. I would like to emphasize once again that we do not see Bolshevism as an ephemeral phenomenon that could be easily debated out of the world or dismissed in thought, according to our wishes. We know him, the Jew: the people who, gathered together from the waste products of all the peoples and nations of this globe, have set on all the stamp of their Jewish blood, whose wish is world-rule, whose pleasure is destruction, whose will is extermination, whose religion is godlessness, whose idea is Bolshevism. We do not underestimate him because we have known him for centuries, and we do not overestimate him because we believe in a divine mission of our people and in our strength resurrected through the leadership and work of Adolf Hitler.

---

[27] *Sicherheitsdienst* and *Geheime Staatspolizei*, respectively.

The Schutzstaffel

We, the Schutzstaffel, have now, according to the command of the Führer, been grounded and developed within this newly revived nation. If I attempt to describe to you today what the organization, structure, and task of the SS is, no one who does not attempt to understand us inwardly with his blood and his heart will yet be able to comprehend us. It cannot be explained why we, so few in numbers—of the German people, only around 200,000 men— have this strength in us. It cannot be explained logically why today each of us who wears the black uniform, no matter where he is, is borne by the strength of our community—whether he sits in the saddle of a racehorse, contests on the sports field, whether he serves as a bureaucrat, whether he lifts stones as a construction worker, or rules in the highest political position, or serves as a soldier, or has to stand his ground somewhere as a man per- haps unseen. Each of us knows that he does not stand alone but that this enormous strength of 200,000 men who have been sworn together lends him immeasurable strength, just as he knows that he, as a representative of this Black Order, has in his turn to be a credit to his community, through the best performance.

In this way, we have risen up and march according to unchanging laws—as a National Socialist Order of Nordic men and as a sworn commu- nity of their customs—along the path to a distant future. We wish and hope that we may be not only the grandchildren of past fighters, but beyond that, that we will be the ancestors of the most distant future generations that are required for the eternal life of the German people.

THE JEWS AND THIS WAR

Ezra Pound
(1939)

Editor: The war in Europe began on 2 September 1939 when Germany crossed into Poland in an attempt to resolve a centuries-long border dispute. As a result of preexisting treaties, England and France then declared war on Germany. Two weeks later, the Soviets invaded Poland from the east, effectively partitioning that country into halves. For the next six months, Germany would take no further major military action.

American poet Ezra Pound (1885-1972) was living in Italy at the outbreak of war. He was well aware of Jewish involvement in the war, having been critical of Jews since at least 1910 when he was briefly living in New York. He moved to Italy in 1924 and would stay there through the end of the war, writing often in defense of Italian and German nationalism and against Western imperialism. Many of his critiques referenced Jews in one way or another. In mid-1939, for example, Pound wrote, perceptively, that "Democracy is now currently defined in Europe as 'a country run by Jews'." When the war began in late 1939, he wrote with increasing harshness against Jews and Jewish policy. By early 1940, he was ready to publish a short essay directly challenging the Jewish role in the burgeoning war (Italy would not formally be engaged until June of that year.) In March, he wrote the present essay, *Gli Ebrei e questa guerra* ("The Jews and This War"), which was published on March 24 in *Meridiano di Roma*, V.12.

As one can tell from the style, Pound writes more as a poet than a formal historian or social scientist; regardless, his message comes through loud and clear. He cites and quotes the notoriously 'anti-Semitic' Russian Jew, Jacob Brafman, who had published in 1869 a book titled *The Book of the Kahal*. The Kahal (or qahal) was an ancient Jewish term for a Jewish governing body; in Brafman's context, it referred to the ruling power of global Jewry. Pound adopts this same usage. When he cites the 'Kahal' in the present essay, it refers to the interconnected network of worldwide Jewish power. For Pound, the Kahal is "centered on Wall Street," with 'branch offices' in London and Paris. In a key paragraph near the end of the essay, he writes that "Roosevelt's governing instincts are those of the Kahal," and that "England and France are governed as the Kahal would rule them." The thesis that the Western powers are working under Jewish control is the best explanation for recent events in Europe, he argues.

This essay has never before appeared in English. The Italian text was taken from *Ezra Pound's Poetry and Prose* (vol. 8), 1991, pp. 19-21. All notes are those of the editor.

"Freedom is not a right, it is a duty."

Few young people go so far as thinking that the ideal of good governance is the highest meditation that can bear fruit in this world; and among young people 30 years ago, no one was less inclined than myself to these reflections. I fully understand the young poets and aesthetes who grumble when I speak of the *idea of the state* or of any economic problem: *et ego in Arcadia,* "swapping cheap love for poor apples," *viles pomis mercaris amores.*

Yet the relative capacity of the different races is of great importance. And when any race, during a period of a thousand, two thousand, or five thousand years, has shown a singular inability to evolve a social form, this fact must be acknowledged. One should take great care before entrusting the prosperity of one's nation to the members of such a race, without, in any case, first subjecting the situation to close and prolonged observation.

These subjects are dangerous. In the space of seven days, a reputable American agent threatened to abandon me to a publisher, also an American, who threw lightning bolts at my attempts to pass "propaganda" through his presses. "Nothing," he says, "that can be interpreted in good faith, etc ..."

Indeed, almost the only friend I have left with whom I can discuss this subject had the surname Levi at birth, and still carries it. An even more eminent Levi sends me his articles printed in France dealing with the same subject. If the Jews I have met during the last 30 years are the symptomatic representatives of Jewish culture, there must be thousands who are ignorant of their racial past, of what the ghetto was from dispersion to 1600 and from 1600 to the recent past, as well as their Christian and pagan contemporaries.

The points that I now propose to highlight are translated from an English publication that gives information about what the Jewish Encyclopedia calls "well-organized communities."

> At the head of the Jewish community was a government directorate..., the members of which belonged to the richest families whose members invariably chose their wives from among these same families. The members of the directorate established the link with the local princes and rulers, occupying the posts of finance ministers, advisers to the sovereign, and doctors. Dual position: administrators of the wealth of both the Jewish community and of the nation in which they lived.
>
> The annual elections of the members of the directorate were surrounded by an infinite number of rules and ceremonies...but they were but a simple succession in the administrative functions of the owners of the directory.
>
> These leaders were content to govern anonymously as a directorate...

Education consisted mainly in teaching "The Law" and in the legal exposition of the contents of the Talmud. Maimonides says: "God has commanded the practice of usury towards the Goy and the loan of money only if he agrees to pay the interest".[1]

The right to tax follows from the right of usury.

In what is said above, there is something in stark contrast to the mentality of some Jews that I consulted a few years ago. One said to me: "No usury. The Law of Moses forbids it." And another: "I am against usury to the detriment of the Gentiles. It would give them a foothold."

Without hesitation, I acquit G. L., the musician, of having desired this war. Without hesitation, I absolve Dr. G. L., physician, of having desired this war. And Dr. B., physician, of having desired this war. And I acquit all three for all the acts they may have committed during their existence to lead to this war. I could make a long list of Aryans from England and America who brought us to this war.

---

[1] Maimonides (1138-1204) was a prominent and influential Jewish theologian/philosopher.

Let me go back to the historical process. Jacob Brafman "declared that taxation was the keystone of the organization of Jewish communities".[2] Every Jew was obliged to belong to a fraternity and to pay his taxes. Failure to do so meant being fined or ostracized, which, at the time of the ghetto, meant ruin. They paid 10 per cent property tax... and, at times, forced loans to the Kahal.[3] Each newcomer had to pay for the right of residence, thus making it nearly impossible for the poor Jew to change residence.

"Tax on tobacco, tar, herring etc. at Kahal," handling of alms, right of decision regarding the distribution of subsidies, often hereditary offices. In Russia, at the time of Disraeli, many tasks of the secret police were entrusted to Jews.[4] (I abbreviate).

The Jewish authorities were authorized to arrest all Jews without passports and to enlist them to complete their quota of recruits for the army.

Did these oligarchies advance the material and intellectual prosperity of their communities? Answer: The only study encouraged was that of the Talmud. "During all the centuries of the ghetto, there is neither literature, nor art, nor Jewish science." Your English critic [i.e. Pound] postpones the discussion on the value of post-ghetto literature, art, and science for a better time.

Brafman finds in the ghettos a uniform standard of poverty far below that of the Gentile communities around them. He describes some ghettos, including that of Frankfurt. Disraeli also called his people "a splendidly-organized race." It is, undoubtedly, not our European concept of splendor.

An article in the *Journal du Nord* says that in Russia, in 1892, only 10 or 12 thousand Jews had secured the means of existence. It is from these ghettos of Russia that, in 1890, hundreds of thousands of Jews moved to the Western world, demonstrating socialist and liberal tendencies everywhere—with the result, as stated in EE Cummings' poem:

Every kumrad ["comrad"] is a bit
Of quite unmitigated hate[5]

---

[2] As explained in the introduction, Brafman (1825-1879) was a Russian Jew highly critical of global Jewry.
[3] The Kahal, or qahal, is a synonym here for organized, global Jewry.
[4] That is, in the 1800s.
[5] From the poem "kumrads die because they're told" (1935). Cummings makes the connection between emigrating Jews and their hatred for their hosts. This is

Your English critic believes that today's Kahal is centered on Wall Street.

For my part, I think it makes little difference to Christianity and European races if the central office is in London with the Rothschild clan, while the branch office, with the Ikleheimer clan, and in New York as in 1863, or if the head office is now in New York under the Schiff & Kahn company with a director named Wiseman, 12th baronet, and Mr. Belisha, just out of the British Cabinet, but easily replaceable with another delegate with the same origins and kinship.[6]

Britain's Slander Act, infamously crafted to protect the criminal and which disregards public welfare, forces some of the more honest British newspapers to print simple lists of names without comment. Just to remind the vassals who their masters are. Rothschild is still interested in gold; Sassoon in silver; and Mond (Melchett) in nickel and chemical industries.[7]

Cry, cry—I say, parenthetically—over the unfortunate Finns. In Petsamo, there are nickel mines belonging to a company whose owners also have a hand in the Imperial Chemical Co and therefore in the *Manchester Guardian*. If the Finnish mines were destroyed, this company could raise the prices of Canadian nickel and thus the losses would be offset. We believe that the Finnish mines were held as a threat to Germany. I am of the opinion that Uncle Stalin's savages should be kept out of Europe, but the point of view of Russia and Germany, opposed to letting Melchett's "gang" retain ownership of all the nickel in the world, is perfectly understandable.

A peaceful settlement of Europe, outside England and the Kahal, could be achieved by nationalizing the Finnish nickel mines, with a pact between Germany, Russia and Italy, each of which would be allowed to buy a third of the product.

I read that the mines have been dismantled. If so, the Kahal wins, at least for the duration of this war that it has done all it can to cause; and that a relentless campaign of lies and agitation from its rotten press does everything it can to exacerbate things more and more.

---

an old story, going back millennia; for details, see *Eternal Strangers* (T. Dalton, 2020).

[6] Leslie Hore-Belisha (1893-1957) was the Jewish-British Secretary of War under Chamberlain from 1937 to January 1940.

[7] The Rothschilds and the Sassoons were prominent and wealthy Jewish families of Europe. 'Mond' refers to British Jew Henry Mond, 2nd Baron Melchett (1898-1949).

I don't get to Latin clarity. I don't reach Latin simplicity in my thinking. I undress naked. I spare neither Jew nor Aryan. And I offer you the flaws of my own thought process—that is, the long parenthesis; compare it with that of Henry James. Use it as best you can.

I have bundled two things together. The archbishop once told me that I try to put too much stuff in one article. All right. There are two subjects here. One is the racial disposition of Jewry. This gives an indication of how they have governed their communities in Europe and Russia over the centuries. Second, a particular case: When it comes to individual crimes and accusations, I cannot convince myself that the Jew suffers much more than the Aryan. The Dantist will be able to give you the complete quotation of the verses that I quote by ear: "Yes, that the Jew among you does not laugh".[8]

When it comes to making money, there is always a fresh memory of the Merton firm of Australia, which was founded in 1914, and which happily sold lead to Germany at half the price of England. You can find old Morgan (an Aryan) who, during our American Civil War, was convicted of selling bad guns to the government. It was something so sly that not even a Jew would have done it. He bought discarded rifles from the War Ministry and resold them—getting paid even before he paid the Ministry himself—to an army corps in the West. This is not Semitism, it is mercantilism. The Jews already have enough trouble of their own, and there is no need to blame them for sins they have not committed.

But they lack a sense of state order. The complex of Roosevelt's governing instincts are those of the Kahal. In our times, England and France are governed as the Kahal would rule them. With no other system of government could their history of the past 20 years be explained.

In contrast to the Kahal system, we have Roman law, and Continental Europeans have all the tradition of the "arts", the "guilds", the "trade unions". We Americans of Anglo-Saxon descent have the scales built to perfection on the work of John Adams.

This is not the time for unnecessary hatred or excitement.

We must weigh these things carefully, analyze the causes as best our abilities allow us, and when we are perfectly enlightened, decide which system suits our needs. The fascist and Nazi programs are based on European dispositions and beliefs that evolve and move towards ever-higher developments. The American system is but a dark and profaned memory, one that

---

[8] Actual quotation: "that in your midst no Jew may laugh at you"—Dante, *Divine Comedy*, Paradiso V.

we Americans have a duty to pull out of the grave, hidden under piles of trash. But no man in any country, unless he is an idiot or an illiterate, has the right to disregard investigating the organism of today's events; he would be worth even less than a louse if he allowed himself to be imposed on a fictitious system, out of true ignorance or pretense.

"Freedom is not a right, it is a duty."

INTERNATIONAL MELTING POT OR UNITED NATION-STATES OF EUROPE?

Robert Ley
(1941)

Editor: One of the brightest and best-educated leaders of NS Germany was Robert Ley (1890-1945). Born into a working-class household, he attended college at Jena, served with distinction in World War One, and eventually earned a PhD in chemistry in 1920. Ley joined the National Socialist party in 1925, becoming a loyal follower of Hitler. In Cologne in 1928, he established a NS newspaper, *Westdeutscher Beobachter*, focusing on anti-Jewish themes and stories. Rising quickly through the party ranks, Ley was named *Reichsleiter* in mid-1933—the second highest civilian rank in the party.

Owing to his working-class background, Ley was assigned to develop German labor policy via the newly-formed German Labor Front (DAF). He played a major role in the establishment of the "Strength Through Joy" initiative which was very popular among German workers. Ley managed to retain Hitler's support throughout the war, serving as one of the Führer's 'inner circle.'

Though not active in either military or Jewish policy, Ley spoke out vehemently against Reich enemies, particularly the Jews. Should Germany lose, he said, "Funeral pyres would be built on which the Jews would burn us"—prophetic, given the many Allied fire-bombings late in the war. Elsewhere he stated that "the Jew is the great danger to humanity." After the war, Ley was captured and held for trial at Nuremberg, but managed to commit suicide prior to the start of proceedings.

The following essay, addressed to the German working-class, was published as a pamphlet in mid-1941. Here, Ley offers one of the sharpest, clearest, and most forceful attacks on international Jewry ever published. It is a truly remarkable statement against internationalist Jews and in favor of German nationalism. Notes are the editor's and translator's.

If men wish to live according to reason, and to live correctly, they must first learn to live clearly and logically. If someone were to give me the task of encapsulating our present age and our National Socialist will in the briefest formula, I would answer him thus: *National Socialism is the idea of clarity, naturalness, and logic.* The National Socialist revolution [of 1933] was the turn and transformation from an obscure, confused complexity that reached the point of lunacy to a simple but, for that reason, clear and true way of thought and action of the German people. The individual must create order in his own mind so that he may indeed clearly express the problems, tasks, men, and topics in a fitting manner.

National Socialism is clarity of concept; National Socialism is logic; National Socialism is the purposefulness of nature; National Socialism is simplicity and lack of complication. Everything else that confuses and clouds our thoughts and action is our mortal enemy, especially when, in this confusion and fog, there lies *a system*—and one then commits the devilry of buttressing this system, and tries to firmly establish it through so-called science.

For this reason, the Jew is our mortal enemy. This is so because the Jew is the master of distortion, the master of lies and deception, and also the master of hypocrisy, camouflage, and masking. If the German man, as the expression of the Nordic race, raises National Socialism—and with it, truth and logic on his shield—the Jew is and must be an antipode, for his worldview is superstition, falsehood, and mysticism.

These two worlds—the German and the Jewish—are both grounded in the racial manifestation of their bearers. In the German is manifest the highest percentage of Nordic blood, whereas the Jew represents the clearest expression of a great mixture of races. Miscegenation in the Jew is so strong that one can no longer even consider him a bastard; rather, in Jewry, through the course of millennia, the bastard has turned into a parasite. The parasitical character of Jewry is the basis of the distracted nature, lack of clarity, and near-lunacy of the Jewish world.

The parasite is the strongest expression of a biological chaos. Even the molecules and atoms—that is, the basic elements of the blood—have been corrupted among Jewry through repeated miscegenation. They constitute only fragments of their prior form and type.

In earlier millennia, the international stock-exchanges of the three continents of Europe, Asia, and Africa lay in Palestine. There, Nordic men exchanged their products with Asiatics and the inhabitants of Africa; in this way, the preconditions existed for the greatest racial miscegenation of all time. And because the mongrels in Palestine were driven into the desert by the racially pure and brave people of the Caucasus Mountains, they were hermetically isolated. From this necessary inbreeding of the mongrels of Europe, Asia, and Africa, a parasite arose—the Jew. The Jew is not a special race; rather, he is the antithesis of all races, exactly as the parasite is the antithesis of all species in the animal and vegetable kingdoms.[1] From this chaos arose also the chaotic world of the Jew, one that is expressed in his scientific, cultural, and political thought.

If the Jew wished to sustain himself among the other races, especially among the Nordic race, he had to elevate conceptual confusion, lies, and camouflage to a life-ideal. When the Jew's character was revealed to the other races, it had to repel them all and arouse disgust in them, exactly as the parasite and vermin arouse disgust in healthy and normal creatures. The Jew had to lie and conceal himself; the Jew had to drag down the ideals of other men to blur the gap between themselves and the pure races. The Jew had to establish baseness as his ideal in order to drag the noble and the great into their excrement because he himself could only be base. And when he was at a loss, he had to arouse pity and raise pity as his human ideal, in order to protect himself from destruction at the hands of the racially pure.

Above all, the Jew had to condemn the nation as an amalgamation of men of equal sort and race, because he himself can never create a sense of community from his parasitical nature. All order is, for him, worthy of detestation, since he, as a parasite, represents the natural expression of the greatest disorder. So he had to despise, combat, and destroy everything that is sacred to the people as a racial community—'the sacred' being that which is required simply to live. His natural existence as a parasite demands this. Just as a parasite eats into the vital organs of living creatures, the Jew eats into the vital organs of the people by virtue of his parasitical constitution.

*****

---

[1] For more on Jews as an anti-race, see Alfred Rosenberg's book *The Myth of the 20th Century* (2021), pp. 275, 277, and 427.

Henceforth the political battle of nations against Jewry will become increasingly crystallized around two concepts: *the national* and *the international*.

'International' means—translated literally—that which is between nations. The Jew has now inscribed this word on his flag because, to him, everything national is hateful. But it's not enough for him to stand between nations. An insane dream—of being the eternal continuation of those crazy Old Testament prophets who, in their superstition, prophesied to the Jewish people that Jehovah, the god of the Jews, had declared them to be the chosen people of the Earth—drives the Jew to lunatic ideas and the deepest superstition. Therefore, typical of Jewish criminality, a little fiddling had to be done with the word 'international'; and so 'between the nations' was transformed into '*above* the nations.' 'International' in Jewish jargon no longer signified the relations of nations among themselves but instead that the Jew established organizations, concepts, strata, and classes *above* the nations. Everything that the Jew established, that he mastered and directed, served the Jewish International. This had to exist in order to allow the prophecies of the Jewish prophets to become reality and thus to establish the international supremacy of Jewry over nations.

From the universalism of the Jew Saul, called Paul, to the Marxist International of the Jew Karl Marx, everything is the same idea: the destruction of nations, the undermining of national authority, and therefore the establishment of internationalist phantoms, internationalist false doctrines, and internationalist lunacy.[2] The Jew Paul wanted, through his [Christian] universalism, to establish Jewish world supremacy, exactly as Karl Marx and his Jewish followers wanted to establish it through proletarian internationalism.[3] From Moses to Karl Marx, it's always the same eternal Jew, the same dream of Jewish world supremacy, and the same goal: chaos among the nations of the Earth.

The weapon is also always the same: the establishment of international currency, the declaration that even gold represents an international value. With this lie, the Jew establishes his international capitalism in order to make

---

[2] An "International" is an old designation for an international organization that attempts to unify groups of similar ideology under a single framework or structure. The "First International" was formed in 1864 to unify various communist and anarchist groups. It disintegrated in 1876, and a "Second International" formed in 1889.
[3] Paul's brand of Christianity was "universal" in the sense that it was open to all people and that it claimed universal truths for all humanity.

the work of men and nations serviceable to himself and to exploit them according to his desire and ability. Six international Jews set the gold standard daily in London under the Jewish king Rothschild, and consequently so too the value of the currency of all countries and, further, the price of labor of men and nations. With the help of this mendacious devilry—namely, that gold possesses some value—the Jew dispossessed all productive men and enslaved them.

But even that was not enough for him. Nations regularly brought forth nationalist men, politicians, and soldiers who, in spite of this ingenious system of international capitalism, established nations in a nationalist and ethnic manner. For that reason, the nations had to be deprived of all leadership; this was the final goal of the Jew. He had to overthrow kings and emperors, dukes and princes; ministers had to eat out of his hand. Deputies and members of parliaments were bought by the Jew.

But above all, the Jew organized the mass of productive men against their national leadership. Through his capitalist system, the Jew exploited the great masses. The masses became discontented, and they sought to revolt against this capitalist exploitation. The Jew collected this discontent in his political parties and organizations, redirecting the energies of the masses— not against capitalism itself but against the *nationalist leadership*, against the *nationalist leaders* of the people. That was the second great weapon that Jewry created in an international way. The first was international gold, international currency, international capitalism; and the second were the international Marxist and proletarian parties.

Now, between the two there lay a large middle stratum, the bourgeoisie. This middle stratum was mobilized by Jewry. First, it was atomized by a large number of groups and groupings that were all incorporated in an international manner. But since the Jew knew the bourgeois' propensity for romanticism, the Jew captured this bourgeoisie characteristic in his Freemasonry. He exaggerated romanticism into mysticism and superstition. Fear and terror, conceit and arrogance, vanity and envy, were mobilized in the so-called 'better' social stratum, which was then mastered by Jewry in their mystical, terrorizing Freemasonry.

And when the Jew—with the help of his money, with the help of his Marxist ideologies, with the help of Freemasonry, with the help of political universalism—had disintegrated peoples and nations, the states were ripe to condemn the nationalist idea as political ideology and to bow down in the

Jewish Temple of Jewish world supremacy in Geneva.[4] The League of Nations, which ought to be called the Melting Pot, gave Jewry its final triumph.[5] Here, all nationalist promptings and all ethnic and racially-conditioned characteristics of state and law were condemned as abominations. What the Jew had done thus far, through disguise, hypocrisy, and lies, was now proclaimed in the most celebratory manner before the whole world as the proper national worldview. The Jew relished the triumph of his world supremacy; he had fully confounded men and nations, he was the master, and now the thousand-year-old Jewish world empire predicted and divined by the prophets was to commence.[6]

*****

A nation is the conceptual determination of a community that is homogeneous in type and race. A nation is the totality of men who feel racially bound to the same feelings and thoughts, to the same conception of work, honor, industriousness, sacrifice, loyalty and other virtues, and who call the same moral customs their own.

The strongest expression of a national community is a common language. Language is the expression and therefore the distinguishing mark of the goodness, elevation, and capacities of a race. The more clearly and the more unequivocally that a language gives the possibility of expressing men's thoughts, the more superior it is. We Germans can declare, with pride and inexpressible gratitude to fate, that we call our own the finest, strongest, and richest language in the world. Ultimate philosophical knowledge and ultimate life-wisdom, logic, and clarity can only be expressed in the German language. The versatility of our German language, the way it constantly subdivides concepts and subtleties—as we often have almost a dozen words expressing different features of a single concept—is proof of the unequalled logic of the German race.

Our nation is a natural community of a race connected through character and blood. Every member of our nation must confess, in his inner being,

[4] The World Jewish Congress was founded in 1936 in Geneva.
[5] The League of Nations was created in January 1920 as a part of the Paris Conference, in the aftermath of World War One. It would later be dissolved and replaced by the United Nations after World War Two.
[6] "Today the Jew rules the world by proxy. He gets others to fight and die for him" (Mahathir Mohamad, 2003).

his inexorable membership in this community determined by fate and life. Either the individual will live within the nation, or he will perish alone. This knowledge is eternal, true, and unchangeable.

Creation is the product of natural law in which everything serves progress and development. From the primordial cell and cosmic energy, or from energy through the primordial cell to the highest living creature, everything is subject to an eternal divine law and order; every progress and every development is dependent on the principle of 'leader' and 'follower.' Nature has no intention and cannot be combated through accomplishments, but it is characterized by a multiplicity of forms and life; and yet everything is ordered sensibly and is wound like one cog into another. One who ignores this diversity and validity will not comprehend nature and will wither under nature's law, and thus perish.

Here lay the fallacy of the international Jew in believing that he could disturb the natural order of rank, and, in place of space, energy, race, heredity, and nation, set up an artificial construction of liberalistic economic order, democracies, and parliaments. For the international Jew, people are not living men; in their cabalistic intrigue, men are lifeless figures that can be moved around here and there, like digits on their calculators. For that reason, the international system—or in Jewish jargon, the supranational system—that the Jew set in motion, according to a finely-elaborated scheme in Geneva, must collapse if creation and the world-order are to retain meaning. We National Socialists base our worldview on the natural laws of race, heredity, the biological laws of life, and the laws of space and soil, energy and action. In a word, we bow with humility and insight before the eternally unchanging divine order of Nature. We believe in reason, and we subject our thought and action to it.

*****

The Führer internally destroys the Jew and his internationalism. Thus, the Führer's methods to lead Germany and the German worker out of distress and misery, out of powerlessness and collapse, were completely different from those of the earlier Jewish parliamentarian system. The former [Weimer] Germany divested itself of every value, it disarmed itself completely, and it plundered the people through the state and the law for the benefit of international capitalism. It always believed in the miracle of international justice and the conscience of the world. The power-holders of democratic Germany begged for mercy and hoped to earn the world's pity. It worshipped the Jewish god Mammon and the Jewish Temple in Geneva, in submissive dependence. Post-war Germany delivered itself and the people, the economy, culture, and politics totally to the Jews. In abject slavery, it fulfilled every request of Jewish international Freemasonry or of Jewish international Marxism and Jewish international Universalism.

Who could forget the controversies of Sacco and Vanzetti:[7] Somewhere in America, a couple of Jewish criminals were hanged because this could no longer go on, because their crimes and their wickedness cried out to the heavens; and incredibly, here in Germany, millions of German workers demonstrated for the release of these Jewish international criminals. Indeed, this madness got to the point where one was ready to dislocate the German state and the German political system in order to pay homage solely to the international parasite. In Germany, there were millions of such German men who were incited and stirred by the Jew in such a way that they were always ready to betray and sell out the Fatherland and the people for his internationalist ideology.

As mentioned, the Führer ruthlessly broke with all that. The parties, trades unions, and entrepreneurial unions were forbidden under penalty of death. The parliaments were dissolved, Freemasonry was totally smashed, Pauline Universalism was condemned to impotence. National Socialism destroyed internationalism in Germany without mercy. We struck the Jew wherever we met him, and now we have, thank God, come so far that the greater part of Jewry has either already emigrated from Germany or resignedly await their chance to leave. The Jew has no more influence—neither in politics nor in culture, nor in the economy, nor in the supervision of men. His party institutions, unions, and his capitalistic instruments have been destroyed and smashed, once and for all. The Jewish-international poison has been burnt out in Germany, and totally up-rooted, branch and stem.[8]

Only in this way could the Führer build up the German ethnic community. Every bacillus and every bacterium were destroyed in the German nation—in its classes, strata, religious groups, tribes, and clans. Germany and

---

[7] Nicola Sacco and Bartolomeo Vanzetti were Italian American anarchists who were accused of murdering a guard and a paymaster during an armed robbery in Massachusetts in April 1920 and were executed seven years later. They were apparently inspired by Jewish anarchists, but it remains unclear if either man was Jewish.
[8] Ley's usage here of the terms *vernichten* (to destroy) and *ausrotten* (rooted-out) mirrors Hitler's usage of the same terms. Ley is clear that such terms mean a destruction of Jewish cohesion and power, and not the physical killing of Jews.

its people have been freed of the international Jewish poison. That is the great and unimaginable record of National Socialism after just eight years of Adolf Hitler's leadership, our Führer.

*****

Likewise, Germany's foreign policy is designed as an instrument of reason, insight, and clarity. The National Socialist Führer of the new Germany did not convene any conferences, nor did he attend any conferences, as for example those of the League of Nations or any other roundtable conference. His intention was to show the world, once and for all, that for National Socialist Germany and its politics, the time for platitudes, conferences, and speeches is over. The Führer despised sitting down for hours with a circle of diplomats in order to cultivate fine intellectual conversations and discussions; for him, this was a monumental waste of time. We National Socialists have no time for that. Here, each person is given a task that he must fulfil according to his capacity, industriousness, commitment, courage, and dedication. This is also how things are handled in the interactions between peoples and states. It is senseless to bring together 30 or 40 people of the most diverse opinions and interests, simply in order to clarify some problem. Every problem always interests only two men, or at most three or four; and only one person can solve a problem.

Why then bring together 50 or more states? Nothing is achieved, as the gossip chamber in Geneva called the League of Nations has clearly shown. For that reason, the Führer has established a firm hold in Europe through the alliance between Germany and Italy. Two powerful states had to decide that they wished to establish a new order in Europe. The Führer found in Italy's *Duce* [Mussolini] the same revolutionary qualities of reason and insight, and in this way alone it was possible to give Europe, through the Axis, a solid foundation based on the friendship of these two men, their clarity and commitment.

Jewish internationalism also had to be destroyed externally. Fanatic nationalism and pacifistic internationalism are like fire and water, and cannot coexist. Since they are like fire and water, it had to come to a conflict between these two worlds, sooner or later. It had to be shown through this conflict whether Jewish democracy and Jewish internationalism could maintain itself, and was thereby the stronger, or whether a nature-bound nationalism and fascism based on natural law would win. Here there was only an either-

or. If the National Socialist and Fascist Axis wished to survive, the Jewish democratic-parliamentarian system had to be destroyed.

England is now the most pronounced prototype of this system, since it is governed mostly by the Jew and his money. The battle is now already decided. Reason and natural law have triumphed, and Jewish schematism, Jewish internationalism, and Jewish superstition have been smashed. The followers of Jewry on the European mainland are gone. England is on its last legs. The English people must pay dearly and hard for following Jewry. For its fundamental mistake in thinking that man can defeat nature with artificial constructions and schematism, England must pay with death. The power political battle has been decided. The Jew and his power have been broken. Germany and Italy are right because they acted according to reason.

Now the Führer is ready to immediately begin the reconstruction of Europe. The Führer does not misuse his victory, like the Jew in 1918, to fabricate senseless humiliations for the opponent and celebrate grotesque orgies; rather, the Führer uses the great power that fate has given him to immediately put Europe in order. The National Socialist Führer of Germany has the preconditions and possibilities to aid the reappearance of reason in our continent. The pact of the three powers has been concluded. Already other powers have joined it, and others will follow.

In a very short time, Europe will be an image of stability and rational order. There will be no 'victors' and 'defeated' in the manner of Versailles, but there will one victor, and that is rationality and the peoples of Europe; and one defeated, that is the Jew and his internationalist lunacy.

This is Hitler's goal: his sacred, unique mission, and his will, is to put this poor European population, tormented through the centuries and millennia, in order, according to the sensible laws of development and progress. Only Nordic man can build states, and Europe has a common Nordic root. As different as the people of this continent may be in their appearance, in their communal life, even in their culture and their economy, they all still have a common root of life, of blood, and therefore of culture. It is obvious that 85 million Germans—with such high racial standing—must, in conjunction with allied Italy, claim the leadership of Europe. An Adolf Hitler had to be born so that Europe could be put in order, and this Adolf Hitler had to be born among the German people so that the German people were given to him in order to be able to fulfill his mission. With the victory of our arms and our soldiers, we claim leadership, and we have it. We will happily bear the responsibility of putting Europe in order, once and for all.

*****

German workers, in this brief essay I have sought to reveal the Jew's lunacy and the irrationality of his worldview, in contrast to National Socialism and to the worldview of the German man—the worldview of reason, logic, and law. Once again fate has preserved Germany from downfall. You stood already with one foot in the abyss. The masters of Versailles had already passed judgement on you. The Frenchman Georges Clemenceau spoke the frightful words: "There are 20 million Germans too many"; and the Englishman David Lloyd George rubbed his hands in glee that the hunger blockade would devastate the German people, even into 1940.[9] They were all slaves of the Jew, in the service of Freemasonry and international Marxism; they knew only one mission: to destroy Germany.

And you yourself, German worker, offered yourself in your blindness as the executor of this Jewish international death sentence. Germans stood against Germans, class against class, stratum against stratum, religious group against religious group, North against South, and East against West. The whole nation was gripped by a sinister political fever. Factories fell into disuse, chimneys no longer smoked, the wheels stood still, and the phantom of unemployment arose everywhere. Hunger and misery imprinted their frightful furrows on the German face. Children died like flies. Millions of Germans died of undernourishment, tuberculosis, and epidemics; and the Jew grinned at everything. In Germany there was fraternal murder, as the Jew incited everyone against everyone else. Everything that had once been sacred to the German man was laughed at, and scorned. That was the abyss.

And the German people did not stand at the edge of the abyss but they stood within it. If this fraternal murder, this sentence of famine, this dreadful unemployment, this political sedition and this cultural decay had continued just 20 years longer, it would have been impossible to save Germany from this abyss. Death ate into our people with increasing rage, and the Jew's jazz band played the dance of death for the German people. It is frightful to imagine, when we look back on this abyss. The German man trembles when he is reminded of this period of social, political, cultural, and economic decay.

German worker, do you still remember how ready you were to sacrifice your nation, your people, and even your family, simply for your 'international ideals'? In this way, for example, international pacifism created monstrous

---

[9] Clemenceau was French prime minister from 1917 through 1920. Lloyd George was British prime minister from 1916 to 1922.

and devastating ideas in the German mind regarding honor, freedom, and the Fatherland. Men who were brave soldiers in World War One, and to whom a soldier's honor signified the highest fulfilment of duty and the ultimate commitment, were no longer recognizable in the years after the world war. It was enough to make a man give up hope in his own nation. It was incomprehensible how this internationalist poison had turned brave soldiers—men who spent four years in the trenches under the harshest conditions—into committed pacifists. Most importantly, one could not understand this way of thinking and mentality because this ideology was fraudulent and completely illogical. Externally, one was a pacifist; and inside, one was ready to crack the skull of one's German brother if he held another opinion. In his diabolical baseness, the Jew understood how to make the bravest German man into a cowardly traitor, and internally into a brutal civil war soldier.

But even the Socialists did not understand this Jewish ideology. It was not evident why socialism had to be coupled with pacifism and what, in general, socialism had to do with pacifism. It is illuminating and clear that socialism trains a man to be a fighter. One who wishes to be a Socialist must defend the community, and one who defend the community must fight against the mistakes, inadequacies, and deficiencies of man. Thus, battle is the first and highest law of every Socialist. But it was never explained how battle could be reconciled with pacifism. One who is a Socialist can never be a pacifist, and one who is a pacifist will always have to betray socialism.

Do you see now, German worker, how fraudulent was the international Jewish slogan of international pacifism? It served nothing but to break your spine, and to soften your bones as an honest and fanatic Socialist. Your untamed strength and your fanatic will are well-known; therefore there had to be a means of destroying and annihilating the energy and ideals of the German worker. That was the result of the slogan of international pacifism.

Do you still remember, German worker, how they hammered in, repeatedly and everywhere, the slogan of the international solidarity of the working class? The Jew did not tire of holding before your eyes, in full color, the blessings of the international proletariat. But above all, the international Jew appealed to your invincible and untamed strength; he, the Jew, knew that as a simple and straight-thinking man, only one thing impressed you: strength, energy, and will.

Consequently, the Jew had to dangle the strength of the international proletariat before your eyes and explain to you that this phantom signified real power and energy. According to the Jew's desire, there was a worldwide working class. "All wheels stand still when your strong arm wishes it." Thus did they speak to you. On this apparent psychosis they built an international structure. You know, German worker, that the wheels actually stood still, and you became unemployed. Seven and a half million Germans had to take welfare, and were subject to destitution and misery. The wheels indeed stood still. But not because you, German worker, wanted it, but because the international Jew and his international capitalism ordered it so. The slogan of the international solidarity of the working class was the greatest fraud and the basest lie that the Jew ever concocted. Do you remember, German worker, whether your French colleague fought for you on the occasion of the Versailles Treaty? Or did the English worker Lloyd George embrace you on the occasion of the insane Treaty of Shame that subjugated, shamed, and exploited you? At the time of the Versailles Dictate, where was the international solidarity? It would have been an opportunity for the international proletariat, if there really existed this international solidarity.

You, German worker, believed the internationalist apostle Woodrow Wilson, and you took his pseudo-sacred Fourteen Points as an innocent confession of faith in a new and better world.[10] In your good-naturedness and good faith, you truly believed in an international solidarity and union of the nations. However, you quickly and bitterly learned that all talk of these internationals was lies and deception. "The Germans will pay for everything," said the Frenchman—and not only the French bourgeois but also the French worker. "The Germans will pay for everything"—here was your international solidarity. "Loot the German, blockade the Hun"; this is what the English worker said. Thus they were all united against Germany in a single will to destroy.

God only knows how many million undernourished children and old people had to pay for your good nature and good faith in the international solidarity. The fact that you have not been destroyed by your good nature is not due to the internationalist apostle, and in no way to the international Jew; rather, it was prevented solely by the will to live and will to strength of the German people. They tried to conceal and camouflage the Versailles failure

---

[10] The Fourteen Points were principles of peace formulated by the US president Woodrow Wilson in January 1918 to be employed in negotiations to end the First World War.

282 Classic Essays on the Jewish Question

with pathetic Quaker Relief supplies,[11] but we Germans will never forget what crime the Jewish International committed against the German people, and especially against the German worker.

*****

German worker, do you still know the slogan of the international Jew: "Everything that bears a human face is the same"? I know that today you are ashamed that you ever believed in it. Your racial instinct has been awakened, and you don't want your errors to be recalled. Nevertheless I must tell you again, and I will not stop reminding you, that it is not true that everything that has a human face is the same. The difference between a great man of our race, like Schopenhauer or Richard Wagner, and an African bushman is greater than the difference between a bushman and an ape.

The Jew has concocted this international slogan, "Everything that bears a human face is the same," only to hide himself. He had to hide his hooked nose and his flat feet in front of the racial beauty of German and Nordic man. In order to raise his value, he had to invent a general melting pot of equalization; and therefore the Jew, of a different racial value than yours, had to drag you down. You, fool, did not realize that, through this slogan, you dispossessed yourself, and even unmanned yourself. German worker, what do you possess? The strength for work is your finest and proudest possession, and this strength and the accomplishments that are associated with it come from your racial worth.

If this worth is reduced, your racial possession is taken from you. You are robbed. Therefore, you have the greatest interest, arising from a primordial and natural instinct, in not allowing your racial worth to be diminished in any way. Cry out to the world: "I am a German, and I have received from God a lofty racial value that enables me to achieve the highest accomplishments. I therefore demand, on the basis of my accomplishments and my abilities, that place in the sun that is due to me."

And not only you, German worker, believed in this internationalist slogan. The bourgeoisie, as I already said, had the same inclination towards internationalist romanticism. If we wish to fully capitalize on the victory of our soldiers and if we wish to fulfill the mission that Fate places before us,

---

[11] The religious society of Quakers organized relief for the undernourished German people after the blockade against Germany was lifted following the Treaty of Versailles in June 1919.

we must mercilessly and ruthlessly break with this reprehensible German inclination to chase after internationalist phantoms.

I recall some equally false slogans: that *science is international*, that there is an *international law*, that there is an *international art*; indeed, this lunacy went so far that one wished to gradually obliterate every artistic difference. It is false that all these things are bound to internationalist slogans and internationalist constructs. Rather, science, law, art, and culture are all bound to race, to the nation. The law is that which is useful to my people; science arises only from the capacity of a race; art and culture are produced only through the creative gift of superior races. The undeniable cultural differences between peoples are an unmistakable proof of the differences between races, of the fact that there are higher and lower races among the nations. The Jew lies, and the slogan of the Jew Karl Marx—"Everything that bears a human face is the same"—was an extreme deception, no matter whether it emerged from a proletarian or bourgeois mind.

How many internationalist phantoms have you, German worker, chased after? We know the second, the third, and the fourth Internationals. Where then is the first? Up to now, we have never thought of that, why the Jew has never yet spoken of the First International. The second was held in Amsterdam, and the third and fourth were held elsewhere. But we won't forget the First International. The First International was established by the Jew Saul, baptized as Paul; it signified a Jewish Universalism that has fought in all centuries and throughout a millennium against the German nationalist people.[12] Everything that was German was the mortal enemy of this Internationalism. The great German emperors have, through the centuries, held high the flag of the sacred German Empire and defended this German Empire against the First International, the Pauline Universalism.

The Second International was that of the bourgeois Social Democracy. I once had, in my life, the opportunity to see at close quarters the representatives of this International during a conference of the International Labor Office in Geneva. In 1933 I was sent as leader of the German delegation to the conference of this International Labor Office. The International Labor Office was a class institution recognized and authorized by the official states. Employers of all countries were all included in it and the employees of the countries equally. And in this way, they made the initial attempt to set the two classes—the employers of the whole world and the employees of the whole

---

[12] Ley is speaking metaphorically of a "First International" going back to St. Paul. As noted above, the official First International was formed in 1864.

world—against each other. There I had the opportunity to become acquainted with, and see in operation, the all-powerful trade union leader of France, M. Jouhaux, and the extremely active trade union leader of Belgium, C. Mertens, and the workers' representative of England, Mr. Hayday.[13]

There, everything that the most daring workers' dreams could imagine was decided: the forty-hour week, plans for housing construction, social insurance, and much else. But everything remained on paper and nothing was realized. This entire international institution of the International Labor Office in Geneva served the capitalists of the world; it was nothing else than a regulation for their international capitalist intentions. Countries like Germany and Italy were restricted in their production with the help of internationalist slogans and international agreements, and were thus held in check in international competition.

This recalls to my mind the only demand of the USA in the Peace Treaty of Versailles. They demanded that all defeated nations, and especially Germany, be forced to participate in the 1920 New York labor conference, and be subjected to its agreement. The agreement at that time said that they wished to introduce a 48-hour-week—not indeed to help the worker but because the American industry had, through the war production, come to such a potential that it could not utilize a longer work week because the world market could not accept the production. That's why they wanted, through this international arbitration, to prevent the defeated and impoverished countries, especially Germany, from dumping products on the world market through increased production. The clause regarding the introduction of a 48-hour-week was nothing more than a capitalistic means to prevent Germany from rising. This diabolical intention was now to be perpetuated by the International Labor Office in Geneva. As victor states, England and France wanted to be forever in control of how much they would allow Germany to participate in production and in international trade. This was their international solidarity!

Thus every one of the Internationals, whether it was the first, second, third, or fourth, had some purely selfish goal. On the one hand, they all were to *prevent* the actual unity of the international proletariat; and on the other

---

[13] Léon Jouhaux (1879-1954) was a French trade union leader of the *Confédération Général du Travail*. Corneel Mertens (1880-1951) was a Belgian trade unionist and member of the Belgian Labor Party. Arthur Hayday (1869-1956) was a member of the British Labor Party and president of the Trades Union Congress from 1930 to 1931.

hand, to help realize the different goals of Jewry. And it is no coincidence that not a single one of these so-called Internationals had their conference in Germany, even though the German proletariat was the most cohesive, numerically by far the strongest, and ideologically the most believing. For example, in 1933, when Germany, at the time of our accession to power, withdrew from the Second International, the Amsterdam institution collapsed.

*****

German worker, you now understand how right National Socialism was when it conducted a fanatic battle against this internationalist mentality and corruption. We had to free you from the internationalist poison. There is no international solidarity, there is no international working class; there is only international Jewry. There is a German national community that is racially-conditioned, and it is thus independent of human constructs, mistakes, and contingencies. God and Fate have brought us together and gave us an unchangeable and inexorable destiny. We belong together, whether we wish it or not. If we bristle against it, we are destroyed. If we acknowledge this unchangeable fact, we will fare well. Not we but the heavens postulate these slogans: blood against money, race against parasitism, nationalism against internationalism, work against exploitation.

Therefore, German worker, understand that Fate gives you today the greatest victory of all time. It calls on you, through the heroism of your soldiers and the genius of the Führer, to lead Europe. But if you wish to lead Europe and thus to fulfill your mission, you cannot be a proletarian and allow yourself to be mastered by internationalist phantoms and bone-softening solidarity nonsense; rather, you must be a master. You are a leader only if you wish to lead, and you can lead only if you train yourself to leadership and mastery.

Thank God this internationalist ghost is now past and everything that we paid homage to, and that oppressed us like a harsh nightmare, seems now like a frightful dream image. A savior came to our people, a man from the depths of the broad masses. A citizen and soldier like you and me, and he undertook, as an individual, against 85 million Germans, the apparently almost impossible task of saving Germany—that is, you and me. He believed in us all. He was inspired by an unrestrained belief in us all. Only this belief in we German men, in the German worker, bourgeois and peasant, gave him the strength to strike the monster of decay and to protect you—the German worker, the German peasant, and German manual laborer, and thus the entire German people—from collapse and downfall.

Thus we stand at the height of our power. Germany has never been as great, powerful, and strong in its unity. German soldiers stand at the North Cape, in Trondheim, Bergen, Antwerp, Calais, Le Havre, Brest, Bordeaux, Biarritz, and along several thousand kilometers of the Atlantic coast, all to keep guard over Europe. They protect Europe against the Jewish monster. Not only is Germany protected by these soldiers, but all the peoples of Europe will eventually feel grateful that Adolf Hitler has established this German army to free Europe from the international Jewish polyp.

German worker, I call you to the roll-call for our true Socialism. The Führer has rescued you from the proletariat, he has freed you from your distress and misery, and he makes all of us a clean, respectable, industrious, and superior German man. Our socialist slogan is: *From a proletarian to a master.* Now do your best, do your duty, take hold of yourself, step up and march towards a new and better future, to your happiness, and to Germany's glory!

— 14 —
GERMANY MUST PERISH!

Theodore N. Kaufman
(1941)

Editor: Ever since Hitler's emergence on the global scene in the mid-1920s, Jews everywhere expressed hatred and outrage toward him, and against the German people generally. When Hitler took power in 1933, Jewry declared "war" against the German people, and Jewish journalists spread horrible and hateful lies about the National Socialist program in order to bias the public against Germany. One particularly incensed Jew was a native New Yorker and small-time ad agent, Theodore Newman Kaufman (b. 1910). When the European war commenced in late 1939 (but prior to US involvement), Kaufman took it upon himself to lead a one-man propaganda effort against the German people. He created his own publishing outfit, Argyle Press, and then proceeded to write and self-published an extended tract, in the form of a small booklet, entitled "Germany must perish!" It was published in March 1941—again, well before Pearl Harbor and the US engagement in the war. Excerpts from the booklet are included below.

Kaufman's thesis was extremely radical, and indeed genocidal: he advocated the literal sterilization of the entire German nation, in order to make a permanent end of the German people and to utterly destroy the German "war-soul." Anticipating eventual German defeat, he sketched out an argument and a plan to subsequently and systematically obliterate the German people within, say, 100 years, by physically and permanently eliminating their ability to give birth. It was an outrageous and incredibly despicable proposal, his "final solution" to the "problem" of German aggression. It would have been collective punishment of a civilian population—a war crime of the highest order.

Kaufman's booklet garnered only small attention in the US, at least initially. He submitted it to the *New York Times* for a review, but they declined. But the Germans soon got word, and they made a huge publicity project of it. For them, it was proof of a literal genocidal plan by Roosevelt and American Jews to exterminate the Germans completely. Goebbels mentioned it in his diary at least a dozen times, beginning in late July 1941; he quickly directed the German press corps to publicize it extensively, and this, in turn, generated attention in the Anglo nations. For example, a short NYT news story of July 24 stated, "The [German] press continued today its anti-Roosevelt campaign with violent attacks upon the president as the alleged promoter of Theodore Kaufman's book *Germany Must Perish*. Both press and radio denounced Kaufman's book as an 'orgy of Jewish hatred'..." A second short story appeared on September 9, in connection with the expulsion of Jews from Hannover. The story was subtitled "Mayor cites American book, *Germany Must Perish*." The mayor's order "cited, as one reason for the ousters, a book written by 'the Jew Kaufman in New York,' demanding 'sterilization of all Germans and employment of German soldiers as coolies in foreign lands'." Also in September, Goebbels had directed the publication of a summary and critique of Kaufman, in the form of a small booklet titled *The War-Goal of World Plutocracy*. The Germans published an astonishing 5 million copies of it, far exceeding the volume of Kaufman's original—this text is reproduced in chapter 15.

The following covers about half of the full booklet—sufficient to see Kaufman's malicious and pathological intent. The text suffers from many defects: it is poorly argued and logically fallacious; it is rife with bald-faced assertions and unjustified implications; it is very poorly cited, with many bogus "quotations" from prominent Germans, citing only a book title (wrongly) as the source; and more broadly, it simply projects Jewish hatred onto the German people. As such, it is a classic study of casting one's own biases and pathologies onto one's enemy. And of course, the explicitly genocidal "remedy" is criminal in the extreme. In the end, Kaufman does indeed justify many of the German fears about the Jewish plutocrats in the West; his book can rightly be seen as an unusually explicit manifestation of a widely-held but rarely-expressed Jewish hatred of Germany.

Introduction

Today's war is not a war against Adolf Hitler.

Nor is it a war against the Nazis.

It is a war of peoples against peoples; of civilized peoples envisioning Light, against uncivilizable barbarians who cherish Darkness.

Of the peoples of those nations who would surge forward hopefully into a new and better phase of life, pitted against the peoples of a nation who would travel backward enthusiastically into the dark ages.

It is a struggle between the German nation and humanity.

Hitler is no more to be blamed for this German war than was the Kaiser for the last one. Nor Bismarck before the Kaiser. These men did not originate or wage Germany's wars against the world. They were merely the mirrors reflecting centuries old inbred lust of the German nation for conquest and mass murder.

This war is being waged by the German People. It is they who are responsible. It is they who must be made to pay for the war. Otherwise, there will always be a German war against the world. And with such a sword forever hanging overhead the civilized nations of the world, no matter how great their hopes, how strenuous their efforts, will never succeed in creating that firm and solid foundation of permanent peace which they must first establish if ever they intend to start the building of a better world.

For not only must there be no more German Wars in fact; there must not even remain the slightest possibility of one ever again occurring. *A final halt* to German aggression, not a temporary cessation, must be the goal of the present struggle.

This does not mean an armed mastery over Germany, or a peace with political or territorial adjustments, or a hope based on a defeated and repentant nation. Such settlements are not sufficiently conclusive guarantees of no more German aggressions.

This time Germany has forced a TOTAL WAR upon the world.

As a result, she must be prepared to pay a TOTAL PENALTY.

And there is one, *and only one*, such Total Penalty:

Germany must perish forever! In fact—not in fancy!

*****

Daily the truth is being impressed upon us by observation, and upon others less fortunate by bombs, that the German doctrine of force is not one based upon either political expediency or economic necessity. The personal war-lust of those who lead the German people is but a component part of the war-lust which exists as a whole in the German masses. German leaders are not isolated from the will of the German people because apart from this will they could not come into being or exist at all. The personal inspiration, the motivation, even the acquiescence to their deeds are one and all drawn by German leaders from the very depths of the German national soul.

Far too often the claim has been made that the present German drive toward world-dominion is only street gangsterism practiced on an organized national scale, deriving principally from the lowest classes, the dregs of Germany. Such a claim is not sustained by facts, for the same lust, the same brute force which the Germans display today under the rule of the so-called "low class Nazis," they also displayed in 1914, at a time when the "highest classes" and the "noblest specimens" capable of being produced by the German nation, the Junkers, ruled that land. And a vast number of Germany's intellectuals, another German "high-class," sat as members in the German Reichstag!

No! The problem of Germanism must not again be passed along to the next generation. The world must never again be stretched and tortured on the German rack. Ours is the problem; ours the solution. The world has learned, with a knowledge born of tragedies too numerous, too horrible to record, that regardless of what leader or class rules Germany war will be waged against it by that country, because the force which compels it to action is an inseparable part of the mass-soul of that nation.

True that soul, at one time, might have been otherwise fashioned.

But that time was in the civilizing cycle of a thousand years ago. Now it is too late.

We know that. Our men of 1917 did not. They had no precedent on which to base their experience. We have not that excuse today. Their futile sacrifices and their empty efforts must today dictate our own actions and decisions.

We are paying today for the lack of experience of the last generation in dealing with the peoples of the German nation. When and if the time comes for us to take similar decision and action we must not repeat their mistake. The cost is far too great; not alone for us, but for all future generations.

We must bring ourselves to realize that no leader can govern Germany at all unless, in some manner, he embodies the spirit and expresses the war-soul existent in the majority of her peoples. "Majority" is used advisedly for in speaking of the masses which compose a nation it must be impartially conceded that some fraction of that mass must perforce vary from it. Consequently no unfair contention is here being made that everyone in Germany is guilty of its heinous offenses against the world. In fact we shall, in pursuing our point, favor Germany by allowing that as much as 20% of her population is entirely guiltless of complicity in her crimes, as well as being foreign to any share of her war-soul. We therefore grant, for argument's sake, that some 15,000,000 Germans are absolutely innocent.

BUT—shall Poles, Czechs, Slovaks, Austrians, Norwegians, Dutch, Belgians, Frenchmen, Greeks, Englishmen, Irishmen, Scotsmen, Canadians, Australians, and Americans—for we too may ultimately feel the spike of the German boot—shall all these peoples, numbering some 300,000,000 of the most civilized, most enlightened on earth suffer constantly and face unnatural death every generation so that some small part of Germany's populace may continue to exist? Are those 15,000,000 Germans so valuable, so indispensable to mankind that 300,000,000 guiltless men, women and children shall fight a War with Germany every time she so decrees? Shall perpetual struggle against the German be the only future facing civilized peoples? Why breed children while Germany breeds War?

Are not the Dutch a sober and thrifty people? Are not the French cultured? Are not the Czechs industrious? Are not the Poles deeply attached to land, family, and God? Are not the Scandinavians a decent people? Are not the Greeks brave and fearless? Are not the English, Irish, Scotch, and American freedom-loving and progressive people? And in very simple arithmetic are nor these 300,000,000 more than 15,000,000 Germans?

If Democracy as Americans know it is majority rule in a national sense, it must be so in an international sense as well. The greatest good for the greatest number is Democracy's rule of thumb; to fight for world Democracy is to secure the rights of the majority of democratic peoples against the incursion made upon them by any autocratic minority.

If this is not so, why conscript a vast army for Democracy's defense? Why train American soldiers to murder a hypothetical enemy of Democracy, when the Will which spawned this enemy waxes and grows with each successive blood-bath?

In 1917 American soldiers, as those of every other major nation, were forced to murder by the millions. What for?

Suppose we are forced again to kill? For wars are won only by such killing, not by dying. Again what for? Another sell-out? Is selling-out our soldiers to become a national habit? *For quite patently, to fight once more in democratic defense against Germany with any goal in view save that country's extinction constitutes, even though it lose the war, a German victory. To fight, to win, and not this time to end Germanism forever by exterminating completely those people who spread its doctrine is to herald the outbreak of another German war within a generation.*

Let us then beware, for it is not illogical to assume that some day the soldier may emerge from underneath the heavy cloak of "duty" and come, like labor, capital, and civilian to demand his "rights." It must not be unreasonable to conjecture that a soldier must have rights too, as well as duties. Certainly, a man forced against his instinct to kill has rights; perhaps not the rights of wages and hours, nor the rights of profits, nor the rights of untrammeled speech against his superiors, which in a military sense spells catastrophe. No, none of these; just a few simple rights—three of which would appear his incontestable duty to demand: one, that he be adequately supplied with the proper arms in sufficient quantities so that there be a minimum of waste attached to his "killing,"—secondly, that he be not betrayed by fifth-columnists who must, in war time, be summarily dispatched, by imprisonment or execution, and lastly, of the primest importance, *that he receive a definite avowal by his government guaranteeing him once and for all time that this whole ghastly, horrible business of killing the Germans is at an end; that his son may know peace without having to kill for it.*

If such a guarantee be not vouchsafed him before his struggle, or be not upheld after his struggle, as it was not the last time, (though the Generals knew, among them our own Pershing, that Germany at that time should have been unalterably snuffed out) may he not then take such action in his own hands? Granting labor has the right to strike when its rights are violated, granting that capital withhold itself from circulation when it feels its usage unprofitable, granting that the civilian feels tyrannized when his civil liberties are jeopardized, what course may the soldier not take once he realizes he has been cheated, once too often, out of that for which he killed?

When the day of reckoning with Germany comes, *as come it will*, there will be only one obvious answer. No statesman or politician or leader responsible for post-war settlements will have the right to indulge in the personal luxury of false sentiment and specious sanctimony and declare that Germany, misled by her leaders, shall deserve the right of resurrection! He will not be permitted this time to forget so easily the bomb-blasted, earth-entombed millions of women and children who lived through a hell on earth; the bullet-ridden, tank-crushed bodies of soldiers; the many countries whose energies were sapped and resources drained. And most of all, he will not be permitted to disregard the unselfish sacrifices made by the common people so that the beast that is Germany shall never roam on earth again!

It is a definite obligation which the world owes to those who struggled and died against the German yesterday, and to those who are fighting him again today, as it is the bounden duty of the present generation to those yet unborn, to make certain that the vicious fangs of the German serpent shall never strike again. And since the venom of those fangs derives its fatal poison not from within the body, but from the war-soul of the German, nothing else would assure humanity safety and security but that that war-soul be forever expunged, and the diseased carcass which harbors it be forever removed from this world.

There is no longer any alternative:

Germany Must Perish!

This war, with its harrowing miseries, its indescribable German devastations, its unutterable German atrocities, is born of the war-soul of those barbarians of whom Machiavelli, writing over four hundred years ago, observed:

> German towns are at little or no expense in any thing, but in laying up military stores and making good their fortifications on holidays instead of other diversion, the Germans are taught the use of weapons.

History repeats itself.

We can remove a tiger from his natural environment, his lair in the jungle, and with patience so tame him that eventually he will respond to our caress, feed from our hand and perform at our command. The more acquiescent he becomes in response to this outward conditioning, the more deceived are we in believing that his jungle days have been forgotten. This is a fatal deception. For inevitably there comes a time when the tiger-soul within the tiger drives him again to the use of fang and claw. In that inexorable response to that irresistible soul-force, the tiger reverts once again to jungle lore. He becomes, again, a killer.

And so it is with the people of Germany. They may respond for a while to civilizing forces; they may seemingly adopt the superficial mannerisms and exterior behaviorisms of civilized peoples but all the while there remains ever present within them that war-soul which eventually drives them, as it does the tiger, to kill. And no amount of conditioning, or reasoning, or civilizing—past, present, or future—will ever be able to change this basic nature. For if no impress has been made upon this war-soul over a period of some two thousand years is it to be expected that of a sudden, on the morrow, this miracle will occur?

This analogous linking of the people of Germany with savage beast is no vulgar comparison. I feel no more personal hatred for these people than I might feel for a herd of wild animals or a cluster of poisonous reptiles. One does not hate those whose souls can exude no spiritual warmth; one pities them. If the German people wish to live by themselves, in darkness, it would be strictly their own affair. But when they make constant attempts to enshroud the souls of other people in those fetid wrappings which cloak their own, it becomes time to remove them from the realm of civilized mankind among which they can have no place, or right to existence.

We need not condemn the Germans. They stand self-condemned. For it suffices us to read and hear those words written and spoken only by Germans; to observe deeds performed solely by Germans; to endure sufferings and dislocations caused solely by the German people in pursuit of their megalomaniacal ideals and daemonic aspirations to realize that it is the Germans themselves who decree, almost demand, their ostracism from their fellowman. They have lost the wish to be human beings. They are but beasts; they must be dealt with as such.

This is an objective viewpoint, carefully considered and factually sustained. It is the view taken of them in this book.

*****

Naturally there are men in the World, our own country included, who think otherwise and who would deal differently with the German menace. It is the custom of such men to take, what they term, a "sensible" view of the problems and progress of humanity. These men would rely upon fate to fashion the future. They would, in effect, permit the Germans to conquer and enslave the world by explaining, in terms whose degree of vociferousness is dependent upon the extent of their own personal motive or gain, that German world-dominion cannot last forever; that at some future date Germany would ultimately lose its iron grip upon the world and then enslaved mankind would come to free itself again. Or , if neither collusion nor surrender seems palatable to their listeners, they would suggest a compromise with the Germans, the so-called "Negotiated Peace."

These are soulless postulates. They can originate only in men whose hearts and souls are still held captive by the marine life of their origin; human species of spineless jellyfish floundering about in the waters of yesteryear. These are men of the past forever living in that past. Men who, being incapable of mastering their own intellectual and spiritual primitivism, seek to drag others down with them to the murky depths and stygian blackness which surround their own pitiful existence.

These are the men, indeed, who witnessing the actual enslavement of such civilized and humane peoples as the Austrians, Czechs, Poles, French, Dutch, Norwegian, and Belgians would all too willingly close their eyes and simulate disbelief in that which is stark and dread reality. These are men who with fatalism as their creed come intellectually to be anesthetized by it; who, proclaiming fate an ally, have become its most pathetic servants.

Fortunately, such men are not yet in the majority nor will they be unless Germany can harness, employ, or bribe enough of them to spread the German netherworld doctrines throughout the earth. But even as a minority the danger which these "appeasers" represent is nonetheless real and they must be harshly dealt with. For by such actions as they may take under the cloak of "unquestioned patriotism" it is apparent that they would not do so unless, within their own soul there existed some part complementary to the war-soul of the German. Those other appeasers whose integrity is doubtful and patriotism questionable—those who advocate the principles of Germanism—are downright traitors to their country. And when, as and if a government cannot or refuses to treat them as such, may it not come in time to depend upon the people, whose lives and liberty are at stake, to do so!

I have no desire that this work be considered as a means of encouraging war for this or any other nation.

As a human being I deplore war; as a civilized member of a civilized nation, I hate it.

I hate War not alone for the sufferings, misery, tragedy, and senseless waste which follows in its path, but even more because I consider it to be the still-unsevered umbilical cord which binds the moral and spiritual embryo of man to the physical womb of the beast-instinct. And I know that so long as that cord remains uncut social evolution and human progress must rest forever upon an impermanent and insecure basis. And too, that so long as war persists there will never come into being that world peace out of which, some day, a world confederation of nations will be born. For it is such a confederation which is the ultimate aim of the human race.

Peace! Hardly a man, woman or child lives who has not heard the word! Throughout the ages it has been a subject of more discussion and debate than any other single problem of mankind. In the halls of government great orators have loudly extolled its virtues. The great prophets of every religion on earth have preached its gospel and catalogued its benefits to world humanity. And in all the world we find that peace is the one common denominator which binds together the people of all nations, of all color and races, in common thought and prayer.

Why then, after passing through thousands of years of such great desire and yearning have we failed to find peace? Why is it that after such a prolonged period of time not one single practical and enduring step has been taken toward its absolute realization? Certainly no one man or group of men shall be born tomorrow who shall exceed in knowledge and excel in ability all those great men who have written, spoken, and preached about peace over the long past. What shall we do then? Throw up our hands and give up? Shall we have done with peace by exclaiming that it does not exist because it *cannot? That it is an unobtainable abstract?*

I do not believe that it is any such thing. I sincerely believe that peace on earth can come to exist as a permanent condition of living. But believing in it as I do, I would not expect it to arrive, on some fine morning, knock on my door, and suddenly announce its presence! No, it will never come of itself!

I believe that peace can be produced, not merely conceived. But never so long as war persists.

Then why does war still exist?

Simply because it has not been made impossible for it to be waged.

There is only one way to abolish war: impose a penalty of such dire magnitude and frightful consequence upon aggressor peoples as to render it virtually impossible for any nation to start a war.

War must be fought not with weapons of ever-increasing destructiveness but with penalties infinitely more frightful and hazardous than war itself.

This book sincerely believes that it has found such a penalty; and by its imposition upon the people of Germany, this book believes that not only

would a great scourge be removed from the world, but a great good born to it.
1

The Background of Germanism

For it must be patent by now that while all the Germans may not approve of the means being employed by the Nazis in achieving German-world-dominion, they are practically unanimous in agreeing that that goal must, now or in the future, be definitely achieved by Germany. There is only one way to frustrate such a desire: the goal of world-dominion must be removed from the reach of the German and the only way to accomplish that is to re-move the German from the world!

Therefore it is most essential that we realize as an irreconcilable fact the truth that the Nazis are not beings existing apart from the German people. *They are the German people!* For to the German, Nazi or not, the Mailed Fist is as stimulating and meaningful a symbol of all the aims and aspirations of his nation as the Statue of Liberty is to the American. Make no mistake about it; world-dominion is not a mirage to the German; it never was, and so long as Germany exists as a nation, it never will be. A belief to the contrary, if too long sustained, may well result in the world's enslavement by the German.

As fantastic and as cyclonic as Nazi "accomplishments" might seem, it is still more fantastic to note as a fact that in the entire annals of history no doctrine ever existed which had all its major beliefs so clearly defined, its methods so concisely detailed, and its aims so vividly, comprehensively, and boldly stated beforehand. It is, in every respect a deliberate, ruthlessly calcu-lated plot to rule the world or, failing that, *to annihilate it!* And so long as the German nation exists it intends, in one form or another, now or later, to bring about just such a catastrophe.

---

[1] The majority of authors dealing with Germanism have treated that subject purely as a product of modern times—born after the last world war—and since developed solely by Hitler and his Nazis. The reader, in pursuing the subsequent chapters on Germanism, will find out for himself just how mistaken those authors are in their viewpoint. And since the German quotations and German writings are so contem-poraneously apropos—though they were all written prior to the last world war—I have thought it advisable, lest they be considered "fabricated," to append a bibliog-raphy to this volume.

The unfortunate neglect displayed by the various governments in preparing for the cataclysmic events brought about by the German Nazis becomes all the more startling and tragic when we examine records existing by the thousands and emanating solely from unbiased German sources, some written as far back as fifty years ago, clearly indicating the precise course of procedure to be some day adopted by the German in his march to world-conquest. These documents are not pedantic treatises expressing theories or extravaganzas dealing in fables or fancies. They are substantial, sober outpourings from the very soul of Germandom. And as such they define lucidly its structure, and interpret frankly its yearnings.

Moreover, these records are so exact in their theme and comprehensive in their scope that the Nazis have adopted and embraced them almost ad verbatim. In searching through these original papers one is struck by the realization that *Mein Kampf* is nothing more than a clumsily-written hodge-podge collection of the writings, opinions and teachings contained in those records and expounded by Germans years before Adolf Schickelgruber was born! As we shall see later, even Hitler's much-publicized *mystic prophecies*, and his *time-tables of conquests* are merely reprints of those published, too, long before his time.

If Hitler was able to make such rapid strides in resurrecting again the monstrosity that is Germanism, it was only because the German people, long before his birth, had already become completely instilled with each and every principle and precept, with every yearning and desire which he himself, later, came merely to express and advocate. The poisonous wine of destruction had long before been distilled; Hitler is merely the agent decanting the poisonous fluid from its bottle, which is the German war-soul, into the jug that is world humanity. In detailing those ingredients which combine to constitute the toxic formula of Germanism the author shall quote, wherever confirmation of his statements may be deemed advisable, principally from German sources. For after all no one can explain the German so well as he himself. He has made no secret of his character, his ambitions and his intentions. By his acts he has himself bared his heart and soul; by his words, by his own hand he will someday come to dig his own grave.

*****

It is not to be wondered at that the nations of the Western world regard the avowed program of the German for world conquest and dominion with a great deal of amazement and incredulity. For such an idea is entirely alien to those basic principles and instincts of the western civilization which, painfully and gradually, arose out of the chaos of the past thousands of years. Such civilized nations regard individual rights, the sacredness of human life, liberty and the pursuit of happiness as the virtues of mankind and itself, the individual States, as guarantor of those rights. And though, at one time or another during their existence nations may have sought political and economic adjustments, even territorial aggrandizement through force of arms, it must be noted that no Western nation has ever made such a religion of war, such idolatry of armaments, and such a cult of mass murder and destruction as has Germany and her peoples.

According to her own writers, teachers, and statesmen Germany has but one great reason for existing; that of achieving world-dominion! Since that is its highest aim, therefore, Germany constantly claims that it has every right to make free and liberal use of chicanery, deceit, intolerance, lust, persecution, and oppression, in order to achieve that goal. Consequently such a perverted nation, such a State of human negation, views its vices as being the only true virtues in life, whereas to the Germans the virtues as they are known and may be practiced by the rest of the world are merely vices due to the latter's decay and degeneration![2] As though there exists anywhere in the world a nation which can boast of degeneration in the same degree as Germany!

The primary reason which stirs German lust for world-dominion was best summarized by a German professor who declared that since Germany will never be able to understand the world, *the latter must be conquered and reformed so that it will be able to conform to German thought![3]*

It is just such mass megalomania, crass egoism and intellectual aberrancy which stirred the demented brain of the German of yesterday to foment his wars; which animates the insane Nazi today in continuing those wars and which will, if the schizophrenic Teutons continue to exist, direct the policies and actions of any party in control of Germany in the future. For, to reiterate, the German idea of world-dominion and enslavement of its peoples is no political belief: it is a fierce and burning gospel of hate and intolerance, of murder and destruction and the unloosing of a sadistic blood lust. It is, in every literal sense, a savage and pagan religion which incites its worshippers first to a barbaric frenzy and then prompts them to vent their animal ferocity in the practice of every horrible, ruthless, and unmentionable atrocity

---

[2] *Thus Spake Zarathustra*: Friedrich Nietzsche.

[3] *Die Politik*: Heinrich von Treitschke.

upon innocent men, women, and children. Such are the true Germanic virtues! And the World will feel their sting so long as they continue to tolerate Germany and her peoples on the earth, for those Germanic traits are the same as those which, emanating from the German soul, animated the Germanic tribes of yore. We have but to examine the development of those tribes to perceive just to what extent within the German soul, the German ideal of world conquest and dominion really lies.

The German slave-holding tribes were noted for their unnaturally passionate love of war and destruction. Seeck, a noted German historian, writes with pride that the Germans of ancient days were notorious for their villainy and treachery and "their faithlessness became almost proverbial with the Romans",[4] who found that the Germans were adept at breaking a pact or a peace whenever it best suited them to so do.

Lamprecht, another German historian, recounts that even among themselves the Germans held no pledge valid![5] Is it so much to be wondered at then that a nation whose people distrust one another, would hesitate at double crossing any of its fellow nations

Those ancient Germanic tribes, like the peoples of modern Germany, were unable to assimilate and accept the humane ideals, civilized aims and social aspirations of their neighbors as constituting the desirable, natural goal of life. "Warlike, as then, have the Germans ever remained!"[6]

We can understand, therefore, why to a German peace is not an objective but merely an interlude to be used by him to prepare for a war in which he can assuage the thirst for mass murder which burns in his soul. The German has absolutely no regard for life; there is no such expression in his language as "sacredness of human life."

It would be impossible, even between the covers of a thousand volumes, to list and describe the daemonic brutalities practiced by the Germans upon innocent peoples, and though records of the last war are replete with numerous actual incidents illustrating the innate cruelty and viciousness of the Germans we have but to refer to one recent occurrence, the sinking of the British vessel "Lancastria" to realize just how and why the German earns his reputation for such cruelty and viciousness.

For assuredly, after sinking a vessel, the aviators of no other Western nation would have deliberately and cold-bloodedly dropped incendiary

---

[4] *Geschichte des Untergangs der Antiken.*
[5] *Deutsche Geschichte*: Lamprecht.
[6] *Unsere Muttersprache*: Prof. D. Weise.

bombs on the oil-covered waters which surrounded the ship in order to roast alive the desperate women and children struggling below. But the German aviators did not hesitate to do so; it must have been with a perverted gleam in their mad eye that they boiled those women and children alive in oil! This from a "modern" and self-styled "cultured" nation! A nation whose press heralded such cannibalism as an illustrious example of German courage and heroism!

Such is the "Master-Race" of the world!

"Blessed Are the War Makers"

THE GERMAN SOUL

> Ye have heard how in old times it was said, Blessed are the meek, for they shall inherit the earth; but I say unto you, Blessed are the valiant, for they shall make the earth their throne. And ye have heard men say, Blessed are the poor in spirit; but I say unto you, Blessed are the great in soul and the free in spirit, for they shall enter into Valhalla. And ye have heard men say, Blessed the peacemakers; but I say unto you, Blessed are the war-makers, for they shall be called, if not the children of Jahve, the children of Odin, who is greater that Jahve.[7]

Thus out of the Bible of Germanism cometh the German Sermon of the Mount, as interpreted by Friedrich Nietzsche, prophet of the Superior Soul, by whose Apostolic sword millions of people in the past year have been cut down, bleeding to earth.

But the world even then was blind. It looked on saber-rattling Prussianism not as a continuance of the German war-soul developed throughout the ages, but simply as a transient period of political history. For had not the spirit of Christ, in the image of Love and Brotherhood, walked the earth for nineteen centuries, softening men's hearts and tempering men's souls? Could civilized man fall heir to such a spirit and not pay heed? In Germany great cathedrals housed the Cross, but though others did not, German thinkers knew they housed but a great emptiness of soul. For they well knew that the German gods of pagan days were not dead; that they but slept; that even

---

[7] *Ed.:* Source unknown. This is likely either a paraphrase or a false attribution to Nietzsche.

in their slumber they were still charged with a fire inflaming the barbaric instincts of those people.

Heinrich Heine, in 1834, had this to say of Christ in Germany:

> Christianity—and this is its fairest merit—subdued to a certain extent the brutal warrior ardor of the Germans, but it could not entirely quench it; and when the Cross, that restraining talisman, falls to pieces, then will break forth again the ferocity of the old combatants, the frantic Berserker rage whereof Northern poets have said and sung so much. The talisman has become rotten, and the day will come when it will pitifully crumble to dust. The old stone gods will then arise from the forgotten ruins, and wipe from their eyes the dust of centuries, and Thor with his giant hammer will arise again, and he will shatter the Gothic cathedrals...when ye hear the tramping of feet and the clashing of arms, ye neighbors children, be on your guard...it might fare ill with you... Smile not at the fantasy of one who foresees in the region of reality the same outburst of revolution that has taken place in the region of the intellect. The thought precedes the deed as the lightning with thunder. German thunder is of true German character: it is not very nimble, but rambles along somewhat slowly. But come it will, and when ye hear a crashing such as never before has been heard in the world's history, then know that at last the German thunderbolt has fallen. At this commotion the eagles will drop dead from the skies and the lions in the farthest wastes of Africa will bite their tails and creep into their royal lairs. There will be played in Germany a drama compared to which the French Revolution will seem but an innocent idyll. At present everything is quiet; and though here and there some few men create a little stir, do not imagine these are to be the real actors in the piece. They are only little curs chasing one another round the arena...till the appointed hour when the troop of gladiators appear to fight for life and death. And the hour will come.[8]

---

[8] *Ed.: On the History of Religion and Philosophy in Germany* (1835/2007), pp. 116-117.

German intellect, German culture, German emotion, industry, economics, politics, in fact all things German, are each but a tiny rivulet feeding with its water the mighty rushing stream which is the German war-soul. The war-soul itself is thus become a mighty torrent against which no dike can be built sufficiently high or sufficiently strong to stem its onrush.

Our problem then is not the course-altering or damming up of any of the rivulets but in contending with and in subduing that power which they have produced, the power of the German war-soul.

Let us hold in abeyance for a moment the question of the all too obvious sufferings which the German war-soul has inflicted upon the world, and examine it objectively from the standpoint of its justification as regards world benefits. In short, is the war-soul of Germany and its spread of Germanism worth more to civilization than its cost in human life and freedom? Will the world, derive more from its perpetuation than from its extinction?

The answer requires no guesswork on our part. Once again Nietzsche in his role of spiritual Baedeker of Germanism leaves no vestige of doubt concerning German blessings. Following are random excerpts from his *Ecce Homo*:

> Where Germany spreads, she corrupts culture…
>
> Every great crime against culture committed during the last four hundred years lies on the German conscience… The Germans incurred the responsibility for everything that exists today—the sickliness and stupidity that opposes culture, the neurosis called Nationalism, from which Europe suffers…; the Germans have robbed Europe itself of meaning and intelligence and have led it into a blind alley….
>
> In the history of knowledge Germans are represented only by doubtful names, they have produced only 'unconscious swindlers'… 'German intellect' is bad air, a psychological uncleanliness that has now become instinctive—an uncleanliness which in every word and gesture betrays the German. And if a man is not clean, how can he be deep? You can never fathom their (the German) depths, they have none; and that ends it…
>
> The German soul is small and base.[9]

---

[9] *Ed.:* Kaufman here quotes from four separate passages in *Ecce Homo*. Specific locations are: (1) "Why I am so clever," sec. 3; (2) "The case of Wagner," sec. 2; (3) "The case of Wagner," sec. 3; (4) unknown.

There is nothing to add to these words. The myth of German intellect and culture explodes under the hand of their outstanding product. German-proclaimed culture is not worth its, or any, cost.

However, is there yet some fine point about the Germans that we do not understand? Over a generation ago, the late American historian, Charles Francis Adams, disturbed by this very question, undertook to examine it.

> Suspecting in my own case (that I did not think like a German) I have of late confined my reading on this topic almost exclusively to German sources. I have been taking a course on Nietzsche and Treitschke, as also in the German *Denkschrift*, illumined by excerpts from the German papers in this country and the official utterances of Chancellor von Bethmann-Hollweg. The result has been most disastrous. It has utterly destroyed my capacity for judicial consideration. I can only say that if what I find in those sources is a capacity to think Germanically, *I would rather cease thinking at all*. It is the absolute negation of everything which in the past tended to the elevation of mankind, and the installation in place thereof of a system of thorough dishonesty, emphasized by brutal stupidity. There is a low cunning about it, too, which is to me in the last degree repulsive.[10]

Germanism was born ages ago, its growth has been proceeding for centuries, and it has now reached an advanced stage of flowering. Hitler is but a bud indicative of what kind of "flower" when it comes to full bloom, the world may expect to see!

Because she made no effort thousands of years ago, to become civilized as did her neighbors, Germany today is an outsider among all civilized nations. The processes which it has taken other nations thousands of years to absorb, cannot be suddenly absorbed by Germany overnight. Consequently, the continued existence of Germany among them becomes increasingly inimical to the best interests of civilized nations.

The deliberate and perverse distortions of what should have been a sane and normal course of development—as in other nations—now gives to Germany and her people a capacity unexcelled by any other peoples on earth, for fostering and propagating every indecent and inhuman precept of

---

[10] *Ed.:* Source unknown. Likely a false attribution.

life. And as she seeks to distribute her own poisonous brew she has herself become so intoxicated by its ingredients that she can no longer escape the ever-constant desire, the urgent compulsion and the burning lust which it incites in her to extinguish any and all signs of good which she sees developed or practiced in other lands. Thus in self-justification Germany would excuse her own unnatural and perverse life by polluting others with her malignant infection. Germany is now well beyond all saving. The world had best look to its Own preservation and welfare, lest some of those German poisons run through her system also and come to destroy it!

With each succeeding world war which she plans, plots, and starts Germany comes over closer and closer to her goal of world-dominion. At the present time Hitler, who has merely striven to remedy mistakes which previous German leaders made in attempts at world-subjection, may bring the German people very close to realizing their goal. And Hitler is not the last of the Fuehrers!

How much misery, suffering, death, and destruction are needed before it becomes apparent to the world that any compromise with Germanism will, of itself, be a certain guarantee that soon thereafter, Germany must again embark upon her unholy crusade to dominate it. How many more chances will be vouchsafed it to beat back Germany? Suppose there comes a time when Germany cannot be halted? Dare we risk waiting? One never knows the exact hour one is scheduled to die; can we, with any more certitude and assurance tell which opportunity shall be our last? It may well be that this is our last chance. Suppose we pass it by; look ahead. Next time, the so-called elder generation of Germany will be the Hitler-trained youth of today, and this elder generation, now mothers and fathers, will already have instilled and encouraged their children with the idea of world-dominion. For it is only natural for parents to want their children to succeed where they themselves failed. And as a consequence of all this there may come to be welded a machine so gigantic in proportions, so overwhelming in destructive power, that it may well overcome every possible obstacle in its path. For assuredly the German youth of the next generation—today schooled in Fuehrer schools—will find a leader, as past generations of German youth have always found a leader, to incarnate and personify the body and soul of that nation and dominate its collective Will.

A leader who will feed that German body and soul the only food upon which it can subsist: War!

Death To Germany

When an individual commits premeditated murder, he must be prepared to forfeit his own life in consequence. When a nation commits premeditated murder upon its fellow nations, it must be prepared to forfeit its own national life.

On that point the laws of man and God are explicit:

"An eye for an eye, a tooth for a tooth, and a life for a life."

But what is the law of man or God to Germany? Nothing.

She recognizes only German law; so be it.

It must then be German law, if such a law there be, which decrees her penalty—the penalty of death.

And there is such a German law which decrees that death to her:

> As in all human affairs, there must also be in every system of punishment a last limit, a ne plus ultra that no punishment can overstep. Thus even from the point of view of pure theory the necessity of the death-penalty is postulated; it is, as the ultimate punishment on earth, the indispensable keystone of every ordered system of criminal law. No apparent reasons which are alleged against it can withstand any serious criticism. The State, which has the right to sacrifice for its own protection the flower of its youth, is to feel so nice a regard for the life of a murderer? We must rather allow to the State the right to make away with men who are undoubtedly injurious to the common weal. That the powers that be must bear the sword is an expression which runs deep in the blood of the honest man; if this truth is to be banished out of the world, great wrong is done to the simple moral feeling of the people. The ultimate problems of the moral life are to be solved in the domain of the practical, not of the theoretical, reason. The conscience of every earnest man demands that blood be atoned by blood, and the common man must simply grow doubtful of the existence of justice on earth, if this last and highest punishment is not inflicted. The State makes itself ridiculous and contemptible if it cannot finally dispose of a criminal. There must be a limit for mercy and indulgence, as for the law, a last limit at which the State says: 'This is the end, humanity is no longer possible here.' It must be possible to inflict at last a punishment

beyond which there is nothing, and that is the punishment of death. (Heinrich von Treitschke)

Let German Will be done!

*****

There remains now but to determine the best way, the most practical and expeditious manner in which the ultimate penalty must be levied upon the German nation. Quite naturally, massacre and wholesale execution must be ruled out. In addition to being impractical when applied to a population of some seventy million, such methods are inconsistent with the moral obligations and ethical practices of civilization. There remains then but one mode of ridding the world forever of Germanism—and that is to stem the source from which issue those war-lusted souls, by preventing the people of Germany from ever again reproducing their kind. This modern method, known to science as Eugenic Sterilization, is at once practical, humane, and thorough. Sterilization has become a byword of science, as the best means of ridding the human race of its misfits: the degenerate, the insane, the hereditary criminal.

Sterilization is not to be confused with castration. It is a safe and simple operation, quite harmless and painless, neither mutilating nor unsexing the patient. Its effects are most often less distressing than vaccination and no more serious than a tooth extraction. Too, the operation is extremely rapid requiring no more than ten minutes to complete. The patient may resume his work immediately afterwards. Even in the case of the female the operation, though taking longer to perform, is as safe and simple. Performed thousands of times, no records indicate cases of complication or death. When one realizes that such health measures as vaccination and serum treatments are considered as direct benefits to the community, certainly sterilization of the German people cannot but be considered a great health measure promoted by humanity to immunize itself forever against the virus of Germanism.

The population of Germany, excluding conquered and annexed territories, is about 70,000,000, almost equally divided between male and female. To achieve the purpose of German extinction it would be necessary to only sterilize some 48,000,000—a figure which excludes, because of their limited power to procreate, males over 60 years of age, and females over 45.

Concerning the males subject to sterilization the army groups, as organized units, would be the easiest and quickest to deal with. Taking 20,000 surgeons as an arbitrary number and on the assumption that each will perform a minimum of 25 operations daily, it would take no more than one month, at the maximum, to complete their sterilization. Naturally the more doctors available, and many more than the 20,000 we mention would be available considering all the nations to be drawn upon, the less time would be required. The balance of the male civilian population of Germany could be treated within three months. Inasmuch as sterilization of women needs somewhat more time, it may be computed that the entire female population of Germany could be sterilized within a period of three years or less. Complete sterilization of both sexes, and not only one, is to be considered necessary in view of the present German doctrine that so much as one drop of true German blood constitutes a German.

Of course, after complete sterilization, there will cease to be a birth rate in Germany. At the normal death rate of 2% per annum, German life will diminish at the rate of 1,500,000 yearly. Accordingly in the span of two generations that which cost millions of lives and centuries of useless effort, namely, the elimination of Germanism and its carriers, will have been an accomplished fact. By virtue of its loss of self-perpetuation German Will will have atrophied and German power reduced to negligible importance.

Reviewing the foregoing case of sterilization we find that several factors resulting from it firmly establish its advocacy.

Firstly, no physical pain will be imposed upon the inhabitants of Germany through its application, a decidedly more humane treatment than they will have deserved. As a matter of fact it is not inconceivable that after Germany's defeat, the long-suffering peoples of Europe may demand a far less humane revenge than that of mere sterilization.

Secondly, execution of the plan would in no way disorganize the present population nor would it cause any sudden mass upheavals and dislocations. The consequent gradual disappearance of the Germans from Europe will leave no more negative effect upon that continent than did the gradual disappearance of the Indians upon this.

Here again, a German attests to this point, Spengler's famous: "A nation or an individual may die and leave no gap!"

*****

A detailed program of the manner in which the outraged victims of Germanic onslaught might make certain that Germany leave no gap might be put hypothetically:

Germany has lost its war. She sues for peace. The imperative demands of the victor people that Germany must perish forever makes it obligatory for the leaders to select mass sterilization of the Germans as the best means of wiping them out permanently. They proceed to:

1. Immediately and completely disarm the German army and have all armaments removed from German territory.

2. Place all German utility and heavy industrial plants under heavy guard, and replace German workers by those of Allied nationality.

3. Segregate the German army into groups, concentrate them in severely restricted areas, and summarily sterilize them.

4. Organize the civilian population, both male and female, within territorial sectors, and effect their sterilization.

5. Divide the German army (after its sterilization has been completed) into labor battalions, and allocate their services toward the rebuilding of those cities which they ruined.

6. Partition Germany and apportion its lands. The accompanying map gives some idea of possible land adjustments which might be made in connection with Germany's extinction.

7. Restrict all German civilian travel beyond established borders until all sterilization has been completed.

8. Compel the German population of the apportioned territories to learn the language of its area, and within one year to cease the publication of all books, newspapers, and notices in the German language, as well as to restrict German-language broadcasts and discontinue the maintenance of German-language schools.

9. Make one exception to an otherwise severely strict enforcement of total sterilization, by exempting from such treatment only those Germans whose relatives, being citizens of various victor nations, assume financial responsibility for their emigration and maintenance and moral responsibility for their actions.

Thus, into an oblivion which she would have visited upon the world, exits Germany.

THE WAR-GOAL OF
WORLD PLUTOCRACY

Wolfgang Diewerge
(1941)

Editor: As one of Goebbels' top aides, Wolfgang Diewerge (1906-1977) was an important if largely unknown figure within the Ministry of Propaganda. Born in Stettin, Germany (now Szczecin, Poland), Diewerge went on to study law at Jena, eventually earning a law degree. While still in his teens, he wrote for regional National Socialist journals and newspapers, joined the NSDAP in 1930 at age 24, and then later the SS, in 1936. With his newly-earned law degree, Diewerge began working as an attorney for Goebbels' organization, defending party and government officials. He worked on a number of prominent cases (van Meeteren, Gustloff, vom Rath), both as a legal consultant and a press officer. He moved rapidly up the ministry hierarchy, becoming head of the prestigious radio department in 1941, at age 35.

One of Diewerge's many tasks was to write short pamphlets on the issues of the day, especially as they related to the Jews. Earlier he wrote pamphlets on his trials (two of which—Gustloff and vom Rath—featured Jewish assassins), but in 1941 he was assigned to write a small booklet in response to Theodore Kaufman's book, *Germany Must Perish!* (see chapter 14). The result was a compelling piece, *Das Kriegsziel der Weltplutokratie* ('The War-Goal of World Plutocracy'), translated here in full. All notes are the editor's.

Diewerge was allegedly present in the Führer Bunker at the very end of the war, when both Hitler and Goebbels committed suicide. Diewerge then fled to the west, managing to avoid capture and prosecution. He worked as a lawyer and journalist for many years, and eventually in the advertising industry. He died in Essen in 1977, at the age of 71.

At almost the same time that the two chief warmongers Roosevelt and Churchill were meeting on the American president's luxury yacht "Potomac," singing pious songs and praying for the victory of Bolshevism, leading personages in the United States and England received a small, long package that contained a miniature black coffin. Upon opening it, they found a card telling them: "Read the pamphlet 'Germany Must Perish!'" The day after this announcement, they received a 104-page booklet with a red cover, with "Germany must perish!" in gold lettering. The author was the president of the "American Federation of Peace," the American Jew Theodore Nathan Kaufman from the ghetto of Manhattan.

The book called for exactly what its title suggested: the extermination of the entire German people, including women and children, and the partitioning of the territory of the Greater German Reich among its neighbors. As the way to exterminate a nation of 80 million people, the Jewish president proposed the disarming of the German people and the sterilization of all fertile men, women, and children.

Who is President Kaufman?

The Jewish president Kaufman is no anonymous loner, no fanatic rejected by World Jewry, no insane creature, but rather a leading and widely-known Jewish figure in the United States. He belongs to Roosevelt's so-called "Brain Trust," the staff of politicians who provide intellectual and political advice to the American president. This circle provides the material for the hate-filled speeches against National Socialist Germany that President Roosevelt likes to give. It is the center of activity for those warmongers who expanded the war into the Balkans in the spring of 1941. The half-Jewish mayor of New York, La Guardia,[1] along with Roosevelt's close confidante and friend Bernard Baruch (the "unofficial president" of the U.S.A.) also belong to this group, which maintains the closest ties to the leading men of the Soviet Union. They provide the impetus for the agitation for American military and material support for Bolshevism.

---

[1] Fiorello LaGuardia (1882-1947) was mayor of New York from 1934 to 1945. His mother, Irene Coen, was Jewish.

Theodore Nathan Kaufman belongs to this circle.[2] He has appeared as a writer before. His influence on the American president has greatly increased in recent months. He is thought to be behind the meeting between Roosevelt and Churchill. The name Kaufman has also surfaced in connection with recent American terrorist actions in South America.

President Kaufman — Spokesman for World Plutocracy

It is indisputable that his book and his demand that "Germany must perish" is the official opinion of the leading circles of world plutocracy. In supposedly free America, a book not to the liking of world plutocracy has no hope of being published. It is either banned or bought out. Neither happened in the case of Kaufman's book. To the contrary, it has been promoted in every way. Kaufman, of course, did not pay for the expensive propaganda—for example, the sending of those black coffins we previously mentioned. He claims to be the sole author, publisher, and distributor. He even tries to make it appear that he gave this program of extermination to the world from a pure "love of humanity," and that he would prefer to die in poverty rather than withhold these "noble thoughts" from others.

That is an old Jewish trick that no longer works on Germany. All the Jewish murderers who have been previously caught used the same methods, which they learn from the Talmud. The Jew Frankfurter, who shot Wilhelm Gustloff, claimed that he planned the crime alone and carried it out by himself, despite all the evidence that he had an exact map of the area, that he was in debt, and received money from large Jewish organizations.[3] The Jew Grünspan, the cowardly murderer of the German embassy employee Ernst vom Rath in Paris, never admitted to his links to the "Jewish World League," although his close cooperation with this Jewish organization could be proven by the documents our troops found after occupying Paris.[4]

---

[2] There seems to be no evidence for this claim.
[3] David Frankfurter shot and killed Wilhelm Gustloff on 4 February 1936. Gustloff was the head of the Swiss NSDAP party.
[4] Vom Rath was killed by Herschel Grünspan (or Grynszpan) in early November 1938. This assassination triggered the *Kristallnacht* reprisals against Jews in Germany.

World Jewry Affirms Murder as a Political Tool

The murderers' racial comrades from the first announced that they did not approve of the crimes of either Frankfurter or Grünspan. At the same time as they were making these hypocritical statements, however, Jews from all over the world, along with major Jewish organizations, were sending the murderers letters and telegrams, praising them in newspapers, providing them with money and goods, and hiring the best-known and most expensive lawyers. Bernhard Lecache, the president of the Jewish World League, had this to say from his then-office in Paris about the Grünspan case on 9 November 1938, nearly a year before the beginning of the war:

> Our task is to declare pitiless war against Germany, the state enemy #1. One may be sure of this: We will fight this war until the Grünspans no longer need to go to gun shops to revenge with blood the misfortune of being a Jew![5]

It is therefore to be expected that, at the moment the Jew Kaufman is revealed as an inciter to murder and his close relations with the president of the United States are uncovered, world plutocracy will deny it. This trick is obvious and has been used so often that it is recognized from the beginning. Just as Frankfurter and Grünspan remained admired figures for World Jewry even when they were in prison, Nathan Kaufman only wrote and demanded that which is the goal and the dream of world plutocracy in this great battle that it has forced upon us.

The American Press on the Book's Appearance

There is one other option. Just as with the *Protocols of the Elders of Zion,* the Jews could claim that *Germany Must Perish* is a clever anti-Semitic forgery. One in fact could not imagine a worse charge against World Jewry than a plan to exterminate 80 million culturally advanced, industrious, and decent German women, men, and children. But this pamphlet is not the product of the hate-filled mind of a loner, but rather the capstone of thousands of years of Jewish plans for world domination. The Jews can no longer dispute the existence of the book. English and American newspapers have already promoted its distribution and discussed its contents. Copies of the

---

[5] Diewerge cites no source for this quotation.

book have also been flown to Germany. An original copy will be shown to the foreign press when this pamphlet is published. The picture on the cover of the author is also indisputable. And the publisher (Argyle Press, Newark, New Jersey) is also established.

Close Relationship with the Potomac Declaration

The book *Germany Must Perish* is the background music to the major foreign policy deception that the leaders of world plutocracy—President Roosevelt and his business partner in international warmongering, Prime Minister Winston Churchill—have launched to support their ally Stalin. While from the yacht "Potomac," the peoples of Central Europe are promised raw materials, open shipping channels, peace and freedom, happiness and prosperity, the call that "Germany must perish and vanish forever from the face of the earth!" echoes through America and England.

Publication of the Jewish Book in the German Language Prohibited!

These tunes are not in harmony, and are also not intended for the same audiences. The alluring slogans from the "Potomac" were spread to German by lying radio stations. The Jew Kaufman's book, on the other hand, has an interesting note on an interior page that bans any distribution or translation in foreign languages. The author further prohibits even excerpts of his book from being translated into German. That is further evidence that it is intended only for the internal use of Americans and Englishmen to help them understand the hypocrisy coming from the "Potomac." The Germans first are to be persuaded to lay down their weapons. The promises Roosevelt and Churchill made are valid up to then. But once Germany is defenseless, the Jew Kaufman takes over.

The plan is carefully thought out and clever. Both the simultaneous publication and the inner consistency are important. The common source cannot be missed. World plutocracy's hate speaks clearly from these documents. The international connections of world plutocracy are clearly visible.

New York, London, and Moscow are a Single Front

Just as Reaction, Bolshevism, and liberalism were allied through their common Jewish foundations in the domestic German struggle against National

Socialism, so today London, New York, and Moscow are arm-and-arm in the effort to create a second, more terrible Treaty of Versailles. This second Treaty of Versailles will bear no more relationship to the Potomac Declaration than the first Treaty of Versailles bore to Wilson's declarations. World Jewry in New York, Moscow, and London agrees on the complete destruction of the German people. The Jew Kaufman has made himself the spokesman for this "peace proposal."

Education about this Murderous Plan is Necessary for Germany

It is, therefore, fortunate that his book fell into German hands in so timely a fashion for the entire German people to learn about it. Although reprinting it is forbidden under international law, there is no objection to printing the central parts of a publication that concerns a community, in order to help that community form its own opinion.

Of course, this publication is unpleasant for the Jew Kaufman and particularly for those behind him. They will certainly attempt to interfere with this publication by legal tricks. As previously mentioned, Kaufman particularly feared that his book would become known in Germany. And now this Jew, who calls for the extermination of the German people, demands that the laws of the very people he wants to condemn to death for "lack of culture" and lawlessness" protect his filthy work. This by itself is enough to show the intellectual nature of the Jew Kaufman and his ilk. It is the same kind of shameless Jewish behavior we saw earlier in Moabit,[6] when Jewish murders were defended by Jewish attorneys. They wanted to ignore the law as long as they were carrying out their dark deeds. But as soon as they faced a verdict, they relied on German law.

It would be a terrible mistake to withhold this pamphlet from the German people. International law recognizes that the rights of an individual cease when the survival of an entire people requires the lifting of copyright regulations. That is the case here. The German people can fully understand the full significance of its fateful struggle only when it is a witness to the revealing of the Jew Theodore Nathan Kaufman.

---

[6] Moabit is a prison in Berlin.

The Jew as Pseudo-Scientist

Millions of American and British readers thus have a book in their hands that clearly demands the murder of the German people. Even in countries in which years of constantly growing agitation against everything having to do with Germany and National Socialism has corrupted judgment to the greatest degree possible, and in which public opinion has suffered under the greatest terror, such a brutal murder plan cannot be proclaimed without covering it with moral, historic, and philosophic justifications. Thus the Jew Kaufman does not begin his book with the demand to sterilize the German people, but rather presents himself in Talmudic fashion to his readers as a patriot, philosopher, anthropologist, and general friend of humanity.

After proclaiming his love of peace, the Jew Kaufman next takes an interest in American soldiers. He hypocritically regrets the possibility that they might have to go into the field, and writes:

> If our soldiers must go forth to kill or die in battle, at least let them be given not alone a Slogan, but a Solemn Purpose and a Sacred Promise. Let that Purpose be an Enduring Peace! And, this time, that Promise must be kept!

Who broke Wilson's promises from 1917, which also proclaimed enduring peace? It was the powers that today once more demand the disarmament of the German people. Trusting in Wilson's 14 Points, the Germans laid down their weapons in 1918. Today, on the basis of publications, laws, and documents, the world knows that the German people were systematically betrayed. Instead of a just peace, world plutocracy's leading men dictated a program of destruction, based on ice-cold hate, the pinnacle of which was to lay all the blame for the war on the German people.

The Jew Hates Front Soldiers

Kaufman is so concerned about the "holy goals of the soldiers," but who is it in all countries on Earth who has insulted and betrayed front soldiers? We will not even speak of November Germany,[7] when they were the targets of crude Jewish mockery and miserable jokes, when communist bands incited by the Jews tore their medals from them, when military pilots with the *Pour*

---

[7] Meaning, November 1918, when Germany surrendered in WWI.

le mérite were murdered as deserters, when the cabaret Jews poured their filthiest thoughts on German heroes. No, even in the so-called victorious nations, the front soldier was betrayed and the Jew was the war profiteer.

The War against the German People

The Jewish peace president Kaufman begins by discussing the reasons for the war the plutocrats wanted:

> Today's war is not a war against Adolf Hitler. ...[8]

The Jew openly admits that this war is being waged against the entire German people. He thereby reveals the swindle that worked in the World War and is now being tried again: separating the leadership from the people. In 1918, the German people believed that the abdication of the Kaiser and the elimination of the monarchy would bring them "a life of beauty and dignity." The enemy exploited Germany's lack of leadership for shameless oppression, which never would have been possible without the November revolt. Today, English agitation is attempting once more, this time in vain, to separate the German people from its leader. The Jew Kaufman cynically makes plain what one should think of the slogans of Roosevelt and Churchill. They are a trap for the stupid, a reaching back to the moth-eaten methods of the World War. Kaufman openly says what World Jewry wants: the hatred of world plutocracy is directed not only at the Führer, but against the entire German people.

And thus he adds the "proof" that the whole German people is guilty for this war, and is responsible for it:

> This war is being waged by the German People. ...

Who Wanted this War?

A digression is in order here: Who declared war on 3 September 1939? *England and France* used the local conflict over Danzig and the Corridor, where justice was indisputably on the side of Germany, to declare war on Germany

---

[8] Diewerge cites, here and below, extended quotations from Kaufman's book. These passages are reproduced in chapter 14, and thus only the leading sentences are included here.

and thus cause a world conflagration.[9] And the United States has been trying to "get into the business" for months with repeated provocations. It prays daily for another "Lusitania," and regrets that in the case of the "Athenia," German attentiveness ruined their finely spun plans.[10]

Murder from the "Love of Peace"?

Since the provocations did not succeed in making the war mood in the United States agree with the will of the Jews, moral arguments had to be found. The Jewish president Kaufman calls for world peace, and says that the death of the German people is the precondition for that.

> For not only must there be no more German wars in fact...

The "War Lust" of the German People

To justify the murdering of 80 million people, Nathan Kaufman is forced to ascribe irremediable criminal tendencies to the German people. He declares that a lust for war is the most prominent characteristic of German men and women.

> The personal war-lust of those who lead the German people is but a component part of the war-lust which exists as a whole in the German masses. ...

Nothing is less true than this claim that the German people lust after war. At most, one can accuse us of being too good-natured and peace-loving over our history to take advantage of opportunities. The German people have always gone to war only after exhausting all other possibilities. Even during the current struggle, how often did the Führer extend his hand of peace, not

---

[9] An important and often-overlooked point: When Germany invaded Poland to settle a centuries-long border dispute, it was then England and France who declared war on Germany (owing to existing treaty obligations with Poland). It was not Germany who initiated hostilities with the Britons and the French, but vice versa.
[10] The Lusitania was a British ocean liner sunk by a German U-boat during WWI, on 7 May 1915, killing 1,198 people. The Germans justified the sinking by the fact that the ship was carrying nearly 200 tons of ammunition. The Athenia was a cargo and passenger ship that was sunk by the Germans on 16 August 1917, killing 15. Ironically, there was a second ship named Athenia that was sunk by the Germans during WW2, killing 117.

because of defeats, but after brilliant victories! Each time the Jew spat on the hand that offered peace.

The Desire to Destroy Women and Children

To deal with the response that one cannot hold babies and old women responsible for German war lust, Kaufman performs some genuine Jewish calculations:

> In fact, we shall, in pursuing our point, favor Germany by allowing that as much as 20% of her population is entirely guiltless ...

Who Should Die — Germans or Jews?

Here a modest point may be permitted: There are about 20 million Jews in the world. How would it be if one wanted to treat 20 million Jews according to the proposal of their racial comrade Kaufman, rather than 80 million Germans? Then peace would certainly be assured. For the Jew is the troublemaker, the warmonger, everywhere in the world.

Nowhere was that as plain than in Germany after the [NS] takeover of power. As long as the Jew controlled the parties, owned the press and film industries, and had captured the intellectual leadership of the masses, Germans fought one another. Since the Jews have been expelled, the German people's community is unshakable. No one today thinks of murdering a fellow citizen because he has a different occupation, or of hating someone because he was born somewhere else. Eliminating the Jews from the German people's body has given peace to the German people.[11]

The same is true of Europe. France is the plainest example. Today, it is indisputable that France was driven into this war against its will and against its interests by a Jewish clique. Since the influence of the Jews in France has been limited, the door to mutual understanding is slowly opening.

It is not necessary to waste words discussing the value of the German people. And American Jews are hardly in a position to judge the cultural values of the German people. The names from intellectual history that

---

[11] "Eliminating the Jews" (*Die Ausmerzung des Juden*) obviously does not mean killing, since the official Holocaust in Germany did not start until early 1942. *Ausmerzung*, like *Ausrotten* and *Vernichtung*, simply means removing Jewish presence and Jewish power in society.

Germany can place on the scales assures it a unique place in this area, one that Jewish complainers can hardly alter.

Kaufman next wonders whether the victories Jews have won in the past, at most with their mouths, have been properly used. In typical Jewish fashion, he uses expressions from business when discussing war, and speaks of "selling out." He asks:

> Is selling-out our soldiers to become a national habit? …

The Jew and Treason

Despite ranking Germans with predatory animals, Roosevelt's confidante cannot entirely ignore the fact that despite all the agitation in the United States, there are still people who do not accept these conclusions. He simply calls these Americans 'traitors.' Of course, for the Jews, treason is only a "gentleman's offense," but when it helps, the Jew is happy to appear as a concerned friend of the fatherland. We know this method from German domestic politics. For years the Jews mocked everything that had to do with the front soldier. But as the "Iron Front"[12] was about to collapse, as the democratic parties were decaying, the Jew suddenly remembered "nationalism." It was almost moving to read what the filthiest Jewish papers had to say about the "heroic" march of "bourgeois" front soldiers in 1932, because it promised a weakening of the "Nazis."

And so now the Jew Kaufman presents himself as an American patriot out to protect the United States:

> Naturally there are men in the world, in our own country included, who think otherwise and who would deal differently with the German menace. …

The Jew as Punishing Judge

To carry out this judgment, the Jewish peace president recommends, of all people, he and his racial comrades, who have the primary responsibility for preparing and conducting this war. Throughout their history, the Jews have presumed to be the chosen people. They constantly present themselves as the moral arbiters for others. Jehovah is the great judge, the God of revenge,

---

[12] The Iron Front was an anti-Nazi group formed in Weimar Germany in 1931.

who punishes Gentile peoples without pity. The Jew Kaufman is pleased to imagine himself as such a punishing judge.

With genuine Jewish self-righteousness, he writes:

> War must not be fought with weapons of ever-increasing destructiveness but with penalties infinitely more frightful and hazardous than war itself. …

Who Wants World Domination?

As further justification of punishment, Kaufman claims that the German people are striving for world domination. To accuse Germany of having plans for world domination is an old Jewish swindle. The Führer has branded this a lie in all of his statements on foreign policy and clearly stated what the German people want: living space for its population, self-sufficiency on agriculture, and the protection of its peaceful labors. It is perverse when the rulers of the United States, the British world empire, and the enormous Soviet Union accuse Germany, a nation whose size can hardly be compared to theirs, of plans for world domination, as the Jew Kaufman does:

> For it must be patent by now that all Germans, without exception, are unanimous in agreeing that world-domination …

The German People are National Socialists

Now comes the most remarkable passage from this book that demands Germany's destruction. It is the only place in which the Jew says the truth about the German people:

> Therefore it is most essential that we realize as an irreconcilable fact the truth that the Nazis are not beings existing apart from the German people. They are the German people!

The Jew Kaufman continues:

> For to the German, Nazi or not, the Mailed Fist is as stimulating and meaningful a symbol of all the aims and aspirations of his nation as the Statue of Liberty is to the American. …

Roosevelt's confidante presents this terrifyingly-portrayed people as one quite incomprehensible to the "peaceful and civilized" inhabitants of the Soviet Union, the "law-abiding gangsters" of Chicago, and the Indians and Arabs who, in the British colonies, enjoy "all the privileges of freedom."

> Such civilized nations regard individual rights, the sacredness of human life, liberty and the pursuit of happiness as the virtues of mankind ...

No Comparison Possible

This objective and loyal representative of world plutocracy now asks whether it is possible to work out some sort of agreement with the German people, despite their "bad characteristics," that would enable the world and Germany to live together peacefully and justly. He has no hope of that. That Germany is a "gruesome reality" is not a foundation for peace. Kaufman complains that the traitors of 1918 have vanished. On this point, he writes:

> For, in the first place, there is no longer living in Germany that so-called 'older generation' with whom reasonable talk might be made. This woeful handful is gone and forgotten and in its stead stands that brown-shirted legion singing that glorious Horst-Wessel paean: "Today Europe, tomorrow all the world!" Enlightened reason with perverted chanters of a world-dirge composed by a drunkard, written in a brothel and dedicated to a pimp.

"Today Germany and tomorrow the entire world" does not happen to be in the Horst Wessel Song, but comes from a National Socialist march.

Once Kaufman has established that peace would not be possible even with a democratic Germany, he examines as a last possible solution the control of Germany by an international armed force. But that does not seem sufficient to him. Even as a Jew, he perhaps feels that the German people could not bear such oppression over the long run, since he writes:

> Even if such a huge undertaking were feasible life itself would not have it so. As war begets war, suppression begets rebellion. Undreamed horrors would unfold.

324   Classic Essays on the Jewish Question

Thus we find that there is no middle course; no act of mediation, no compromise to be compounded, no political or economic sharing to be considered. There is, in fact, no other solution except one:

> That Germany must perish forever from this earth! And, fortunately, as we shall now come to see, that is no longer impossible of accomplishment.

World Plutocracy's "Peaceful Solution"

To world plutocracy, this solution means: Death for Germany. The following passages from the book by President Roosevelt's adviser are so clear in their thinking, so hate-filled in their conclusions, and so typical for the manner of thinking of the powers that want to exterminate National Socialism, that they should be printed in full. Here the enemy speaks clearly, without any concealment or caution. This is the source of enemy war propaganda. Here is revealed the deepest cause of this great war that the Greater German Reich today must fight for its life and its freedom.

Now President Kaufman has the floor to plead for the sterilization, and therefore the death, of Germany:

> When an individual commits premeditated murder, he must be prepared to forfeit his own life ...

The Most Practical Death Sentence

Kaufman understands that you cannot hang someone unless you have him. In view of the strength of the German *Wehrmacht,* it seems to him impractical to carry out the death sentence by force. Apparently, he does not think his racial comrades suitable to defeat German soldiers on the battlefield. To be moral and civilized, the Jew proposes the following way to carry out his crime, once the German people has been disarmed:

> There remains now but to determine the best way, the most practical and expeditious manner in which the ultimate penalty must be levied upon the German nation. ...

Perhaps there are those who still doubt the seriousness of the Jewish murder plan. Perhaps they simply cannot believe that the famed "conscience of the world" would permit this mass crime against a cultured nation, once Germany was disarmed. But the conscience of the world has accepted other things, for it is a Jewish invention, not an Aryan one. No one would be concerned about a disarmed Germany and its allies if those in power in New York, London, and Moscow carried out sterilization.

Jewish Murder of Nations

As monstrous as a plan to cold-bloodedly exterminate a people of 80 million is, and as much as one may be inclined to consider it impossible and unbelievable, World Jewry is serious. We would not be the first people to be murdered by the Jews. A look at world history, beginning in biblical times and continuing to the present, shows that numerous peoples have lost their lives and disappeared from history because they drew the enmity of the Jews. And in recent days, murder plans of this nature have been part of the political demands of our enemies for our people.

We need only think of the statement by the Frenchman Clemenceau, whose Jewish cabinet chief and close confidante Mandel[13] whispered to him that there were "20 million Germans too many." That was not an empty phrase, but threatened to become reality. Millions of Germans died in the post-war period, and millions more were never born because of poverty. The army of seven million unemployed with their 20 million family members would have been condemned to starvation, had not National Socialism saved them. The suicide rate had reached alarming levels.

Mass Murder in the Soviet Union

Or we may remember the Soviet Union. Millions of the intelligentsia were slaughtered. Jewish commissars played a central role. Millions of people were intentionally starved to death. And now during the great battle for freedom in the East, Jewish commissars with machine guns stand behind the Bolshevist soldiers and shoot down the stupid masses if they begin to retreat. The Jew has always avoided honest, open combat, not from a love of peace, but from simple fear. Instead, he has always chosen murder—the cowardly and treacherous crime—from the rear, even when in power. The list of

[13] Georges Mandel (1885-1944), born Louis G. Rothschild, was an Alsatian Jew.

Jewish murders is very long, stretching from biblical times to the present day. Every opponent of Jewry, whether an individual or a people, has always been at risk of being murdered.

This Plan is not Fantasy, but Jewish Realpolitik

Thus it is not unbelievable, only all too understandable, that the Jew Kaufman has said what World Jewry wishes and hopes for: The murder of the German people. It does not bother the Jew that one day, the last aged survivors of the German people will crawl among the ruins of German cities, speaking Polish or Czech, speaking a few German words only when it seems safe. No, that is his goal. That is what he incites other peoples to do, that is why he reaches into his wallet to pay those in every nation. The cost of bribing a statesman is never too high for him, no lie about National Socialism too filthy, no crime against German women and children too cruel. The Jew feels that German victory in Europe would make his position impossible. Thus, he attempts to mobilize the world. To eliminate forever any danger to his parasitic existence, he has decided to exterminate the German people.

The Murder Program

Roosevelt and Churchill outlined their plan for world improvement in a number of points. The Jew Kaufman wants to do the same. To systematize the extermination of the German people, he has proposed nine articles of a detailed program of murder, which is as follows:

> Germany has lost its war. She sues for peace. ...

Partitioning the Greater German Reich

The Jew Kaufman's book provides a map, which we include on the back cover of this pamphlet. It corresponds to article 6 of the murder program and shows how World Jewry wants to partition Germany. Each German should study and remember this map. That is how Germany will look if the plutocrats win the war. Consistent with its dreams of great power status before the war, Poland receives East Prussia, West Prussia, the Warteland, Pomerania, Mark Brandenburg, Silesia, and the Reich capital Berlin. The Czechs move into Vienna, Dresden, Leipzig, and the Alpine areas of the Reich. France stretches into the Ruhr and Thuringia. The Hollanders get Hamburg and Lübeck, while the Belgians will have to satisfy themselves with most of the Rhine provinces. And in all these areas, adults and children will have to learn and speak the language of the occupying state until the last German dies.

Such a map may seem to be the dream of a crazy fanatic, but it is hard reality. We remember that, during a visit by the American Sumner Welles to the then-French Prime Minister Renaud, a slip on the part of the censors revealed a similar plan to the public. The publications of the former Polish warmonger clique, with similar "scientifically based" demands, are generally known. The Greater German Reich, with its natural and historic borders, is a bulwark of peace and progress, of honor and social justice, but it is the deadly enemy of those forces allied with world plutocracy. If they ever have the opportunity, it will be their greatest triumph to follow Kaufman's plan for partition.

Just as Polish and Bolshevist murders stabbed and clubbed even the corpses of ethnic Germans who had been tortured to death, the so-called statesmen on the enemy side take sadistic glee in drawing borders and setting up control commissions for the condemned German people, even before the end of the war. The Jew Kaufman's map is a clear formulation of the territorial war goals of our enemies. Polish bands as victors in Berlin, Czech legionnaires marching into Vienna and Dresden, French colonial troops in the Führer's buildings in Munich, Queen Wilhelmina as the victorious field marshal in Hamburg—that would be the final chapter in the history of the German people, according to the will of world plutocracy.

The Last Act for the German People

This is the picture that the Jew Kaufman and his racial comrades in New York, London, and Moscow have of the final fulfillment of their political desires:

In long, gray columns, the regiments and divisions of the disarmed German *Wehrmacht* appear. The weapons are broken, the aircraft destroyed, the big guns empty. The glorious flags have been sent to New York, London, and Moscow, there to be mocked by sub-humans.

Slowly, column after column is taken into the barracks and tents where mocking Jewish doctors carelessly sterilize them. Each German soldier has to pay the Jews for the operation. Then the troops march, under Jewish and Soviet supervision, to forced labor in the wild mountains of the Balkans, to Siberia, or the Arctic Sea. There, the heroes of this war, the Führer's soldiers who bear the Knight's Cross, will be tortured with the "tested" methods of

Soviet forced labor, serving as slaves under miserable conditions, until starvation releases them from this life.

Meanwhile, Jewish doctors will be set loose on German women and children. Whatever perverse lust have been imagined in the dark minds of the Jewish people will be unleashed on defenseless German women and children. All the bestial horrors that were previously conducted in the dungeons of the GPU, far from public view, can then be carried out in the "offices" of Jewish humanitarians. No one will defend the honor of these tortured women and children.

The only place to which they could turn might be Mrs. Eleanor Roosevelt. Just as after the World War, she would certainly send a few cans of condensed milk and rancid bacon to make herself seem a shining example of "Christian charity." But that would not stop the horrible misery that would prevail in Central Europe. The only power that could hinder it, German soldiers, would be wasting away as slaves abroad.

Victory or Death — That is What This War is About

One must know this to know what this war is about. It is not a war of the past, which can find its end in a balancing of interests. It is a matter of who shall live in Europe in the future: the white race with its cultural values and creativity, with its industry and joy in life, or Jewish sub-humanity ruling over the stupid, joyless enslaved masses doomed to death.

World plutocracy succeed in 1918 in betraying the German people in the most infamous way. While Marxists organized demonstrations in favor of Wilson's 14 Points behind the lines, the vultures gathered in the capitals of the Jewish alliance to fight over the spoils. While naive citizens or bribed subjects, who were then presented to the world as heroic representatives of the German people, either did not see through the swindle or even propagated and promoted it, Jewish writers, sure of their triumph, confident that a tortured and demoralized Germany would never rise again, revealed the recipe for their victory. The Kaufmans of 1918 wrote their memoirs as the German people lay in the dust. Every word in their mocking memoirs is today part of the knowledge of the politically educated German people.

World plutocracy today faces the fact that the German people once again cannot be defeated militarily. To an unprecedented extent, the strength of the whole nation has been mobilized. All of Europe supports the Führer's efforts to build a new order. Blow by blow, the accomplices of world plutocracy's warmongers are beaten down. England's final fortress on the continent, the Bolshevist Soviet Union, is crumbling. The war speculators in England and America think that the time has come to trick the German people *a la* Wilson. They believe they can use their lying slogans to reach a people that is still in the spiritual state of 1918. They think the German people are as they were when Jewish emigrants fled the National Socialist revolution.

To Victory!

But today the German people knows what is at stake. It knows how to distinguish between the lying humanitarian slogans that come from the "Potomac" and the real plan of extermination by Jewish President Nathan Kaufman. The German people knows that the International Jew stands behind the war-will of world plutocracy, and behind warmongers throughout the world. It knows that these hate-filled opponents have only one chance of success: The disunity of the German people. National Socialism has eliminated this possibility. If world plutocracy believes that this struggle can end only with the deadly destruction of one side, then it must know that the German people will not die. All German men and women are fighting and working together in an inseparable people's community until the victorious conclusion of this struggle. As the Führer said on 30 January 1939:

> The peoples no longer want to die on the battlefield so that the rootless international Jewish race can earn money from war and satisfy its Old Testament lust for revenge. A higher knowledge will triumph over the slogan "Proletarians of all nations, unite!": namely "Creative members of all nations, recognize your common enemy!"

German People!

Now you know what your eternal enemy and foe plan for you. There is only one defense against their plan for destruction: Victory! Reading this Jewish murder plan for the German people will only steel your strength and increase your will for victory. And now, back to your weapon, your plow, your workbench or desk. Our slogan is:

Fight, Work, Win!

— 16 —
NEVER!

Heinrich Goitsch
(1944)

Editor: This extended essay was written in late 1944, when the war was going badly for Germany and it was apparent that it would not end well. This was a kind of final plea to the German people, to keep fighting, to keep up morale, and to struggle until the bitter end. The author, Heinrich Goitsch, is an obscure figure, of whom little is known. Still, as a product of the Zentralverlag, it evidently received official blessing from Goebbels and the NS hierarchy. The essay paints the horrors of possible German defeat, and the tortures likely to be inflicted by the Judeo-Bolshevik-Capitalists. Many of Goitsch's prophecies failed to materialize, but many did occur, in one form or another; millions of Germans were killed or raped under postwar conditions, Germany was partitioned and occupied, and the dreaded Soviets took control of East Germany, oppressing those residents for over four decades. This would be one of the last major National Socialist statements on the Jewish Question.

Their Hate Knows No Bounds!

The echoes of the first shots that began the war had hardly faded when Germany's enemies began their war of nerves, conducted on the battlefield of the spirit, one just as important as the soldiers' battle. In modern war, a people's spiritual and moral state plays an important role; indeed, on it depends victory or defeat. Total war uses not only all military means, but also all the forces of the spirit. In the end, stronger nerves, greater faith, and firmer steadfastness determine the outcome.

National Socialist Germany, which over five bloody years has been forced by its opponents into a war that has spread to the entire world, was prepared for spiritual warfare. The German people knew its enemies and their hate for the German Reich that under Adolf Hitler had once again become a world power. It knew the background that led to the declaration of war against Germany. Those who pull the strings in the world's backstage are not unknown to us. The Reich's political leadership saw to it that they were revealed. If our enemies believed that the war of nerves they so carefully began and steadily intensified would lead to victory, they soon had to realize that we were immune to this enemy poison. Twenty years of National Socialist education had sharpened our hearing. The tricks of 1918 that our opponents tried to reuse failed. Germany in this area is invulnerable!

That certainly did not stop our enemies from continuing their war of nerves, using ever stronger weapons. Using thousands of channels, they carried on a subterranean campaign of destruction to once again mobilize the thoughts and feelings of the whole world against us. The world press, the world radio, and the world film industry were engaged. National Socialist Germany was accused of being "World Enemy #1" in thousands of newspaper articles, over hundreds of radio stations, on the screen, and in mass meetings. Germany is guilty! Germany must be condemned to death! That was our enemies' battle cry.

But what had this Germany actually done? It overcame Versailles and regained its rightful place in the sun. That is our "sin"! The Führer forged the Greater German Reich through peaceful labor. He won German unity, thereby fulfilling the dreams of all Germans, the deepest longings of the nation. He did not want war. He wanted peace. But our enemies wanted war! "Germany is becoming too strong. We must smash her!" said Winston Churchill as early as 1936, to the American General Wood.[1] That was our enemies' real reason for war. Germany was to be excluded, it was to be destroyed, because it endangered the world dominance of the great powers. British representative McGovern hit the target when he said in the House of Commons: "This war is imperialist through and through!"

We have been engaged in this world-wide struggle for five years, and have again proved our manhood against our hate-filled enemies. German soldiers achieve deeds unique in world history. But behind the fighting troops stands the fighting homeland, for this war is a true people's war, a battle of worldviews, a struggle of the new forces seeking the light of world history against the outdated powers of a dying epoch. We therefore know that this war concerns us all! Each of us is fighting for his life! We are

---

[1] Recalled by Wood in a US Congressional testimony in February 1941. Cited in J. Doenecke, *Storm on the Horizon* (2000, Rowman and Littlefield), p. 440.

fighting for Germany! This knowledge makes us strong and unconquerable as our enemies reveal their goals of war and destruction. Both as individuals and as a nation, we would cease to exist if the enemy should triumph over us. They themselves have told us repeatedly what they want to do to us. "We are determined," Churchill said on London radio, "to expunge Hitler and any trace of Nazism. Nothing will stop us from doing that—Nothing!" And he added: "We will never negotiate or parlay with Hitler or one of his band. Every man and every state that fights against the Nazis will have our help. Every man and every state that is with Hitler is our enemy."

Their hatred for the Führer, whose peace and disarmament proposals they always rejected, is almost sick. Because they have no stature themselves, neither human nor political, they envy the genius, the unreachable, the creative spirit, that seeks a new world. They know and sense that this man has guided the German people to its true inner greatness. As British Foreign Minister Anthony Eden said, "Hitler is no accident; he is a symptom." The former British production minister Beaverbrook once expressed this deep desire for destruction in this way: "We want to bring about a deep hatred for the Germans, for German soldiers, sailors, and airmen. We must hate until we win."

We Germans are second-class people for these creatures. As British publicist Reginald Hargreaves wrote in the London magazine *The National Review*: "From the beginning, the Teutonic peoples have qualified only for the role of pariah, the outcast mad dogs of Europe." So says a European, who perhaps on that same day was deeply moved by Beethoven's immortal symphonies! Their understanding is defective. How else can one understand this wild outburst by Sir Neville Henderson, former ambassador to Berlin, and thus a diplomat of standing and education: "As my last act, I would like to do in Germany's leading men with a few bullets and a gun stock, and I would aim at their bellies." That is what he said to British students at the famed Oxford University! Churchill betrayed the same bestial sentiments in a speech at a conference of so-called Allied governments in London in June 1941: "Nothing is more sure than that every trace of Hitler's footsteps, every stain of his corrupt and corroded finger, shall be wiped, and if necessary blasted, from the surface of the earth."

Well, world history pays heed to a different clock than the one Churchill carries in his vest pocket. After his name has faded, the name Adolf Hitler will shine more brightly than before over humanity! The great have always been disdained by the mediocre, but it is also true that the fame of the genius endures for centuries!

The Common Denominator of the Enemy's Destructive Goals

It is still necessary and useful, and consistent with the goals of our political war leadership, for the German people to have exact knowledge of the goals our opponents have for war and destruction. Over the past years, many statesmen in the enemy camp, many official diplomats and professional politicians, along with a swarm of publicists and newspaper writers, have spoken, written, or negotiated on this theme. Numerous conferences, committees, and commissions dealt with the matter. An enormous army of professionals and amateurs investigated the war aims of the "United Nations," and if one were to collect everything that reached the public, one could fill four thick volumes. Even average newspaper readers like Mr. Smith in London or Mr. Parker in New York concern themselves with the matter.

If one averages together all the official, unofficial, and half-official plans, proposals, and goals, the result is the classic sentence that appeared directly before the war in the Jewish *Alliance Israelite Universelle*: "This German-Aryan people must vanish from history's stage."

That is the alpha and omega of the enemy war aims. Everything leads back to this, whether from official or from private sources. This formulation reveals the real, the true war goals of our enemies, their political attitudes, their basic attitude about us Germans.

For years the English, American, and Soviet side has repeatedly said in the most brutal way that the German people, as the center of order and construction in the middle of the European continent, stand in the way of the enemies' imperialist will. They must therefore be destroyed with a brutality unrivalled in world history. That is the united war aim of our opponents, and it is what holds the plutocratic-Jewish-Bolshevist world coalition together.

The Jew Ilya Ehrenburg, Stalin's favorite journalist, proposed in his book *Trust for the Destruction of Europe* a dreadful picture of the future that corresponds precisely to these enemy war aims, seen with Jewish eyes. He writes:

> Europe must vanish. A year will be enough to destroy the continent and its 350 million people. The remains of the European peoples who escape our tanks and flame-throwers—and not

only the Germans—will be sent to work as slaves in the mines of Siberia.

The enemy war leadership has proved in these five years that this is a concrete plan, not mere fantasy. The extermination and enslavement of not only the German, but all the European peoples, is at the center of the enemy goals. Stalin made a beginning with Rumania, Bulgaria, and Finland. Churchill and Roosevelt are assisting him. We are not only aware of their goals, we have had experience with their Bolshevist allies, as the Führer said on Heroes Memorial Day at the Berlin Zeughaus on 21 March 1943:

> The extermination of all nationally-aware continental peoples, our own German people above all. It is all the same, whether English or American papers, parliamentarians, popular speakers or writers speak of the destruction of the Reich, the seizure of our people's children, the sterilization of male youth, etc., or if Bolshevism actually practices the slaughter of whole peoples, men, women and children. Behind it all is the eternal hatred of that race that for thousands of years has presented itself as God's gift to the peoples, until at times of renewed awareness, the peoples again defend themselves against their torturers.

The truth of the Führer's words—that the eternal Jew is the real inciter of war—is proven by Bernard Lecache, the president of the "International League against Anti-Semitism," who wrote in his Paris newspaper *Le Droit de vivre*: "Our task is to declare pitiless war against Germany, world enemy #1. One may be sure of this: We will lead that war!" The Jew wrote this on 9 November 1938, and the chamber pot biographer Emil Ludwig Cohn wrote this in the magazine *Les Annales* as early as 1934: "Hitler does not want war, but we will force it on him, not this year, but soon."

The Jew Mirelmann revealed in an article in the *Standard*, the newspaper of the British community in Buenos Aires, the fact that this war is the war of International Jewry, whose connection to both Anglo-American high finance and Bolshevism has been proven. He wrote that the British government must recognize "that it is fighting a war of the Jews, one that it can never win without the help of the Jewish people."

Apparently the Jews are hoping for a new "national homeland" in Germany. At least the Jew Maurice Perlzweig, the head of the British section of the "Jewish Federation," assured the general meeting of this Jewish association in Atlanta (USA) in February 1941: "The British government has assured us that Jews will receive their old rights back again once Germany is defeated." Here the wish is the father of the thought. We do not need to speak of what the realization of this Jewish dream would mean for the German people. The Jews would bathe in blood! Such thoughts are not utopian. The Jewish writer Louis Adamic, now living in the USA, writes in his book *Two-Way Passage* (1941) that the Jews who have emigrated to America from Germany and the rest of Europe since 1933 should be trained at the expense of the American government and sent to Europe after the war to be a "governing upper class." Adamic is not insignificant; he is a friend of Mrs. Roosevelt.[2] His plan is typical of Jewish war aims, which Jewry is pursuing along with the British, Americans, and Soviets.

Occupation Until the Year 2000!

The German people should and must know the truth about the terrible dangers that threaten us. One can only overcome a danger after it is recognized. Otherwise one falls victim to it. What is true for the individual is also true for the whole people: a recognized danger brings forth the greatest defensive efforts.

Our enemies have already lost the war of nerves. There is agreement on this even in the enemy camp. They know that the Germany of 1944 is not that of 1918. Their political strategy has failed. Germany will never capitulate! They know that too. They thus seek a decision on the battlefield. But here, too, the last word has yet to be spoken! Still, it is good for the German people to know what the enemies of the Reich plan, should we be defeated.

First and foremost, the enemy's military plans require that Germany be disarmed. Then the Reich will be occupied. Finally, there will be economic depopulation. But the final goal is the biologic destruction of the entire German people, the literal extermination of a nation of one hundred million.

The English magazine *New Statesman and Nation* put it plainly. In November 1942 this magazine, which has a wide circulation, published a rabble-rousing article with the attractive title "Free Europe." It began by calling for the complete disarmament of Germany. That is the most important foundation for the post-war order in the British-American view. "In any case we must totally disarm all German states," Weekham Steed proclaimed in an

---

[2] Adamic indeed seemed to have had top-level access in the US government. See, for example, his book *Dinner at the White House* (1946).

article headlined: "What Will We Do With the Enemy?" It is significant that this Briton speaks of "German states," ignoring from the start the sovereignty and unity of Germany. According to Emil Ludwig Cohn, Germany should be disarmed "down to pistols." He wishes an "Allied occupation army to see to it that the Poles and Jews get their rights." Another Jew, Felix Langer—and this is not his private thinking, but rather officially inspired—wrote in his major work *Stepping Stones to Peace* that Germany's disarmament must be total. Not even a woodsman may be left with his hunting rifle. This proposal was discussed seriously in the USA magazine *News Review*, since it had "come from the work of psychology and science." ...

The Jew Leopold Schwarzschild goes the furthest. In his book *Primer of the Coming World* (1944) he writes:

> Germany must be occupied not for five or twenty years, but until the year 2000. Only then will all the Germans who led the troops or built the weapons have died out. All military organizations, clubs, or similar organizations will be banned. No German may serve in any nation as a military trainer, whether as a pilot or armaments engineer.

That was only a small selection of comments on the disarmament and occupation of Germany. What follows shows even more clearly what our enemies plan.[3]

Ten Million Unemployed Overnight

The last force behind our enemies' perverse war aims comes to clearest expression in those questions that have always been close to the hearts of these grocers and clothing merchants: The future of world trade.

In but a hundred years, German industry conquered the world in peaceful competition. Good and inexpensive German goods dominated every market. Germany had some monopolies. German drugs and the products of the German optical industry were, for example, unequalled. That aroused the envy of the British and Americans. They see in this war a good opportunity to once again put an end to our economic strength, to block us from world

---

[3] Indeed, Germany is still occupied today; some 35,000 American troops are permanently stationed there, now 80 years after the war. Clearly the occupation would continue well beyond the year 2000.

markets. They did not entirely succeed in 1918. This time their motto is: Do it better! German industry must fall under our control, they say. Why does Germany need trade relations? Why does Germany need a merchant marine? The Germans are "not seafaring people like us British!" So away with the German merchant fleet!

On this basis the Jewish economist Paul Einzig proposes a plan for German economic disarmament in the *Economic Journal* (London). He thinks that economic disarmament should follow military disarmament. Einzig therefore proposes not only the elimination of the German armaments industry, but also the destruction of the German tool-making industry.

England's true spirit speaks in these words—the spirit of greed and revenge! Its goal is to plunge Germany into the deepest economic night.

"Even from a pure social standpoint, it would be short-sighted to leave the German people with the least economic prosperity. We must completely destroy and plunder the enemy," demanded the Jewish editor of the leading British economic paper *Financial News* on 13 November 1941. There are already firm plans to plunder the German economy. The previously mentioned London Jew Einzig thinks that 51% of the stock in German companies with over 29 workers must be in Allied, that is Jewish, hands. Paul Goodman, the chair of the political committee of the Zionist Federation, said in London in February 1942: "The reestablishment of the Jewish economic position on the European continent must be one of the war aims of the British and Allied governments."

The Jewish USA Secretary of the Treasury Morgenthau proposed a plan to destroy Germany to Roosevelt and Churchill at their meeting in Quebec in September 1944. It was fully in accord with Moscow's aims. Germany is to be wiped out as an industrial nation, its machines destroyed or dismantled and shipped to the Soviet Union. The plan at the same time restricts the rebuilding of the German economy. The Associated Press reports from Washington that Roosevelt approved the plan. The leading USA government officials and Churchill also approved. London supplemented the news by adding that large-scale deportation of German workers was planned.

They want to take over our advanced German industry and run it for their own benefit. The venerable Archbishop of Canterbury, Dr. Temple, stated it openly:

> The industrial wealth of the Rhine and the Ruhr must be put to other uses. I am impressed by the suggestion that the industrial

> resources of this area along with those in neighboring areas—
> including those outside Germany—be administered by an in-
> ternational syndicate. Whether this be done under private or
> social ownership can be determined later.

The British of course want the best of it. That would be the coal of the Rhine and Ruhr and the mines! Just as always! They had similar ideas 25 years ago! They think that the German people are just good enough to produce industrial goods to export to them at the lowest pay. True, the American magazine *New Statesman* proposes taking the might of German industry "out of the hands of the big industrials and use this wealth for the general benefit of Europe and the world," but it is not hard to replace the words "Europe" and the "world" with "America" and "England." The *New Statesman* also recommended that German industry be reorganized after the war, since 90% of the Germany economy was involved in the war effort. The American writer continued: "It would require enormous investments to convert the German war industry to peaceful production. That is the proper point for the Allies to make their influence on the German economy permanent."

They want to use the same methods they used in 1918, only a thousand times "better." Thus the London magazine *Free Europe* proposed that the greater part of German heavy industry, particularly the metal, machine, and chemical industries, should be "moved to the lands of Central Europe." This would allow the former agricultural nations "to develop their own industries and thus break Germany's economic dominance." Once their heavy industry has been taken from them, the Germans will have to develop other branches of industry, but not for themselves. "The Germans must cover the costs for the rebuilding of what has been destroyed in Europe from their own resources." More reparations! In any event, *Free Europe* wants Germany to lose its economic leadership on the continent. Why? "Production in Great Britain must be simultaneously reorganized to replace the loss of German production."

The concern these humanitarians have that we never recover economically was evident in a passing remark by Sir Arthur Greenwoods at the Roundtable Conference on 18 December 1941. This British minister said: "I do not believe that the German people after the war should be permitted unrestricted importation of raw materials or finished goods. The Germans are the greatest productive geniuses on Earth. We must remember that. I doubt whether certain industries can be permitted the Germans at all." As early as 13 November 1939, the *Financial News* declared that the war and blockade against Germany would favor England's conquest of the export markets throughout the entire world. Germany must be driven from world markets.

From this standpoint, Douglas Miller, former commercial attaché at the USA embassy in Berlin, told the American press that Germany's economic future would have "insurmountable difficulties." He wrote that the Germans must receive no new capital, that we must "exclude them from productive cooperation after the war." All means of transportation are to be eliminated, metal and machines seized, "strategically important railway lines kept in the hands of the victorious powers." And the future borders should be drawn so as to ensure that the coal and iron ore districts in the east and west are outside the Reich's borders. ...

Biological Extermination of the Germans!

If one adds together the enemy war aims, their plans for the political, military, economic, and finally cultural and spiritual annihilation of Germany, the sum is the complete extermination of the German people, its biologic disappearance. The German people should disappear numerically from the surface of the Earth! London, Moscow, and Washington are agreed. In practice, it will happen through simple murder. Look at what authentic sources have to say:

William Barkley, parliamentary correspondent of the *Daily Express* on 9 February 1943:

> Germany is a nation of the insane. Were one to read one day in the paper that a natural catastrophe had destroyed the Germans, turning Germany into a Libyan desert, there would be a smile on every English and American face. After the war is over, one must cut the German claws, take away all their industry, establish a quarantine around Germany, and let the Germans stew for a generation in their own juices. No one in Britain or America needs to concern himself if they perish as a result. Whole nations have been exterminated in the past. What remains of the Aztecs, for example?

Duff Cooper, former British minister and one of the most influential warmongers: "However this war ends, let us be sure that there is no longer a German nation" (Speech in London, cited by the *Daily Mail*, 8 March 1943).

Picture Post on 9 December 1942: "If there is to be real peace after this war, nothing must remain of Germany on the map of Europe."

British union leader George Gibson in a speech in Leeds: "England can only win this war by killing Germans. That sounds blood-thirsty, but it is true, and one can kill them best where they are concentrated" (29 September 1941).

Daily Mirror, 5 September 1940: The Reverend C. W. Whipp from St. Augustin in Leicester writes in his church paper: "The orders for the Royal Air Force's bombers should be: Wipe out the Germans! I say it plainly. If I could wipe Germany from the map, I would. The more Nazis are killed, the happier I am."

Sir Robert Vansittart: "Stalin was of the opinion that one must kill Germany" (Speech in the House of Lords, 10 March 1943).

London: *Nineteenth Century and After*, November 1943: "The belief that the German problem can be solved only by slaughtering Germans grows ever stronger, however drastic it may seem. It is a hard and frightening thing, but as many as 500,000 young German men must be executed under martial law, without any particular formalities."

[Jew] Ilya Ehrenberg, Moscow, in his book *Trust D.E. Liquidates Europe*, in the chapter "Death Sentence for Berlin," which depicts with bestial lust the invasion of Berlin by 300 enormous tanks: "Germany finally ceased to exist. Of its 55 million inhabitants, at most 100,000 remain. There is now a desert between the Rhine and the Oder in which robber bands roam." British Vice Consul Blackwell of the British embassy in Peking, in a letter captured by the German navy on a British ship in February 1940: "I see this war as an enormous tragedy in which the German people must be sacrificed for the good of humanity. I think that Germany, not only Hitler, must be destroyed so that it can never again recover. It is clear that two peoples as England and Germany cannot coexist in the same world. The world is not big enough for them; one must go."

This gruesome extermination list could be continued for pages. It may be sufficient to demonstrate our enemies' goal of annihilation to cite the enemy magazine *News Review* of 6 April 1939, that is, even before the war began: "If we fight Germany again, give it the blow it deserves; wipe German manhood out and divide Germany between Britain and its allies. Let German women marry men of various nationalities and thus hinder pure Germans from growing up in the future."

That British and American war policy aims at the destruction of Germany was known to us even in the years before the war. Churchill, Eden, and Duff Cooper worked out plans for Germany's destruction in public since 1934. In the ten years since, the plans have not changed, only intensified systematically. For example, a reader wrote to the London *Sunday Express* at the beginning of February 1944 on the notorious theme of "German reeducation":

> When we have won the war, we must spread all German children between three and 14 years around the British Commonwealth. Every childless couple must accept and educate at least one of these German children. Children born during the ten years after the end of the war in Germany must be educated in the same way as soon as they reach the age of three.

This devilish plan follows the proposal of the Jew Theodor Nathan Kaufman, who published a book in 1941 that provided a detailed plan for the biologic elimination of the German people. The title was *Germany Must Perish*. This book demands nothing less than the sterilization of all able German men. The plans that were later circulated in our enemies' camp for the annihilation of Germany are based on this documentary book.

Who is Kaufman? Wolfgang Diewerge's pamphlet *The War-Goal of World Plutocracy*, millions of copies of which are in circulation, reprints the larger part of Kaufman's book *Germany Must Perish*. Diewerge writes:

> The Jewish president of the American Federation of Peace is no anonymous individual, no fanatic rejected by world Jewry, no mentally ill crackpot, but rather a leading and widely known Jewish personality in the United States. He belongs to the so-called Roosevelt Brain Trust, which provides intellectual and political education and advice to the American president. It is therefore beyond question that his book and its demand that 'Germany must perish' corresponds to the official opinion of the leading circles of world plutocracy.

Kaufman writes:

> When the day of reckoning with Germany comes, there will be but one obvious position. No statesman, no politician, no leader who is responsible for things after the war will have the right to engage in false personal sentimentality or sanctimoni-

ousness by declaring that Germany, deceived by its leaders, may rise again! It is the sacred duty of the present generation to those yet unborn to ensure that the poisoned fang of the German serpent can never again kill. Since the fang's poison and its deadly power rests not in the body but in the war psyche of the Germans, one can ensure the prosperity and security of mankind only by finally extinguishing this soul and the rotten body that houses it, removing it finally from the world. There is no other choice: 'Germany must perish!'

With Jewish lust for revenge, Kaufman continues along these lines, calling the Germans "animals" that must be treated as such, and proposes the following "no longer impossible solution": Sterilization, that is, rendering them unable to have children (by castrating men or removing women's ovaries):

> When one remembers that health measures such as immunization and inoculations are seen as blessings for the community, one can certainly view the sterilization of the German people as a major hygienic measure that will forever protect mankind from the bacterium of Germandom.

Diewerge adds:

> Perhaps there are still doubters who think that these Jewish murder plans cannot be serious. Perhaps they simply cannot imagine that, once Germany was disarmed, the world and its famed 'world conscience' would allow these crimes against humanity in a civilized nation. The conscience of the world has accepted such things already, for it is a Jewish invention and therefore not of Aryan origin. No one would raise his hand for a defenseless Germany or its allies if those in New York, London, and Moscow carried out their sterilization plans.

The president of the Jewish Peace Federation [Kaufman] has concrete plans as to how to carry out sterilization. His plan sees to it that no fertile German escapes. He writes:

The population of Germany, not including the conquered areas, is about 80 million, equally divided between the two sexes. To extinguish the Germans, one need sterilize only about 48 million, for men over 60 and women over 45 do not need to be included, since they are fertile only to a limited extent.

Sterilizing the men could most easily and quickly be done by treating army groups as organized units. Assuming that 20,000 doctors were available and that each could perform at least 25 operations a day, it would take at most a month to sterilize the army groups. If one had more doctors—and when one considers the many participating nations, there could be far more than 20,000—less time would be necessary. The remaining male civilian population could be finished within three months. Since it would take longer to sterilize the women and children, one should allow at most a three-year period to sterilize all German women and children. In view of the current German doctrine that a single drop of genuine German blood makes a German, the complete sterilization of both sexes must be viewed as necessary.

Population growth through births will cease in Germany after all have been sterilized. Given the normal death rate of 2% annually, the German population will decrease by about 1,500,000 souls annually. Within two generations we will accomplish what would otherwise cost millions of human lives and centuries of effort, namely the elimination of Germandom and its carriers. Lacking the ability to reproduce itself, the German will die as it shrinks and Germany's power will become reduced to negligible importance.

As monstrous as the extermination in cold blood of a people of 80 million sounds, and as much as one is inclined to think the plan unreal and unbelievable, World Jewry is in dead earnest. Diewerge demonstrates that we would not be the first people to be exterminated by the Jews. It is therefore not unbelievable, but rather all too understandable, that the Jew Kaufman has expressed what world Jewry wishes and hopes for: The murder of the German people!

Dictate! No Negotiations with the Germans!

These witnesses from our enemies testify to our enemies' destructive intentions toward Germany. They will open our people's eyes and stiffen the national conscience. No one should believe that these theories or views come from people with no influence on the enemy side. We have presented the views of top enemy witnesses such as Churchill, Stalin, and Roosevelt, leading diplomats, politicians, and journalists, representatives of the Church, of international Jewry, of the Bolshevist regime. Even average newspaper readers are part of the huge army of hate-filled enemies of the Reich who are working for the extermination of the German people. Whatever the human mind, the human imagination can devise, is here visible. But it is only a part of the whole, a sample, a foretaste. Reality would throw it all into the shadows! Reality would surpass the horrors of Nebuchadnezzar! World history would hold its breath!

Still, some may think that London, Moscow, and Washington simply cannot go that far. That is a dangerous conclusion, a completely incorrect view. Our enemies want blood—that is the truth! There are epochs in world history where reason seems to disappear. Every trace of humanity dies, the lust for power and blood rule. We live and fight in such an epoch. Woe to that people that is not prepared to do its utmost to preserve and protect its life. It is lost beyond hope and will be extinguished!

Wilson's 14 Points that murdered nations are but a trifle in comparison to the enemy demands that shall be carried out by these political hyenas without forgiveness or pity. London announces: "There will not be a peace conference immediately after the armistice. The Allies expect rather to hold the peace conference three years later, or even further in the future."

Earlier, one occasionally said that there was a difference between the German people and the "Nazi hierarchy," but today this Jewish-plutocratic-Bolshevist hate is directed against everything that is called, speaks, or thinks German. "Do not show any sympathy for the Germans at the negotiation table on the coming peace," said Lord Halifax, the man with the pious look and a bible in his hand. The London *Evening Standard* wrote on 30 October 1941: "We are not fighting Hitler, but rather for the destruction of the entire German people." The leading English magazine *Nineteenth Century* made it unmistakably clear in July 1942: "We are fighting not a German idea, but rather with the German nation." The notorious Jewish-English warmonger

Augur-Poljakoff, a spokesman for Churchill's group, told the Antwerp newspaper *Metropole* as early as April 1940:

> The English have realized that Hitler is Germany. They no longer speak of waging war against Hitler. Our revenge must be directed against the German people. The German people must pay the bill. Victory must be total. The Reich must be irrevocably destroyed. Peace will be dictated, not negotiated!

In this war, too, our enemies have repeatedly attempted to conceal their destructive aims, to lull us through bluff, promises, and pretty words. The *New York Daily News*, for example, suggested in August 1944 that Germany be encouraged to lay down its weapons by pretty words, as it did in the World War [One]. Once the Germans have given up the fight, one can be as ruthless as one wishes. The main thing is to encourage them to stop fighting, and the end justifies the means. But the enemy had to recognize that such a bluff was of no use this time. Still, we should remember the methods they used before. There is good reason to do so! *Before* the German collapse, Churchill gave a speech in Glasgow on 9 October 1918 in which he said:

> The thought of peace must be made more alluring for the enemy than the continuation of the war. No opportunity may be missed to make the German people understand that they are fighting not for their existence, but rather for the ambition of their Kaiser. One must guarantee the Germans certain basic rights.

In a speech in Manchester six days later on 15 October of the same year he said: "We do not want to reduce the German people to a state of slavery." *After* the German collapse, he gave a speech in Dundee on 26 November 1918:

> The German attempt to make the former government responsible for everything is of no use. They were all there, they must all pay! Their punishment will be terrible, more terrible than ever before!

And that is what happened. These deceivers put us in the chains of the dictates of Versailles. They certainly know today that a repetition of this betrayal is impossible. Therefore they have taken off their masks and show what they really are—implacable, unforgiving, revengeful enemies of the German Reich and the German people! They no longer make distinctions. *Globereuter* reported from London on 17 July 1943: "The Labor Party congress today discussed the difference between the war guilt of the German people and that of its leaders. A large majority voted to make no distinction between the German government and the German people. The decision was strongly applauded." Lord Vansittart, according to a dispatch from the *German News Agency* in New York dated 18 November 1941, which cited a report by Larry Rue of the *Chicago Tribune*, said that "the German people, not their leadership, were responsible for German policy, and that the Germans as a result would receive not peace conditions, but a hard dictate." Mr. Brandscome from London, an average Englishman, wrote as follows to the *Daily Telegraph* in May 1944:

> The so-called innocent Germans are a minority. The great majority has participated in the bloodshed. From the hundreds of conversations I have had in London and the provinces, I can assure you that the English do not want to work together with the Germans after the war. We will give them the most thorough beating a nation has ever gotten. No punishment can be severe enough! Their teeth must be pulled!

That is the view of the overwhelming majority of the British and North Americans, not to mention the Bolshevists. British Foreign Minister Anthony Eden expressed this general sentiment at a public meeting in Leeds on 5 July 1941: "We are not ready to negotiate with Hitler at any time about anything." USA Secretary of the Interior Ickes, according to the Associated Press, made the same point on 18 December 1941: "Any pause for negotiation with Germany is unacceptable!" One of his earlier colleagues, the late USA Naval Secretary Knox, gave a speech at Harvard University on 11 June 1942 in which he said: "I reject completely those who want to extend the hand to Germany after the war. That is a stupid, reactionary idea." London's major political weekly *John Bull* therefore wrote in February 1942: "This time there will be no negotiations with Germany other than those on the basis of unconditional surrender."

The nature of the German government plays no role. After the signing of the Atlantic Charter in August 1941, the English newspaper *Daily Mail*, which has a circulation in the millions, wrote:

> We are at war with Germany, not only the National Socialists. The war against Germany will continue, regardless of its government. Germany's strength must be broken, regardless of whether Germany is National Socialist, conservative, democratic, or socialist, or else we fight in vain. Germany must be rendered incapable of ever again determining its governmental system.

This thesis was emphasized by Eden himself, the English Foreign Minister, one of the leading statesmen in the enemy camp. He said in the House of Commons on 2 December 1942: "It would be madness to allow any kind of non-National Socialist government in Germany. The old and false German gods must be uprooted." That is Roosevelt's program as well. USA journalist Lindley wrote in the American magazine *Newsweek* in August 1944 that Roosevelt had no intention of granting milder conditions to a Fourth Reich than he has for the present German government. The USA government wishes neither a German government after the Vichy model, nor any other German government!

The Jew agitates and incites behind the scenes. Great Britain's leading rabbi, Dr. J. A. Hirtz, made this call in a statement on the occasion of the Jewish New Year in 1942: "We must ensure that there is no compromise with the Nazis." It was stated even more clearly in Nr. 7426 of the *Daily Herald* on 9 December 1939: "Stop talking about peace conditions! Break Germany in pieces!" The *Manchester Guardian* wrote along the same lines in April 1944: "The worst thing about Germany is that there are too many Germans. There are too many Germans in the world!" The article's author, A. J. P. Taylor, proposed that one should eliminate this German strength through "careful peace terms." The same paper had made plain what that means as early as March 1940: "The destruction of the Nazi regime is seen as an essential element of any peace with Germany. To remove Hitler and a few other holders of high positions would be useless if the large sympathetic army of lesser officials remains." The oft-cited *Nineteenth Century* was even clearer and plainer:

> There is but one war goal, breaking the power of Germany,
> and only one peace goal, to keep that power down. Proposals
> for a new or united or federated or better Europe are useless.
> Any peace proposal that leaves Germany's power unbroken
> must be rejected absolutely. If this power is not broken, the
> war is lost. And if German power is not kept down, the peace
> will be lost and we will have fought the war in vain.

This all means Germany's unconditional surrender! It means a dictate of hatred and the destruction of Germany and our entire people! "Humiliated," the USA Jew Felix Langer wrote in his book *Stepping Stones to Peace*, which had a high circulation in the United States, "A humiliated German supreme command will have to beg for an armistice." Then a dictate would come like a bolt of lightning with devastating force and harshness, a Super-Versailles with all its details worked out in advance! No negotiations! No parlay with Germany! That is the firm intention of our enemies.

The official British news agency Reuters reported on 18 September 1944: "Eisenhower will exercise supreme legal, judicial, and executive authority in the Allied military government in Germany." The *Svenska Dagbladet* adds news from Quebec that the British and North American governments have decided to treat Germany harshly. Roosevelt is reported to have rejected the first draft of guidelines for handling Germany a week before the Quebec conference because it was too mild. He demanded a new draft within 48 hours.

It would therefore be insane to think that our enemies will not be as harsh as they say. The German people must be thoroughly convinced, the German people must know, that our enemies will demand "unconditional surrender" if we lay down our arms. The German people must further know that, at that moment, unimaginable misery would descend upon us Germans. We would be disarmed, occupied, economically plundered, torn into many small states, dominated and ruled by the Bolshevists, Americans, and British, forced to send ten million German men to the Soviet Union and other countries for forced labor, forced to send our children, our most precious possessions, to all the world, sterilized by Jewish physicians, castrated, rendered sterile, so that the German people will literally perish within a few decades. We would be forced to surrender our National Socialist idea that we carry deep in our hearts as the idea of the century—that would be the fulfillment of the dream of hate that the former English ambassador to Berlin, Sir Neville

Henderson, has been dreaming for a long time: "There may never be a land named Germany! Call it what you will—anything but Germany!"

German man! German woman! German boy! German girl! Do you want our enemies' hateful dreams to become reality? Do you want Germany to perish, as the Jew Kaufman demands?

No—a thousand times no!
We want Germany to live!
We want to be free as our fathers were!
Better to die than live in slavery!

EPILOGUE

There is a short story, perhaps apocryphal, about the final days of the Hitler bunker in Berlin. It was obvious to all that the war was quickly coming to an end, and that Hitler himself would not be surviving. One of his generals came to him and said, "*Mein Führer*, what will we do after the war?" And Hitler replied, "Prepare for the next one."

Whether true or not, this says something important both about Hitler's ethos and about the human condition. Consider the following:

> A man fights hand-to-hand on the battlefield. He stands or falls. Either way, the battle goes on.

> The battle continues. It is ultimately won or lost. Either way, the war goes on.

> The war continues. But a war is not an end. A war is won or lost. Either way, the larger struggle goes on—the very human struggle for one's place on this Earth.

Hitler was not arguing for endless war for the sake of war. He was not some mad killer, intent on world destruction. He was acknowledging the simple reality that, in the present day, the human condition requires constant struggle in order to secure the well-being of oneself and one's people. Today it may be the Jews, but tomorrow it could be the Chinese or the Russians. Someday it could be the struggle against an over-populated Earth, or against Nature herself, in the form of disease or environmental collapse. All life struggles for survival; all life wants to flourish, expand, and grow. This is the nature of human existence, like it or not.

A defeat by the Jews one day—unless final and absolute—means little more than a chance to learn and to prepare for the next day. The hand-to-hand combat, the battles, and the wars will go on. Life's struggles do not end.

Learn, and prepare.

BIBLIOGRAPHY

Adamic, L. 1941. *Two-Way Passage*. Harper and Brothers.

Adamic, L. 1946. *Dinner at the White House*. Harper and Brothers.

Dalton, T. 2019. *The Jewish Hand in the World Wars*. Castle Hill.

Dalton, T. 2020. *Eternal Strangers: Critical Views of Jews and Judaism Through the Ages*. Castle Hill.

Doenecke, J. 2000. *Storm on the Horizon*. Rowman and Littlefield.

Dostoyevsky, F. 1877/1949. *The Diary of a Writer* (vol. 2). Scribner's Sons.

Dühring, E. 1881/2017. *The Jewish Question as a Racial, Moral and Cultural Question* (A. Jacob, trans.). Ostara.

Emerson, R. 1860/1919. *Conduct of Life*. E. P. Dutton.

Heine, H. 1835/2007. *On the History of Religion and Philosophy in Germany* (T. Pinkard, ed.). Cambridge University Press.

Kant, I. 1798/1978. *Anthropology*. Southern Illinois University Press.

Langer, F. 1943. *Stepping Stones to Peace*. London: L. Drummond.

Lessing, G. 1779/2020. *Nathan the Wise*. Nick Hern Books.

Luther, M. 1543/2020. *On the Jews and Their Lies* (T. Dalton, ed.). Clemens & Blair.

Marx, K. 1843/1978. "On the Jewish Question," in *The Marx/Engels Reader*. Norton.

Maser, W. 1974. *Hitler's Letters and Notes*. Harper & Row.

Nietzsche, F. 1989. *On the Genealogy of Morals and Ecce Homo* (W. Kaufmann, ed.). Vintage.

Pound, E. 1991. *Ezra Pound's Poetry and Prose* (vol. 8). Garland.

Rosenberg, A. 1930/2021. *The Myth of the 20th Century* (T. Dalton, ed.). Clemens & Blair.

Schiller, F. 1801/1967. "On the sublime," in *Naive and Sentimental Poetry, and On the Sublime; Two Essays* (J. Elias, ed.). F. Ungar.

Schwarzschild, L. 1944. *Primer of the Coming World*. Knopf.

Shaftesbury, A. 1711/2001. *Characteristicks of Men, Manners, Opinions, Times*. Liberty Fund.

Toaff, A. 2007/2020. *Passovers of Blood*. Clemens & Blair.

INDEX